Domesticating Youth

Integration and Conflict Studies
Published in Association with the Max Planck Institute for Social Anthropology, Halle/Saale

Series Editor: Günther Schlee, Director of the Department of Integration and Conflict at the Max Planck Institute for Social Anthropology

Editorial Board: Brian Donahoe (Max Planck Institute for Social Anthropology), John Eidson (Max Planck Institute for Social Anthropology), Peter Finke (University of Zurich), Joachim Görlich (Max Planck Institute for Social Anthropology), Jacqueline Knörr (Max Planck Institute for Social Anthropology), Bettina Mann (Max Planck Institute for Social Anthropology), Stephen Reyna (Max Planck Institute for Social Anthropology)

Assisted by: Cornelia Schnepel and Viktoria Zeng (Max Planck Institute for Social Anthropology)

The objective of the Max Planck Institute for Social Anthropology is to advance anthropological fieldwork and enhance theory building. 'Integration' and 'conflict', the central themes of this series, are major concerns of the contemporary social sciences and of significant interest to the general public. They have also been among the main research areas of the institute since its foundation. Bringing together international experts, *Integration and Conflict Studies* includes both monographs and edited volumes, and offers a forum for studies that contribute to a better understanding of processes of identification and inter-group relations.

Domesticating Youth

Youth Bulges and their Socio-political Implications in Tajikistan

Sophie Roche

berghahn
NEW YORK · OXFORD
www.berghahnbooks.com

Published in 2014 by
Berghahn Books
www.berghahnbooks.com

© 2014, 2016 Sophie Roche
First paperback edition published in 2016

Library of Congress Cataloging-in-Publication Data
Roche, Sophie.
  Domesticating youth: youth bulges and their socio-political implications in
Tajikistan / Sophie Roche.
      pages cm. -- (Integration and conflict studies; volume 8)
  Includes bibliographical references.
  ISBN 978-1-78238-262-1 (hardback) -- ISBN 978-1-78533-212-8 (paperback)
-- ISBN 978-1-78238-263-8 (ebook)
1. Youth--Tajikistan. 2. Youth--Tajikistan--Social conditions. 3. Age distribution
(Demography)--Tajikistan. I. Title.
  HQ799.T3R63 2014
  305.23509586--dc23

                                                              2013042952

British Library Cataloguing in Publication Data
A catalogue record for this book is available from the British Library

ISBN: 978-1-78238-262-1 hardback
ISBN: 978-1-78533-212-8 paperback
ISBN: 978-1-78238-263-8 ebook

Contents

Figures and Tables

Tables

Foreword

The Construction of Life Phases and Some Facts of Life

Günther Schlee

In all sorts of statistics, including demographic ones, social constructs and 'givens' that resist being constructed and deconstructed interpenetrate. Hard-core constructivists would always claim that statistics do not reflect numbers but create them. In fact both processes are at work. Statistics make us observe things we would not otherwise have observed – or, at least, we would not have counted and calculated them as averages, such as pets per household or per capita beer consumption. But statistical calculations of such frequencies for these units might appear artificial to many. When it comes to pets, we normally do not add canaries to dogs. Nor do we think about the many households without any pets; and we may forget to ask how household splitting – the tendency of more and more people to live alone or in twos rather than in larger units – influences the average number of pets per household. When we think of beer consumption, we do not have old ladies and little babies in mind, who are included in nationwide statistics, but the prototypical beer drinker, the (more or less) adult male. How much less beer we drink if we include all the babies who drink no beer at all in calculating our average consumption! Such thoughts rarely occur to us, unless we are already familiar with statistics.

So, the units we include in our count are a matter of choice and plausibility, and many of these units are not simply there but have to be agreed on. To give just one more example: There are no 'lower-income families' unless we have a definition of the family and a way of deciding which kind of income to call low; and, even if we do, such categories may misdirect our perceptions. Would members of a rural family with a low monetary income but a large vegetable garden and lots of rabbits (not as pets but for food) agree that they are poor, as such a categorization implies?

I am fully aware that statistics about household pets, preferably broken down by species and other categories, can be of great interest to pet shops and animal-feed producers – and that the marketing branches of big breweries have good use for figures on per capita beer consumption in nation-to-nation comparison. Also statistics about poverty are important, even if they can be misleading. I merely want to point out that these examples reflect a way of looking at things that is unfamiliar to those without an earlier exposure to statistics. The categories that are used here are constructs. They are products of a whole series of choices made about definitions.

These elements of construction, however, do not lead to arbitrary findings that are subject only to the will of the investigator. Once we have agreed on meaningful categories, and if we have designed our investigation procedures carefully enough, numbers come in that are beyond our control and cannot be deconstructed. The real world in which we live and to which we have to relate imposes itself on us. The statistics may, then, reflect numbers that are real enough to hurt us. For example, we (in the post-industrial world) may find out with the help of demographic statistics that the high living standard that we pay for by not investing in enough children to replace our own numbers cannot be maintained when we are old, because there are not enough people who pay taxes, contribute to our pension funds and work where these pension funds have been invested. Once we make this discovery, we could still redefine some categories and apply some cosmetic touches to our statistics; but sooner or later we would bump up against some hard facts that can neither be deconstructed nor dreamt away.

Sophie Roche is a demographically minded anthropologist (a far too rare species – many anthropologists abhor numbers). Her work beautifully illustrates the interplay of social construction and hard facts (which may result from earlier social construction or may simply be there). Her theoretical point of departure is the 'youth bulge' in Tajikistan. It may, therefore, be appropriate if my introductory comments start with 'youth' and other phases of life.

In the last century, life expectancy in the developed world has increased dramatically. Joshua R. Goldstein has discussed what this means for life phases.[1] Does an increase in life expectancy from 70 years to 80 years mean 10 more years of senility? We hope not. What we hope for is a longer middle phase of life: healthy, active adulthood. Some people call that youth: they want to look and to feel young for a longer period of time. They may have forgotten how it actually felt to be young. In fact, the age of physical puberty has decreased dramatically, as life expectancy has increased. If, according to our definition, a girl's childhood ends with the first menses, then a reduction in the average age for this event from 16 to 11 would mean the loss of roughly a third of childhood.

There are two basic possibilities. First, the increase of life expectancy results in the proportional lengthening of all life phases, as if a rubber band with sections in different colours was stretched (the case $a => b$ in Figure I.1). This model, obviously, does not describe the reality to which we have just referred. And, second, the increase in life expectancy affects different life phases in different ways. Some expand with the overall gain of time, but others may even shrink (the case $a => c$ in Figure I.1).

Joshua R. Goldstein:

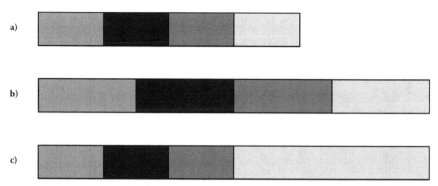

Figure I.1: Life phases according to Goldstein.

If, in our post-industrial world, characterized by an overall increase in life expectancy, the absolute and relative length of various life phases may change, then it is also possible that life expectancy is stable or decreasing. Our present situation is just a good starting point for thinking about life phases: a rapidly increasing life expectancy must affect all life phases somehow, since the length of a life is the sum of the length of its various phases. But, in principle, there is nothing special about our present situation. That life phases can be stretched, and that they can shrink, holds true for demographic situations with stable, growing or shrinking life expectancy alike.

The question of how to define a life phase is not an easy one, and people answer it in different ways. In other words, there is cultural variation. The apparent lengthening or shortening of life phases is affected by cultural definitions to no lesser extent than by observable physical events such as birth, menstruation, growth of a moustache, parturition or menopause. Very often, life phases are defined without reference to physical maturation or loss of a faculty. The entry into full legal adult status takes place years after sexual maturity and the end of longitudinal growth. In Germany, in my youth, it was legally fixed at the age of 21; now it is 18, irrespective of whether people actually have matured faster or not.

Jennifer Johnson-Hanks describes how several changes occur simultaneously to mark the transition of a young American male from youth to adulthood:

> When a U.S. boy turns 18 . . . he becomes eligible for the draft and
> responsible for his own debts. He is newly authorized to vote and run
> for office. He typically graduates from high school and moves away from
> his parents' home for the first time. Although his transition to adulthood
> is neither complete nor uncontested, the coordinated interventions of

school, bank, family, and state largely succeed in making this temporal coincidence of major life transitions feel intuitively natural. (Johnson-Hanks 2002: 865)

But the coincidence of different changes marking the transition to adulthood is, as Johnson-Hanks makes clear, an institutional artefact. The different changes have been made to coincide. In the Vietnam War, many young Americans fought and died, for their country it was claimed, before they had reached the age required for the right to vote. This was perceived as an inconsistency, and the voting age was lowered to coincide with the age of eligibility for the draft.

Johnson-Hanks then goes on to describe the absence, among the Beti of southern Cameroon, of this synchronicity of events marking the entry into a life phase or the exit from it. Sex, childbirth and the different forms and stages of marriage take place at different ages and even in different order. What is more, the timing of any one of these events has little influence on the timing of the others. The same person can, therefore, be a girl from one point of view and a woman from another; and persons can and do revert from the status of a woman to that of a girl.

Against this broader background, let us now turn to the work of Sophie Roche, which shows the interplay of demographic, cultural and political factors in the production of 'youth' in Tajikistan. The youth bulge in post-civil war Tajikistan is a deformity of the age pyramid. A stable or growing population is represented by an age pyramid with a regular conical shape, but in Tajikistan there is a protrusion less than halfway up the pyramid. There are an unusually high number of 'youths' in relation both to older adults and to children.

In the secondary literature, 'youth bulges' have been discussed as a problem. There are too many young people in proportion to the societal positions and the economic resources that they will take over from their seniors. There is unemployment and social tension. Youths are of fighting age. There is violence.

Having gone through a gruesome civil war, Tajikistan has seen much violence. And it does have a youth bulge. This is the starting point for Sophie Roche. What is the relationship between the two? Jumping to the end of the book, we find her answer. She does not reject the hypothesis of a link between youth bulges and political violence, but she argues that this link is not deterministic: 'There is no revolution if young people do not want it to happen, and there can be a huge youth bulge without any unrest'. This means that other variables come in, and these may be broadly classified as cultural. '[Y]outh bulges are a useful analytical tool', writes Roche, 'if analysed within a cultural context'.

Culture comes into play if we consider 'youth' in light of systems of classifying ourselves and our fellow humans – and in the light of resulting social identities. Viewed in this way, 'youths' can be seen to behave just like any other category used for social identification. Ethnic identifications may widen to include remote

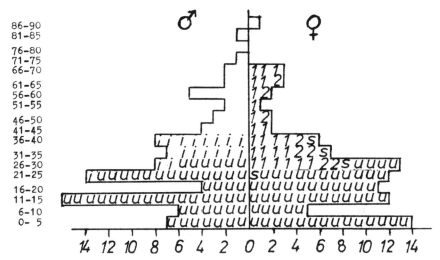

Figure I.2: An age pyramid.

This example of an age pyramid is from my research among the Rendille camel-herding nomads of northern Kenya in the 1970s. In this case, the bulges and dents are due to the age-set system. Rendille men do not set the date of their first marriage individually; rather, they all marry at the same point in a fourteen-year cycle. A normal age-set pyramid (without such effects) of a pre-modern farming or herding society would look like a perfect pyramid, becoming increasingly narrow toward the top. In this diagram, the symbols lined up in each row represent individuals of varying status, such as first wife, second wife or uncircumcised (Schlee 1979).

linguistic relatives with whom only older, perhaps merely putative relations exist; or they may shrink to include only people who share a long list of rigidly defined features. Religious groups open up to court potential converts; and they shrink in periods of purification or rigidification, during which only strict adherents to a complex set of rules are regarded as members. 'Youth' does the same: it widens and shrinks and thus behaves like a perfectly normal social identity. (See Figure I.3, where in diagram *d* the second phase, 'youth', following 'childhood', lengthens, whereas in diagram *e* 'youth' shrinks and the third phase, 'adulthood', lengthens.)

Thus, life phases may join other domains of social identification in the comparative framework provided by other previously published books in this series, which deal, for example, with the variable logic of Anywaa and Nuer ethnic identification (Dereje Feyissa 2011) and with changing identifications and alliances in Northeast Africa (Schlee and Watson 2009a, 2009b).

The social forces behind this widening and shrinking of categorical boundaries are inclusion and exclusion, which are strongly affected by the interests of

Sophie Roche:

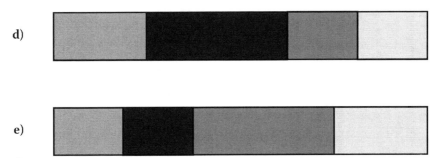

Figure I.3: Life phases according to Roche.

various groups of actors. In the introductory, historical part of her book, Roche takes us back, for example, to the 1920s and the establishment of Soviet rule in Tajikistan. For that, a vanguard of young people was needed to fight 'tradition' and 'feudalism' – or whatever the reigning negative stereotypes were. As was the case throughout the Soviet Union, the Komsomol, the Young Communist League, was established and helped 'to collectivize youth under a common ideology, turning them into a group that could be moulded under a specific youth concept'. The definition of 'youth' changed in this context, not only in terms of ideological load and political expectations, but also technically. The Komsomol was found so useful that the age limit for membership was pushed up to 28, so that more members (and perhaps more mature ones) could be included.

A youth organization, serving as a political vanguard, has ambivalent effects on the agency of young people. On the one hand, it is an enabling structure that enhances their agency as long as their activities promote state ideology. Here, youth is a mobilizing concept. Young people are told that they are progressive and the agents of change, and they unite under the banner of a youth organization. On the other hand, youth organizations help to keep youths under control. Here we can distinguish two types of control: control by inclusion and control by exclusion. Members are subject to the discipline of the organization and the indoctrination and the collective expectations they experience within it. Others are disciplined by exclusion. Roche gives the example of a young man whose family was thought to be too religious and who was therefore not admitted into the Komsomol. In terms of Anthony Giddens' (1979) distinction between enabling and limiting structures, we can identify a limitation of agency here. Youth activities inside and outside such an organization are monitored and closely directed by its representatives.

Not only in the Komsomol but in many other cases around the globe, 'youth' has been used propagandistically as a mobilizing concept with a basically inclusive appeal, and Roche is aware of these parallels. She mentions the Young Turks and the Young Bukharians. Of course, it is important to distinguish between a broad category of youth, which comprises a relatively large number of young people, and youth as a social or political force. To become a political force, 'young people need to collectivize, crystallize, and form groups around ideologies or identities'. Often, youth movements do not comprise an age bracket but a cohort, the members of which age from year to year, as we all do. When I met them, the surviving members of the Somali Youth League, formed in opposition to British colonialism, could certainly no longer be described as young.

Mobilization or political control are not the only factors affecting the definition of youth. A look at the resource base is helpful for identifying other important variables. As long as one is a 'youth', one is not expected to marry or to reproduce. Instead, one is expected to contribute to the maintenance of one's parents and the upbringing of one's younger siblings. Therefore, with a low or shrinking resource base, one would expect a high or rising age of marriage and an increasingly comprehensive youth category. 'The fewer the resources, the larger is the youth category in local constructions', writes Roche. From an individual perspective, this simply means that it takes longer to save for one's marriage.

More examples of the two points we have discussed so far – namely, the shrinking and widening of concepts of 'youth', and the control emanating from such classifications – are provided in those parts of Roche's theoretically inspired empirical study that deal with the present post-civil war period. At this point, however, the keyword 'control' may lead us to one of her central concepts, perhaps the most central, as it has found its way into the title of the book. 'Domestication' is used literally to refer to the way in which someone is made part of the house (Latin *domus*) – that is, the ascription of a role in the household and in the domestic reproductive cycle. Nevertheless, this word also carries the connotation of taming, as in the domestication of wild animals. The extension of the phase of life referred to with the term 'youth', or local equivalents, keeps young men, to whom youthful roles are ascribed, from marrying and having a household of their own. Marriage and having a household of one's own is, then, the reward for a long period of preparation, postponement, subordination and patience. The agencies that achieve this domestication are not exclusively domestic. Because of the status difference between parents and children, and the respect due to elders, parents tend to know relatively little about their children. The teahouse (*choykhona*) is a domesticating agency at the village level because it is there that status differences among generations are played out. One even has to look at the international level to identify forces of domestication. Russia domesticates the many young Tajik men who go there as labour migrants. In Russia, they mature to self-sufficiency, a prerequisite for future household heads. Russia also provides them with the financial means for being respectful sons who support their parents in the present and, ideally, save for their own households and for the often crippling expenses of marriage ('conspicuous consumption') in the future.

Roche's analysis of domestication leads straight back to her main argument about youth bulges, namely that the youth bulge hypothesis requires further differentiation. Viewing youth bulges in strictly demographic terms may cause one to assume that one young man equals another – that differences are merely quantitative. Roche's case material, which is too rich to be summarized here, convinces us with compelling force, however, that young men are not interchangeable. Within the family, birth order plays a major role. Oldest sons are providers for their parents and younger siblings. In most cases, they are labour migrants and send money home. In contrast, the youngest son usually inherits the house of the parents and cares for them in their old age. The chances for receiving more than a rudimentary formal education are best for middle sons, who seem to have the most options in life. Middle sons are also potential recruits of pressure groups, militias and gangs. This, however, should not lead us to the premature conclusion that, being 'surplus' or somehow 'superfluous', they may be regarded, primarily, as conflict potential. Rather, they must be seen as part of a group and as elements of a group strategy. 'Siblings . . . are the strongest social unit and ensure a family's social security through diversification'.

The strongest image for the complementary relationship among brothers or, rather, among the different roles accorded to them by order of birth is the Tajik saying that 'brothers are different like the fingers of one hand' – which Roche uses to illustrate diversification as a family strategy. Whether or not youth bulges become a problem and lead to political disruption, depends, as she clearly demonstrates, not only on absolute numbers but on the many different ways in which youths can be integrated into larger wholes, the roles provided for them and the opportunities given to them.

Roche's study shows, among other things, that different values are attached to different phases of life. According to a widespread idea, the early phases represent an upward progression that culminates in full maturity and high status, while the latter phases are visualized as a downward movement, as in the late nineteenth-century illustration reproduced below (Figure I.4). In contrast to this folk view, Roche shows that the curve taken by this upward and downward movement is subject to historical changes in the values attached to different phases of life; and she shows that the length of each phase is subject to variation (which would result in strange stairs with steps of unequal height and width).

For a broader review of variation in the social construction of life phases (*Lebensaltern*), one might consult the volume edited by Martin Kohli and Georg Elwert (1990). East African age-grading systems of the *gada* type represent an extremely rigid ordering of life phases.[2] These proceed according to cycles of years (multiples of seven in one case and eight in another) that mark the passage of new groups into age-sets endowed with social and reproductive rights and charged with military, political or ritual duties. Age-grading systems of the *gada* type contrast vividly not only with equivalent institutions in Western society but also with

Figure I.4: *Lebenstreppe* (© bpk – Bildagentur für Kunst, Kultur und Geschichte)

those of the neighbouring Nilotes, where the initiation of new age-sets does not follow a rigid order but is subject to social pressures (Müller-Dempf 2008). The idea of an upward and downward movement, as represented in the image of the bridge (Figure I.4), is alien to all these age-grading systems. They are pervaded by a gerontocratic spirit, and social status increases, at least ideally, with each upward movement from one age-grade to the next. Due to the collective nature of age-set promotion rituals, the room for individual re-affiliation to life phases ('I am as young as I feel!') is very limited in such a cultural environment. Thus, Sophie Roche's fine study inserts itself into a broad field of possible comparisons.

Notes

1. For recent work on life phases, see Lee and Goldstein (2003), Vaupel and Loichinger (2006) and Goldstein (2011).
2. Recent research on *gada* systems at the Max Planck Institute for Social Anthropology has been carried out by Andrea Nicolas, Ambaye Ogato and Günther Schlee.

Acknowledgements

This book would not have been possible without the help of numerous people. First of all I would like to thank the Max Planck Institute for Social Anthropology and its director Günther Schlee for their support for this study. Having chosen to explore a subject that is not well established within social anthropology, I was very appreciative of Professor Schlee's guidance and openness. Amid the unique and generous atmosphere of the Institute, it was my good fortune not only to have benefited considerably from many colleagues, but also from the help of librarians, secretaries, technicians and student assistants. I would also like to express my profound gratitude to Ildikó Bellér-Hann, who provided insightful comments and advice, and to Laura Bernardi, who showed enthusiastic interest in the topic and the region, and encouraged me to engage in demographic anthropology.

I am also indebted to the Max Planck Institute for Demographic Research in Rostock. In 2007 I attended introductory courses offered by the European Doctoral School of Demography, where I learned techniques both for modelling population data, and, with the knowledgeable assistance of several researchers, for handling small quantities of data. During my stay in Rostock, I discovered the value of the statistical analysis of ethnographic material and the intriguing possibilities it offers for understanding population through its demographic processes.

I was the very fortunate recipient of a three year contract at the Max Planck Institute and a grant from the graduate school's 'Society and Culture in Motion' programme. I especially profited from this opportunity due to the school's intellectual environment and the generous support of Professor Ralf Elger, who agreed to read and comment on my work at several stages. I am also grateful to the Zentrum Moderner Orient in Berlin, which kindly granted me time to work on the book and thus completing the long path of scientific production.

Likewise, I must gratefully acknowledge the helpful and critical interest of many colleagues and friends during various phases, whose questions and discussions sharpened the text considerably. Although, unfortunately, I cannot name all of them here, I would like to mention Barno Aripova, my teacher and dear relative who helped me at various stages with the translations; Stéphane Dudoignon, who shared with me his expansive knowledge of the Bukharan period; Madeleine Reeves, with whom I had inspiring discussions and who kindly edited the demographic appendix; Thomas Zitelmann, one of the great conflict researchers, who allowed me to present my work at his colloquium in Berlin, from which I benefited tremendously; Payam Faroughi, for his comments and regular updates on the current situation in Tajikistan; Sergei Abashin, with whom I discussed the Tajik kinship system; and Paul Tyler, who edited the manuscript, making it agreeable to read. I also owe special thanks to Hartmut Lang, who helped me with statistical operations, and to Aksana Ismailbekova, with whom I not only discussed many topics but from whom I received welcome encouragement at various stages.

Without doubt, I owe my greatest thanks to the people in Tajikistan, who trusted me and helped me to realize this project. My assistant was able to overcome many prejudices that existed between urban and rural people and thus become well integrated into the male community of different villages, providing me with many helpful contacts. Further, without the families who allowed me to stay in their homes and with whom I developed cherished friendship ties, research would have been impossible. The communities supported my research, integrated me into their lives, and even protected me against the unpredictable members of the secret service. My deep gratitude to all those wonderful people can hardly be expressed in words. For reason of security I cannot name them here, yet their words, ideas, habits and thoughts have shaped this study.

Finally, my family has offered continuous emotional support, encouragement, love and phenomenal patience. Special thanks go to my sister, Marie Roche, who not only supported me emotionally but also read and commented on the chapters several times. Last but not least I would like to thank my son, Nasim, for helping to keep me motivated. With his wonderful laughter and inexhaustible energy he eased the work considerably, and during our stay in Tajikistan it was thanks to him that we were welcomed so warmly in every community and left the country having made many valuable friends.

Notes on Transliteration and Usage

Transliteration is a problem in Central Asian scholarship, mainly due to the language policies of the past. In the pre-Soviet era, most Central Asian languages were written in Arabic script. In the course of Sovietization, however, many of these languages began to be transcribed using the Latin and/or Cyrillic script, due to which some terms that were commonly used in several Central Asian republics acquired a distinct written form. For an excellent and detailed description of this development of the Tajik language, I would suggest Rzehak's (2001) book on the creation of a standardized Tajik language at the beginning of the twentieth century. Although there was a kind of standardized Tajik language already in existence at that time, people often continued to write in their own local dialects, which resulted in multiple written variants of numerous common terms – for example, the word for 'mosque' might be written as *masjid, mazjid, maschid* or *mazchid*, and 'mullah' as *mullo, molla* and so on. In my study, however, I have endeavoured to maintain regional specificities when applying certain terms (such as *mujohid, mullo*).

For purposes of readability, I have not separated the genitive -i and the vowel -u (and), typically written at the end of the word following a dash, as is done in more linguistic-oriented works. For those who are interested in the linguistic aspects, it is sufficient to know that in most cases if a word ends with an -i and followed by another term, it is probably a genitive denominator of the noun. For plural nouns, I have retained the singular forms in Tajik, with the addition of a pluralizing -s, as is common in English. In the case of common words, I have used the spelling provided in the *Standard Tajik–English Dictionary* (Randall and Olson 2000). For transliterations, I have used the system suggested by Edward Allworth in *Nationalities of the Soviet East* (Allworth 1971). Well-known Arab and Persian words have been simplified into their common English spellings (such as Koran, mullah). I have retained spellings when quoting from various texts. Unless otherwise indicated, interviews and quotations from the literature are translated from Tajik. In a few cases, however, I have used Russian quotations (mainly from the published literature) and terms in accordance with the International Scholarly System – one of the simplest transcription systems for Russian, based on the GOST and ISO systems. Although there are some inconsistencies in my use of transliteration, these reflect not only scholarly problems but also the flexible nature of language. I am responsible for all translations in this study. All terms marked with * can be found in the glossary at the end of the book.

Introduction

Youth (Bulges) and Conflict

On 8 April 2011 I received a call from Dushanbe. A young colleague excitedly told me that he was on the way to a demonstration in front of Barki Tojik, headquarters of the state energy supplier, to protest at its inability to provide a reliable service. He intended to watch from afar at first, and only join in after gauging the state's reaction. The flash mob that eventually took place, involving about thirty young people from Dushanbe, lasted no more than twenty minutes and my colleague had no time to join in. The participants carried posters with words of mourning (in Russian). They lit candles and laid flowers at the main entrance in a 'symbolical funeral for the Tajik energy system'.[1] Thanks to the presence of a couple of journalists, this flash mob – the first of its kind in Tajikistan, according to the news report – was brought to the attention of the international press.

The young men who participated knew each other well, and belong to a group of well-educated urban youth who prefer communication in Russian to Tajik. They criticize the regime and its politics, not only concerning energy but also education, labour and the economy. Usually they do not appear collectively, yet they share many ideas and frustrations in personal communication and on internet platforms. My colleague, for instance, had been handed a note about the planned event at Barki Tojik, but he also spends a good deal of his day moving among internet cafés to participate in virtual discussions. The young activists are all known to the government, which keeps a close watch on them, and some are regular visitors to the offices of the secret police (formerly the KGB). Under such circumstances, participation in the flash mob took courage, and those in it wondered what might happen if others chose to join them in a spontaneous protest. While the activity in the end was too brief and small to attract the masses or security officers, it nonetheless alarmed the regime. These young men believe themselves to be the vanguards of a movement towards democracy for Tajikistan, but they have yet to connect with the great majority of the deprived countrymen they claim to represent.

Similarly critical of the regime, but drawing upon a different source of influence, is Eshon Nuriddinjon, one of the most popular religious authorities, who has caught the ear of large groups of young people. In 2010 it was not uncommon to hear his recorded sermons playing from the mobile phones of Tajiks in Tajikistan and in Russia as they lay idle from lack of work. For almost a decade religious practices had become a central topic to many young people. On Fridays the mosques were packed, often causing roads and even neighbourhoods to be closed to traffic because of the crowds. In villages the small mosques erected during the perestroika period (1986–1991) were being replaced by cathedral-like mosques that still failed to accommodate the masses of the faithful.

The mosque headed by Eshon Nuriddinjon held several thousand young men who arrived from distant villages and towns. While some saw this as a normalization of religious life in post-Soviet Tajikistan, the regime was very concerned by these large religious gatherings. Thus it came as no surprise that at the peak of this enthusiasm for Islam, the state passed a law restricting youth participation in live religious events. At the sight of these large congregations of young believers, the state feared that it was losing control over the religious sphere. The goal of the Law of the Republic Tajikistan on Parental Responsibility for the Education and Upbringing of Children passed in 2011 is to call upon parents – who represent a generation that tends to view the Soviet era as a relatively prosperous and stable period – to help the state regain its hold over the nation's youth.[2]

It is not clear to what degree such religious gatherings were and are capable of being mobilized for purposes of violence, and there is no reason to assume that believers in Tajikistan tend to be more violent than believers in other countries. And yet, the anti-Islamic politics of recent years, including the bans on youth attending mosque prayers until the age of eighteen and restricting Eshon Nuriddinjon from leading prayers, reflect the anxiety of the regime in light of the demographic potential of the country's youth. Today there is no subject more capable of bringing together youth than Islam. At the same time there has been no religious leader who has used this demographic potential to bring about a violent confrontation, either because they want to avoid bloodshed (such as the Islamic Revival Party) or because they do not have the necessary charisma to rally the large plurality of believers (such as various youth movements). Yet, there is no doubt that competition over youth is a key factor in recent political developments and that demographics play a major role in shaping the dynamics of Tajik society.

What is the role of demographics in political and social change? Tajikistan is in the midst of a demographic transition, experiencing a youth bulge vis-à-vis other age groups, due to a decreasing birth rate and the postponement of marriage, which has freed up a substantial amount of young people of working age from family obligations. Along with this demographic change we can observe youth groups that challenge ways of categorizing and organizing youth. This is most visible in politics, like the young men in the flash mob mentioned above, but such engagements are not restricted to politics and equally affect social relations within the community and family. Attempts at domesticating youth by elders, traditions, community, parents and the state are rejected by certain young people, who crystallize in groups through which they articulate their resistance to political and social pressures. These groups, which claim to represent large segments of youth, or even large segments of the overall population,[3] call upon other youth to join them in taking action.

Under what circumstance do categories of youth crystallize into active groups? What is the relation between demography and the mobilization of youth? This study seeks to examine closely the relation between a 'youth bulge' and conflict within society.[4] Thus far, social anthropology has generally neglected to address the impact of population pressure on social change, and in particular the presence of youth bulges as a possible cause of social conflict. For the most part, this topic has been discussed from a political perspective; my intention, however, is to approach the issue from an anthropological viewpoint. In this study, I examine the concept of 'youth' in Tajikistan, focusing on how it has been used, shaped and modified over the last two decades. In order to bridge the abstract concept of demographic youth bulges and the reality of active young people, I intend to present 'categories' and 'groups' (which I will define shortly) as two distinct but related entities out of which the dynamism of youth bulges evolves.

It is the contention of this study that the tendency to see youth bulges as a source of conflict is related to the widespread perception that youth must be 'domesticated'. Domestication suggests that the lives of young people are manipulated, controlled and modelled by means of defining, shaping, negotiating and evaluating their roles at the political, community, family and ideological levels. Thus, I argue that what is meant by 'youth' is constantly being renegotiated. Out of such negotiation processes emerge various definitions of youth, each representing a socio-biological category during a certain historical period, under a specific political regime, and within a particular established society.

Jean and John Comaroff (2000, 2005) have asserted that the category of youth is socially constructed and politically shaped. They have raised the important question of how youth have entered public perceptions and discussions, concluding that 'youth, as we speak of them here, are the historical offspring of modernity' (Comaroff and Comaroff 2005: 20; cf. Bourdieu 1993: 137). In their study, they indicate that there has been much scientific discussion on the relationship between 'youth' and unrest, as contrasted with the relatively harmless connotations of 'teenager' – a term that is reserved for white (civilized) adolescents.[5] 'Youth' seems to simultaneously suggest mistakes in the past, terror in the present, and a vision of hope for the future.[6] Hence, the Comaroffs remark that youth is now viewed as a more distinct, independent group than ever before. This has become possible due to the marginalization of youth, they argue, referring to numerous studies on the difficulties experienced by young people in their attempt to enter into traditional economic arenas, and an eventual perception among youth that they lack future prospects. The position of youth in society thus becomes a matter of situational interpretation, shifting unpredictably from young people as vanguards to young people as vandals. I believe that this has less to do with their biological maturity than with the way in which the socio-demographic category of youth is constructed, shaped and used, and to what degree young people participate in political activities.[7]

Terms such as 'group', 'cohort', 'category' and 'collective' have different implications and lend themselves to various interpretations. In order to use these terms analytically, I adhere to a precise distinction: While the concept 'group' in this study refers to individual members who remain in a specific relation to one another as defined by the group's identity, 'categories' are used to order society and classify people by age, sex or other markers that are independent of their personal relation to each other. In demography, the term 'cohort' is commonly used to refer to individuals of the same age, sex and so on, whereas the term 'population' embraces a larger entity, usually including people of all ages. In this study, I use 'cohort' only in a demographic context. Regardless of how society constructs youth categories, young people can be part of different groups at the same time; they can be highly active as individuals but still be denied the role of agency due to the categories to which they belong. In this sense, youth are no more of a category than adults are; hence the concept of youth suggests that 'young people are perched on the brink of an equally promising adult life, and all they have to do is to make the right choices for themselves' (Wyn and White 1998: 318).

Youth is sometimes a category of analysis, sometimes a category of practice; it refers to groups, cohorts, conditions and so on. In short, youth as a category is malleable and context dependent. In Tajikistan we find different ways to think of youth. All of the terms suggested below not only describe young people under certain conditions but also in relation to other age groups and society. While the terms provide a basic idea of how age is constructed in Tajikistan, throughout the book we will see the malleability of the concept of youth and the consequences that this can have in situations of conflict.

Tajik Life-stage Categories

Those aged approximately between 14 and 25 are in their youth (*davrai javonon*, sing. *javon**), and this phase is followed by what is called the period of maturity (*davrai kamolod*). By this stage, a man should have spent much time learning everything and should marry. His life changes considerably: he now starts thinking about starting a family and about the future; gradually the person gains maturity. Then at around the age of 29, his behaviour changes completely, and he begins to care about his family's future. This period continues until the age of 40 or 50, when he attains maturity. During this period, he gains further knowledge and starts to make plans for his future. It is believed that in the period of *kamolod*, people work until about the age of 60, after which their life changes drastically due to old age.[8]

S.R.: Until what age do you consider someone 'young'?
UMAR: From 18 to 25.

S.R.: Why?

UMAR: As a youth, you tend to think only of yourself, but once you have passed the age of 25, you are married.

S.R.: Once you have married, are you not young anymore?

UMAR: You then move to *mardak**. At the age of 25 years, you are still young, but differently.

S.R.: Could you give me an example?

UMAR: As a young boy, you think of nothing but other young people and hanging out. Once a boy becomes *mardak* [married], he does not indulge in the acts that he used to in his youth, and he begins to think of how to improve his life. He then has to fulfil many responsibilities.

S.R.: Would a young man prefer youth or *mardak*?

UMAR: Being young is good.

S.R.: Why is being young good?

UMAR: A young man can do as he pleases and go wherever he likes. After marriage, you cannot continue to go everywhere; you stay at home for the sake of your wife.

S.R.: From what age do you call somebody *miyonsol** [middle aged]?

UMAR: From 35 to 60 years of age. At the age of 60, you become *oqsakol** [elderly man].

S.R.: What is the role of *miyonsol* in the family?

UMAR: He stays at home and works, if there is any, not difficult work, only in the house.

S.R.: So work is divided?

UMAR: For example, my father says: 'My son, do this work, go there, and say that'; then he prays his *namoz** and sits at home.

S.R.: What age group do you consider as youth (*javon**)?

TOHIR: From the age of 18 to 30 years.

S.R.: Why until the age of 30?

TOHIR: Because until the age of 30, a man is young; after 30, committing mistakes is shameful.

The most widely used term for young people in Tajikistan is *javonon* (sing. *javon** – young). It is often used interchangeably with the term *bachaho*,[9] yet *javonon* has more of a political connotation and hints at youth as a social category rather than at the relative status of young people within their families. Although *bacha** is correctly translated as 'unmarried boy', it may also be used to describe young married men behaving in a 'wild and undomesticated' manner, and even more often refers colloquially to 'guys' (several more or less young people).

The next step is the intermediate stage, *mardak**, which emphasizes both a young man's marital status and his subordinate position to elders; it is the period of gaining psychological maturity (*davrai kamolod*). During this period, young men are at the peak of their physical power and are expected to use their labour to serve the family and community. They may try different jobs and take chances, without the risk of being judged, because mistakes are considered a part of maturation. Hence, it is only much later that full maturity is acquired – somewhere between the ages of 35 and 50. While those *mardak*s are no longer *javonon* in the same sense as a *bacha* (unmarried man), they are still *javon* in terms of social conceptions of maturity.

Old age is marked by withdrawal from physical work and the attainment of a new position: as a wise and oft-consulted person. Older people are expected to dedicate their time and effort to a religious life as they slowly approach death. Sometimes the term *miyonsol* bridges the period between the ages of 35 to 40 and 60. In the psychological construction, changes occur smoothly during old age – *müisafed** or *oqsakol** (white-haired men); *kampir** (elder women).

The short description of the linguistic terms provided above shall suffice for now. The following chapters will provide not only a much wider scope of concepts and categories but will also link them to social and political changes.

This study seeks not only to examine the role of youth in Tajikistan, but also, more generally, to determine how this social category itself was and continues to be shaped and reshaped. The Central Asian republic of Tajikistan provides an ideal arena for such a topic, because it has gone through a civil war, has a high proportion of youth, and is beset by problems related to a scarcity of resources. As part of the former Soviet Union, Tajikistan was previously integrated into a larger political, scientific and economic system and profited from well-structured educational and medical systems. Hence, we should not forget that scientific and political discussions regarding youth have developed differently in the former Soviet Union than in Europe and the United States. All of these factors make Tajikistan an interesting arena for research with respect to competing categorizations and the crystallization of groups emerging from such categories.

To date, there have been numerous anthropological studies in the field of youth and violence (social and political violence), some of which have mentioned the problems associated with youth bulges; however, to my knowledge, very few studies in this field have addressed the complex issue of a 'youth surplus', both as a social category and social group. For the purposes of this study, I have relied upon literature from various fields in order to determine how problems pertaining to youth bulges, population and conflict have been discussed in security demography and social anthropology.

Since this study is based on first-hand information and observation, and supplemented by the available literature, it does not claim to represent the whole of Tajikistan, but rather only phenomena that have been encountered by the author in certain areas of Tajikistan. My interest lies solely in investigating the negotiation of relationships between individuals and groups and the construction of categories, not in judging and arguing about the value of certain political practices or the accuracy of various historical representations. Nevertheless, I believe it is often impossible to consider my field sites in isolation from the political context and historical events, mainly because the influence of politics and historical events are strongly felt at the local level and play significant roles in contemporary constructions of relations and social groups. For this reason, the present study ranges beyond the restrictive compass of contemporary local villages to include a larger political framework and historical period.

The Emergence of Youth Concepts

The research problem addressed by this study is located specifically within the field of theoretical debates on the subject of youth and conflict. It is beyond the scope of this book to deal with the varied discussions within youth studies that have taken place over more than a century. However, I consider it necessary to explore the youth bulge argument as it has evolved with regard to youth concepts in the social sciences and psychology. Youth bulges suggest a demographic approach to society, but at the same time it provides links to various categories of actors and groups. I am aware when using the term that, throughout the Islamic world, societies are experiencing youth bulges. That these youth bulges have been accompanied by social and political change (such as the 'Arab spring') is of interest, yet it is not necessarily a causal result. How socio-political changes link to the demographics of a population demands careful investigation, and that is the intent of this book with regard to Tajikistan.

Concepts of Youth and Generation

Let us begin the discussion with the most obvious questions: What is youth? Should it be constructed based on age, rituals, psychological stages, economic success or biological maturity?[10] Age in many societies is understood not in terms of chronological age (that is, simply the number of years lived) but rather in terms of relative age, measured by the individual's position within society.[11] Abbink contends that since age limits, for pragmatic purposes, cannot be set, 'the category of "youth" in Africa [is limited] to the 14–35 age bracket' (Abbink 2005: 5). Furthermore, demographers as well as politicians create age groups for practical reasons. In this sense, Cincotta, Engelman and Anastasion (2003) refer to youth bulges as comprising people between the ages of 15 and 29, while Heinsohn (2006) limits youth to 15 to 24 years. These varying definitions indicate that there is a basic uncertainty regarding what comprises youth as an analytical category, in comparative studies as well as in local contexts.

A closer look at the history of the concept 'youth' will clarify its contemporary use. According to some authors, youth culture in Europe and the United

States can be said to have begun in the nineteenth century (Gillis 1974; Wyn and White 1997: 21).[12] At that time, youth was identified as a socio-demographic category and became the subject of study during the course of industrialization and urbanization in England; thereafter, the concept of urbanization has remained central to the emerging category of youth. It was in urban centres that differences and clashes between classes and social groups over ideas were most apparent; articles of that time already dealt with issues related to the loss of parental control over children (Fortes 1933: 15). Youth, or to be more specific, single groups of youngsters, mainly males, were portrayed as a category of people who experienced difficulties in achieving a smooth transition to adulthood. 'The history of youth studies is replete with case studies of (usually) male "delinquent gangs" and student "resisters"' (Wyn and White 1997: 78; cf. Chicago School).[13] Increasingly, youth became the creators of a so-called 'subculture' by demonstrating youth-specific consumption behaviours, as in the work of those associated with the Centre for Contemporary Cultural Studies (CCCS) in Birmingham. The concept of 'subculture' entailed that the category of youth was seen as subordinate to the dominant culture.[14] However, these ideas regarding dominant culture and subculture were subsequently contested by the study of subculture as a source of creativity in youth (Wulff 1995).[15]

Other schools have developed youth concepts based on consumer behaviour, such as the Frankfurt School. Strongly influenced by Stanley Hall's (1904) study of adolescence, discussions of 'youth' began to revolve around the idea of a psychological stage (which a person usually enters and leaves by way of certain rites of passage). From this social Darwinist perspective, adolescence is seen as a period of emotional storm and stress, representing a passage from 'stone age baby' to the rational and enlightened state of 'modern man' (Cohen 1999: 184). Cohen concludes that, 'In this view the youth question is by definition diversionary, deflecting public attention and resources away from what can and should be changed (political and economic conditions) and towards something which is essentially unchangeable (adolescent behaviour)' (ibid.: 192). Thus, the concept of youth in the social sciences came to be discussed in relation to the problem of adolescence.[16] In this way, youth first emerged as a socio-demographic group in social science studies, constructed as a phenomenon that occurred in industrial societies.

The generation concept has been another approach toward structuring society and creating arbitrary youth cohorts.[17] Mannheim (1970) suggests that societal generations are conceptualized in relation to specific 'breaks' in history; in other words, shared experiences separate one generation from the next. In the social sciences, as well as in popular parlance, this is often indicated by adding qualifiers to the word 'generation' – for example, first-, second-, or third-generation migrants, the last Soviet generation, the postwar generation, generation X and so on. In contrast to Mannheim, the communist approach constructs a theory of continuity across generations, oriented around the concept of progression rather than breaks or ruptures.

In the context of the former Soviet Union, the concept of generation was based on Leninist interpretations: 'The entire purpose of training, educating, and teaching the youth of today should be to imbue them with communist ethics ... the generation of those who are now fifteen will see a communist society, and will themselves build this society. This generation should know that the entire purpose of their lives is to build a communist society' (Lenin, quoted in Pilkington 1994: 46). Every generation was to absorb only the best traditions from the older generations, providing a sense of forward movement, which would then be transferred to the new society, complemented by new practices and ideas. Based on a materialist conception of history, Elster in his study of Marx claims that, 'History is nothing but the succession of the separate generations, each of which uses the materials, the capital funds, the productive forces handed down to it by all preceding generations, and thus, on the one hand, continues the traditional activity in completely changed circumstances and, on the other, modifies the old circumstances with a completely changed activity' (Elster 1986: 182).

Pilkington explains that youth in the Soviet Union emerged as a socio-demographic group in the social sciences only in the 1970s – not as a 'problem group', as labelled by the 'bourgeois approaches' of the West, but as a problem rooted in class divisions. It is against the backdrop of this ideology that we should analyse the youth question in contemporary Tajikistan. Therefore it is not unusual for Poliakov to state that: 'it must be stressed that no "youth problem" exists in Central Asia. Young people are always controllable' (Poliakov 1992: 91; cf. Harris 2006; Stephan 2009). Rather, he writes firmly within the Soviet tradition that regards youth problems as an issue of the West (Europe and the United States); as per the Soviet definition, there is no rupture between generations. Pilkington explains that this assumption comes from the emphasis of Soviet scientists that, 'Soviet society [is] free of generational conflict' (Pilkington 2004: 120). In this light, it is not surprising that youth were put forward as vanguards and as builders of communism: 'From the hands of the old generation our youth takes the great and precious legacy. Entering life, boys and girls of the country of Socialism must remember that their sacred duty is to carry on the cause of the older generation' (Anon 1950: 7). The Komsomol, the youth organization of the Soviet Union, was crucial in the early years of establishing the Communist Party's authority within industry and the military and among the rural peasantry (see Chapter 3).

The Tajik discourse on youth has remained within this interpretative framework. However, when civil war broke out in Tajikistan in 1992, analysts appeared to agree that high fertility (rising birth rates and a population explosion) and economic problems had fuelled the conflict.[18] In other words, population pressure was seen as one of the main causes of the social unrest that had dragged the country into a civil war (that lasted until 1997), and youth were regarded as the principal troublemakers during the war.

The concept of generation therefore should be regarded as vague, because it mixes categories and groups (distinctions that are essential for the discussion of youth as a demographic factor) – that is, family relationships and politico-historical groups (Abbink 2005: 3–5). While domestication largely concerns groups, it is also based on categories that are shaped through domestication processes. 'Generation' says little about the people themselves, whether they are a social, political, biological or religious category or part of a concrete group in opposition to another group (such as pupils and their parents). In Tajikistan, for instance, people believe that the parent–child relation is, by definition, conflict free; however, the 'civil-war youth' is said to be a problematic generation (*nasli javonon**). Since the concept of generation is more confusing than clarifying, I will not make use of it here.[19]

In effect, the notion of a predictably constructed world, in which youth pass through adolescence to adulthood guided by rite and tradition, appears to be endangered today, and not merely due to globalization.[20] For instance, Abbink mentions that, 'Being young in Africa is widely and consistently perceived as problematic in essence' (ibid.: 2). Politicization of the topic has compelled researchers to revise the term 'youth' as a constructed category, replacing the more psychological approaches to the discussion on adolescence with economic, historical or political approaches.

Conflict Studies and Youth

We can see that, from the beginning, youth studies focused on the deviant and troublemaking tendencies of youth.[21] Thus, a specific socio-political problem gave rise to a distinct socio-demographic group. In line with this view, young people were seen as needing guidance and attention, so they were analysed either as psychological subjects or as the producers of a subculture. It should be noted that in both cases, however, they were regarded as marginal people in need of special treatment. This perception of youth, however, did not exist in non-Western societies. For Margaret Mead (1973) and many anthropologists thereafter, youth, in opposition to Western concepts, represented a more or less well-integrated social group that was able to move smoothly from one social status to the next. Young people's use of violence was portrayed as part of culture, and anthropologists interpreted the extent of institutionalization and social embeddedness of young people in terms of the idea of the 'noble savage'. Violent conflicts were organized along social rules such as those characterizing feuds or warfare. Age-grade systems or generation-set systems were portrayed as structuring society and restricting the use of violence to a specific time in life.[22] Thus, warfare provided youth with a space in which they could be active and learn skills that were considered important acquisitions on their way to adulthood. This transition – or at least the way it was portrayed in many African societies – was controlled by the elders, who retained the right to allow youth to enter adulthood formally.

Conflict studies represent a wide field that includes the entire range of non-violent to violent clashes between groups with differing opinions.[23] While this study considers the term 'conflict' in all of its implications, there is one specific type of conflict that is central to my argument: civil war. The civil war in Tajikistan in the 1990s will be analysed with regard to how young men engaged in it and how it affected youth concepts. This study does not focus on the cause of the conflict; rather, it seeks to determine the ways in which the civil war moulded the socio-demographic category in question (youth).

Agadjanian and Prata argue that: 'few demographic studies have been conducted in [war-torn countries] and the literature on the demographic consequences of wars is relatively scarce. Fertility responses to wars in developing countries are especially rarely studied' (Agadjanian and Prata 2002: 215). Certainly, the key reason for this scarcity is the inaccuracy of demographic censuses in times of civil conflicts – that is, when such censuses are possible at all – and the necessity of using different methods to collect data or statistically model the available data (Li and Wen 2005: 480).[24] Agadjanian and Prata's claim regarding fertility in the context of conflicts is also applicable to many other aspects such as gender constructions, youth concepts and rituals.

In conflict studies, the main focus has been on leadership approaches. Hence, according to some authors, such top-down approaches miss the dynamics in the field.[25] 'It is important to point out, however, that top-down (para) military orientations do not control the character of the war as it is played out on the ground' (Nordstrom 1999: 167).[26] The idea that behind every conflict exists a (super)power that is pulling the strings derives from cold war perceptions, Waldmann (2002: 370) explains.[27] The leader approach overshadows the common person's participation in a conflict. Therefore, this study concentrates on the role of ordinary youth rather than on biographies of exceptional leaders. In fact, every young man with whom I have talked seeks social recognition in some way, and many are determined to engage actively in gaining such recognition. Keeping the issue of social recognition in mind, I look at the ways in which Tajik society structures the passage through one's life; how it shapes, negotiates and deals with categorizations of ages; and how it identifies group formation processes out of these categories. What is important for young men (and women) is access to social status and positions that are accepted and recognized within their social context.

In order to mobilize and motivate young people to join combatant groups, their roles and positions are redefined in such a way as to legitimize the use of violence. A relevant example has been given by Lamphear (1998) in his work on the Maasai. Lamphear shows how the age system of the Maasai changed due to the external intervention of the so-called *Laibons* (chief prophets) and became a source of organized violence. 'It was the centralized leadership of the *Laibons* which provided the means of maximizing the demographic potential of the synchronized age-class system and the *manyattas*, and of transcending the inherent limitations of the old concepts of warfare' (ibid.: 88). Later, the *Laibons* were co-opted by the colonial regime. While the domestication of young people seems to have failed at the community level, it was achieved at the societal level, in that the restructuring of youth was successfully realized by politically motivated leaders (or leading groups) who transcended the limitations of local concepts.

One central problem in youth studies has been the mixing of two distinct entities – social group and demographic, political or analytical categories – which has led to a conceptual confusion. This problem has been previously mentioned only for ethnicity; however, it also applies to youth. Jenkins, discussing ethnicity, writes, 'Social groups and social categories are different kinds of collectivities existing in the social world' (Jenkins 2003: 61–62).[28] The study of social movements has been a field in which the borders between categories and groups have become blurred, to the point where they are often regarded as congruent. By accepting and uncritically reproducing modes of categorization, we overlook the nature of such categories – for instance, the state as a strong identifier, psychological categorization, traditional constructions of the life cycle, and so on. We also fail to notice the shift from a mere category to concrete movements or groups. The matter becomes even more complicated with the distinction between relational and categorical modes of identification (Brubaker and Cooper 2000). Transferring this to youth, we need to distinguish between, on the one hand, young people living in relational webs such as kin, friendships and classmates, or in groups such as combatant groups and peer groups, and, on the other hand, young people subsumed into social, political or religious categories. Out of these two modes of identification emerges the dynamic of youth as a demographic factor.

Youth Bulges as Security Problem

The concept of youth bulge developed out of the debate in social science circles regarding delinquent youth, as well as from the Malthusian idea of ecological (im)balance; today it is used exclusively as a politico-demographic term, connoting a (male-dominated) security problem. The debate over 'youth bulges' (a relatively recent coinage) as a source of conflict has developed only in the second half of the twentieth century. The French conflict researcher Bouthoul (1968) is sometimes cited as the first researcher to explicitly discuss the connection between youth bulges and violent conflicts. Through the concept *le Complexe de l'Encombrement*, he argues that while the French population underwent only a moderate increase in the 1950s, the number of students tripled a decade later, giving rise to enormous competition for the same resources. 'For the *Complexe de l'Encombrement* leads to impatience and furore; those who suffer believe themselves to be "surplus men"' (ibid.: 16).[29] For them, everything becomes an obstacle, but first it is other men who block their way. Bouthoul's approach to youth is psychological, thus corresponding to anthropological and sociological discussions of youth and adolescence. According to Bouthoul, conflicts are an inevitable fallout of the destruction of the demographic–economic equilibrium: 'Until recently, men were in natural equilibrium with their environment. This equilibrium increasingly crumbles in front of our eyes' (ibid.: 18).[30]

A similar approach was taken by Moller (1968) in his analysis of European revolutionary movements, the driving forces of which he attributed to youth. In this regard, we should also consider Goldstone's *Revolution and Rebellion in the Early Modern World* (1991), where he examines four aspects that he believes are responsible for state crises as well as revolutions: the problem of taxes and severe financial crises in the state; the inter-elite conflicts that arise from these state crises; the increasing population pressure and competition for land; and the emergence of ideologies of 'rectification and transformation'.

Goldstone limits his definition of youth – and this supports the discussion in this study – to the ages of 10 to 30 (though in his analysis of England, he uses the age cohort 25 to 35, thus indicating that youth as a socio-demographic group is also a cultural category). His approach is the most complete to date; however, like most other approaches, he assumes that 'youthfulness' (that is, youth bulges) is a demographic concept and that young men are naturally aggressive. Such an approach makes it unnecessary to explain why violence emerges in some 'youthful' societies and not in others. Nevertheless, the author does remind the reader that population growth alone explains little about population dynamics.

In this context, Tiger and Fox deny a causal relationship between population density and male violence: 'Man was violent *before* he had dense populations . . . Density is not a basic *cause* of violence, but it remains a possibility' (Tiger and Fox 1992: 224, original emphasis). The question of violence and demography then has been considered in previous studies, which have discounted a linear causality. Rather than asserting a connection between density and violence, Tiger and Fox suggest a closer look is needed at the conditions of density for humans, who create and shape their own social environment.

There continues to be much discussion regarding a causal relationship between youthfulness and competition or conflict. Mesquida and Wiener have further developed Bouthoul's approach, suggesting that male age composition is a decisive factor in civil conflicts: 'competition for mates is greatest just before the usual age of marriage; young males must compete for connubial resources among themselves, and also with older males who control the political and economic resources of society' (Mesquida and Wiener 1999: 183). Collective violence happens against a background wherein young people feel they have nothing to lose. Mesquida and Wiener suggest looking at male population ratios (for the ages of 15 to 29) as a variable to be plotted against the severity of conflicts. Apart from their attempt to classify the 'severity' of a lethal conflict, their argument is similar to later youth bulge approaches.

About thirty years after Bouthoul and Moller, studies of Arab countries have presented the situation of the 'deadly impasse between demography and history' (Ajami, quoted in Vakil 2004: 45; cf. Winckler 2002). Vakil refers to Iran as 'a pressure cooker ready to blow off steam' (Vakil 2004: 53). In addition, Fuller's (2003, 2004) analysis of the Middle East brings together the factors developed thus far: high fertility levels ensure the continuation of conflicts associated with competition over resources and with the grievances of young people against their state or the international community.

According to the sociologist and genocide researcher Gunnar Heinsohn (2006: 14), youth bulges provide the impetus for civil war.[31] His research, based on historical studies, led him to conclude that if a society has young people (aged 15 to 24) constituting more than 20 per cent of its population, it will probably experience a civil war. One of his central arguments deals with inheritance patterns. If a father has more than one son, he may be headed for trouble if his wealth is not sufficient to satisfy all of his sons' needs and their demands for a decent future. As a result, the dissatisfied sons will begin to stir up conflict within the household and eventually in the world outside the household. Although this idea appears to be based on European inheritance practices, it invites discussion on how other societies with high fertility rates regulate inheritance.

Recent studies by Henrik Urdal, moreover, claim the presence of a 'clear statistical relationship between youth bulges and the increased risk of ... internal armed conflict, terrorism, and riots' (Urdal 2007: 91). The demographers Cincotta, Engelman and Anastasion (2003), in their study of civil conflict, present youth bulges as one of three stress factors that make civil conflict more likely (the other two factors being the rapid growth of large cities and conflicts over cropland and water).[32] Here, we see a parallel development in conceptualizing the youth problem as an urban economic one resulting from the inability of society to domesticate young men.

Some analyses blame religion for the problem. Huntington (1998) and Heinsohn (2006) explicitly formulate a connection between youth bulges and Islam.[33] However, such a connection necessitates a cautious approach, particularly when it suggests the possible conceptualization of youth as troublemakers. Most other authors distance themselves from such a linear correlation. For instance, the Middle East Youth Initiative has suggested an 'inclusionist' approach to youth. They argue that in most Middle Eastern countries (basically meaning all Muslim countries in the dry belt), birth rates have considerably decreased in the last decade, creating large youth bulges with a low dependency ratio (Dhillon and Yousef 2007).[34] Historically, this has been identified as a chance for the accumulation of wealth; therefore, the organization suggests that the '100 Million Youth Challenge' should be seen as an opportunity, not a threat.

The so-called 'greed and grievance concept' has gained popularity as a measurable politico-economic approach to young people's violent expression of political dissatisfaction (Collier and Hoeffler 2001).[35] However, upon empirical testing the concept has proven not very useful since it ignores the specific context that shapes each conflict (Collier and Sambanis 2005). What all of these studies have in common is that they view youth as a group that seems to exist outside culture and social norms.

The mono-causal approach to youth bulges and conflict has also been refuted more recently in a statistical study by Stephan Kroehnert (n.d.) of the Berlin Institute for Population and Development. Based on data from 156 countries, Kroehnert has shown the total absence of any exponential correlation between population growth and violent conflicts; he has also demonstrated that the rate increases linearly – which means that the proportion of six to seven conflicts per million people has remained constant during the last fifty years.

Kroehnert has presented a critical analysis of the apparent correlation (youth bulges and conflict), finding that the probability of having a conflict rises linearly and peaks when youth comprise 19 to 21 per cent of the population, while again showing a sharp decline for countries with a youth bulge (defined here as from 15 to 24 years) of over 21 per cent. This leads to speculation that it is not merely the quantitative aspect of youth that gives rise to unrest. Urdal (2006: 615) has recognized the problem of correlating youth bulges to the total population, and instead suggests that in order to gain reliable data, youth bulges (ages 15 to 24) should be measured in relation to the total adult population (ages 15 years and above), along with the addition of the dependency ratio measurement.

Urdal (2004, 2007) has provided the most detailed approach to this problem, taking into account numerous factors. He makes an important point – namely, that 'identity groups are necessary for collective violent action to take place' (Urdal 2004: 2). In other words, a large category of youth in and of itself is not sufficient to declare youth a risk factor; for this to occur, young people must first collectivize, crystallize and form groups around identities. This study departs from the assumption that youth categories serve to domesticate youth, and also provides the necessary collective reference to allow for the crystallization of groups around vanguard identities.

A central problem in the youth bulge discussion is the incongruence of categories of practice and categories of analysis. Similar to the approach taken by Brubaker and Cooper (2000) in their discussion of ethnicity, the study of youth needs a serious re-examination of categories of analysis (usually derived from Euro-American historical analysis) and categories of practice (which are constantly reshaped, transformed and negotiated). The mixing of various categorizations and classifications leads to confusion and imprecise assumptions about the role of youth in society. Categories do not act, they create social order – and youth groups use categories to change, negotiate and contest social order. That is to say, we should not lose sight of the actors behind the events, and we should continue to question how categories and groups are used as identifiers.

Youthfulness in Context

'Youth bulges' or 'youthfulness' is considered to be a source of insecurity in countries in transition – that is, moving from a developing to a developed state. 'Several researchers have argued that a "youth bulge" of unattached, unemployed men encourages generalized violence and terrorism because they are easily recruited by radical causes' (Jenkins, Crenshaw and Robinson 2006: 2011). Similarly, a report on the security dynamics of demographic factors argues that 'unemployment rates tend to be higher in developing countries' which can pose a security risk to the concerned population (Cincotta, Engelman and Anastasion 2003: 41).[36]

Urban studies claim that the presence of a distinct political, demographic, economic and social group of youth can be responsible for destabilizing entire political systems. According to this argument – which also exists in social anthropological approaches – young people who are excluded from legitimate economic activities may either turn to illegal activities or become easily mobilized by opposition parties.[37] When discussing youth and war in Sierra Leone, Maxted writes, 'The marginalization of youth was a key factor in the causes and modality of the civil war in Sierra Leone' (Maxted 2003: 69). The concept of educated young people lacking opportunities to join the job market is also a theme of research on the Asian continent. Mahmood (1996), writing about Sikhs in India, states that many young people who experienced exclusion from the mainstream job market were either pushed into the informal sector or drawn toward more radical movements. An inflexible social structure with regard to upward mobility, and scant options for entering the mainstream job market and thereby attaining respectable social positions, are certainly among the most critical issues existing in present-day Tajikistan. However, if we accept the literature, the economic situation was less dire before the civil war – at least for young people – than it is today.

Abdullah coined the term 'lumpen youth' to describe 'the largely unemployed and unemployable youth, mostly male, who live by their wits or who have one foot in what is generally referred to as the informal or underground economy . . . [T]hey are to be found in every city in Africa' (Abdullah 1998: 207–8). Initially, these 'lumpen youth' mainly consisted of youth from the lower classes, who began to be noticed as distinct youth cultures following the end of the Second World War; this changed in the 1970s, as discussed by Marguerat (2005) in his project on street children. He contends that the urban youth problem is much more class independent than has come to be expected or usually assumed.

Despite the popularity of the urban unemployment argument among conflict researchers, this theory is not adequate to explain why in some urban centres young people become violent while in other contexts it is rural people who are blamed for behaving in a 'wild and uncivilized' manner, as in Tajikistan. The urban argument that figures prominently in youth bulge approaches has been explicitly criticized and deconstructed by Sommers, who, in his comparison of

Somalia, Sierra Leone, Sudan and sub-Saharan Africa, argues that those wars 'have been largely rural-based conflicts at their roots' (Sommers 2006: 141). Hence, it is not necessarily urban youth 'losing' their traditional ties who are at the root of conflicts; conflicts are equally likely to be started by rural young people who apparently are well established in their own communities. This is also true for Tajikistan. Thus it must be kept in mind that approximately three-quarters of the population in Tajikistan – about 5.5 million out of 7.5 million people – reside in rural areas, 97 per cent of which is mountainous (Olimova 2000: 60), and the country has very few urban centres. The majority of educational institutions and political activities are concentrated in Dushanbe, the capital of Tajikistan, which therefore also has a significant concentration of young people.

While Malthus doubted in the late eighteenth century society's ability to adjust to new situations and predicted that humanitarian catastrophes and wars would result from population growth (see Malthus 1999),[38] Boserup (1965) showed that a certain population density and population pressure were prerequisites for the acceleration of technical development (cf. Bengtsson et al. 1998: 70). Applying this insight to youth bulges, we might ask whether, in various countries, an overabundance of youth provided the necessary social pressure to push through social, political and technological developments.[39] However, anthropologists tend to avoid macro approaches and prefer more precise and detailed micro-analyses. Although many scientists have complained about the lack of micro-analyses in the field of social pressure and change – especially in the study of conflicts (see Macfarlane 1968; Lang 1997; Agadjanian and Prata 2002; Li and Wen 2005) – some aspects have been studied by social anthropologists.[40]

In this context, the anthropologist Hartmut Lang proposes that population growth by itself does not necessarily lead to a drastic change in society; rather, it is the relationship between population increase and the society's resources – that is, population pressure – that provokes changes (Lang 1997: 17).[41] Lang, relying on ethnographic material, discusses how changes in population size appear to exert a considerable influence on cultural features: 'demographic sizes act upon the formation of cultural entities' (ibid.: 18). This leads to the question of population size and specific 'cultural types'; further catastrophic events may have an important role to play in the regulation of these relations (Lang 1982).

The possibility of a connection between the size of (kinship) groups and the level of available economic resources as sources of conflict has also been addressed by Günther Schlee (1989, 2006, 2008). He develops Hechter's (1988: 37) idea of cost-sharing as a principle that can be used to create group solidarity and restrict size. Schlee (2006, 2008) has applied this rational-choice-theory approach to conflict studies. He argues that ethnic and other forms of collective identification are shaped by economic considerations of sharing costs and benefits. Although his argument does not take into account demographic composition, it hints at the importance of intra-group social stratification and the role of resources and the consequences of limited access to them; it can therefore be applied to demographic cohorts and age structures.

As can occur within linguistic, ethnic or religious groups, the concept 'youth' can be modified either to maximize the demographic potential by including as many (young) people as possible (inclusion strategy) or to minimize it by emphasizing an elite status (exclusion strategy). An example of such strategies can be found in the Soviet youth organization Komsomol (see Chapter 3). The more limited the resources, the larger the youth category becomes in local constructions.[42] Hence, once the notion of 'youth' is accorded value in the marketplace, the other boundaries become blurred and everyone gains potential access to 'youth' as a conceptual resource.

In this regard, the more interesting phenomenon is not the way in which the Tajik population has progressed far beyond its economic resources but rather its social responses to this progression and the consequences in terms of redefining social positions, work divisions and the use and shaping of categories such as youth. As long as the elders and the Soviet state controlled the attributes of status and resources in Tajikistan, and as long as the state was able to provide mainstream positions of some status in the job market and successfully excluded non-conforming young people, youth remained in a subordinate position. Demographically speaking, even though young people constituted a large majority, they were, nonetheless, a liminal, powerless minority (Sommers 2006: 155). However, much seems to have changed during and after the civil war. Today, many young men are the main breadwinners of their extended family (siblings, parents and children) and therefore their power within the community has increased, as compared to their prior situation under Soviet rule.

Returning to my earlier statement of purpose, this study is less concerned with the origin of conflict than it is with the transformative power of conflicts themselves. Youth concepts are created and shaped by conflicts which, due to their disruptive nature, provide the necessary foundation for the radical transformation of concepts. This study considers youth as individual young people, as a socio-demographic group, and as a political, religious, biological, demographic and, most important, cultural category. How these categories have been framed and redefined, co-opted and rejected, over the last twenty years in Tajikistan, and how they continue to relate to group formation processes, will be the central themes of this study.

Domesticating Youth

At this juncture, having shown how youth has been conceptualized as a source of social pressure in conflict studies and security demography, it is helpful to advance the discussion by introducing the concept of 'domestication'. The term 'domestication' is used here in a metaphorical sense, as a process, alluding to the ways in which authority views and deals with youth. However, the structural and authoritative domestication of youth at the same time suggests that people – unlike animals – negotiate positions and may reflect upon how they are treated by those in authority. Consequently, the domestication of youth refers to a process that is contested by young people. Domestication is, first and foremost, a top-down perception of the problem, and this approach is useful because it mirrors the way in which young people are believed to grow up, namely under structural and authoritative control and guidance. It is also how politicians and scientists tend to approach the socio-demographic group (the concept of liminality, discussions on subculture, adolescence and so on).[43] The approach reflects the difficulties inherent in controlling and shaping youth, because they are social actors who act, not as a unified category, but as different groups and individuals who thereby shape as well as challenge the top-down constructions. Thus, domestication is not an emic but an analytical term that I use to capture complex processes. We may differentiate between authoritative domestication, in which a (numerically small) social group controls the process of maturation of the large socio-demographic group 'youth', and structural domestication, which refers to institutions that are said to guide youth in their socialization and maturation (such as kinship and the education system).

To accompany this concept of domestication, I have adopted a holistic approach to youth that reflects these domestication processes. Various distinct processes (such as socio-political, religious and economic ones) influence these domestication processes; therefore, domestication processes are not static but are constantly remoulded by way of shifting local and global contexts (Christiansen, Utas and Vigh 2006). In this sense, studies engaging with the subject of 'conflicts and youth' must first contextualize young people and specify those different contexts (kin, economic, religious, political, urban, rural and so on).

Assuming that conflict can alter group composition (Schlee 2008), I argue that changes within a population and its age composition are the result of domestication processes that, although primarily authoritative in nature, have to be negotiated between respective age groups on different scales – that is, between individuals and collectivities. Often this is an asymmetric relationship, with negotiation processes occurring between an authoritative minority and a subordinate majority, which means that any interaction within domestication takes place between unequal partners. Much of the strength of youth in structural and authoritative domestication then must lie in its relative demographic size. How demographic size is manipulated through negotiations of categories defines the dynamics of domestication processes. In other words, I use youth bulge not only as a demographic phenomenon but in its political sense, as a specific condition of youth mobilization. This is independent of the actual number of youth vis-à-vis other age groups but depends on how individuals or groups use 'youth' as a social and political term to generate categories. Youth groups that translate categories into action play a central role in transforming 'youth' into a vanguard identity.

Domestication is not necessarily a face-to-face process; it simply describes what happens between individuals and/or social groups when they redefine their positions in asymmetric relations. This redefinition can, in some cases, be violent and involve conflict, but it can also occur peacefully, democratically and even through mediators.

Whether perceived as aggressive due to psychological causes (adolescence), a structurally defined period (for instance, warrior age), a natural characteristic (according to local concepts), a demographic risk group or a political source of grievance, youth are constructed as wild and potentially violent actors in a very destructive sense. In this study, I wish to approach the question of youth from many different angles, including the different interpretations of youth in modern society. In this context, I am interested in how individuals as well as groups of young people become collectives and representatives of categories. I believe that psychological local constructions of youth, their role in political discourses, and demographic pressures influence each other in the creation of youth concepts with which young people themselves (as individuals or groups) need to negotiate. Note that a purely top-down approach can never do justice to this issue. Youth concepts and identity have to be negotiated with respect to – or at least adapted to – the concerned social group, which may then accept, reject or reshape the suggested concept. This process often takes place between economically and demographically unequal partners and therefore resembles authoritative domestication. However, any domestication process in this context will provoke a more or less strong counter-reaction by some young people and thus force the adaptation of domestication strategies, even when the overall process is presented as successful authoritative domestication.

In this sense, the term 'youth', as it is used in this study, is a collective reference to which society has accorded certain values and expectations. The category of youth is ascribed an identity by external actors – it is this ascribed identity that is internalized by individuals or groups of young people. Being a collective term, it is open to manipulation, which can be used by other actors to organize and mobilize young people for collective (violent) action.

Youth as Vanguards

The concept of youth as a vanguard is accorded a key role in opposing domestication attempts. Large groups of highly motivated young people can be mobilized by the prospect of becoming a vanguard group in society.[44] The vanguard concept pits youth against the existing order and systems, and places them in a position to oppose or challenge local constructions of youth. Although most vanguard groups strive for the transformation of society, vanguard status, as a whole, is lost as soon as the vanguard group becomes a mass organization and rises to the level of a national ideology or is transformed from a group into a category.

These vanguard concepts relate to what Eisenstadt (1988) has described as the development of a specific generational consciousness. The emerging of a revolutionary movement, argues Eisenstadt, is a process of 'the growing impingement of the periphery on the centre, by incorporation of orientations of protest into the centre' (ibid.: 101). He identifies generational consciousness as the driving force behind historical changes and the cause of ruptures. Yet, for him, youths are not initiators; rather, revolutionary movements emerge when new ideas undergo a process of crystallization, often finding expression in (youth) movements and youth groups.

I argue that categories of youth matter when looking at how young people are mobilized in a violent conflict; in this way a 'vanguard' can be viewed as a concrete group in which concepts of youth crystallize and generate strong identities. Domestication in this context refers to the concrete practices used to create and maintain categories that allow a minority (elders, the regime and so on) to exert control over young people so as to avoid vanguard groups from challenging existing youth categories. I believe that categories are malleable, and thus youth groups are able to claim to be representative and challenge existing categories, even if numerically these groups are a small minority. That is to say, I am interested in the capacity of youth movements to create strong identities by manipulating youth categories in order to mobilize the masses. This refers to the concept of inclusion and exclusion, as discussed by Günther Schlee (2008), because these strategies elevate a youth movement to vanguard status. What Schlee has suggested for ethnic and religious identities, among others, also applies to classifications of youth – namely, that strategies for regulating the size of groups make use of inclusion and exclusion methods. Categories of 'youth' behave like ethnic groups because they have the same potential to be mobilized. When we distinguish between categories and groups as interdependent entities, we can see that category definitions precede group formation. To put it another way, strategies of inclusion and exclusion are used to maximize the demographic potential of the category 'youth'.

For example, Roy shows that Al Qaida represents itself as the 'vanguard of the Muslim Umma', but since few Muslims share this perception, the group has so far remained a relatively liminal group with regard to their success demographically (Roy 2004: 69–72). In other words, not all vanguard youth movements are able to mobilize the demographic potential of youth by skilfully balancing inclusion and exclusion strategies. Thus, Roy suggests that what matters most to the young men joining such a group is not ideology but rather the need to participate in revolutionary activities. Twenty years ago, these activities would have taken the shape of leftist movements. In this way, Roy's suggestion supports the more general concept of vanguard that will be explained in the course of this study, and the difficulties faced by vanguard youth movements in their attempts to manipulate youth concepts and regulate membership and access to resources.

Turkey's history presents a successful example of how a new status for youth had been created by reformulating negative concepts of youth into positive political vanguard identities of a new social system. 'Single young men tended to circulate in Ottoman society as seasonal workers, apprentices, and students. Unlike householders, single young men (like roaming nomads) were viewed as a potential threat to organized society. Young men formed the backbone of revolts that broke out in Anatolia from the 16th century' (Neyzi 2003: 362). At the end of the Ottoman Empire, the concept of the 'Young Turk' was fostered during student movements. It became a symbolic image of the new generation – the 'Young Turks' – who were expected to revolutionize the system and replace the old generation. (By the time the revolution had succeeded, some twenty years later, those who attained influential positions had already reached the age of 40; nevertheless, they still held on to the label of 'Young Turks'.) 'However, what seems true is that the revolution of the young Turk has given the necessary signal to provoke a renewal (and juvenescence) of the leading classes, even if it did not happen at once' (Georgeon 2007: 160).[45]

Georgeon (ibid.: 155) describes the importance of introducing early schooling and age-based classes in universities, which allowed young people to form a common spirit and group identity. Although Koranic schools had been age-based as well, the *madrasas** (schools for higher education) were composed of students from a wide range of age groups, with older people having the dominant influence. It is through the use of youth at the political level, he argues, that 'the notion of "youth" (*genç*) suddenly became popular in discourses . . . Indisputably, the young people and youth assume a new position within the society and politics' (ibid.: 161).[46] In other words, it is through organizing systems of education according to age groups that the youth of Turkey could be mobilized on such a large scale.

Şenı has added to this discussion an analysis of the writings of Agâh Sırrı Levend (1894–1978), who actively created a youth model to fit Turkish national propaganda. The youth of the 1930s were perceived as something that could be moulded and formed (*infiniment malleable*, Şenı 2007: 243) in accordance with the needs of the country. This example from Turkey most clearly reveals how youth can be formulated as a separate generation in its own right and converted into a strong force that can be politically co-opted. In schools and through the discipline of sports, both of which were within the control of the state, the youth, including the country's children, could then become the 'beautiful generation' in a militaristic sense. This does not imply that concepts of youth did not exist beforehand in Turkey, but there was no systematic organization at the national level, and individuals interacted in terms of patron–client relations – for instance, young people were regarded as apprentices and students (*shogird**) (cf. Dağyeli 2008). Thus 'youth' changed from being a pejorative term implying a subordinate position in the older system to representing the driving force and vanguard behind the emergence of the new system.

The history of Germany also provides examples of the highly strategic use of youth to accomplish political goals. Sternberg, in the context of Nazi Germany, mentions that, 'the second and third sons of peasants were often enlisted in the SS and SA' (Sternberg 1981: 152).[47] At that time, there was much social unrest due to laws that aimed at proletarianizing villages by declaring the eldest son as the only heir. Younger sons were forced to find work, but there was not enough land to accommodate them, unless they were willing to work for the large land-owners (*Großgrundbesitzer*), whom the Nazi state preferred to leave untouched. In this way, young people were obliged to engage in farming 'voluntarily' (*freiwilliger Arbeitsdienst*), most often on the farms of large landowners, who profited from the arrangement. 'It (Fascism) received the support of the first-born peasant sons by forcing the process of proletarianization on the younger peasant sons' (ibid.: 153).[48]

Sternberg's analysis is noteworthy in that it reveals the state's specific strategy to gain the loyalty of the elder brother at the expense of his younger brother(s), who later joined the SS and SA (*Sturm-Abteilung*, the Nazi's paramilitary force) en masse. This highly strategic use of siblingship may be a specific Germanic occurrence, but it still fundamentally adheres to the idea of youth bulge – namely, that a military structure can profit from the inability of parents to provide all of their sons with an adequate inheritance (Heinsohn 2006).

Similarly, Thomas Zitelmann (1991: 269) has shown that the violent rebellions of the Oromo Liberation Front (OLF) in Ethiopia were due to familial tension. He finds in those activities, on the one hand, recognition for acting in accordance with traditional male life-cycle activities (violence) and, on the other, the opportunity to fight for their own position, which they define by reviving old myths and combining them with new ethno-political symbols. The expansion of the Oromo since the sixteenth century, he argues, is grounded in status and resource conflicts within the household and the extended family, whereby inheritance patterns, access to women, and the taking of power from the elder generation, politically as well as economically, played a major role.

In the African context, it has been argued that the status of youth changed from that of freedom fighters (vanguards) to troublemakers because of their inability to enter the job market and hold respectable social positions. In Kenya and many other African countries, young people secured various positions for themselves by carrying out wars for independence (d'Almeida-Topor et al. 1992; Kagwanja 2005; McIntyre 2005).[49] Nevertheless, as Kagwanja (2005) has shown in the case of Kenya, the very generation that secured those positions was then unwilling in turn to make those positions available to the younger generation succeeding them, hence creating enormous social pressure. In the traditional *ituika* system, political leadership would be handed to the next generation every thirty or forty years, thus ensuring that the younger generations would eventually succeed to the positions of preceding generations. However, the change in political circumstances during the colonial period (for instance, the banning of certain key rituals) and the introduction of central regimes meant that the ruling generation could refuse or abolish (informally) the traditional handing over of power, thus intensifying social pressure that in turn would be politically exploited by opposition groups.

To conclude the discussion, the concept of a 'vanguard', in this context, implies that a small group claims to represent a majority and is ready to fight for the future of those they have included in their category as disadvantaged. The existence of such youth movements has been responsible for the distorted view of youth in many contexts – due to the aggressive or dominant public posture of such movements, the majority of more compliant youth are ignored (Wyn and White 1997: 19), and those movements are accorded the categorical identity 'the youth'. Hence, in the course of this study, we will see the extent to which these vanguard youth movements are important in mobilizing youth through negotiating, challenging or replacing category definitions.

Research Methods

Qualitative Research

Participant observation is a central tool in social anthropology, and if done systematically and properly, it is considered to be of high scientific value. Unlike the use of the interview method to understand a society, participant observation allows the researcher to experience people's activities firsthand. Although every foray into fieldwork should be guided by the primary inquiry of the researcher, an inductive approach can open up additional avenues through which to investigate central aspects of social life. This is especially significant in the field of youth. Thus far, very few anthropologists and sociologists have written about youth in Central Asia.[50] Most commonly the topic is dealt with as a subordinate subject or treated with an ideological focus. The aim of this study has been to allow youth to take part in the discourse while engaging in their own activities, whether work or leisure. In this sense, I mostly interviewed people informally, while joining them in their activities.

Georg Elwert (1994: 7) has mentioned the importance of conflicts in the study of society, as it is in the breaking of rules that rules are revealed. However, in the case of Tajikistan, previous studies have mentioned the desire for harmony that is not only expressed towards outsiders but also internalized as a value (Stephan 2008).[51] Therefore, conflicts are often perceived as negative and not fitting to discuss with an outsider, and even someone who participated in a conflict and is willing to discuss it may not be reliable when relating their individual motivations for joining the conflict and the role(s) they played during it.

It benefited this study that I was able to listen to different narratives from many segments of society. Men and women, for example, express their memories in different ways and thus follow different narrative paths. Every history is shaped by and reflects gender roles within society. In Tajikistan, a man is a political entity – even if he refuses to actively engage in politics, he still is regarded and treated as such. Male accounts lay claim to a certain 'objectivity', distancing themselves from the 'subjectivity' of the female narrative, or in the words of Bjerg and Lenz (2008), men are believed to retain factual knowledge while women recall everyday stories (cf. Jonker 1997: 192–93). As a Tajik saying goes, 'Men are the clothes one wears outside the house, while women are the clothes one wears at home'. Thus, men fulfil this expectation of their role in society by providing more chronological and often politicized accounts of events, whereas women are neither expected to be political subjects nor are their accounts, by definition, considered true or relevant in political discourse.

I recorded more than four hundred conversations, including casual conversations, interviews that ranged from a few minutes to several hours, and oral records of genealogies (census data). I recorded the stories that were told during discussions of genealogies because they help to explain and add important details to the technical data. Of these, I have transcribed 107 interviews and conversations; the genealogies, to a large extent, have been used as statistical data. In my view, the observations and experiences, casual talks – whether occurring on the street or at an informal occasion – which have been documented in the form of field protocol and field notes (presented also under the summary heading of 'fieldwork experiences'), and group discussions are as important as classic interviews for the gathering of information.[52]

For the interviews, I have tried to retain the use of local symbols to express ideas and thoughts. The glossary explains selected terms and provides their linguistic origin. Most words, whether Arabic or Turkic in origin, have been influenced, however, by the Tajik language, especially with regard to the vocals. The words that can be found in the glossary are indicated by an asterisk (*).

Quantitative Approaches

I have included quantitative analysis at a basic level, extrapolated from the genealogical census data. Although demographers claim that statistical data on Tajikistan is reliable, this is only partially true. In Tajikistan statistics are politics and hence do not necessarily reflect social practices in all their variations; an example is the change in marriage patterns that accompanied change in the law on marriage (Roche and Hohmann 2011).

Although there were detailed censuses of Tajikistan during the Soviet era, it was very difficult to get access to them. I tried to obtain some very basic data (birth rates from the 1980s to the present) at the *rayon* (district) centre archives, but was refused. Furthermore, many families do not register their children until they need the necessary documents (for schooling), after which the children may be registered under the name of any relative; hence, the official data may differ from that which I have gathered on my own. Children can only be registered under their parents' name if the parents have been married according to state law, the Record of Civil Status Act (*Zapis Aktov Grazhdanskogo Sostoyaniya*, ZAGS*). If this is not the case, for instance in the circumstance of a second wife, her children would be registered as those of any other relative (such as the mother's parents, her husband's first wife).

Censuses and Genealogies

Hans Fischer (1996, 1997) discussed the historical evolution of the terms 'census' and 'survey'. As components of demographic anthropology, both census and survey methods have been used rather indiscriminately and, at times, even inter-changeably. While a census refers to the systematic collection of data from a clearly defined locality, the survey method is less territorially bound.[53] The survey method was rejected by van der Geest because it is based on closed questions and 'does not lend itself to the complexity of the respondent's own ideas and experiences and thus escapes the correction of its wrong presumptions' (van der Geest 2004: 43).[54] I have followed Fischer's suggestion and concentrated on the census method; however, since I chose to use genealogies, territorial boundaries are blurred because many children today settle outside the census area where their parents were registered. This study is based on three neighbourhood (*mahalla**) censuses that I took through the collection of genealogies during 2006 and the beginning of 2007.

Genealogies can be used to collect different types of data such as names, kinship, history and demography. Each of these types demands a slightly different procedure as well as its own group of questions. Apart from data on entire kinship genealogies, I mainly collected information regarding sets of siblings. The older the data, the greater the chances that my informants would not be able to remember accurately; hence, in my view, reliable demographic data do not include any information earlier than the twentieth century. Also, the quality of the information varied according to the willingness of people to talk candidly. Often, it was necessary to leave the defined locality in order to visit an interview partner's sibling who lived in another area, in order to improve the quality of the quantitative and qualitative data.

The quantitative data I have attempted to collect systematically can be classified as basic data (items 1–7) and supplementary data (items 8–12).

1. Sex
2. Date of birth
3. Date of death
4. (Name)
5. Data regarding children
6. Date of marriage(s)

7.   Household units
8.   Type of marriage (state registration, traditional marriage, religious marriage)
9.   How the marriage was managed[55]
10. Education and profession
11. Date of moving out of the parents' house
12. Migration data

In the course of analysis, I have maintained the links between the census data and individual information; thus, it is possible to see who produced the data and in what way. Through this approach, it is interesting to note how different strategies, ideas and ways of life may still produce the same result – for example, a delayed marriage, economic difficulties, housing problems and birth order may all influence fertility decline.[56]

In this study, I have presented only portions of my quantitative results, instead relying mainly on the qualitative data for the presentation of the argument. It should be noted, however, that quantitative procedures and approaches helped me to identify key questions such as how and why marriage behaviour has changed in society over the years, and to understand the idea of a youth bulge in the Tajik context and how it relates to groups of young people, life-course constructions and various discourses.

As Bernardi (2003) mentions in the case of fertility, abstract models and questions do not possess the necessary reach and flexibility to capture the social influences of decision-making. In open interviews and unstructured discussions, people are given the chance to return to certain points in order to explicate them further, thus providing additional clues into the factors influencing their decision-making (such as the experiences of their friends and family members, and how these experiences influence mutual relations).

In this study, I would like to elucidate what Bernardi (ibid.) calls these 'channels of social influence'. This aspect will be covered in the course of this study, which deals with the situation of young men in Tajikistan, who find themselves torn between parental expectations, community pressure and their experiences during labour migration to Russia.

Reflections on the Study

Conflicts occupy an intermediate position between public denial and public fascination, and it is the extremity of these two positions that makes it difficult to conduct research into them. While some sciences claim 'objectivity' by letting the numbers talk and thereby escape individual responsibility, this is not possible for an anthropologist. Anthropologists have a heightened sense of responsibility towards the people about whom they write, because they work closely with the people who are willing to share their knowledge and because they are allowed to take part in their lives – very often the anthropologist's most significant breakthroughs in awareness emerge from participation in daily activities (Elwert 1994).

Each person who has shared some of their intimate life expects me to treat those confidences appropriately. However, there is no single 'correct' manner – otherwise there would be a total coherence of views and an absence of argument. Nevertheless, throughout this book, I have made every effort to be as accurate as possible. That being said, this book does not claim to present an authoritative political analysis, and any discussion related to political situations is limited to information gathered during my fieldwork.

Unlike in countries such as Sierra Leone, the subject of civil war is considered taboo in Tajikistan, and the state has used repressive methods to control the spread of individual versions of the event. In light of this situation, I greatly appreciated people's courage in telling me the version of events they believed to be true. Due to several incidences involving the secret services, I have exercised caution when providing individual accounts and have made every effort to preclude any possible identification of an account with a particular individual.

At times, I was asked why I was so interested in conflicts (which were understood as negative events), and why I didn't choose instead to write something 'nice' about Tajik culture. The idea of folklore in the study of *ethnografia* in the Russian tradition had a very different purpose from that of social anthropology today. Hence, while (older) people were eager to help me gather information on 'ancient rituals' and encouraged me to collect cultural information, they became uncomfortable when asked questions dealing with contemporary problems. I have attempted herein to describe the rich and diverse culture of the villages I visited, but for theoretical purposes I have also included sociological interpretations of social interactions. In the last decade, the term 'conflict' has become irrevocably associated with politics, making analytical approaches increasingly problematic. Therefore, I have referred to Elwert's (2004) definition of conflict, wherein he correlates the grade of institutionalization and the relative use of violence to identify four general types of conflicts: legal proceedings, wars, shunning and genocide.

Route Map of the Book

Following the introduction and theoretical outline of the argument and the discussion of research methods in this chapter, Chapter 1 presents my research locations and their demographic developments. Although Tajikistan's mountain areas have not always been as densely populated as they are today, economic conditions seem to have forced a large part of the population to remain mobile over the centuries. In relation to these demographic developments I present some statistical data for the villages being studied, and describe fertility and mortality patterns, particularly in connection with the civil war as a 'break' in Tajik history. Further I have included a statistical presentation related to the youth bulge, so as to introduce the concepts of population composition and dependencies between generations and to provide a numerical overview of the actual dimension of the youth bulge. To illustrate how youth bulges are not solely a demographic problem for social scientists, an interview with a teacher is included to reveal not only the changes that have occurred since his youth but also his insight into a solution to the density and youth bulge question in Tajikistan.

Chapter 2 discusses Tajikistan from a historical perspective. Various examples from Central Asian history aptly demonstrate the relationship between cultural youth categories and the emergence of vanguard groups. I have used the *jadids**, the Komsomol and the *mujohids** to advance my argument that domestication efforts by society and the political leadership motivates youth movements to redefine themselves as vanguards. This has demographic consequences, which can be observed in the minimizing and maximizing of the size of the youth category.

Chapter 3 engages with domestication within community and family. Starting with the developmental cycle of domestic groups the chapter identifies the position of youth within the household. It is by moving out of the parental home that a young man becomes a full member of the community – and in that way domestication is fully achieved. The chapter continues with siblingship as one of the central cultural institutions through which young people's scope of choices is negotiated. Within youth bulge discussions, Heinsohn sees siblingship as a key factor for civil unrest – namely, that in high-parity societies the birth of many sons results in a male surplus. When fathers are consequently unable to provide all of their sons with an adequate inheritance, the surplus sons look for alternatives, which often lay in violent and/or expansive activities, such as military conquest, colonization or migration. Although Heinsohn's thesis sets forth some interesting points, it fails to analyse sons within the family context. In this sense, Tajik families perceive brothers as the strongest social unit, which does not exclude individual paths. The diversification strategy captures best how high-parity families deal with many sons, a practice dependent on culture and politics throughout history.

Against the background of youth within the family, Chapter 4 suggests a closer analysis of three different ways of categorizing youth: work, religion and migration. Youth is the physically strongest segment of society and hence the struggle over youth is also a struggle over the society's workforce. Categories and terms used to denote youth thus capture these specificities of youth. Similarly, local religious authorities praise the physical ability of youth to fulfil God's duty. Yet, these ideas of youth domestication are challenged by new movements which suggest that Islam liberates youth from community domestication and family bonds. Youth here is an individual chance to become active in society and engage with other young people as 'brothers'.

Today, migration also strongly influences parental and the community's domestication of youth. This has led young people to increasingly decide to postpone marriage in favour of greater freedom in Russia (the European idea of youth) and greater respect as the primary breadwinners (the local perception of adulthood). This leads to strongly diverging discourses on the role of youth within the local community. The elders argue that it is neither appropriate nor dutiful for young people to migrate to other regions and that this hardship over-burdens them; instead, they should remain at home and serve the family and community. The relative freedom that young men experience in Russia and their changed status back home, however, appears to be very attractive to hundreds of thousands of young men every year – even though the kind of work that most Tajik do in Russia is certainly not among the easiest.

With Chapter 5 we move to a classic topic of anthropology – marriage – which is often perceived as the key event marking the passage from youth to adulthood. Marriage in Tajikistan, however, is only one step on the path towards maturity, albeit an important one. Whereas during the Soviet period the life course of young people became more or less standardized, the legal vacuum of the civil war made it possible for young people to adapt nuptial rituals to their own needs. Rituals are central to domestication, and thus their analysis is a case in point. The increasing postponement of marriage in the post-civil war period is the result of this manoeuvring with regard to marriage rights and wedding practices, which has considerable effects on demographic developments and the negotiation of youth concepts. The relevance of studying rituals in order to understand demographic processes can be seen in the adaptability of life-course constructions and thus in the formation of youth categories.

Chapter 6 deals with the state's interest in youth. Adhering to the Soviet definition of youth, the Tajik state today continues to treat young people in a paternalistic way. I have attempted to determine the sectors (military, education, criminal) in which the state can directly influence youth and show how this is done. The example of the failed Arash concert demonstrates how young people can, within a single evening, be transformed from representing the hope of the country to being feared as a threat – that is, in psycho-cultural terms, being perceived as unruly and uneducated. Hence, this chapter discusses how groups must crystallize around identities to transform a youth bulge from a cultural or political category into an active movement.

In the Conclusion, I discuss how the previous chapters have illuminated the question of whether a demographic bulge of young people increases the likeli-hood of violent confrontation. Instead of taking a detached approach based on abstract statistical analysis, I have pursued the issue in the contexts of history, terminology, kinship, politics and culture. To demonstrate that a youth bulge is a cultural concept that relates to kinship structures, economic conditions and political claims, I assert that it has yet to be proven that the identification of a large youth bulge necessarily places a society at a higher risk of experiencing a conflict than a society without one. Here the categories that define the life course of people relate to individual socio-political groups. These groups transcend the negative connotation of youth by assuming a vanguard status – an exclusive status – the ideology of which aims then to recruit as many people as possible, that is, to mobilize the demographic potential through inclusion and exclusion strategies. In other words, the demographic argument around the concept of youth bulges needs to be analysed in its social, cultural and political contexts in order to understand the dynamics of youth.

To conclude, youth concepts are the result of different perceptions and practices within the family, community and state. Different categories have come to be shaped over many decades (centuries), and they continue to be shaped and reshaped even today – through domestication processes that, while remaining authoritative and top-down, have to take into consideration, and in some cases adapt to and incorporate, the demands and needs of young people. From the demographic point of view, the youth constitute a large majority of people who are either placed in unsatisfactory positions or experience problems of social mobility after completing school, thus creating the risk of being co-opted by political groups who seek to maximize their potential in professional organizations. While youth typically constituted the workforce that was subordinate to the elder generation during the Soviet era, the newly emerging concepts of youth accord young men a high level of responsibility. Domestication is a concept that suggests looking at youth not only as a concept but also as individuals. In successful structural and authoritative domestication, young people internalize the roles dedicated to youth. Hence, young people often reject top-down domestication and increasingly take charge of their own lives, resulting in changing concepts of youth.

Notes

1. See: http://www.rferl.org/content/tajikistan_flash_mob_energy_shortages/3553230.html; http://www.avesta.tj/main/8058-fleyesh-mob-po-tadzhikski-ili-kak-v-dushanbe.html.
2. In 2011 the government passed the Law of the Republic Tajikistan on Parental Responsibility for Education and Upbringing of Children (*Qonuni Jumhurii Tojikiston dar borai mas'uliyati padaru modar dar ta'limu tarbiyai farzand*). The law holds parents responsible for, among other things, educating their children and restricting them from attending illegal religious lessons and praying in mosques.
3. One of the posters at the Barki Tojik protest was a collage stating 'nepotism + tribalism = corruption – the people oppose' (*narod protiv*).
4. A 'youth bulge' is generally understood to refer to a demographic phenomenon in which the proportion of youth has increased significantly when compared to other age segments in a given population. It is a characteristic of a society in demographic transition such as the majority of Arab and Central Asian societies.
5. Gillis (1974: 170–1) argues that the concept of adolescence emerged as distinct from the concept of juvenile delinquent at the end of the nineteenth century. Hence, the adolescent,

as the concept was developed in Europe, came to represent a stage of immaturity that was susceptible to various, sometimes fantastic interpretations; however, within the context of a global North/South opposition, adolescents have been portrayed as the noble revolutionaries of the North in contrast to the wild (criminalized) youth of the South.

6. This phenomenon – of using contrasting terms for describing youth – has been incorporated into the titles of numerous works, such as *Vanguards or Vandals* (Abbink and Kessel 2005) and *Makers and Breakers* (Honwana and de Boeck 2005). Hebdige's *Hiding in the Light* (1988) is a more symbolic title, while other examples include Harris's *Muslim Youth: Tensions and Transitions in Tajikistan* (2006) and the section of Fuller's demographic study (2003) titled 'A Youthful Population: Benefit or Hindrance?' Tiger and Fox argue that 'in every human population, the adolescent and post-adolescent males are at once a resource and a threat' (Tiger and Fox 1992: 112). Thus, previous studies indicate that this dual perception is a universal view of young people.

7. See also Dracklé (1996), Liechty (2002) and le Meur (2008).

8. The age of 60 is symbolic and refers to the Prophet's age at death. From this age onwards, people retreat from household obligations and are expected to dedicate their lives to spiritual matters.

9. Interesting here is Baldauf's (1988: 11) comments on the neighbouring Afghans, in which he states that *bacha* (used synonymously with *javon* by Abdullo Qodirij) only applies to boys in the stage of physical puberty (between ages 11 and 18). This seems to be related to the tradition of *bachabozi* (the relationship between a young boy and a grown man, wherein the man finances the boy who in return acts devotedly towards his master and performs dances for him), for which only boys in this age group were considered. I surmise that after age 18, they would simply be too strong and self-confident; furthermore, by this age they have lost their 'childlike appearance' and become visibly men (for example, beard growth). It is possible that the term *bacha* changed in the 1930s when this tradition ended in Soviet Central Asia; it now refers to the time that leads up to marriage and more generally to youthful masculinity (whether someone is married or not).

10. The word 'youth' in English has several meanings (*Oxford English Dictionary* 2009: s.v.). From among the given definitions, only two meanings are reflected in this study: (1) 'youth' indicating a period in life-cycle constructions (singular – 'youth is'), and when expanded, 'youth' as a term for a socio-demographic cohort within the period of youth; and (2) 'youth' referring to young people collectively (plural – 'youth are').

11. Dorman and Last demonstrate the malleability of the concept 'youth' within each cultural context. Dorman (2005: 194), in her studies of Eritrea, mentions that youth (18 to 40 years) is defined in terms of recruiting sufficient people for military programmes. Last (2005: 39) studied the Hausa, who use *yara* to refer to age (youth) as well as to a lower status in general, in contrast to the higher status implied by *dattijo*. See also Stewart (1977), Eisenstadt (1988), Elwert, Kohli and Müller (1990), d'Almeida-Topor et al. (1992) and Bräunlein and Lauser (1996).

12. I will not provide a literature review of this period, since this has been done competently by others (e.g., Gillis 1974; Hebdige 1988; Pilkington 1994; Wyn and White 1997). Gillis (1974: 170–1) argues that, at the end of the nineteenth century, the concept of adolescence emerged as distinct from the concept of juvenile delinquents.

13. Cohen complains about the gender blindness of the term 'youth', in that it is usually applied in the context of 'boys being boys' (Cohen 1999: 202). The Chicago School of Sociology was ground-breaking for its sociological and anthropological approaches concerning urban, migration and subcultures in the beginning of the 20th century. Robert E. Park was one of the school's mayor founder.

14. The notion of youth culture was introduced by Talcott Parsons in 1949 'to mean a distinctive world of youth structured by age and sex roles' (Parsons, cited in Wulff 1995: 3). For a critique of this concept, see, e.g., Wyn and White (1997: 72–77) and Bennett (2004).

15. Hebdige (1988) has criticized the American approach that distinguishes between youth as peaceful consumers and youth as dangerous political agents, described as a 'moral panic' by Cohen (1973: 9). According to Hebdige, the aforementioned dichotomies are repeatedly used in public to portray and discuss the question of youth, with respective political consequences. While punks and skinheads were seen as somewhat rebellious but marginal subcultures in the United States, black youth were stereotypically portrayed as more threatening and disruptive to the society at large (cf. Comaroff and Comaroff 2000: 100; Bucholtz 2002).

16. See Ariès (1962), Gillis (1974), Kłoskowska (1988), Amit-Talai and Wulff (1995), Dracklé (1996) and Wyn and White (1997).

17. See Eisenstadt (1956, 1988), Mannheim (1970), Mead (1973), Abélès and Collard (1985), Müller (1989), Nora (1996), Burkart and Wolf (2002) and Alber, van der Geest and Whyte (2008).

18. See Fierman (1991), Poliakov (1992), Bushkov (1993), Niyazi (1994, 1999, 2000), Olimova (2000), Harris (2002, 2006) and Nourzhanov (2005).

19. The Tajik term that is primarily, though not exclusively, used to denote generation is *nasl** (*avlod**), which refers to father–child succession as well as to a societal generation – e.g., the young generation (*nasli javonon*).

20. The effects of globalization on youth have received little attention thus far, according to Maira and Soep (2005), who have compiled a volume dedicated to this topic (cf. Comaroff and Comaroff 2000; and Kirmse 2009 on Kyrgyzstan).

21. The pejorative view of youth goes even further; as Wyn and White discuss, young people were assumed to be 'naturally rather animalistic and uncontrollable', while at the same time they represented hope and optimism and were regarded as vulnerable (Wyn and White 1997: 19). The popularity of such a view can be seen even in recent publications. For example, a leading German journal, *Der Spiegel*, made it the cover theme of its 7 January 2008 issue: *Junge Männer: Die gefährlichste Spezies der Welt* (Young men: the most dangerous species in the world).

22. For a comprehensive introduction to age-group systems, see Stewart (1977) and Müller (1989).

23. Most anthropological studies on youth and conflict have been conducted in African and South Asian contexts; hence, there are numerous interesting studies in the field, including, among others, Schiffauer (1987), Zitelmann (1991), Cruise O'Brien (1996), Mahmood (1996), Richards (1996), Elwert, Feuchtwang and Neubert (1999), Abbink (2000, 2001), Koehler (2000), Orywal (2002), Honwana and de Boeck (2005) and Collins (2008).

24. Despite the limitations, there have been studies on fertility and nuptiality, such as Lindstrom and Berhanu (1999) on Ethiopia, Eloundou-Enyegue, Stokes and Cornwell (2000) on Cameroon, and Randal (2005) on the Tuareg.

25. It is significant that Tajik opposition leaders admitted to having 'no control over some twenty per cent of their forces' ('Civil War in Tajikistan: Diary of Events', *Central Asia Monitor*, No.5, 1992 (p.6)).

26. Cf. Peters and Richards (1998) and Benda-Beckman (2004: 236).

27. Another external influence that has affected social groups and the development of conflicts is freer access to small arms. The circulation of small arms has affected the traditional control of young people, since young people not only have greater access to such weapons

but also have a greater say in deciding when and how to use them. See Benda-Beckmann (2004) on Ambon, Indonesia; Simonse (2005) and McCaskie (2008) on Africa; and Heathershaw (2005) on Central Asia.

28. Jenkins sees this deficit as specific to post-Barthian anthropology, in which processes of group identification are favoured over social categorization.

29. '*Or le* Complexe de l'Encombrement *suscite l'impatience et la fureur, ceux qui en souffrent ont le sentiment d'être des 'hommes de trop'. Pour eux, tout devient obstacle, mais surtout les autres hommes qui leur barrent le chemin*' (Bouthoul 1968: 16).

30. '*Jusqu'à présent l'homme était en équilibre spontané avec son milieu. Cet équilibre se détruit sous nos yeux chaque jour davantage*' (Bouthoul 1968: 18).

31. '*Ein* youth bulge *findet sich überall dort, wo die 15–24-Jährigen mindestens 20 Prozent . . . bzw. die Kinder (0–15-Jährigen) mindestens 30 Prozent der Gesamtbevölkerung ausmachen*' (We can identify a *youth bulge* in all those societies in which the 15–24 year olds make up at least 20 per cent . . . i.e., the children (0–15 year olds) are at least 30 per cent of the total population) (Heinsohn 2006: 15).

32. An interesting point is raised by de Boer and Hudson's (2004) additional criterion of the sex ratio. In Asia especially, the ratio of men to women is high, which is perceived as an increased risk factor. The authors argue that socially manipulated sex ratios result in the male surplus becoming a source of conflict, due to competition among men for women.

33. Huntington writes: 'The numerical expansion of one group generates political, economic, and social pressures on other groups and induces countervailing responses'; he argues that the Tamil insurgency 'coincides exactly with the years when the fifteen-to-twenty-four-year-old "youth bulge" in those groups exceeded twenty per cent of the total population of the group' (Huntington 1998: 259).

34. The dependency ratio reflects the relation of the dependent segment (children and elderly of the population) to the productive segment (population of working age).

35. The 'greed and grievance concept' assumes that economic interests drive young men to join rebel groups, without giving much consideration to the quality of available work and expected income. My contention is that when making such decisions, young men value status above economic ends.

36. Compare de Boer and Hudson (2004: 27) and Makhamov (1996) for Badakhshan, Tajikistan. After Tajikistan achieved independence in 1991, the economy collapsed and unemployment rose rapidly, especially among young people. Makhamov (ibid.: 197) reports that, in the autonomous province of Badakhshan, 76,000 out of 161,000 people were unemployed. Women were especially hit hard. They were left with no choice but to give birth to one child after another in order to receive state subsidies, which for many families was the sole source of income.

37. Max Gluckman (1963) considers the question of youth and civil war (although he uses the term 'civil war' interchangeably with rebellion rituals, which is somewhat confusing). He observes that the periodicity of civil wars (rebellions) is twelve to seventeen years – which corresponds to the periodic transfer of power from the elders to the warriors' generation. The limited number of positions in society motivates the maturing youth to compete: 'the whole question of the effect on wider political relations of the movement of men through grades of age clearly needs investigation even where these grades are not institutionalized . . . This has made me wonder whether the growing of younger men into adulthood, in which they found their path to power blocked by their elders, has some influence on the total situation, in that this pressure from below tends to lead to rebellion' (ibid.: 38). Cf., e.g., Abdullah (1998), Comaroff and Comaroff (2000), Maxted (2003) and Peters (2010).

38. Malthus (1999) placed the problem of food production and population growth at the centre of his research. According to his work, populations cannot exceed the supply of food; any population that reaches this limit will be vulnerable to disease, famine or war – which he refers to as 'positive checks'. The question of ecology and war has been contested by Paul Richards (1996) in his study of Sierra Leone.
39. The rebellions of 2010/2011 in the Arab world are a case in point. Young people took to the streets for social, economic and political rights. From an economic perspective, the youth in these countries represent important mass consumers, but socio-politically they continued to be treated as a peripheral minority.
40. Especially in kinship studies, there is a tradition, following Rivers, to relate (statistical) micro-analyses to social dynamics (Rivers 1900; Chibnik 1985; Bernardi and Hutter 2007; Heady 2007).
41. There are many similar studies, mainly focusing on fertility (cf. Pauli 2000; see also Winter 1992; Kertzer and Fricke 1997; Basu 2004; Eloundou-Enyegue, Stokes and Cornwell 2000; Randal 2005).
42. This seems to be the case in traditional systems that concentrate wealth in the hands of the elders and regard youth as having a 'deprived minority status'. The situation rapidly reverses when wealth becomes potentially accessible to everyone, independent of age, because then youth becomes a valued target of marketing efforts and attains the status of a highly desirable economic sector.
43. See Ariès (1962), Gillis (1974), Bourdieu (1993: 136–46), Turner (1995: 97), Dracklé (1996) and Wyn and White (1997: 67–70).
44. A 'vanguard group' is a distinct group (usually of young people) that claims to speak in the name of youth, or those youth who comprise a concerned social or political unit, and that sets forth demands and calls for changes. Not every youth group is necessarily a vanguard group; they become such a group when they achieve political and public attention, which in turn increases their chances of success. It is significant for vanguard groups that their ideas are publicly understood as representing the demand or needs of a social category (such as youth, children, or ethnic, political or religious minorities).
45. '*Mais en tout cas, ce qui est sûr, c'est que la révolution jeune turque a donné le signal d'un renouvellement (et rajeunissement) des classes dirigeantes, même si cela ne s'est pas fait d'un coup*' (Georgeon 2007: 160).
46. '*[L]a notion de "jeune"* (genç) *se trouve soudain popularisée dans le langage ... Incontestablement, les jeunes et la jeunesse prennent une place nouvelle dans la société et dans la politique*' (Georgeon 2007: 161).
47. '*[I]n der SS und SA sind häufig die 2. und 3. Bauernsöhne*' (Sternberg 1981: 152).
48. '*Er (der Faschismus) erkauft sich die Stütze, die er an den ersten Bauernsöhnen hat, durch eine Forcierung im Proletarisierungsprozess der jüngeren Bauernsöhne*' (Sternberg 1981: 153).
49. Young people played a central role in the struggle against colonial regimes in Africa, as demonstrated by numerous examples in d'Almeida-Topor et al. (1992).
50. See Poliakov (1992), Olimova (2002, 2006), Harris (2004, 2006) and Stephan (2008).
51. Heathershaw (2009: 75–76, 82) refers to a concept of 'harmony ideology', which fittingly captures the intention and efforts of people to create a peaceful society despite numerous dissonances and conflicts.
52. Interviews were usually conducted by myself (S.R.). All names of my informants have been changed to protect their person.
53. Howell prefers the anthropological census 'microanalysis' and defines it as 'the study of particular populations of a group of locally bounded people defined as small enough that they can be studied by one or few investigators over a period of a few months to a few

years' (Howell 1986: 226). In other words, microanalysis can be conducted in a local community bound by territoriality (and not by kinship), such as a village or neighbourhood – i.e., a common settlement.

54. Van der Geest cites an example concerning birth control in a Ghanaian community. In this case, he realized that the data which had been collected in a medical survey were actually the official data, which drastically differed from the information that van der Geest (2004: 44) himself had obtained through discussions, observations and interviews. In light of the huge discrepancy with regard to the number of children calculated by the two sources, it was as if there were two different populations.

55. This item refers to questions that go beyond quantitative data collection: 'By whom was the marriage arranged?'; 'Was it a love marriage?'; 'Did you perform the state marriage registration, and if so, after how much time?'; 'What was the marriage procedure?' (details regarding bridewealth, marriage rituals, organization and so on).

56. While demographers take these factors into account as variables, I have attempted to identify their qualitative roles in influencing demographic changes.

Chapter 1

Placing the Field Sites in Their Context

A Demographic History

This chapter discusses the demographic context of the field sites researched in this study. After a brief introduction to the four research locations, I will provide an overview of their demographic history. The material presented here has been gathered, to a large extent, from interview narratives and genealogies collected to represent demographically relevant census data. The ensuing discussion revolves around three key inquiries: When and why did fertility increase in these regions? What constitutes a youth bulge in this context? What are the mortality patterns in these regions?

During the Soviet period, fertility rates rose almost without interruption, while since the mid 1980s a steady decline in fertility has occurred. According to Dhillon and Yousef (2007), if, due to decreasing fertility, a youth cohort exceeds any other cohort, the society is considered to be experiencing a youth bulge. Thus, youth bulges are not (only) a high percentage of children and young people in the populace but also a specific phenomenon associated with the demographic transition from high fertility to low fertility. In order to approach the question of 'size' from a demographic anthropological point of view, I will make use of different methods such as genealogies, narratives and basic statistics.

The interview excerpts with Zikir reproduced below, which pertain to demographic changes and their relevance to youth, constitute a narrative upon which I place great importance. The interviewee, a teacher, not only gives voice to the core questions analysed in this book but also confirms that the main theme developed here reflects daily concerns and discussions among Tajiks. In other words, demographic issues have not only become political and scientific matters but also matters of concern to the local population.

The Field Sites

My original plan entailed conducting research only in the Jirgatol district, but I ended up spending time in other locations as well. For instance, I had not intended to stay in Dushanbe, but due to several incidents (among them, visa problems and my child's serious illness), I had to remain in the capital for quite a while. During my stay, I realized that my urban experiences were of great relevance to understanding the role of students and, in particular, state concepts of youth (Chapter 7). The capital plays a central role in the lives of rural people. As the economic centre of the country, and the centre of education (universities are located here), Dushanbe is also considered the ultimate symbol of modernity. Since young people from rural areas come here to study or work, Dushanbe has a high concentration of them.

The main research locations that I selected are situated in rural areas, although Shahrituz could be classified as a small town. In each of the locations a large part of the population was sympathetic to the United Tajik Opposition (UTO) during the civil war.[1] They include the area referred to as Lakhsh (two villages), Shahrituz (a neighbourhood within the small town) and Shahrigul (a village).[2] Lakhsh, which lies in the Jirgatol district, is linked historically to Shahrituz. Several villages from this mountain district had been relocated to the cotton plantations in the Vakhsh Valley during the 1940s and 1950s.[3] One of these villages constituted the neighbourhood where I conducted my research in Shahrituz. The neighbourhood had continued to maintain social relations, through intermarriage and economic exchanges, with those who had remained in the mountain regions. Moreover, during the civil war, many people from this neighbourhood in Shahrituz took refuge with relatives in Lakhsh.

Jirgatol is said to be Kyrgyz, and thus people from these areas are labelled with the ethnonym 'Kyrgyz' by outsiders, even if their native language is Tajik.[4] The Kyrgyz constitute the majority of the population in Jirgatol, although their proportion has declined over the last decade due to a considerable increase in the number of Tajik people in many villages and to the extensive migration of Kyrgyz to Kyrgyzstan.

It is important to mention here that what constitutes an 'ethnic' identity is anything but clear in the context of Central Asia. Many of the 'ethnic groups' in this region evolved through census taking in the early twentieth century.[5] Census categories and the politics of nationality transformed various fluid identifications into more fixed ethnic categories, officially declared in the passports of Soviet citizens. Ethnic cultures, within the realm of ethnographic research, came to be celebrated in folkloric representations, while at the same time they were marginalized as a remnant of the past, soon to give way to a single, common identity, *Homo sovieticus* (Mühlfried and Sokolovskiy 2011).

In Tajikistan national identifications have been described as weak because Bukhara and Samarkand were seen as the cultural centre of Central Asia's Persian speakers, both these cities being were incorporated into the Uzbek socialist republic in the course of nation building in the 1920s (Rubin 1998; Roy 2000). Regional identification had historically served as an important marker of identification and, at least to a certain degree, laid down the dividing lines among militant groups in the civil war.

Administrative Divisions

Tajikistan is divided administratively into provinces. Khatlon province in the south includes the research site of Shahrituz. Sughd province is in the north, the main town of which is Khujand. The easternmost Pamir province enjoys a certain degree of independence as the Gorno-Badakhshan Autonomous Oblast (GBAO). The central region – including the capital Dushanbe and the Rasht (or Qarotegin) Valley in the east, right up to the Kyrgyz border – is called the central province (Region of Republican Subordination).

The two research locations in the Rasht (Qarotegin) Valley are Shahrigul, situated in the district of Gharm in the Kamarob gorge, and Lakhsh in Jirgatol,[6] which lies high up in the mountains, near the border with Kyrgyzstan. In geographical terms, this valley is usually referred to as the Qarotegin (Karategin in Russian). Politically, the name Qarotegin has been changed to Rasht. However, I will retain the geographical name of Qarotegin because it is more common and includes Jirgatol, which was my main area of research in 2006. The specific characteristics of the Jirgatol district will be dealt with in subsequent chapters. Every district is divided into *jamoat*s* (municipalities) comprised of several villages, with one of these villages constituting the main *jamoat* or administrative centre.

A History of Qarotegin

The Qarotegin Valley, situated to the east of Dushanbe, has long been populated by the Kyrgyz. It is not clear when and why they arrived in the valley. According to one local version, the Kyrgyz were refugees who had come from territories further north and were allowed to stay in the mountainous regions by the emir in Bukhara. Another version states that they arrived seeking new pastures rather than refuge. The official version appeared in a book by Baltabaev in the Tajik and Kyrgyz languages in 2006, celebrating the seventy-fifth anniversary of the Jirgatol district. 'The people of this *viloyat* [district] are of two kinds: first, the Özbak (qirgiz), and second, the Tojik' (Baltabaev 2006: 26).[7]

In 1970, excavations were undertaken in Lakhsh, which apparently proved that phenotypical 'Iranians' had once lived there, before a landslide wiped out the entire village. This motivated the local Tajik to lay claim to the land, arguing that it belonged to their forefathers, thus systematically precluding any Kyrgyz claim.[8] Bushkov and Mikul'skiy (1996: 3) identify two time periods during which the Kyrgyz are likely to have come from their place of origin in the south of the Ferghana Valley to Qarotegin, both dating back to the seventeenth and eighteenth centuries – or more precisely, 1665 and 1758.

Thus, the Kyrgyz version of history differs from the historical accounts in Baltabaev's book on certain points. A local historian (who remembers local

Figure 1.1: Map of Tajikistan.

history in the classic Kyrgyz manner, through a recitative song called a *dastan*) mentions that several hundred years ago the Kyrgyz were authorized to live in the area by the central government in Bukhara. According to him, this is evident in the fact that all of the local places bear Kyrgyz names, even if the majority of the population today is Tajik.[9]

> Earlier on, they had assured us that they would never lay hands on us – this was three to four hundred years ago, when Alim Khan [1798–1819] was the emir in Bukhara. At that time, the Tajik could not do anything, because we were in the majority here. Now the Tajik have come here, thinking they can tell us to 'go back to your homeland (*vatan**)' . . . But they came after us, the Tajik. We have been here since 1406 – this year, that makes 600 years.[10]

The Tajik population of Lakhsh came to the region in several waves. According to family genealogies, sets of siblings arrived from the Bukhara and Samarkand regions (possibly as refugees). They first settled in the area of Tavildara; later, they migrated further to the upper valleys of Tavildara (Vakhyo) and Rasht, and the southern shores of the Muk-suu River.

In the 1920s, demographic pressure in the most remote mountain regions resulted in several significant population movements. Persian-speaking families – later to become Tajik citizens – split up, with some members moving to Kyrgyz settlements such as Lakhsh. These migrants came to Kyrgyz villages in search of opportunities. At that time, each village was headed by one or two (Kyrgyz) *biys* (local chiefs) who were in charge of land distribution (Martin 2001: 36). According to Kyrgyz elders, the first Tajik who had come were rather poor, looking for work (*khizmatgor*; n. *khizmat**). They were given land by the land-lords, on which they founded families (in the nineteenth and early twentieth centuries). Other Tajik groups joined them from neighbouring valleys (such as from Khujaitov and Vakhyo) during the Stalin purges of the 1930s. Unlike the earlier migrants, those groups also included rich landowners who had fled the *kulak* persecutions.[11]

Lakhsh

The Lakhsh area is located approximately 300 kilometres from Dushanbe; however, due to poor road conditions, it takes an entire day's journey to reach this remote area, which is only 50 kilometres from the Kyrgyz border. The *jamoat* (municipality) of Muk – named after the Muk-suu River – consists of ten villages, the largest of which is Sasik Bulak, which has a Tajik majority; Sari Kenja has a Kyrgyz majority, and Kara Kenja a mixed population. Muk is home to approximately 7,800 residents, about 2,900 of whom live in two villages (Sasik Bulak and Sari Kenja). The area of Sasik Bulak, Sari Kenja and Kara Kenja is also referred to as Lakhsh (I will make use of the term 'Lakhsh' to refer to the villages, especially Sasik Bulak and Sari Kenja, and their respective agricultural and pastoral land). Although the largest cultivated area is still state property, with its chief appointed by the district government (*hukumat**), the present-day cooperative farm (*khojagyi dehqoni*) does not have to provide the state with agricultural produce on a regular basis; however, an informal transfer of products does occur in a slightly different manner (often on the basis of demand).

Bushkov (1993: 3–4) suggests the following population composition for Qarotegin: approximately 200,000 people lived in Qarotegin, Darvaz and Bald'juan at the beginning of the twentieth century. According to Bushkov, these residents were of mixed ethnicity, and at times, less than 5 per cent of the population was Tajik. It is not the percentage of ethnic groups that is interesting here but the fact that ethnic diversity was a common pattern of settlement and that recent figures show a rapid change in favour of the Tajik population. In the last decade, the Tajik have grown to outnumber the Kyrgyz in this region, also evidenced by more recent statistics of first-grade school pupils.[12]

The climate in Jirgatol is harsh, with a long winter (five months) and shorter spring, summer and autumn. Potatoes are called the 'gold of Lakhsh' because they are usually converted into cash and are valued as the area's most important resource. Wheat, carrots and onions are produced solely for family consumption, and wheat production is usually not even enough to supply a household for the entire year.

Most people have cows (two to five) and goats and sheep (five to twenty) that spend the summer on the pastures (*ailok**) and can be converted into cash at any time, usually when extra money is needed for a feast. Further, the milk is processed into butter and hard cheese. Some people also grow apples of high quality in plots near their houses, but due to the fruit's recent appearance in the region, many people are not knowledgeable about how to store or market them, so the apples often rot in humid cellars and are among the most popular goods to be 'stolen' by children.[13] Labour migration to Russia is relatively new and done on a smaller scale here compared to the other research locations, but the numbers of outbound migrants is rapidly increasing, bolstered by the success stories of those who return.

Shahrituz

Old Soviet maps situate Shahrituz in a forest. Presumably it was not until the 1940s that the forest was cleared to make room for cotton plantations. This does not mean that there were no settlements in this area before that time – villages such as Sayod and Kobodiyon existed – but it was only in the mid twentieth century that Shahrituz developed into a town. According to local people, during the time of the emirs (before 1920), the forest was inhabited by expatriates sent into exile by the regime. Most groups chose this route to go to Afghanistan, and those who did not manage to cross the Amu River remained in hiding in the forest.[14] As a result, Shahrituz is a conglomerate of many different social and ethnic groups, including certain types of 'Arabs', various Uzbek tribes, and Afghans – to name just a few.

From 1949 to the early 1950s, the Tajik and Kyrgyz were forcibly displaced by the communist government from the mountainous regions of Qarotegin and relocated to the plains. Due to the severe climatic differences between the two places, many people died. The inhabitants of one mountain village were together resettled in one village or neighbourhood (*mahalla*) in the new environment. Many of those who were resettled favoured marriage within their group or with relatives who had remained in the mountain regions. It should be noted that the migratory groups hardly ever intermarried with local people (*mestni*). To my knowledge, the first interethnic marriage between a *mestni* (a local girl of the

Kungurot) and a boy from the relocated group occurred in 2002. (While it is possible that there may have been one or two other such marriages in the past, it does not change the fact that the community, on the whole, almost never intermarried with the local population.)

According to Roy (1998; 1999: 112; 2000),[15] relations within a resettled village community were not merely based on a single kinship group (*qavm** or *avlod**); they at times embraced the identity of an entire village – in other words, one or several different kinship groups (*avlod*) were regarded as connected through a common village identity. The *mahalla** where I conducted research basically comprised the settlement of one dominant extended family (*avlod*), together with other smaller groups from the *jamoat** of Muk, as described above.

Regardless of their mother tongue, this group was referred to as 'the Kyrgyz'; thus, a regional marker was used to classify them (see above). Many of them internalized this ethnonym, thereby distancing themselves from neighbouring Tajik groups.[16] These Kyrgyz considered themselves neutral in the recent civil war. They followed the events in Dushanbe (the demonstrations that resulted in war) from a distance without imagining that war could possibly reach them, since they believed themselves to be without political 'sin'.

But civil wars often provide an opportunity for the release of local tensions. In this sense, the local groups that had resided in this area long before the arrival of migrants used the power vacuum to pursue their own agenda, which was 'to send home' (*vatan**) migrants (to their place of origin in the mountains). Local Uzbek groups in cooperation with Tajik pro-governmental groups, and with outside assistance from the Uzbek government (in the form of technical equipment), launched genocidal persecutions of all Tajik and Kyrgyz migrants.[17] Other local groups took advantage of the situation to rob their neighbours' houses, while still others received help from the Popular Front (*Fronti Khalki*), one of the executive arms of the Tajik government. According to Karim, between 13 and 15 November 1992, the various pro-government groups converged 'to clean Shahrituz of the opposition' (Karim 1997: 516). In this way, the 'Kyrgyz' eventually had to flee when war reached their very doorsteps.

The Tajik and Kyrgyz fled to the Afghan border, some crossing into Afghanistan where they joined refugee camps in Qunduz and Mazar-e Sharif.[18] Others managed to join their relatives in Jirgatol. Shortly after the mass exodus, some local forces called for the 'Kyrgyz' to return, promising that they would not be harmed. However, ethnic identities had not been sorted out yet, since regional identities had prevailed for more than forty years. Thus, when some families of the group in question returned, believing that they were emically Kyrgyz, they were declared to be Tajiks from Qarotegin and thus members of the United Tajik Opposition and consequently enemies of the government. The men were massacred on their arrival, whereas the women were emptied from buses somewhere outside Dushanbe. This is how they learned the 'lesson of ethnicity'. Eventually, the president of Kyrgyzstan, Askar Akajev, sent a train (remembered as 'the Askar Akajev train') to collect 'the Kyrgyz' from Tajikistan. While most of those who had fled to Afghanistan and Jirgatol returned after 1994, most of the refugees who went to Kyrgyzstan remained there, with very few exceptions.

As for current living conditions in Shahrituz, the Vakhsh Valley is dry, with little if any snowfall. It is characterized by extremely hot summers and yields two harvests per year. Within their household plots, people grow potatoes, carrots, onions, wheat and many other crops, and have various fruit trees. In Shahrituz people work on cotton plantations that are partly private, partly state owned. Only women work on the plantations – not so much for the money, which is so little as to be considered irrelevant by men in terms of the household budget, but for the firewood provided by the woody stems of the cotton plants. 'I will just buy some clothes for my daughters; this is all I will be able to do with the money', said Jamila, a young mother, during a conversation in January 2007. In Shahrituz most young men migrate to Russia in order to help their parents rebuild their existence; in other words, they work for their parents' generation instead of their own.

Shahrigul

The village of Shahrigul is situated approximately 50 kilometres from the town of Gharm in the picturesque Kamarob gorge along the Sorbog River. It basically consists of several social units comprised of the original inhabitants and migrants from three small villages that were relocated here in 1969 because of the 'difficult and dangerous' conditions in the upper mountains. The steep mountains were believed to erode and cause natural disasters. Although this was certainly not the only reason for the relocation, the mountainous regions are, in fact, frequently affected by earthquakes that lead to landslides.[19]

The valley has good water resources but very little arable land. Almost all of the land has been sold and is now privately owned by property speculators.[20] Only families who do not have sons (employed in Russia or Dushanbe) providing for their basic needs such as food rely on cultivating the steep hills; the harvest is variable, depending on weather conditions and the effort expended. Local agriculture has declined in the last few years, and at the same time migration northwards has risen sharply. The village economy is now highly dependent on financial remittances from those who have migrated to Russia. With this increase in migration, the value of agricultural work has decreased. The livelihood of people in Shahrigul today is balanced between subsistence agriculture (performed by elderly people and children) and a total dependence on migration work (mainly by young men). Thus, the village's demographic composition reflects its economic stratification.

Shahrigul was severely hit by the civil war, in which a considerable proportion of the population participated. They supplied basic necessities to the activists in Dushanbe during the demonstrations, and later during the civil war. The percentage of the population that actively engaged in the war cannot be accurately determined, and also depends on how engagement is defined. The war moved towards Rasht in February 1993, accompanied by the heavy bombing of Gharm and Tojikobod (Karim 1997: 567). In spring 1993, state troops reached the area and declared the entire population to be collectively guilty of conspiring against the government. Eventually, the village of Shahrigul was also taken, and the *mujohids** fled. Although the majority of Shahrigul's inhabitants claimed to be neutral, they were nonetheless denied humanitarian help 'until the last *mujohid* had been captured'.[21]

Although the area of Gharm (that is, the Rasht district) is often portrayed as the centre of evil and a *mujohid* stronghold, the majority of the ordinary population was and continues to be opposed to war. As Karim (ibid.: 587–88) puts it, the people in Gharm had neither weapons nor the will to fight.[22] According to my research, some people did engage in war; however, the majority made every effort to keep their sons away from the war and to protect them from being recruited by *mujohid*s or by state troops.

Demographic History of Qarotegin

The following micro-demographic analysis of the research areas is based on the interviews and census that I conducted there. However, before viewing the statistics, it is helpful to discuss the existing literature on when and why there was such a dramatic increase in the Tajik population.

Until the socialist revolution, which occurred along with increased control over the Bukharan emirate, fertility in Central Asia had been rather low, with high infant mortality (Khan and Ghai 1979; Jones and Grupp 1987; Islamov 1988). The population increased considerably after the establishment of the Soviet Union, in part due to the introduction of its healthcare system.[23] Lublin states that, throughout the 1960s and 1970s, the total population of three Central Asian republics – Uzbekistan, Tajikistan and Turkmenistan – grew 'at least three times faster than they had during the previous two decades' (Lublin 1991: 37). The Tajik were said to have had the highest fertility rate in the Soviet Union, with an average family size of 6.6 members per family, and many families had seven or more children (which was the case for only 1 per cent of Russians) (ibid.: 46). Several other authors have also noted that fertility rates varied to a considerable extent within the entire Soviet Union.

Jones and Grupp (1987) have taken a wider look at demographic policy during the Soviet era, which they regard as Russia-oriented. While the authorities of the time were concerned about the sharp decline in fertility in northern areas of the

Soviet Union, they were very little concerned about high fertility rates in the southern republics. Thus, the Soviet Union implemented laws to counteract the tendency toward decreasing fertility; however, these laws – when applied to the whole of the Soviet Union – failed to have the intended impact, namely, to improve the living standard of the poorest families and to ease the burden of the working mother. While these laws did not increase the size of medium-sized families, they instead encouraged 'high-parity families to produce even more children' (ibid.: 270).

There had been high fertility in the southern territories ever since Brezhnev's policies (in the 1970s) to improve the low fertility levels in European Russia, an argument that is used by Tajiks today to justify their migration to Russia despite the many hostilities they face there. This distinct difference in demographic development between the south and the north was seldom discussed in fertility politics, with only the scientific community showing any concern for the long-term consequences (for example, they were concerned about the status of the Russian language and the authority structure within the army).[24]

While some authors link high fertility to an improved healthcare system, a decrease in local conflicts and warfare, and the pro-natalist politics of the Soviet state, especially after the Second World War, Jones and Grupp (ibid.: 15–22) have developed the idea of a 'cultural filter' that only integrates elements of modernization which are compatible with patriarchal family values. This argument is related to other discussions that attempt to identify causal links between Islam and high fertility.[25]

Although abortion had already been legalized in 1920, the law never prompted the same level of participation in Tajikistan as it did in Russia (Harwin 1996: 8).[26] The high mortality level of the 1930s (due to a severe famine in 1933) led to the identification of population growth as 'an ideological issue . . . regarded as an indicator of the country's well-being' (Barbieri et al. 1996: 70). Since abortion had become the principal method of family planning, it was banned in 1936, with the implementation of pro-natalist measures. These laws were reversed only after Stalin's death, with abortion becoming legal again in 1955.

Beside political programmes, Goody (1972: 10) suggests another influence on fertility rates: that in polygynous unions, women's fertility levels are lower, while monogamy increases the number of children born to each woman. Taking into account the changing conditions of households, where children tend to leave their parents' house earlier than before, and the juridical prohibition of polygynous unions, it can be asserted that the change in housing conditions, accompanied by the decrease in polygynous practices, contributed to the increase in fertility in Tajikistan. An additional factor in this phenomenon is the change in the economic structure, with subsistence farming as the economic base giving way to a collectivized economy. These and many other factors promoted the emergence of a more standardized and secure life course within the Soviet Union, leading to higher fertility.

The Consequences of Soviet Fertility Policy in Rural Tajikistan

The widespread contention that fertility began to increase due to the Russian presence seems less obvious if we look at people's narratives. According to people's accounts, collectivization and the Second World War had a heavy impact on family health and reproduction.

> I was ten years old when I started working on the sovkhoz [state-owned farm]. For one month I had to go to Jirgatol with a donkey during the night to bring the day's quota of wheat – with the donkey carrying bags weighing 120 kilogrammes. Only two people – me and an old man. When the bags fell off, I had to pick them up again, and I cried. My mother had to lead the horses for ploughing the acre; this is a very hard job because you have to push the horses away from each other all the time. She had five sons, and when she was thirty years old she was locked [meaning she could no longer bear children]. In the past women bore few children. Bahrom's mother, for example, had only one child – none of her other children survived. Due to hard work women could not bear too many children; they were locked [infertile] early.[27]

The former Soviet Union experienced a series of demographic catastrophes throughout the first half of the twentieth century (Haub 1994). In Shahrigul, people still remember not only famines, wars and purges but also recall everyday life as hard and painful, especially for the women, who had to handle their household duties as well as the obligation to work on the sovkhoz.

> Women had to leave for the fields early in the morning, leaving their children back home – even the very small ones. They would return only in the evening, with 'breasts full of milk'. After feeding their child, they would bake bread, because the men refused to eat bread older than one day; then they would wash the children's clothes. Before dawn, when it was still night, they would get up to make butter (*dugh kashidan*), prepare tea for their husbands, and then leave for work before the children had woken up. They were officially allowed to stay at home if they were in the ninth month of pregnancy, but the doctors often sent them to work until the very day the baby was born.
>
> I was pregnant with my son and went to the doctor; he said that I was not in the ninth month, and so I went back to ploughing – the same night, I gave birth [this was in 1963]. Then forty days later, I left the baby crying and struggling with its brothers and sisters and went back to work. We raised our children in black days. The situation improved a little bit in the sixties, and became much better in the seventies. They would not believe us if we said that a child was ill, so the children who

were strong enough survived, while the weak ones died. Two of my sons
and one daughter died. [Another mother interjects]: Four of my children
died.[28]

During the Second World War, between 1941 and 1945, 27 million people
perished in the Soviet Union (Winter 1992; Harwin 1996: 19). Whole villages
were emptied of men. Thus, Stalin's main concern was to raise fertility in order
to produce a supply of men for the Soviet army. Even fourteen years after the
war, women outnumbered men by 20 million. This led to the implementation of
stricter laws against abortion in 1944 and the relaxation of laws regarding illegitimate children, whose upbringing until the age of 12 was taken over by the state.

The state also introduced different incentives to encourage higher fertility. A
law established in 1944 introduced a one-time payment at the birth of a child
(Harwin 1996: 19–23). Moreover, monthly child benefit, begun in 1936 but
initially only paid from the birth of the seventh child onwards, was paid after
1944 upon the birth of the third child until their fifth birthday.[29] Motherhood
awards were introduced for all women with five or more children, and eventually, the 'mother heroine' award (usually a gold medal) was bestowed on
mothers with ten (sometimes eight) or more children (ibid.: 20). Jones and
Grupp (1987: 275) have mentioned that depending on the monetary value of
the award at a given time, these payments offered quite a substantial support for
families. Extremely poor families considered them a welcome supplement, but
the payments did not provide an incentive to women who were employed and
sufficiently well-off.

The situation seems to have been different for Tajik women, who were
'aiming for a Jiguli' (a Russian car given to 'mother heroines'). Although, as one
male informant claims, monetary assistance was neither fully responsible for the
increase in family size nor the main incentive to keep having children, nevertheless the public recognition of motherhood accorded women a valued status.
During my fieldwork, women stressed this aspect, contrasting it with the sense
of devaluation they experience today. At that time, motherhood was something
to compete for, even though awards were often handed out arbitrarily. When a
family in Novobod (a village in the vicinity of Gharm and an educational centre
for the region) with twenty-two children from one mother (?) was given a bus
as an award, having 'many children' became the aim of many mothers (and for
some, it still is). In interviews, women would proudly mention it if they had
received any of these awards (usually given only to those who had ten or more
living children).

Having many children, as stated above, was not merely an economic boost –
it also increased a woman's social status (Harris 2002). Only by having her own
children did a young woman gain social recognition. Regarding actual compensa-
tion, however, my informants could tell me little about the official rules, though

most of them seemed to have received child benefit up to a total of about twelve roubles a month, which was equal to the price of a 50 kilogramme bag of flour.[30]

> S.R.: According to you, did women have more children during the Soviet era or today?
>
> ZEBO: It doesn't matter. For example, if we are of the same age (*hamsol**), you have a child and then I have one as well; if you have another one, I will have one as well – it's like a competition. I will always try to have more children than you. In feasts, we are now told to bear fewer children, that four are enough, but the *hukumat** [government; i.e., during the Soviet era] would encourage us to have children – we were aiming for a Jiguli [Russian car].
>
> S.R.: After how many children would they give awards?
>
> ZEBO: After ten children. After a woman had seven or eight children, she would receive a silver medal; after nine children, a gold medal. We tried hard, but it didn't work. I didn't have a good mother-in-law who would tell me to stop working hard, take some rest. Believe me, sister, at one time I had two in the cradle and another child in my womb. My husband was not fair, and in addition to this I had so many guests to look after. In the morning I would get up early and send the cows to graze; then I would bake bread, cook, and at the same time I would also look after my children so nicely – they lived like kings. In one day, I would wash clothes four times – one packet of washing powder (*ayna*) would not last a week.[31]

Demographic Growth until Independence

The Russian premier Leonid Brezhnev (who ruled from 1965 to 1982) 'repeatedly called for the creation of meaningful demographic policy in his speeches before the general meetings of the Communist party' (Kuniansky 1981: 50). In other words, the Communist Party believed that demographic behaviour could be regulated by the state. Reports from the village describe the time under Brezhnev as relatively peaceful and harmonious. It was during this time that the Tajik, in particular, managed to become a significant demographic group.

In 1973, the USSR had the highest abortion rate in the world. Abortion had become the principal means of birth control, since very few people practised contraception (there was a widespread rumour that oral contraception could cause cancer). For the majority of Tajik Muslims within the research area, abortion was and is allowed for poor families or ill mothers, and even local mullahs to whom I spoke never opposed this method if it was done to secure the health and future of the existing children.

The efforts to increase the birth rate finally yielded results in the first half of the 1980s. Political strategies in this regard had not varied much throughout the

USSR; the results, however, varied considerably by region and left each republic to deal with the outcome after independence. In Tajikistan, children were
perceived as not only the family wealth but also as a contribution to the Soviet
nation. Some perceived high fertility as an opportunity to improve the ability of
families to sustain themselves in difficult local conditions, while others believed
that a greater workforce would make it possible to send labourers to areas that
required people, such as Siberia (Barbieri et al. 1996). It was only in the second
half of the 1980s that family planning programmes, aimed at controlling fertility,
began to be implemented in Central Asia. However, the process was interrupted
by the upheaval resulting from the dissolution of the Soviet Union.[32] Like the
other republics, Tajikistan was left to its own devices, with its still increasing
population. This population, however, was no longer part of a larger nation – the
citizens now belonged to a small mountainous country.

A Teacher's Reflections on the Contemporary Youth Situation

The consequences of demographic conditions are not merely accepted by the
people who must live with them; the issue invariably becomes part of local discourse. In this light, it is appropriate to conclude this historical account of population development with a significant excerpt from an interview with Zikir, a teacher,
who reflects on the changing situation of youth in Shahrigul. He is representative
of the fact that local people discuss the phenomenon of the youth bulge in the
context of economic crises and the country's inability to provide decent opportunities for its working population. In the face of such difficulties, parents' and the
community's main concern is how to domesticate their children. This interview
touches on how youth are regarded in the contexts of parental duty, community
concern, state responsibility, and their impact beyond Tajikistan's borders.

> Until 1993, I did not see a pick or plough – I wasn't given any work like
> that, only scholarly work. We received wages and bought food and did
> not have to worry about tomorrow. Now I feel concern for the future of
> our youth. For example, they go to Moscow and work there for six to
> eight months; others stay there for three, four or five years and then only
> return in order to marry . . . You wouldn't believe the kind of difficulties
> today's youth have to face. When it is time for them to marry, the father
> incurs such debts in the process that he ends up spending all his savings.
> Then the son lives with his bride for one or two months, after which
> he leaves for Moscow. My wife and I, in contrast, have been married
> for twenty-six years without being separated even once, except for the
> time when I was studying. We have always been together . . . All those
> young people leave home so early that they do not experience any joy
> in life. Earlier on, young people would spend more time at home; they
> would work at home in the traditional way. Today if you give a young

man a wife, and the wife is young, he still leaves this young wife. His wife will remain here, while he will go abroad and stay there for six to seven months before he sees her again. You can say that half their [young men's] lives are spent on the road – this is absolutely bad.

We help other countries to develop but not ours. There [in Russia] we have built castles, but here – nothing. Look at the state of youth in our country today – what will they do? I mean, in Tajikistan today there are no policies, no laws to generate employment opportunities for youth, which would enable them to earn a decent living, a salary – that's why they have to go elsewhere to earn . . . There, in one day they can earn up to 100 dollars – this equals 350 somoni. Here, we need to work day and night for four months to earn 350 somoni.

. . .

Today, the population of Tajikistan is seven million; hence, this territory and land [of which only 7 per cent is agricultural land] cannot properly look after a population of seven million people. For example, in our village there is no more space left for building houses. If our sons want to move out and build their own homes, there is no more land. This is because half the land has been, little by little, occupied by new families, and now there is no more space . . . Our demographic situation is absolutely impossible! Otherwise, we will have to emigrate to Kazakhstan or Uzbekistan or some other place – there doesn't seem to be any more space for the increasing population in our Tajikistan.

. . .

Earlier on, instead of having one wife, like my father, they would take five or even ten wives. This means that if I, for example, have four sons, then each son will eventually have his own independent household . . . There were so few people at that time; for example, I lived with my four brothers in one house. How could they have relations with their wives while living in the same house? Therefore, in order to have conjugal relations, they would tie up their *lengī** [piece of cloth] outside the door. Then the others would know which son was in the house that night with his wife.[33]

This teacher's reflections on the youth problem show that youth is not merely a political matter; parents are also concerned about not being able to provide the same standard of living for their children as they themselves received. He is also very well aware of Tajikistan's limitations in being able to provide enough work and food for its citizens. He compares the situation to that of his own childhood and his father's life (living in one house with his brothers and controlling the birth of children by regulating a person's access to his wife by being forced, through the *lengī*, to announce his intentions to the entire family).

This narrative excerpt summarizes many of the problems, perceptions and difficulties concerning today's youth in Tajikistan. It also shows that the purpose of this study is not merely to test a predefined model developed in Europe or some other distant place; rather, it deals with the daily concerns of the people in Tajikistan and how they view their history, how they experience current political developments, and how they regard the future.

Demographic Development in Three Villages

Fertility and the Dependency Ratio in Shahrituz

This section presents the family history of Ahad (Figure 1.2) to show how fertility and the role of youth play out in a local family and how the civil war has affected and changed people's views regarding roles and tasks. A statistical data analysis, based on this family history, provides the reader with an overview of the situation in the villages concerned.

Ahad, who was born in 1944, lives in a neighbourhood of Shahrituz where he and his family (including his parents and siblings) were resettled from the Jirgatol district in 1953. Today, he is the head of a household and father to twelve children. He first married in 1968, aged 24; his first wife, Firuza, was 20. Firuza had four children and died in childbirth with her fourth, a son, who died as well. Ahad was left with a son and a daughter (another child had also died at birth)

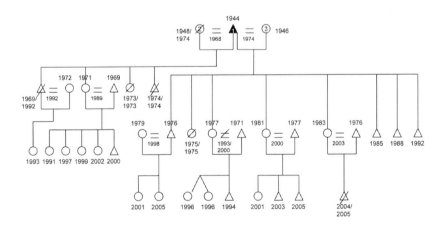

Figure 1.2: Ahad's family (Shahrituz).

and no wife. This kind of situation is usually resolved as soon as possible in Tajik society, since a man is not expected to take care of his own children (cf. Kislyakov and Pisarchik 1976: 161–62).

While family members helped rear his children in the meantime, it was very clear that he would marry again as soon as possible, which he did, within a year. His second wife, Gulnigor, gave birth to eight children. With this figure, she represents earlier fertility patterns that suggest a total fertility rate (TFR) of 6.89 for women aged 45 and above and a marital age-specific fertility rate (MASFR) of 7.16 children per woman for the years 1983 to 1990, which is still far below the maximum reproductive rate.[34]

Gulnigor told me that she had first used contraception from 1977 to 1980, because she suffered from ill health after having delivered three children – one per year. (One daughter died after a serious illness.) Since her husband was against contraception, she used it secretly. She also informed me that breastfeeding in the beginning had not prevented her from becoming pregnant. Then, after having three more children (each spaced three years apart), she again used contraception. Ahad, who was still against contraception, assumed that she had entered menopause. When she finally withdrew the IUD she expected to have no more children, but she had another child when aged 46. By this time, the first wife's daughter had already given birth to a girl. With this fertility history, Gulnigor mirrors the village data, where the birth-spacing average was 2.32 years, with the last child being a latecomer.[35]

In 2006, Ahad had three sons that fit the Tajik definition of youth. In other words, from among his twelve children, three boys (one-fourth of his children) attained the age at which they could be defined as young males. From the outset, they knew that they belonged to the group who were expected to expend their energies in the service of family and community. All three of them work abroad – the younger two in Russia, the eldest in Kazakhstan – in order to help their parents rebuild the house and finance the rites of passage. They also look after their divorced sister and her two daughters. Since their youngest sister has not yet had a child who has survived infancy, she depends on her family's help while living with her husband (a parallel cousin) in their separate household. In this way, apart from themselves, the three brothers look after ten family members (their parents, two sisters, the twin daughters of one sister, the youngest brother, and the wife and children of one of the working brothers).

The dependency ratio measures the number of dependent people in a society. As mentioned in the Introduction, Dhillon and Yousef (2007) have argued that youth bulges serve to reduce dependency, allowing young people to accumulate wealth. How true is this for Ahad's family and Shahrituz? In the villages concerned, the dependency ratio is 84 dependents for every 100 people.[36] This reflects the pyramid-like structure of the society, with a large number of children dependent on the adults. A similar structure can be found in Ahad's family – approximately

23 per cent of the family is entirely responsible for the remaining 77 per cent. What are the consequences of such a dependency ratio? The dependency ratio is based on Western concepts of working cohorts within the population; hence, in agricultural families, children play a central role in the family economy, and Tajikistan is no exception to this. However, due to serious land shortages, families are increasingly becoming almost entirely dependent on the money sent home by family members working abroad. These family members are also responsible for financing the education of their younger siblings (in Ahad's family, for example, the elder brothers have promised to pay for their youngest brother's education).

This overview of Ahad's family reveals that, in fact, about one in four of the family's members need to earn money in order to ensure a decent standard of living (not luxurious) for the family, supplemented by basic agricultural work within the compound and some work on the cotton farm for firewood. Like many other houses in this neighbourhood, Ahad's house had been bulldozed during the war, and all their belongings were stolen by neighbours. It was then that the eldest brother took a job in order to finance the new house, while the next brother, at present, is working to save up for his wedding. At first glance, the dependency ratio in Shahrituz and the responsibilities shouldered by the young people seem to contradict Dhillon and Yousef's argument. However, the current world for these young people has changed considerably from that of the past: while it is true that they are financially responsible for their family, and therefore may not be able to accumulate wealth through work, they are still aware that work earns them a higher social status and greater recognition.

A Statistical Analysis of the Villages

A statistical analysis will help to show how Ahad's history is related to the more abstract data. In order to capture the dynamics of the last two decades, I have divided my data to allow for a comparative approach. However, before present-ing the analysis, it is necessary to provide information regarding the quality of the data. In addition to the data samples collected from the locations mentioned above, data from members residing outside those locations is included, due to my use of genealogies for data collection. Only for certain estimates is the data restricted solely to that collected in the villages. Having personally recorded the information, I excluded data that appeared to be either questionable or incorrect and that I was unable to verify. Even these precautions are no guarantee against the possibility that some people may have been misreported or that interview partners omitted certain people for numerous reasons. In this sense, I suggest that the following estimates should be regarded as tendencies, not necessarily realities, even though a significant portion of the statistics were in accordance with what people told me – with a few exceptions.[37]

The following estimate considers only women from ages 15 to 45 from the two locations: a neighbourhood in Shahrituz and in Sasik Bulak. This age

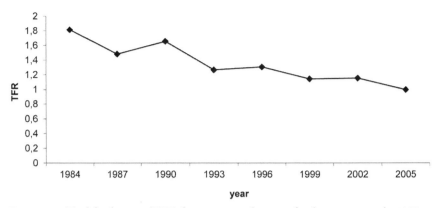

Figure 1.3: Total fertility rate (TFR) for ever-married women for three-year periods, 1982 to 2005 (Shahrituz).

group was selected in order to exclude the effects of representing past patterns (in estimates based on women aged 45 and above). Within this age group, more than half the women had started having children before the civil war; however, all of them had been affected by the civil war and its aftermath. I applied the same methodology to both data sets from Shahrituz and Sasik Bulak in order to compare the TFR for ever-married women at the two field sites. In the case of the neighbourhood in Shahrituz, the results showed a decline in the TFR from 7.16 children per woman between 1983 and 1990 to 6.13 for 1991 to 1998, which again sharply declined to 4.16, on average, for 1999 to 2006. The results for Sasik Bulak showed a similar decline, starting from an average TFR of 6.5 children per woman (1983 to 1990), which increased to 6.9 (1991 to 1998) and eventually declined sharply to 4.1 in the last few years (1999 to 2006). This indicates a TFR decline of 38 per cent in Sasik Bulak and over 40 per cent in Shahrituz, which clearly exceeds the threshold of 10 per cent that, according to Coal and Watkins (1986), represents a substantive evidence of change.

The next estimation refers to Shahrituz only. First, I wish to highlight the fertility decline of the last two decades and, second, I will split the data into its statistical elements, crude birth rate (CBR), crude death rate (CDR) and crude growth rate (CGR).

The data in Figure 1.3 show that fertility in Shahrituz has declined considerably since the era of perestroika in the 1980s.[38] There are numerous reasons for this, all of which cannot be presented here. Chapter 5, however, which discusses marriage, will also consider the postponing of marriage by young people – one of the main reasons for the decline in fertility. Other reasons include socio-political changes (centred on Tajikistan gaining independence in 1991) and economic changes (such as migration, which probably has had the most significant impact on Tajikistan's demographic development today).

Table 1.1: Crude birth, death and growth rates (Shahrituz).

	CBR	CDR	CGR
1992	0.043	0.062	−0.019
1993	0.059	0.032	0.027
1994	0.054	0.014	0.039
1995	0.048	0.014	0.035

Table 1.1 provides a closer look at crude growth rates (CGR) during the civil war period. The table illuminates some interesting tendencies. The crude birth rate (CBR) of over 40 births per 1,000 people is rather high, even by Tajik standards.[39] This may be due in part to the fact that some people were left out of the count, which resulted in an underestimation of the total number of people with respect to registered births (in particular, a CBR of 0.059 seems very high). The crude death rates (CDR) reflect the effect of the civil war within the population studied. The high CDR is responsible for the decline in the CGR in 1992 (during the civil war), but as the table shows, this trend had already reversed by 1993. In the last two years, however, the CGR shows a significant increase. The average estimate for the four civil war years suggests 49 births and 29 deaths per 1,000 people. (In comparison, in 2000, the CBR for Shahrituz was 0.045, while the CDR was 0.009; consequently, the CGR was 0.036.)

The Youth Bulge in the Tajik Context

The Introduction provided the academic context in which 'youth bulges' developed and described the multiple cultural definitions for age groups. Nevertheless, it is necessary to use some form of measurement to conduct a quantitative analysis. According to the census of 2000, 70 per cent of the population was aged 0 to 29 (Olimova 2006: 159). This impressive number, however, must be further divided in order to determine the percentage of people included in the category of 'youth'. Table 1.2 shows how youth bulges vary with age group definitions.[40]

Each of the first two groupings in Table 1.2 identifies a youth bulge according to the respective author's use of the term. If we consider the Tajik cultural definition, we realize that more than one-third of the male population (35.32 per

Table 1.2: Percentage of youth according to different age groupings (Shahrituz, Shahrigul, Sasik Bulak).

	age group	m		f	
		n = 2,336	%	n = 2,291	%
Cincotta et al. (2003)	15–29	710	30.39	731	31.91
Heinsohn (2006)	15–24	491	21.02	535	23.35
Tajik cultural definition	16–35	825	35.32	855	37.32

cent) belongs to the category of youth and thus can be studied in terms of the values associated with youth. Does this latter proportion of young men represent a higher risk of conflict, and on this basis can we confirm a causal relationship between youth bulges and conflict?

Rather than attempting to answer this question through statistical data alone, this study considers many other factors, perhaps none more important than the creation, manipulation and negotiation of youth definitions, which I believe to be central to determining any possible relationship between a youth bulge and a higher risk of conflict. From the outset it is apparent that the Tajik cultural definition of youth encompasses a wider range of ages than international standards that are based on psychological and biological definitions. This forces us to reflect on the domestication strategies to which youth are subject in different societies and the reasons leading to such cohort constructions. Consequently it is necessary to explore numerous areas (such as politics, community, religion and the family) in order to identify these domestication strategies.

The Tajik cultural definition reflects the scarce resource situation and the long process of social, political and religious maturation that one must pass through before gaining access to those resources (see the following chapters). In any event, the statistical analysis does not reveal the values accorded to youth and the possible emergence of movements that might transform youth from a submissive group into a vanguard one.

Figure 1.4 shows another distribution of youth – namely, youth as a relative proportion of the total population over a larger period of time. Here I have used the age group 15 to 39 because these where the 'youth' expected to participate in military activities during the civil war. As we will see throughout the work, youth definitions vary and the age cohort of 15 to 39/40 is the largest possible definition I came across – we may call it the maximal youth cohort.

Figure 1.4 shows the relative size of the different segments within the three communities as they can be culturally defined. It is obvious that youth does not constitute the largest group – children do. Although I have made allowances for errors in the data for the years 1985 and 1992, it is clear that those said to be mature in a social and political sense and consequently hold all social and political rights, comprise around only 10 per cent of the total population. Further, it is interesting to note the large child bulge preceding the civil war. Thus, a discussion of youth bulges and conflicts should involve the process of ageing and its relation to social positions.

If youth bulges are to be detected purely along biological lines, then post-civil war Tajikistan has a very large proportion of young people. However, if youth bulge is a term used to describe a group of people who can be mobilized or who can exert pressure on a political regime and older generations, then it requires a more complex definition. These conceptual variations will be explored further in the course of this study.

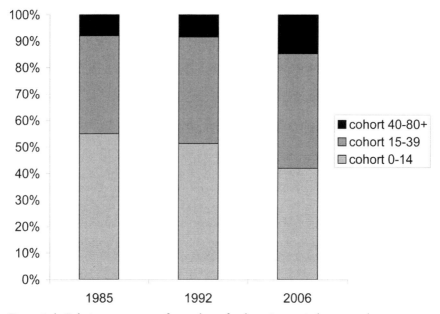

Figure 1.4: Relative percentages of age cohorts for three time periods, men and women (Shahrituz, Shahrigul, Sasik Bulak).

Mortality in the Civil War

Civil wars affect all generations, irrespective of their political investment. Estimates of mortality in a civil conflict can vary by as much as 500 per cent; for Tajikistan, they vary between 20,000 and 60,000 deaths in a population of approximately 6 million during a five-year time span (1992 to 1997).[41] Inaccuracies in estimating the impact of this conflict serves to emphasize the fact that, demographically speaking, little is known about civil wars; however, some current research has progressed further in the study of other conflicts.

The group of people who are most affected by a civil war, and the impact of such a war on gender, is less obvious, when compared to the effects of a larger, 'classic' war. Studies on the Second World War identify a huge gender imbalance and a deficiency of men in all fighting generations (Winter 1992; Harwin 1996: 19). The scenario is obvious: young men leave home in order to fight at the front, which is often far away from home, and in the event of a death, the family is informed by letter. Although most wars at one point or the other victimize civilians, different types of war result in different impacts on gender patterns (Ghobarah, Huth and Russett 2001). Tabeau and Bijak, in their study of deaths in the war in Bosnia and Herzegovina (1992 to 1995), show that 'causes of death taken into account must distinguish in this case between *regular causes of death* and causes responsible for *excess deaths* in this period' (Tabeau and Bijak 2005: 191, original emphasis). A civil war differs from a classic war in the sense that frontlines cut across the entire country, putting the civilian population at permanent risk. In fact, Lacina and Gleditsch (2006: 144) argue that only 6 per cent to a maximum of 29 per cent of the casualties in a civil war are battle-related deaths – the majority of victims die due to secondary, though related, causes.[42]

In Tajikistan, the highest mortality occurred within the groups that were directly affected and targeted in the war: refugees. The community of Shahrituz consists of former refugees – they suffered the greatest number of civilian losses. The mountain areas, however, were more affected by lack of supplies such as food and medical services than by massacres of entire groups (Hohmann, Roche and Garenne 2010).[43] Although it is likely that I have underestimated male deaths due to the fact that I worked with people who had been classified as belonging to the opposition,[44] one can hardly overlook the clear implications of the statistical outcome. From all the deaths registered within the neighbourhood of Shahrituz since 1960, 40 per cent died during the civil war, between 1992 and 1997. Even making allowances for the underreporting of civil war deaths, Table 1.3 shows that a simple estimate of life expectancy ($e[0]$), based on dates of birth and death, turns out to be 13.9 years. This low figure represents the large number of children who died during and after the civil war.

Table 1.3 indicates that children (and the 0 to 1 year old children account for the majority of causalities) are the highest risk group, comprising more than half of all those dead during the civil war. While in the youngest age group, girls seem to be at a higher risk than boys, this relation is reversed in the other age groups. The group of people who are most exposed to risk – youth – are not the second-highest risk group, which is people 36 years and older.

The above data regarding youth is mostly sourced from the Shahrituz neighbourhood; thus, it represents the group that was the longest and most heavily affected by conflict-related activities. The data also suggests that most of the deaths which were not mentioned occurred within the youth group. As stated above, deaths in the civil war have culturally different values and are accorded different relevance. While the death reports of the victim groups (children and elders) seem to be more precise, the highest number of omissions in reporting

Table 1.3: Number of deaths during the civil war (Shahrituz, Shahrigul, Sasik Bulak).

| Age | M | | | F | | |
	0–15 years	16–35 years	36+ years	0–15 years	16–35 years	36+ years
1992	11	11	13	15	2	3
1993	10	7	4	17	1	1
1994	3	4	5	9	1	0
1995	7	0	1	7	1	2
1996	1	0	1	4	1	2
1997	4	0	6	2	0	2
Total	36	22	30	54	6	10

applies to the group that was most actively involved. The only conclusion that can be derived from these estimates, then, is the tendency for children to be the highest risk group in a civil war. However, it is plain that, in general, people of all ages and both genders suffer in a civil war. Further, we should be aware that reporting the total number of deceased in a civil war is a political matter. While reporting the deaths of unarmed victims does not appear to pose a dilemma, active combatants tend to be omitted if the political system has not rehabilitated them.[45]

The level of unreported killings in the civil war is high, and it would be a daunting task to clear up the matter, even by attempting to identify conspicuous gaps in many families' genealogies. The numerous mass graves yet to be unearthed suggest a dark story that remains untold. Systematic killings are often part of civil war strategies, typically used to target an enemy group. In addition, people in Tajikistan have suffered numerous atrocities, and some have even lost entire families. While the number of victims may be reported more accurately, it is the young men who died that are most lamented and mourned by their families. Since I have not been able to provide statistically representative data on the young men who died in the civil war, I will present a story to show how the deaths of young men have been socially integrated.

Making Sense of a Civil War Massacre

To celebrate the New Year (*Navrūz*) on 21 March, the women traditionally prepared a special, time-consuming dish called *sumanak**. First, wheat grains were put to germinate in several plates about a week before the event. Before the wheat sprouts turned green, when they had grown just a few centimetres high, they were plucked out to prepare the dish. The newly germinated wheat sprouts were said to symbolize young people. The sprouts were then mashed and cooked for over a day and a half, by which time the preparation was brown in colour, with a pleasant, sweet taste. During the civil war, this was the only sweet dish available, since sugar was expensive and difficult to get. Thus, many women in Lakhsh prepared this dish for the New Year feasts during the war.

Like many other mountain villages, Lakhsh had become a place of refuge for people from the south (refugees from Shahrituz, among others). Every family hosted some refugees, while hundreds of refugees were sheltered in the teahouses and mosques – they too were looked after by the village population. In spring 1995, the president issued a declaration asking refugees to return to their homes. Shortly after the Persian New Year feast, many refugees staying in Lakhsh decided to return home and boarded buses to take them back to their native places. On the long journey to Dushanbe they were stopped at a (state) military post just outside of Tojikobod, and everyone was ordered off the buses.[46] The young men were then separated from the other travellers and killed. These deaths were shocking not only to the parents of those who were killed but also to the villagers who had hosted the refugees (many of them were relatives of the refugees). In an effort to make sense of this brutal event, the suspicion arose that making *sumanak* must have been responsible for the killings: the mashing of the young wheat sprouts was, therefore, causally related to the massacre of young (innocent) men. After this massacre, no woman in this village has ever dared to cook *sumanak* again.

I was often told moving stories about the death of young men; there was much less talk about atrocities against women. The death of individual young men tended to be overemphasized compared to other deaths – this had less to do with the preferential position of sons than with the idea that men continued descent lines. Thus a deceased young man leaves a genealogical gap; his father's line of descent can no longer continue through him. Further, sons are regarded as the providers of security for their parents in old age. The above story shows us the way in which parents tried to make sense of unexpected death – unexpected because young men are perceived as strong and healthy and naturally less vulnerable than old people and children.

Conclusion

The rural Tajik population continues to increase by an intrinsic, natural rate of growth of 2.55 per cent.[47] However, its fertility rate must be seen in the context of changing economic and migration patterns. Instead of concentrating on the variables of 'education', GDP and other extracted factors, a deeper analysis shows that fertility is influenced by people's past and present experiences, cultural shocks (the civil war, for example), politics, and the constant exchange of ideas and practices intensified by an increasing percentage of migrants. As has been observed in other countries, the colonial period resulted in fundamental changes in childcare systems. During the Soviet era, along with an improvement in medical care and political stability, fertility rates rose considerably – these were compensated for with payments and other awards by the communist government. However, perestroika seems to have heralded a fertility transition, which accelerated during the civil war and its aftermath. Two reasons for this in the post-civil war period have been the migration of large sections of the male population and changing marriage patterns in Tajikistan.

Today, Tajik society has to deal with a huge proportion of young people, which some studies would define as a youth bulge. However, in this chapter we have also seen that at least one quarter of a family need to be employed so that the family can enjoy a modest standard of living and provide for the education and well-being of all of its children. Thus, the problem of youth bulges as a source of conflict must be regarded in a wider discussion on the roles, values and expectations of youth as seen in the context of their environment.

This chapter has explored the demographic circumstances of the research sites, identifying population dynamics and dependencies and introducing their regional contexts. Rather than attempting to answer the question of whether youth bulges increase the risk of conflict, I have tried to demonstrate changes in fertility and mortality as well as different ways of defining a youth cohort. Having presented details of regional history and demographic development, the following chapter investigates a more wide-ranging historical perspective. My interest there will be to identify the demographic potential of youth movements through their inclusion and exclusion strategies.

Notes

1. I will present an account of the civil war in the next chapter. For now, suffice it to say that the civil war grew out of political tensions in the early 1990s, reached its violent zenith in 1992 and 1993, and concluded with the signing of a successful peace agreement in 1997.
2. In order to protect the identity of my informants, I have changed the name of the village that was my field site in the district of Gharm, in the Kamarob gorge. Many people with whom I have become acquainted since 2002 entrusted me with their information and views, and I have promised them to take every possible precaution to ensure their safety.
3. Bushkov and Mikul'skij (1996: 14) contend that in the early 1950s, tens of thousands of farming units were resettled from the mountain regions to the southern plains.
4. I will not go into detail here – the rules behind the use of ethnonyms in Tajikistan are complex and operate on many different levels.
5. According to Marxist historical materialism, societies develop in relation to material conditions in five successive stages: primitive communism, slave societies, feudalism, capitalism, communism. These different developments were further developed by Soviet anthropological theory that would accord each step specific social structures: in primitive communism, tribes and tribal federations arose; in slave societies and under feudalism 'people' emerged which transformed into nations in the two successive stages capitalism and communism. On the arbitrariness of these theories and their concrete application to Kyrgyz historiography, see Tchoroev (2002).
6. I have used transliterations of the Tajik spelling, which differ from Kyrgyz and Russian spellings.
7. According to Baltabaev, citing Mahmud ibn Vali and Bartold, the first written proof of Kyrgyz presence in the area dates back to 1635: 'In the month of Rajab in the year 1045 (11 December to 9 January 1635), 12,000 households of Qaraqirghiz unbelievers came by way of Qarotegin to Hisor . . . Bartold has mentioned that in 1635–1636, the Qirgiz were chased out by Qalmoks, under the leadership of Xuntaishe Batur. Persecuted by the Qalmoks, the Qirgiz fled to Oloi, Qarotegin' (Baltabaev 2006: 28). According to these historical accounts, the persecuted Kyrgyz fled in all directions, and only a part of this refugee population remained in today's Jirgatol and settled there.
8. Baltabaev (2006) strongly emphasizes differences between the ethnic groups. According to his account, the Tajik came to the region in search of work, while the Kyrgyz fled to the region seeking refuge. This kind of classification, with different value judgments attached to the actions of 'coming in search of work' versus 'seeking refuge', clearly implies the ranking of one group over another. Based on honour constructions that favour the strong, fearless labourer over the weak refugee, this interpretation of history – along with this distinction between ethnicities – is maintained to the present day. For this reason, the Kyrgyz emphasize that the Tajik arrived as economic refugees entering bond relations (in

the nineteenth century) and as refugees from Stalin's purges in the 1930s. In their turn, the Tajik regard the Kyrgyz with suspicion because many of them fled during the civil war instead of supporting local parties and enduring the conflict – hence, according to some Tajiks, the Kyrgyz have no right to consider themselves 'Tajik' citizens (for more detail regarding the importance of taking sides, see Chapter 3). These retrospectively justified historical claims are highly relevant today, as resources become increasingly scarce and rights to land increasingly ethnicized.

9. In the last few years, some of these places have been renamed in Tajik, especially in the Gharm region.

10. Interview with Batirbek, an elder man, February 2007.

11. Since the nineteenth century the term *kulak* (Russ. fist) was used for wealthy peasants in Russia. Under the Bolsheviks the term received a pejorative meaning and became central to the campaign against landholders between 1929 and 1932 known as the de-kulakization.

12. See Figure A.1 in the Appendix.

13. A Tatar woman living in Lakhsh explained to me that most of the apples are stolen by children, who suffer from persistent vitamin deficiencies. They either eat them right away, ripe or unripe, or bring them home to their mothers.

14. Dudoignon writes, 'During the period of civil war and endemic terror against the Bukharan "Jadids" (1917–20), the oriental provinces of Qabadiyan and Kulab were often chosen by the Emirs for the deportation and execution of prominent figures and activists of the reformist and revolutionary trends' (Dudoignon 2004a: 80).

15. It was also Roy who first mentioned that kolkhoz organizations were built up along regional and local patterns and not intended as reformative. Roy stressed that the role of the kolkhoz in the building of community identity was diachronic with clan affiliation. According to Roy, the civil war can even be understood as 'the War of the *Kolkhoz*' (Roy 2000: 94).

16. The irony is that all former Tajiks, even those considered Kyrgyz in Tajikistan, are labelled as 'Tajik' in Kyrgyzstan.

17. The interview partners mentioned two mass killings explicitly directed against their group.

18. These two were the largest refugee camps in Afghanistan, according to Karim (1997: 787), with approximately 20,000 refugees in Mazar-e Sharif and 37,040 refugees in Qunduz.

19. In 1949, the village of Hoid in Rasht, located in a ravine, was buried under a landslide. However, it is also likely that remote villages were relocated along main roads to help authorities better control the local people, since mountain people were well known for supporting the opposition and had previously revealed their affinity with the *basmachi* movement (discussed in Chapter 3).

20. Under state law, it is forbidden to build houses on arable land, but the shortage of living space has compelled people to give up cultivation in favour of constructing homes, even though it is illegal. The increasing incidences of migration have allowed young people to bring back enough money to invest in a new house. Thus far, bribing the authorities is the easiest way to get away with circumventing the law.

21. Although it is beyond the scope of this study, it is certainly worth mentioning the heroic efforts undertaken by women to help their families survive during the civil war. Women walked long distances to find food, and during some periods they were the only ones who could do so – girls, boys and men were targets and therefore had to hide.

22. See also Ghufronov and Yuldoshev's (2008) report on women asking militants to lay down their weapons.

23. Islamov (1988: 32, 36) identifies 44 births per 1,000 population between 1897 and 1990 and 20 deaths per 1,000 population between 1897 and 1935 – an increase of 24 per

1,000 population. In 1986 the birth rate appears to have been around 40 and the death rate 7 per 1,000 population – an increase of 33 persons per 1,000 population. The child-to-woman ratio doubled from 1.257 in 1926 to 2.561 in 1970 (Jones and Grupp 1987: 98; cf. Krader 1971; Islamov 1988; Bushkov 1993: 39–40; Olimova and Bosc 2003: 13). Poliakov (1992: 39–40) rejects the use of the term 'demographic explosion' in the 1970s to describe the Central Asian fertility behaviour, since the term does not take into account the gradual increase in population over time. He sees the increase in fertility as the logical result of 'appending the region to Russia'. According to his detailed analysis of the northern Leninabad Oblast of Tajikistan, from 1870 to 1930 the population increased by 3.5 times, and by 1980, it had increased by 10.5 times. The first stage of this increase – up to 1930 –represented the result of greater political stability in the region and 'the end of internecine war'. In the second stage, infant mortality dropped sharply 'because of the rise in standard of living [and] free medical care'. In light of these explanations, Poliakov reconsiders the current fertility transition theories, which assume a high population increase before the beginning of a transition to low fertility, as an explanation for Tajik population developments. Olimova and Bosc, referring to a state statistical committee report from 2001, assert that, 'during the period between the 1989 and 2000 censuses, the working-age population rose by 124.1%, or 2.1% annually' (Olimova and Bosc 2003: 13).

24. Guboglo (1990: 27–31) provides an analysis of the last Soviet census taken in 1989 and compares it to the three previous censuses of 1959, 1970 and 1979. In Central Asia, 'the Russians were the most numerous nationality in each of the capitals, but the most striking fact was the extent of their numerical superiority' (ibid.: 27). In Dushanbe, Russians constituted 47.2 per cent of the population, while the Tajiks only constituted 18.5 per cent. By 1989, however, the Tajiks already outnumbered the Russians – a tendency that was further accelerated during the course of the civil war.

25. For a critical reflection of this argument, see Obermeyer (1992).

26. The abortion rate rose rapidly towards the end of the 1920s: '18–20 women of every 100 who attended maternity clinics were asking for a termination, with poverty as a chief reason' (Harwin 1996: 9).

27. Interview with Batirbek, an elderly man, February 2007.

28. Testimony of elder women during a group discussion, November 2006.

29. According to Harwin (1996: 40), child benefit was 50 roubles per month for the first child and a hundred roubles for the second and third. Moreover, Jones and Grupp (1987: 276) add that non-working mothers received 30 roubles per month for the birth of the first, second and third children. However, new birth payments were introduced into the southern territories in 1983. For the fourth child, the family received a one-off payment of 65 roubles, and for the fifth child, 85 roubles. Monthly payments of 4 roubles per child were given to the family after the birth of the fourth child, which became 6 roubles after the birth of the fifth; these payments went on until the child attained the age of five years (ibid.: 273).

30. A family of approximately eight people needs two to three bags of flour a month (making allowances for occasional guests). There is a currently held belief that the aid of international organizations is no more than a continuation of former state support. Thus, every once in a while I would see people picking up their children's share of flour from school. In discussions, people would compare this 'child benefit' to that given during Soviet rule, irrespective of the very different sources and ideologies behind the two kinds of 'aid' (international organizations respond to child malnutrition and reluctant school visits).

31. Interview with Zebo, 39 years, January 2007.

32. Gorbachev's politics of 'openness' (glasnost) brought disturbing revelations to many people, who learned about the situation of state-run childcare institutions. For instance,

it was revealed that eight out of ten so-called 'orphans' had at least one living parent (Harwin 1996: 65) who had entrusted the child to state care because of their inability to cope with the public stigma of having an illegitimate child or because it was easier to remarry without a child to care for. In 1987, up to one million children were living under state care. (Children in Tajikistan who have only one parent are still legally orphans.) However, Harwin adds, instead of this discussion resulting in the promotion of proper contraception, it was channelled into a moral condemnation of single mothers.

33. Interview with Zikir, 49 years old, October 2006.
34. See Figures A.2 and A.3 in the Appendix.
35. See Table A.1 in the Appendix.
36. See Table A.2 in the Appendix.
37. Two recent dissertations have dealt with larger survey data sets and discussed demographic changes in Tajikistan (Shemyakina 2007; Clifford 2009). The village data lines up with these works in certain respects, but in other respects they do not. (Further discussion of these works, however, is outside the scope of this study.)
38. We have to understand the period of perestroika as a very enthusiastic and energetic one providing new opportunities in various domains but also accompanied by a sense of insecurity concerning political apparatus and ideological directions.
39. Haub (1994: 48) identifies a CBR of 38.8 for the year 1990 and 32.9 for 1993. The CDR rises from 6.2 in 1990 to 8.7 three years later, which seems rather low for a society experiencing a civil war.
40. The official United Nation definition of 'youth' ranges from 15 to 24 years: see www.un.org/youth.
41. According to some accounts, the number of casualties in the civil war were as high as one hundred thousand.
42. Li and Wen (2005: 487), in their article on adult mortality in conflicts, argue that men in civil wars (intrastate wars and severe conflicts) suffer higher mortality than women, while women are adversely affected over a longer period of time following conflicts. However, Ghobarah, Huth and Russett (2001: 25) mention that women, and especially children, constitute a significant proportion of casualties during a civil war.
43. Verwimp and Bavel (2005) observe that refugees in Rwanda show higher parity than non-refugee women, but there is also considerably higher child mortality, especially regarding daughters.
44. Considering the heightened political tension during my fieldwork, people tended to avoid discussing politics, and thus may have omitted certain casualties related to political events.
45. The deceased and veterans of the Second World War are not only openly recognized but celebrated every year, in contrast to the taboo surrounding any discussion of civil war casualties.
46. At that time the entire road was dotted with checkpoints, and often it was unclear who controlled them. Travelling became extremely dangerous, as one could fall into the hands of either a stoned *mujohid* or a drunken state soldier and be killed for no apparent reason. For example, one state-controlled checkpoint was known to be safe only in the morning hours; from noon onwards it was feared as a deadly spot, dangerous to travellers because the commander in charge was considered absolutely unreliable.
47. Official data pertaining to the entire country, including cities, cite a much lower growth rate of 1.893 per cent (2008). Another study by Turner (1993) suggests that Tajikistan has the highest total fertility rate (TFR) of all the newly independent Central Asian countries, with a TFR of 5.1 births per woman, compared to that of 2.7 for Kazakhstan.

Chapter 2

'Why Didn't You Take a Side?'

The Emergence of Youth Categories, Institutions and Groups

Tajikistan is the result of various political processes that occurred early in the twentieth century. Its borders, as they exist today, resulted from the remapping of Central Asia by Stalin in the 1920s. As has been described by many authors, the process of categorizing the population on the basis of certain ethnic identities ultimately turned into quite a difficult undertaking, which eventually led to the creation of territorially based nation-states that were intended to host the majority of the titular population.[1] It is in this way that Tajikistan came into being. Tajikistan – one of the poorest countries in the Union of Socialist Soviet Republics (USSR) – gained its independence in 1991. However, the transition to independence was a rocky one, and as has been noted in earlier chapters, the country soon descended into civil war. Peace returned to the country only towards the end of the 1990s.

This chapter has a dual purpose: to show the emergence of a 'youth' category in Central Asian history; and to look more closely at institutions, movements, political parties and classifications during this process of emerging youth categories in Central Asia and more specifically in Tajikistan. Demographic processes are highly dependent on historical developments, and it is the political context that influences and is influenced by demographic processes. Based on our discussion of youth bulges and the concept of vanguards, this chapter concentrates on several vanguard groups that emerged as political movements out of specific demographic conditions. But it also discusses educational institutions and the reform of those institutions that went along with an emerging youth category which was instrumentalized for political purposes. Special attention is paid to the impact of the civil war during the 1990s on the contemporary socio-demographic developments in Tajikistan. Although it is not the first time in Central Asian history that youth were mobilized, it is the most recent occurrence and the best documented and most accessible, which makes a proper analysis possible. Only a brief historical glimpse will be provided here – a comprehensive overview would demand a book of its own, and furthermore much of the history of Central Asia, especially the history of youth in the region, has yet to be studied in a scientific and detailed manner.

The numerous political changes that have occurred in the twentieth century, to a large extent, have taken place with the participation of young men – they were the *basmachi** who fought against the Russians, and also, by way of the Komsomol*, the ones who helped to introduce communism in remote areas. They were responsible for constructing socialism, and later, they were the *mujohid** who fought in the civil war against socialism. This chapter touches upon the central periods in history, wherein youth was made or became a socio-demographic group through the political concept of the vanguard (*jadid*, Komsomol, *mujohid*). In this context, changes in the education system (that is, from the *maktab** or *madrasa** to the Russian education system) were fundamental to the formulation of youth as a socio-demographic group. These socio-demographic definitions were to become relevant in the civil war and in the way youth were portrayed either as rational actors, as victims of the military authorities, or as inherently undisciplined troublemakers.

Relying upon examples from the Tajik civil war, I examine the manner in which former combatants are framed as victims and perpetrators in the civil war literature. In addition, several examples will be presented to show how young people perceive their own activities, and how these perceptions contrast with the domesticating approaches of older people, politicians and communities. Young people rephrase their relation to their combatant leaders in opposition to kin and community relations, and yet along the lines of the similar relational principle, that between teacher (*ustod**) and student (*shogird**).

This chapter also explores the problem of domestication as reflected in current terminology, concepts and practices. Before discussing any of the numerous strategies to create group sizes and youth concepts, it is important to understand that youth are more than just a socio-demographic group – they are also a political construction, a tool of ideological or religious interests, a social group, and a collection of individuals with unique motivations and constraints.

The Timeline

It is helpful here to provide a brief overview of Tajik history, with a strong emphasis on Tajikistan's civil war. This is necessary because much of the ethnographic material used in this study dates from the three time periods surrounding this conflict – the prewar era, the war itself, and the postwar era. It should be noted that although my interest lies in the creation, use and negotiation of youth concepts over time, my research has been conducted solely during the postwar period. In this sense, the work has a bias, insofar as the war and prewar periods have been reconstructed based on people's accounts and not through direct observation.

The division into three periods corresponds to how Tajik people frame the history themselves: *pesh az jang* (before the war), *vaqti jang* (during the war) and *ba'di jang* (after the war). However, unlike the political version of events, people divide the periods based on their individual realities, since different villages experienced the war in different time frames. In Shahrituz, for example, when people spoke of something that occurred 'during the war', they were referring to the year 1992, while in Shahrigul, 'during the war' meant the years 1993 and 1994, when state troops entered the Qarotegin Valley.

The beginning and end of a civil war are empirical matters, not always consistent with the political version of events. The same applies to the end of the civil war in Tajikistan. In Shahrituz, people place the end of the conflict about a year before the war officially ended according to the political authorities, because this was when the people were able to return to their former neighbourhoods. However, in Shahrigul, people say that the terror unleashed by the war ended around 2000, when the last *mujohid* had been arrested by state troops.

The demographers Agadjanian and Makarova (2003) assert that a representative statistical analysis should begin with an investigation of people's perceptions of time frames in order to establish meaningful divisions, upon which the analysis can then be based. Memory, as Assmann (1999) puts it, often lags behind changes that may be sudden and irreversible, and it takes at least a generation for such changes to be fully processed in people's minds.[2] In this sense, Būrī Karim (1997), politician and author of a monograph describing the civil war, represents the feelings of most of the people in Tajikistan when he states that the civil war had already started by 1990, the year of the first uprising against the government.[3]

It is not problematic here to use local notions of time rather than political markers, since I am neither attempting to reconstruct political events nor seeking to report historical facts but instead intend to discuss the socio-demographic and cultural changes brought about by the civil war, as they were experienced and interpreted by people. This study focuses on how concepts, behaviours and discourses are emically used, negotiated and changed and the manner in which young people internalize, challenge or reject these.

From Pre-Soviet *Madrasas* to the *Jadid* Movement

Until the October Revolution of 1917, Central Asia had been divided in two: the emirate of Bukhara (including much of what is present-day Tajikistan, except for the northern region surrounding Khujand); and those areas (Turkestan) under the Russian protectorate (since 1868). At the time, present-day Tajikistan was referred to as Eastern Bukhara. According to the Russian census of the time, 2.1 million Tajiks inhabited Central Asia (however, only about 700,000 of these became residents of the newly created Autonomous Soviet Socialist Republic of Tajikistan).

The emir in Bukhara served as a quasi 'vassal' of the Russian tsarist empire, with Russia increasingly seeking influence and control of the emirate. The

Bolshevik revolution in Russia dramatically changed the situation in Central Asia. The region was attached to Russia as part of the Soviet Union and the area was fundamentally restructured. Based on arbitrary censuses in 1897 (which used language as the sole marker of ethnic belonging), 1917 and 1926, ethnic categories were created and defined more with regard to political considerations than according to the reality of social stratification and economic niches (Abashin 2007). Turkestan, the Bukharan emirate and the Khorezm republic were dissolved and reshaped in 1924 into Kyrgyzstan, Tajikistan, Turkmenistan, Uzbekistan and Kazakhstan. However, Tajikistan remained a part of Uzbekistan, as the Tajik Autonomous Soviet Socialist Republic (ASSR), for another five years. Upon the approval of Josef Stalin, who regarded the Tajik as the 'oldest inhabitants of Central Asia', they were accorded an independent republic in 1929, which came to be known as the Tajik Soviet Socialist Republic (SSR).

The political aspect of this territorial division has been described by Brubaker (1994), Niyazi (1999), Bergne (2007) and many others. According to residence patterns dating back over centuries, cities such as Samarkand, Khujand and Bukhara were dominated by people who spoke Farsi (Persian); however, the rural areas were comprised predominantly of Turkic-speaking populations. Due to regular exchange, cohabitation and trade, many people grew up to be bilingual – a practice that still exists in many multi-ethnic areas of Central Asia, including Jirgatol.

Farsi was spoken not only in cities but also in certain remote mountainous areas in former Eastern Bukhara, including the Qarotegin Valley and Vakhyo. The predominantly Farsi-speaking urban centres of Bukhara and Samarkand were incorporated into the new state of Uzbekistan, whereas Khujand in the north became part of the SSR Tajikistan in 1930 (cut off from the rest of Tajikistan by two mountain ranges). During the process of restructuring Central Asia, Turkic was portrayed as the language of progress and political correctness, while Farsi was seen as the language of 'backward' people as well as the Islamic elite (Rzehak 2001: 1–38).[4] During the creation of a standard Tajik language and a territorially defined Tajik people, many inquiries were carried out among mountain-dwelling Tajiks (rather than among the urban religious elites in Bukhara and Samarkand, which became part of Uzbekistan). The mountainous areas served as the backdrop for the formulation of Soviet ideology regarding the Tajiks. The new (socialist) Tajik man was assumed to be a person from the mountainous regions.[5]

Tajikistan and the other Central Asian republics proclaimed their independence in 1991. Since then, each republic has struggled with difficult economic and demographic conditions, which have led to migration by many in search of work. Besides localized conflicts in the Ferghana Valley, Tajikistan was the only Central Asian republic that experienced a civil war in the 1990s. To understand the role of youth in these various historical periods, let us start with educational institutions in pre-Soviet Central Asia and successively move from the Soviet period to the civil war in independent Tajikistan.

Students in Madrasas

In Turkestan, there was a widespread and well-developed network of *maktab*s* (schools) and *madrasa*s* (Islamic colleges).[6] Each village had its own local *maktab* for village boys, in which they learned basic reading and writing skills (Aynī 1955). The pupils were 'immediately thrust into a set of hierarchical social relationships' as soon as they entered the *maktab* (Khalid 1998: 22). They improved their status individually, depending on the number of books they had worked through with their teacher.[7]

Only certain students later moved to a *madrasa* for further education. Since *madrasa*s were financed by means of *waqf* (pious endowments), they were often privately run institutions.[8] Teachers (mullahs of different kinds) attracted students to these institutions, mainly on the basis of their lineage and territorial (*qavm**) relations. These teacher–student relations reflected the larger sphere of patronage-based relations between a respected religious authority in (urban) Bukhara and his (rural) *qavm* (Dudoignon 1996: 144–45; 2001, 2004a).

> Central Asian *qavm* or *tā'ifa*s, in the nineteenth – as in the sixteenth – century, were functioning as systems of personal protection and patronage, set up by a strong spiritual authority: the *shayh* of a mystical order, or a prominent figure of the madrasa system (those two figures often being one and the same person). Such a 'faction' used to be made up of a vertical segment of society, whose members were held together by an essentially 'negative loyalty' – that is, the need to defend common interests against common enemies. (Dudoignon 2004a: 73–74)

Education in Central Asia was a lengthy commitment. Sadriddin Aynī (1962: 208–12) writes in his memoirs (*yoddoshtho*) that learning at the *madrasa* was so difficult and slow that it could take up to nineteen years.[9] However, this could vary depending on the student's capacity and degree of specialization in the subject (Dudoignon 1996: 136). From these accounts, we can assume that each class had students of varying ages. Aynī mentions a companion of similar age with whom he shared classes, but also describes sharing lessons with older students as well, who were not necessarily more advanced but who had spent more time in the *madrasa*. According to a Turkic journal of 1914, the average age of students in the *madrasa*s of the Ottoman Empire was 35 years (Georgeon 2007: 154). We can assume a similar average age of students in the *madrasa*s at Bukhara, although Aynī (1962) does mention that there were 'young mullahs' teaching in the *madrasa*s as well.

In fact life at the *madrasa*s until a later period was dominated by a distinctly masculine and turbulent youth, men aged between 15 and 30 years – as proven for instance by the development of the pogrom of the Shi'ite community in 1910 – but the intellectual sociability was marked by a larger generational diversity. The big 'lounges' (*mahafil*) that were held by the main figures of the scientific and educated milieu in Bukhara and in other regional capitals of the Emirate (the most famous being without doubt Ziya [Dudoignon 2004b]) demonstrated that people of advanced age continued to occupy central positions, including within reformist circles (*jadid* [a Central Asian reformist movement at the turn of the twentieth century]*), until the Soviet period. The assumption of power by younger people seems to have taken place twice: first, when an initial wave of students, led by Fitrat, returned from the Ottoman Empire and founded the secret society Tarbiyya-yi atfal; second, after the arrival of the Bolsheviks, who during the 1920s tried to place the youngest figures of the *jadid* movement in responsible posts. The older wave disappeared in the first mass purges of 1932–1934, the younger wave in those of 1936–1937.[10]

In this context the dynamic between master and student plays a central role in the senior–junior relation. *Usto** refers to the master (*ustod** is used to refer to a teacher, whether religious or not) and *shogird** to the student or apprentice. 'Historically, the relationship between elders and juniors was marked in the family, the educational system, the system of apprenticeship, the organization of religious brotherhoods, and the military establishment' (Neyzi 2003: 361), and this is true also for Central Asia (Khalid 1998; Krämer 2002; Dudoignon 2004c; Dagyeli 2008; Stephan 2008; Kikuta 2009). *Usto* (master) does not signify a level that can be reached by an apprentice only, but is always relational, Jeanine Dagyeli (pp. 165–80) observes. Thus an apprentice continues to call his master *usto* even after his professional independence.[11] The education of an apprentice can take anywhere from fifteen to twenty-five years.[12] Through the relationship between *ustod* and *shogird*, knowledge is passed transgenerationally.

Within religious education the relation between *ustod* and *shogird* is initiated by a gift from the family of the future student (*shogird*), signalling the beginning of a lifelong teacher–student relation. Whether concerning a Sufi leader (*murshid*) and his student (*murid*) or a (secular) teacher (*muallim*) and his student (*talaba*), all of this teaching occurred within an individual relation between *ustod* and *shogird*. This relation is a central concept and can be found even today in any relationship where knowledge is passed transgenerationally.[13] Knowledge and skills are developed along with maturing, constituting a process of education. In light of this relation we can understand much of the domestication strategies that take place between social senior and social junior, which depend less on age (although age difference is usually implied) than on a respect for knowledge and skills as a marker of education and status.

Such individualized methods of learning, even if the main lessons are conducted in classrooms, allow for the direct domestication of young boys by their senior master. Youth (as a life-cycle period) here refers to a process of individual learning, not to a socio-demographically distinct group of people. Youth here reflects a subservient position in which young people remain until they are considered to have reached maturity by their teachers and parents. While the democratizing of knowledge has changed it over the last century, the relation between *ustod* and *shogird* has never disappeared, but in more recent times the notion of 'youth' has become increasingly powerful within political and secular fields of education.

The Jadid *Movement*

The *jadid** movement (the members of which referred to themselves as *yoshlar**, 'youth') consisted of scholars who, inspired by the reforms undertaken in the Ottoman Empire and British India, advocated the introduction of new teaching methods (*usul al-jadid*) (in the Russian Empire, this enlightenment occurred from the 1880s onwards).[14] Starting with the Tatars of the Volga and Crimea, the movement eventually spread to Bukhara and Kokand. The two writers Abdalrauf Fitrat and Mahmud Khoja Behbudi are known to have played a central role in stirring up the 'passive attitude of Bukharan Muslims' and making an effort to educate their children properly so that they could catch up with other, economically more successful 'ethnic groups' (Komatsu 2000: 30–31; cf. Allworth 2000).[15]

Dudoignon mentions that there was much tension and competition between these Bukharan reformists (*jadid*s) and the *qadimchī*, traditionalists or defenders of the old system (cf. Fedtke 1998). The Russians disliked the reformist movements and sought to undermine them by diverting the *waqf* incomes, which provided the basic finances for the education system, and concurrently by introducing schools teaching in Russian. However, the *jadid* movement still managed to reform the system to some extent, by placing young people in important positions. Due to this, Dudoignon (1996: 174) mentions the emic concepts of the Young Bukharans as analogous to the Young Turks who led the revolution in the Ottoman Empire.[16] The party *firqa*, which enjoyed tremendous popular support, emerged from these groups of Young Bukharans. Following increasing Bolshevik influence, the Young Bukharans eventually joined forces with the Bolshevik and became more politically active, but they were soon heavily persecuted by the communist regime. Nonetheless, after being appointed to central political posts, they implemented reforms in the education sector, creating universities and reforming *madrasa*s (ibid.). It is important to point out that this restructuring of the education system (classes based on age) demonstrates a systematic and politically motivated reorganization of young people, which provides the first indication of the emergence of a distinct socio-demographic category of youth that is accorded certain values and characteristics.

Dudoignon reminds us that even in the old system and before the arrival of the *jadid* movement, it should not be assumed that young men entirely lacked the agency or ability to develop their own talents, since the old system also provided a platform for young people to develop their skills and intellect, for instance, in handicraft professions (Dagyeli 2008). However, this appears to have been more of a patron–client relation, similar to the one which Snesarev (1963) and Rakhimov (1990) have described as existing in the 'school of youth' in the 'men's houses'.

In the *madrasa* system, students learned by copying their teachers – a method of teaching that remains widespread even today (Fathi 2004; Stephan 2008). This promoted the youth concept of gradual maturation through the internalization of various religious and community values.[17] Although the new teaching methods (*usul al-jadid*) introduced by the *jadid*s attempted to reform this method, it was only later, under the influence of communist ideology, that a radical redefinition of youth took place, which declared youth to be the vanguard of communism and the vessel for transmitting revolutionary ideas and realizing them at the community level.[18]

The Role of Youth in Constructing the Soviet Union

Sovietization began in Central Asia in 1927, according to Roy (1999: 111), with the first five-year plan. By the 1930s, the campaign for collective farming focused on kolkhoz (an abbreviation of *kollektivnoe khozyaystvo*) had reached even the remote area of Lakhsh. Each village had its own kolkhoz, which in practical terms meant that the land became state property, and all production was collected and redistributed according to the amount of work people put into the collective-farming effort (payments were made in kind).[19] The kolkhoz system continued in Lakhsh until 1958, when it was replaced by the sovkhoz (state farming) system, which differed in that all production had to be delivered to the state, for which the people were paid salaries. With these salaries, they could then buy necessary items for their families. In Tajik mountain areas one sovkhoz comprised ten to twenty villages. In Shahrigul, the kolkhoz system is recalled with higher regard than the sovkhoz.

> The kolkhoz was good: however much you brought would be fine. If you had potatoes, you brought them – you were paid according to your work. The sovkhoz took away even the (little) milk we had – the sheep, the cows – everything.[20]

Stalin's first attack on the family took the form of the collectivization programme, as it aimed at destroying the large farming families that continued to remain independent, to a certain extent, by owning land and cattle and using hired labour. It is believed that at least one-eighth, and possibly even one-sixth, of the peasant households, comprising about 25 million peasants, were wiped out during Stalin's purges, which persecuted not only the so-called *kulak* (the wealthier, more prosperous peasant), but also his entire family, including children (Harwin 1996: 14). The persecution of the *kulak* succeeded in changing land ownership patterns, but it did not destroy the social configuration of the community. In Jirgatol, for example, entire villages fled to other regions, reorganizing themselves in safer areas.

Two other impacts often discussed in relation to collectivization are effects on fertility and the displacement of populations. While Creed (1998: 129), in his research on Bulgaria, found a transition to low fertility within one generation during the period of collectivization, this was not the case in Tajikistan, where collectivization had some impact on fertility in the beginning, but after the Second World War the fertility rate steadily increased, reaching its peak in the 1980s. With regard to displacement, collectivization in the remote mountainous regions involved the resettlement of entire villages from the agriculturally unprofitable mountainous regions to cotton plantations in the southern and northern valleys and plains (cf. Loy 2005). These large-scale population movements left deep scars on people's life stories and identity construction, a matter that surfaced again in the recent civil war as a process of sorting out ethnic and regional belonging (see below).

The Basmachi (Mujohid) *Revolt*

Following the October Revolution, the Soviets tried to gain total control over Central Asia; however, the Red Army faced opposition from the so-called *basmachi** – 'bandits' according to the Russian translation, but *mujohid** in the emic Tajik view (Hayit 1992). The *basmachi* movement, which operated against the Soviets in Central Asia primarily from 1918 to 1931, were portrayed by the Soviets as criminal gangs roaming the country, plundering and destroying people's property.

Snesarev (1963: 179) has presented a closer look at the organization of Turkic-speaking groups from which the *basmachi* or *mujohid* were said to be recruited. A local leader, the *beg*, sought to recruit *egit** ('strong and fearless young men'), in order to steal from the rich in other villages. As their leader, the *beg* was responsible for providing the food at meetings; he also performed juridical functions in the village (*aul*). However, the *beg*s were not the only ones who recruited young men from the surrounding regions. Roy (2000: 46) mentions that many other types of armed groups submitted to traditional, religious or local chiefs such as the *kurbashi*, mullahs, *ishan*s (*eshon**), *khan*s and tribal chiefs or local notables.

In Qarotegin, the *basmachi* groups were also based on the 'men's house' institution.[21] Such men's houses (or teahouses) could be found all over Central Asia. The men's houses, as described by Rakhimov (1990), were run according to internal hierarchies. The leader was the *vazir*, a term taken from political vocabulary (Arabic for 'minister'), or *eshon bobo*, a term derived from religion, or *hokim*, a term based on juridical concepts. People met on a regular basis, usually at the home of a wealthy leader. According to Rakhimov, social hierarchy dictated the behaviour of people at such gatherings, which was regularly reinforced by the imposition of social sanctions if anyone acted outside the strict codes of conduct. Once they joined a men's house, its members never left it, unless they moved to another area. Any other reason for leaving would be regarded as an offence.

Rakhimov views these men's house institutions as providing the foundation for the creation and maintenance of social stability and political continuity. Moreover, Snesarev points out the educational character of men's houses, where tradition and social structures were maintained and reproduced; he calls these places 'the school of youth' (Snesarev 1963: 172).[22] For example, a father would bring his son to a teahouse leader and consign him to the leader's care and education with the words, 'I have entrusted this boy to you: his flesh is yours and his skin and bones, mine' (Rahimov 1989: 125; cf. Khalid 1998: 22; Roberts 1998: 682). This address was considered to be 'an oath of allegiance'. According to Rakhimov (1990: 65), a 12-year-old was regarded as fully mature and thus eligible to join a men's house. Hence, instead of being marked by a distinct youth identity, the *basmachi* were perceived as *egit*, mature youthful fighters.

All of these groups were loosely coordinated into a single movement, and the most that they had in common was their cause: to fight for a 'conservative Islam'. This underscores the fact that the groups had no qualms about 'switching camps in line with changing conditions' (Roy 2000: 46), as long as their power was not threatened.[23] The *basmachi* insurgence gradually declined, with Qarotegin being one of the last areas to actively oppose the Russian institutional presence until late into the 1930s.[24]

Although young people made up the majority of the *basmachi*, due to the lack of a common ideological base and lack of coordination among various separate groups (Marwat 1969: 110), the *basmachi* cannot be defined as a single movement. Despite efforts to unite them in their anti-Soviet struggle, the various *basmachi* groups did not develop a shared identity; each group, above all, defended its local interests. Regarding the decline of the movement, Marwat writes that the *mujohid* 'lacked not only military strength but also the sense of organization and unity' (ibid.: 110).

The Komsomol
Youth was always central to socialist politics – a subject that has been thoroughly researched (e.g., Hahn 1969, 1971; Juricic 1994; Pilkington 1994; Yurchak

2006). Youth was crucial to the success of the Bolshevik movement – without support from youth, the movement would have been politically quite powerless. If we remember that it took the Bolsheviks fifteen years to win the Russian students over to their side, we can see that the Bolsheviks had to invest a great deal of effort to obtain youth support in order to achieve their ambitions. 'After fifteen years of trying to dominate the student movement, the Bolsheviks, to the chagrin of other revolutionary parties, succeeded in October 1918 when they coordinated the establishment of the Komsomol' (Juricic 1994: 14).

Among the widespread discontent and activism that was directed against the tsarist regime, the Communist Party of Lenin was only one of the political parties struggling to gain the attention of youth. They were heavily invested, however, in meeting with the numerous student groups and establishing methods of inclusion and exclusion to create a vanguard group. The Komsomol* (*Soyuz Kommunisticheskoy Molodyozhi* in Russian, or the Young Communist League) was the organization for those youth groups that were successfully co-opted by the Bolsheviks in 1918 and soon became central to Bolshevik military activism. Especially during the civil war of the 1920s, young people were recruited en masse through the Komsomol.[25] Later, during the Second World War (dubbed the 'Great Patriotic War'), they again played a major role.

While the Komsomol remained a movement of enthusiastic young people, the roles, responsibilities and autonomy of the Komsomol changed rapidly, as did the direction of the Communist Party itself. These young people became crucial in industrializing society, acting through various brigades such as the 'rationalization brigades' in the early 1920s, the *udarnaya brigada* (shock brigade), and the brigades within the 'Light Cavalry movement' that were enlisted to fight bureaucracy and spread technical and political education from 1928 onwards (Juricic 1994).[26] Especially in the formative years of the Soviet Union, it became clear 'that the rapid industrialization campaign in the Soviet Union relied greatly upon the efforts of Komsomol members' (ibid.: 81).

For many years the Komsomol remained an urban movement, despite efforts to establish Komsomol cells in rural areas. In general, the Communist Party did not trust peasant Komsomol cells that operated within the territorial delimitation of villages, and thus, through the collectivization campaign that was instituted at the fifteenth Communist Party Congress in 1927, rural Komsomol came under the full control of the Communist Party. In this collectivization campaign the Komsomol were to play a crucial role in 'dekulakization'. 'In Central Asia the Komsomol was influential in dividing the land and livestock of former aristocrats, guaranteeing water to peasants through the construction of an irrigation system' (ibid.: 93). Through competition, 'shock-construction' projects and education campaigns, young people were given the task of building communism.[27] Similarly, young people were sent to all corners of the Soviet Union to teach and 'liberate' women from patriarchal domination (Kamp 2008). 'The promotion of physical education, the discouragement of drunkenness, debauchery, and hooliganism, and the agitation to "free young people, and especially young girls, from the influence of the family" were all important components in the Komsomol's drive to create a new lifestyle for the peasants' (Juricic 1994: 93). In short, youth were the vanguards of communism because they were believed to be free from past experiences, and thus they were at least partially entrusted with the building of the new state. 'At the heart of the "constructors-of-communism" paradigm . . . lies the conjunction of the symbolic importance of youth in the process of state-led modernization with a labourist, progress ideology' (Pilkington 1994: 47).[28]

The Komsomol remained an instrument of the Communist Party, which actively exerted control by regulating membership (the Komsomol, however, was allowed a certain amount of internal freedom in this regard, as long as it adhered to party directives) and the maintenance of a cadre. Membership came to be a prerequisite for any career and hence a way to pressure youth who did not conform, or who openly challenged the work of the Komsomol. This often arbitrary practice allowed the more enthusiastic members within the Komsomol to sustain an internal hierarchy in their favour.

The Communist Party's closest allies were members of the industrial Komsomol, who were sent to rural areas to act as leaders. To encourage participation in this faction of the Komsomol, 'the party offered monetary incentives, better food and accommodation, and the privilege of an increase in power and authority' (Juricic 1994: 72). By controlling membership, and through the public denunciation of those who did not conform to or meet the requirements of the Komsomol, the group was also able to exert its power over older workers, who felt resentment against the Komsomol, especially in rural areas.[29]

From its beginnings as a student movement to its evolution into an industrial and military organization, and eventually to its formidable stature as an all-union institution, the Komsomol increased dramatically in number; between 1924 and 1926 Komsomol cells grew sixfold, and there were four times more Komsomol than party members (ibid.: 96). This is significant because it signals the transformation of a vanguard group into a mass organization. Later, as the Young Communist League (YCL) itself put it in 1966, membership of the Komsomol was open to 'any young person from the Soviet Union, recognizing the rules of the YCL, actively participating in Communist Construction, working in one of the Komsomol organizations, fulfilling the decisions of the Komsomol, and paying membership dues' (quoted in Hahn 1969: 220). The age limit was increased from 22 to 24 in 1924 and eventually to 28. Many members remained in the Komsomol long past the later-prescribed age limit of 28 (Riordan 1989: 21), and with a continually increasing membership, the Komsomol reached the scale of a mass movement, constituting up to 65 per cent of eligible age groups in the 1950s, while continuing to espouse the same aim: 'to encompass and organize the entire younger generation' (ibid.: 21).

The Komsomol comprised the third stage in the communist (political) life-course construction: children grew from *oktyabryat** (7 to 10 years) to *pioner** (10 to 14 years) to Komsomol* (14 to 28 years). Although Komsomol membership officially ended when a person turned 28 (as mentioned above), the leaders were often far older. However, the largest number of members were aged 16 and 17, because it was commonly agreed that university entrance required party membership (Riordan 1989: 23; Yurchak 2006: 3). Alexei Yurchak (2006) aptly describes the attitudes of Komsomol members and leaders since the 1970s. Having become a mass organization, participation became 'normalized' and increasingly a ritual performance that marked a person's belonging to the community and to their own people (*svoi*, Russ.: us, ours). Yurchak argues that this belonging was central to the continuation of the Komsomol, while at the same time it allowed for a creative life. The shift from ideological work to ritual performance described by Yurchak became possible under Brezhnev, whose politics were more even-handed, with fewer of the sudden changes that had characterized the Stalin years.

The successive traditionalization of many procedures (meetings, assignments and so on) allowed for the integration of youth without necessarily forcing them to identify with the ideological content. On the one hand they joined the Komsomol because they sensed they could not change these traditionalized procedures; on the other hand they did not believe that by joining they had relinquished their own agency in all domains. In this way the Komsomol of the 1970s to mid 1980s became part of a larger tradition of Soviet culture. Hierarchies were established, and certain rituals marked one's belonging to the Soviet community, but these traditions were not overly restrictive, as they allowed for creativity and change. Because the Komsomol became part of tradition, it was necessary for some members of the cadre to be educated in the ritual procedures necessary to keep this *svoi* alive: 'Komsomol leaders of different levels in the hierarchy received different amounts of training in the techniques of ideological production . . . Among the leading cadres, however, special training was necessary to acquire the skill of reproducing texts and conducting ritualized events and assignments' (ibid.: 83). The 'professional ideological workers' resemble those select few who are initiated into a secret society, such as in West Africa. They assume a leadership position over youth, tasked with incorporating youth into a common society without fully controlling all elements of a youth's life. Overt domestication occurs only in situations in which an individual (described as a dissident) actively challenges the Komsomol tradition (hierarchy, power distribution and rituals). It is in breaking rules that the rules are revealed. The Komsomol institution was effective in controlling maturation and establishing a specific youth category.

At this point, let us consider a concrete example from Tajikistan, namely the story of one of the first Tajik Komsomol members, Mastibek K.A. Tashmukhammedov. To commemorate Mastibek's hundredth birthday,

Kurbanova (2008) published a short biography that describes how Mastibek began his education in a local *maktab* (school) but was then sent by his father to a school where the Russian border guards sent their children. In 1923, at the age of 14, he was one of the first Tajiks to join the Komsomol, and within two years he was sent – along with thirty other activists – to study at the pedagogical institute at Dushanbe. In time he was elected secretary of the institute's Komsomol branch and later continued his career within the organization in Kulob, where the Komsomol were fighting the *basmachi*, who disrupted their work and harassed their members. The account hints at rather serious internal resistance to the socialist system, considering that by the 1930s socialism had already taken root in northern parts of the Soviet Union.

In 1935 Mastibek joined the military, but he was persecuted during the purges of 1937. Pilkington (1994) has mentioned that the Komsomol were not spared from these purges, and this was also true for Mastibek. However, thanks to his connections with Shotemur, an important political figure, Mastibek was released and called upon to fight alongside Soviet troops, all the way to Berlin, in the war against Germany. Kurbanova writes that by the time Mastibek was 35 years old, he was already involved in party work and had become a member of the central committee of the Communist Party in Tajikistan.[30] His story suggests that members of the Komsomol were the vanguard of communism, and had faced local resistance in many cases. Unfortunately, the biography does not provide much information on what motivated Mastibek (and others) to join the Komsomol; thus, we are left wondering whether it was primarily the parents who encouraged their children to join the Komsomol, as Mastibek's father had done, or whether the Komsomol directly recruited children from villages against their parents' wishes, as reported in other regions, particularly Russia.[31]

The Komsomol are given credit for building a Soviet Tajikistan. According to Kurbanova, they built 'the kolkhozes, the village Soviets, the social organization [meaning many cells of Komsomol], with numerous active young people' (Kurbanova 2008); they constructed socialism and were engaged in the communist project. As part of the socialist educational system, the Komsomol helped to collectivize youth under a common ideology, turning them into a group that could be moulded through a specific youth concept which had come to be regarded as 'tradition'. This youth concept had been constructed according to the socialist ideal, with its leaders portrayed as guiding lights. The success of the Komsomol in recruiting masses of young people shows that its organization was effective in maximizing youth potential.[32] It was the very idea of being a vanguard and of increasing one's status despite one's young age that made the Komsomol so attractive and effective, at least in its earlier years. Leaders of the Komsomol (the *komsorg* – Komsomol organizer) continued to profit from their status and the advantages such status afforded. Thus Yurchak (2006) describes how *komsorg* friends arranged to leave lessons to amuse themselves in town, relying on their status as *komsorg* to obtain permission, and how they exerted their authority over any young person who challenged the *svoi* and their right to enforce it.

It is important to note that the Komsomol was targeted at those aged 14 to 28. This implies a youth definition stretching far beyond European concepts of adolescence, and is more in line with the Central Asian concept of youth as a long process of social, political and psychological maturation. Juricic writes that the establishment of schools aimed at recruiting 14- and 15-year-olds was a conscious strategy of the party, '[s]ince many youths are both inquisitive and rebellious at this stage in their lives' (Juricic 1994: 91). It is only in the context of such a process that we can grasp the construction of youth as a top-down domestication effort. Such a youth concept does not focus on allowing a young person's individual talents to be encouraged and developed, as in the *madrasas*; rather, it promotes the idea of young people living for the community and contributing their energy and physical strength to its service. While competitions were held to encourage individual engagement in production and to motivate others to join, this was intended less as a reward for individual talent than as a method for furthering collective goals and encouraging exceptional performances according to socialist values.

The Soviet state, at least earlier on, had a clear vision of 'domesticating' youth on the basis of a carrot-and-stick policy, while rejecting and punishing any kind of open deviance.[33] Unfortunately, the Soviet era produced very few scholarly studies of rural youth in Tajikistan that go beyond giving advice on how to educate Soviet citizens. I was informed by a young man from a family of clerics that membership was important for the pursuit of a political career as well as higher education; he was in fact restricted from studying and from any other form of promotion (via the Komsomol) because of his family's religious background. Thus, as Yurchak (2006) has mentioned, exclusion from the Komsomol could act as a roadblock to a youth's advancement in life, and therefore participation in the Komsomol did not necessarily mean that all of its members agreed with or even engaged in communist ideology.

Eventually, the Muslims of Central Asia appeared to be equally attracted to the popular culture of the West, which became the Komsomol's greatest concern from the late 1970s to the early 1980s. Instead of fighting traditional backwardness and 'harmful' elements – such as traditional healing (cf. Poliakov 1992: 62) – the Communist Party was now faced with controlling the spread of 'unacceptable' Western popular culture (Fierman 1988: 27). With the break-up of the Soviet Union, however, the Komsomol simply ceased to exist in practice in Tajikistan, informants claimed.[34] The year 1985 marks a break in the traditionalization of the Komsomol. By 1988, Yurchak asserts, 'the party had lost its prestige and millions started leaving its ranks – an act that would have been simply unthinkable a year or two previously' (Yurchak 2006: 294).

Although the above analysis of the Komsomol is in no way exhaustive, it still points clearly to the importance of its role in redefining youth as vanguards and builders of a visionary, glorious future. The Komsomol organization thus became a useful tool for the socialist regime to gain control over its youthful population by according them a vanguard status within communist ideology. Furthermore, the organization's defined rules of inclusion and exclusion allowed it to control group size (cf. Schlee 2008), and thus, for the communists, as a demographic instrument, the Komsomol made it possible to manage the life course of the Soviet Union's youth and channel youthful behaviour within a vanguard ideology.

Most importantly, the Communist Party was able to create a youth category under their control. Using the vanguard ambitions of youth movements, they transformed the enthusiasm of young people into a system of youth control. Through the Komsomol they claimed to represent 'youth' as a socio-political category, and at the same time the party pursued strategies of inclusion and exclusion that maintained an elite vanguard group who were charged with both upholding and renewing ideas. In this way they skilfully used demographic potential by controlling and moulding categories and maintaining groups that represented the youth category. A specific youth identity, then, had been created that excluded those young people who did not conform to its requirements. This strategy generated oppositional identities (such as religious identities and 'Western' youth cultures) that intensified from the 1980s onwards. The organization's power lay in its size, as more than half of the eligible age group held formal membership. However, when the Soviet Union collapsed, the Komsomol went down with it. Unlike communist ideology, which to an extent endured the dissolution of the Soviet Union, the Komsomol did not.

In the newly independent states youth increasingly became the focus of the nation-state project (no longer the future of the Soviet Union but rather that of Tajikistan, Uzbekistan and so on). Although mobility did not diminish, it changed in character. During the era of the Soviet Union, mobility had been about joining the military, being part of a youth group engaged in 'developing' another country, or leaving to advance one's education; now mobility was about escaping violence (civil war, violent clashes), seeking economic opportunities (labour migration), or educational purposes (not only higher education but also religious education and primary education). Each independent republic was thus left with its own demographic and economic conditions that were destined to become a central source of future problems. None of these conditions had been taken into consideration when the independent Central Asian states were founded. We shall see in the next section, however, that in Tajikistan a new youth ideology had already gained enough adherents to become the most important opposition during the civil war that followed the collapse of the Soviet Union.

Independence and the Tajik Civil War

The civil war in Tajikistan that lasted for an entire decade, at varying degrees of intensity, left ten of thousands dead and more than half a million persons displaced in and outside the country. The following section provides a general overview of the civil war, and then focuses on the different ways in which youth were portrayed during the war. Earlier we have seen how youth within the Komsomol were proclaimed to be vanguards of communism, while at the same time the Komsomol organization was used to control and domesticate youth within the Soviet Union. The various descriptions of youth in the civil war shed light on similar tendencies – namely, to see youth as vanguards of Islam, as victims of war, or as naturally disruptive.

Civil war is an extreme situation in which roles become more radicalized and – most important for young men – in which choosing neutrality is essentially not an option. Another effect is the 'juvenilizing' effect of conflicts, in that during war men may be forced or are more willing to fight even if by social standards they have already reached maturity. In other words, the civil war enlarged the youth bulge of potentially involved combatants as a result of redefinitions of 'youthfulness' in war situation. How this actually plays out on the ground is discussed later. Before we inquire further into how youth were mobilized and became categorized in (and after) the civil war, it is necessary to provide a short overview of the civil war, based on available resources and supplemented by my own research.

The Civil War in Tajikistan

The era of perestroika had a snowball effect, unleashing a social dynamism that had been developing since the early 1980s, if not sooner. In Tajikistan the first demonstrations took place in February 1990. On the eleventh of that month, people gathered in front of the Parliament building to demand a resolution to the housing problems in Dushanbe. The regime in power did not believe it was obligated to explain why Armenian refugees had been given privileged treatment and offered flats, passing over others who had been on waiting lists for a long time. The demonstrations attracted more and more people, particularly young people demanding that the government heed their public, economic and political grievances – to which the state's response was violence. Sources have reported that twenty-five people died in the altercation, with another eight hundred injured. Instead of causing people to back down, the state's actions antagonized an even larger segment of the population. This event is considered by many to represent the beginning of the greater unrest that, after a period of relative peace, led to increasingly violent confrontations.

As one of the last republics of the former Soviet Union, with only Kazakhstan to follow, Tajikistan proclaimed its independence from the USSR on 9 September

1991. People to the north of Tajikistan had dominated political life in the republic throughout Soviet rule. When Moscow's central control broke down, however, other groups claimed some of the most attractive political posts. Many political parties emerged at this time, forming pro-government and oppositional factions or groups.[35] On the one hand, the ruling party continued a socialist regime supported and later replaced by people from the Kulob region (in the south of the country), while on the other hand various opposition groups formed a democratic-Islamic coalition. The United Tajik Opposition (UTO) was characterized by the inclusion of multiple groups, among others the Democratic Party (Hizbi Demokrati Todjikiston), the Islamic Revival Party (Hizbi Nahzati Islom), Rastokhes (nationalist-democratic party), and the La'li Badakhshan Party (Dudoignon 1994). The Islamic party turned out to be the most significant of the groups, as it was able to mobilize more subgroups than any of the other parties.[36]

With Tajikistan gaining independence in September 1991, demonstrators again began to pressure the government to change certain laws.[37] Rahmon Nabiev was elected president of Tajikistan on the basis of a rather dubious election on 24 November 1991. Nabiev responded to the political demands of the opposition parties by harshly suppressing them. Since the army remained neutral, he built up his own fighting units, the best known under the command of Sangak Safarov – affiliated with the Popular Front (Fronti Khalkī) from the Kulob region – a former criminal who had spent more than twenty years in prison. In addition to these fighting units, pro-government demonstrators were provided with arms at the beginning of May 1992 (Schoeberlein-Engel 1994: 38; Bushkov 1995: 17; Karim 1997: 518). These demonstrators, all supporters of Nabiev, gathered at one end of Dushanbe's main roads, Rudaki Street, in the Ozodī Square. As the urban population hesitantly gravitated towards the square, youth were brought in by bus and even helicopter from rural areas to significantly bolster the pro-government presence. The opposition had already gathered at Shohidon Square at the other end of Rudaki Street, and mainly comprised of people from Qarotegin, Pamir and Kurgan-Tepe, but had interrupted the demonstrations (*miting*). When pro-government activists organized Ozodī Square, opposition actors again gathered at Shohidon Square.

The demonstrations lasted for almost an entire month in spring 1992. Since Dushanbe had already begun to experience food shortages, the demonstrators from Qarotegin asked their relatives to send supplies: 'They collected sheep and goats from us and brought them to Dushanbe', a woman from Shahrigul told me. Food was served to the people in Shohidon Square – this obviously attracted urban residents as well, mainly curious and hungry young men with some connection to the Islamic party (often based on ethnic, regional, emotional and/or religious ties, and sometimes out of political conviction).

While the demonstration of the opposition was heated, it had not yet turned into an armed disturbance. However, the distribution of small weapons transformed the nature of the political conflict. Weapons poured in from individual conflict actors who either took them from armed militias or were given them by the Russian military still stationed in Tajikistan. The more the conflict escalated, the more its actors pushed to advance their individual interests. For instance, the urban leaders of the criminal underworld, who under the Soviet regime had profited from political protection, entered the conflict with well-organized youth groups. Rauf, to cite an example, was the criminal leader of several *mahallas** (neighbourhoods), including the Putovski bazaar. He provided protection to those businessmen who paid him, keeping the violent conflict out of his zone of influence. Recruiting young men in his area, he sent some of them out to rob and plunder outside the *mahallas* under his control, while posting older members of his organization at street corners to maintain order within his *mahallas*.

In such a way, though not restricted to criminal groups, middle-aged men were busy protecting their own neighbourhoods while young men and boys (aged 16 years and above) formed independent combatant groups (outside parental control), causing trouble across the city in the name of their *mahalla*. These groups of youth believed that they were actively defending their *mahalla*, but they also had their own agenda; rather than viewing these groups as fighting for a political cause, some people were 'concerned about local rivalries between their village and the one over the hill'.[38] Hence, some armed young men used their newfound power to take revenge on others who had bothered them in the past, such as an annoying policeman or an unfair chairman or director. The more overtly criminal groups launched attacks on private houses and indulged in looting and plundering; this actually turned into one of the biggest problems of the war and continued until 2000.

From this moment on, a critical segment of the demonstrators (namely youth) were armed and able to turn a political cause into open confrontation. While those specializing in violence were elevated to the level of political actors, such as the presidential guard of Safarov, many youth barely knew how to operate their weapons, which increased the risk of misuse. According to Karim (1997), the terms *vovchik* and *yurchik* had entered popular usage by May 1992 and were used to distinguish between ad hoc individuals and groups as friends or enemies.[39] *Vovchik* included members of the above-mentioned opposition parties – more specifically, people from Kofarnihom, Rasht and Badakhshan – while *yurchik* in the beginning referred to people from Kulob (*kulobī*), and later more generally to all followers of communist ideology.

Apart from conflicts led by numerous violent actors,[40] who were more or less interconnected, many local conflicts took place outside this dualistic concept, under the guise of the civil war. Only occasionally did these conflicts flow outward into the wider context of the war, as I learned from an event at Lakhsh.[41] While ethnicity was one line of argument that emerged from the shadow of the political events described by the vocabulary of ideological opposition – 'communists versus Islamists' – the conflict itself cannot be described as ethnic (Bushkov and Mikul'skiy 1995, 1996). The most common explanation of the Tajik civil war lies in the idea of *mahalgaroi*, which has two dimensions: at the macro-political level, it means 'region against region'; at the local level, it refers to neighbourhoods, especially in areas where these neighbourhoods (*mahallas*) had been created by village populations that were forcibly transplanted in the 1940s and 1950s.[42] While regionalism in and of itself did not promote divisiveness, the conflict prompted local leaders to look for ethno-regional support. During this process, it became important to sort out the issue of people's ethnicity – an undertaking that was not easily accomplished.

The war moved from Dushanbe southwards, to regions where people from the mountains had been resettled in the 1940s and 1950s, which in turn caused masses of refugees to head to neighbouring Afghanistan or to join their relatives Qarotegin, in the east of the country. In February 1993, the pro-government warlords made their first attempts to conquer the Qarotegin Valley, which was the stronghold of the opposition, especially Gharm and Tojikobod. On 2 February 1993, the head of the opposition in Gharm had apparently declared the independent Islamic Republic of Qarotegin (Jumhuri Islomii Qarotegin) (Hetmanek 1993; Karim 1997: 581).[43] However, the Islamic Revival Party later denied having had any ambition to establish an Islamic republic.

President Emomali Rahmonov half-heartedly attempted to re-establish peace, but the fighting continued in several parts of the country, such as Pamir and Qarotegin. Rahmonov had been head of the Parliament since 1992, but he was elected president only on 6 November 1994 – in the absence of any real alternative. At that time, a large part of the Tajik population was still displaced within the country – and also outside it. Meanwhile, the Safarov group proceeded south to the Shahrituz area, 'cleansing' the population as it went. The word 'cleansing' was used by the pro-government militias to refer to the violent measures they implemented because 'they didn't want their children to become slaves of the *qozi**' (Karim 1997: 534).

From April 1994 onwards, several attempts to establish peace between the warring factions failed, and it was not until 27 June 1997 that a peace agreement was signed, under pressure from the international community.[44] However, some opposition leaders were left unsatisfied by the terms of the peace agreement, so a few armed factions continued their activities, mainly terrorizing and robbing people. Two such groups were those under the command of Rahmon Gitler and Rizvon – leaders who had not been integrated into the new coalition and only enjoyed limited support.[45] Despite continual international attempts to re-establish peace, according to Karim, it took a long time for Rahmonov to exert absolute control over the numerous subgroups and even longer before he was able to stop sending tanks and soldiers into opposition areas (ibid.: 897, 948).

As part of the peace agreement, those who fought for the opposition were integrated into government law-enforcement agencies. Their perception of their role within this framework in Rasht district is exemplified by the case of the special unit in Gharm and its leaders Mirzokhoja Nizomov and Mirzokhoja Ahmadov. Apart from being a military unit, the group also assumed the responsibility of moral policing, which first of all meant ensuring that women were kept out of the public sphere and establishing public order on the basis of Islamic principles, including the banning of alcohol and cigarettes. During my fieldwork, I collected many accounts from women who were accused of having 'misbehaved' according to these strictures – either in the role of a teacher or NGO leader, or in holding any political position. The following statement by an informant gives an idea of the extent of this group's power: 'Even the *rais palkom* [chief of the district] is afraid of Mirzokhoja, although he is a higher authority than him'.[46] The former command structure of the Rasht region was headed by Nizomov, who, after the civil war, worked in the customs department and, later, on the border committee. He became increasingly a state agent, losing much of his previous authority over many former *mujohid** groups.[47] Some local leaders and former *mujohid* commanders sided with the government, while others continued to implement their own ideas of law (which they called *shariat*, Islamic law) until 2010, when the government had them killed (Roche and Heathershaw 2010a, 2010b).

Young Combatants: Victims, Actors and Troublemakers

Let us now take a look at the way youth were perceived during the Tajik civil war and how they are portrayed in civil war literature. Classically, population pressure and ideological conflicts are put forth by scientists and political actors as the root causes of the Tajik civil war (Fierman 1991; Bushkov 1993; Roy 1998; Niyazi 2000; Nourzhanov 2005). However, thus far no study on Tajikistan has closely examined how people and the government dealt with these problems or how demographic pressure is empirically connected to conflicts. Furthermore, to state that youth constituted a majority of the fighters does not advance one's understanding of the conflict without exploring how and why they fought. Also, this says little about how concepts of youth change in conflict settings. My intention is to discuss the categories that were created and applied so as to make youth engagement possible. These are based less on socio-economic problems than on ideological, international and cultural constructions of what a young person is or can become in a violent conflict.

Youth as Victims

In the civil war literature, youth move from troublemaker to victim rather easily, a phenomenon which Wyn and White (1997) have tried to grasp through an approach looking at the relationship between agency and structure. They argue that the conceptualization of youth has failed due to an overemphasis on youth's role within politics: 'There is a form of "victimology", for example, which defines young people primarily and exclusively in terms of their status as (passive) victims of circumstance' (ibid.: 317). Such an approach reflects the late-conflict or post-conflict categorization of young people as victims of circumstance. This is also how young people's engagement with violence is viewed by parents, who blame elites for taking advantage of 'youth's natural thirst for adventure' for their own political ends.

Youth were the primary target group in the civil war: young men as potential fighters and young women as 'prey' meant to disgrace the enemy (Tadjbakhsh 1994). This is reflected in some of the local literature on the civil war in which young people are portrayed as victims of the older generations who 'misused' the youth for their own purposes. Tajik politician and author Būri Karim writes:

> Military groups say that the orders of the leader must be followed uncon-
> ditionally . . . Our leaders and generals never fight themselves. Their
> children and kinsmen do not fight. The simple farmer's youth fights.
> Our military youth have not seen life yet, but give their soul [i.e., they
> die] with the words 'we defend the state constitution' on their lips. For
> this, the leader nominates them heroes, heroic pictures emerge, and
> people are forced to build up [those images] because they will follow
> their example. But look, their own children never take up this example.
> (Karim 1997: 672)[48]

Karim's interpretation of how the combatant groups were organized reflects the construction of youth within Tajik society. Youth were the victims of leaders, caught in an irreversible patron–client relation. The older generation ordered the younger ones to do the physical work while they simply strategized and delegated. Karim also refers to the fact that the recruitment of young men during the civil war was perceived as legitimate by all political groups, based on the argument that young men had to do their military service anyway (and could perform such service in any of the combatant groups). Thus every commander felt they were in the right when forcibly recruiting young men. Generally, *mujohids** – and I surmise it was similar for other groups – recruited youth from the age of 14 ('officially' from 17) upwards.

Karim complains that combatant leaders reflected little on youth's other social roles (future fathers, security for their parents, and so on). Instead, they identified themselves as legitimate leaders and thus laid claim to young men's physical participation in war. This shows us that in the civil war, mass recruitment was legally conducted under the assumption that it was the duty of young men to defend the country against an (internal) enemy. Even if it was not the only recruitment pattern, it was one way to present the participation of youth in the war as a normal consequence of the political life course of those youth. This also explains why, in 2003, I was told by several people that the *mujohids* were young men born in 1975 and later (in 1992, the oldest of those were 17 years old and thus, by law, the new recruits).

Muhiddin is a young man from Lakhsh who had been recruited by the opposition forces while fulfilling his military service. He embraced a rather strict version of Islam. Continuing to serve in the army after the war ended, he eventually returned home. However, life has been difficult for him as neither his family nor many of his co-villagers share his ideas. Dependent on his younger brothers' help, he feels vulnerable and at the same time a better person due to his devout life. His primary activity is teaching young boys Islam.

> MUHIDDIN: I had tried to go to Dushanbe and study, but since I didn't have money and thus I could not enrol,[49] I went into the army. I served on the border of Afghanistan. We did not go on the wrong track; we took lessons in a *madrasa**.
>
> S.R.: When did they recruit you?
>
> MUHIDDIN: In 1994 [1992?] during the war, when there was unrest on the squares. I was on neither side; on the contrary, they would advise us not to fight against our brothers (*barodaron*) and instead to follow 'a good path'.
>
> S.R.: Where did they take you to fight?
>
> MUHIDDIN: Around Gharm, during the war we got mixed up, and when we left for the mountains, we bought their words [we believed what they said], those called the opposition. Then we went to Afghanistan and saw that they were good upright people. They gave us lessons. They were our people, Samarkand people, who had fled after the persecution of 1917.[50]

Another woman in Jirgatol explained the distinct roles ascribed to youth and grownups in the civil war: *mujohids* recruited young boys by force to fight against the *hukumat** (state), whereas older *mujohids*, such as a *qozi*, for example, felt responsible for educating the ordinary population. The latter would force people to get up for prayer, and women were only allowed outside the house fully covered by a neck scarf (*faranji, lengi**). In other words, the work of youth was to join a combatant group, whereas elder political activists took care of the rest of the population by educating them.

Youth as Actors

Some accounts show that young people had been organized long before the war started. The underground youth organization, Sozmoni Javononi Ozod (Organization of Free Youth), was founded by Said Abdullo Nuri, later a leader of the Islamic Revival Party of Tajikistan (IRPT) (Bashiri 2003; Rashid 2003: 97). According to Olimova (2000: 65) it is from this youth organization that the IRPT emerged in 1978: 'The objective of this young group was to study and disseminate the reformist teachings of Hasan Al-Banna (founder of the Muslim Brotherhood movement in Egypt) and the ideas of Abdul Ala Mawdudi (the ideologist of a Pakistani branch of political Islam)' (ibid.: 65).[51] Nuri headed the youth organization, which began with educational and cultural activities and later became an active group, sending students abroad and collecting literature and textbooks about Islam (Olimova 2004: 248). Based on these materials, they formulated their own goals and methods of struggle.

Throughout his life, Nuri supported young students and taught them in his house. One of his students said that Nuri was like a father to him. When I met this student, he was on his way to a commemoration feast for his teacher, who died in summer 2006. The young man had not only taken classes with Nuri for four years, but also lived in his 'small and decent' apartment. Having served as one of Nuri's troops, the young man claimed that it was Nuri's effort alone that stopped the fighting; it could easily have continued otherwise.[52] He also warned that if a new war should break out, no one would have the charisma to stop the war as Nuri had been able to do. Nuri's lifelong suffering in the political struggle surrounding his religious beliefs has been integrated into the narratives of many former combatants.[53]

Young people reflecting on the civil war mentioned two central relationships: between their leaders and them, usually as teacher and student (*ustod** and *shogird**), and among combatants (brother relations). The teacher–student relationship was described emotionally by young people and perceived as a lasting relationship, similar to the way Nuri's student described his relationship with the leader. This represents a classic Central Asian form of relationship, in which knowledge is passed transgenerationally; this leader–follower relationship was recalled by many former combatants, who although they had escaped parental subordination, nevertheless accepted religious tutelage.

During my research, I have tried to reconstruct combatant groups in order to explore the social relations that existed within them. I will restrict my accounts here, with regard to youth as actors, to a more age-based analysis; a detailed description of youth within Tajik society will be discussed in the following chapters. Let us start with one *mujohid* group, whose origins lay in the Gharm district and whose influence remained strong until 2010.[54] The group was rather large, with around sixty people (groups of around ten people were more common): 'the oldest was our commissar, who was almost 50, then another commander was in his forties and yet another was 30 years old. The others were all between 14 and 27 years of age. Three were very old, one 70 and two others 60 years of age. The youngest was called *malish*'. In response to the question of how they had become *mujohid*s, one informant – let us call her Safarmoh – said: 'They came out of their own will and became *mujohid*s; if you liked to fight, you would go out and join ... [T]hey came from everywhere, from Qurgan Teppe, Dushanbe, here, and we also had Afghans with us'. Safarmoh appreciatively called the group leader a 'psychological specialist' because he skilfully managed a group of varying ages and backgrounds. As a leader of a heterogeneous combatant group, he took existing group concepts (such as the family and religious brotherhoods) and applied them to unify people with diverse social background and regional origin with different motivations (refugees, recruiters, volunteers and so on).

Violence was also used to both keep the group together and to sanction group members. Simons claims that solidarity and bonding 'in non-regimental militaries ... comes from soldiers sharing pain-filled, miserable, frightening, exhilarating ... dangerous experiences' (Simons 2000: 17). She further argues that group solidarity is located in traditional experiences and common ritual practices. The groups under study not only created a whole set of new rituals but also actively reformulated old ones. For example, a new member had to walk under the Koran while declaring, 'I will be following your message' (*Man kafoi tu meravam*), and thus symbolically became subordinate to the holy book and its holy words. Yet it is less the submission aspect that creates the bonding than the conditions tied to it, namely, accepting fellow combatants as brothers and sisters.

Eventually, violence against members who strayed was used to prevent the group from being weakened internally: 'If one fled the group, [the person] was brought back. Since [they] already knew everything, [they were] taken far from us so that we wouldn't see and [they were] killed. However, he was a really fair commander', Safarmoh said. In all of these reports young people are portrayed as rational actors who participated in the war less as victims of politics than for various reasons, such as solidarity, revenge, ideology, hunger, longing for power and defending one's honour.

Young people came under enormous pressure to take sides; not taking a side was even worse than taking the 'wrong' side. As Mirzokarim explains, 'Then gossip would reach you – "why didn't you take sides, you were afraid" – so that would mean at that time you had to take a side, you didn't have a choice'.[55] This (postwar) explanation of youth participation in conflict is balanced by a very different perspective, offered by a young man (aged 22) who described the sensation of carrying a weapon: 'It was cool to have a weapon because older people would greet you. Those *mūisafed** that usually did not even look at us now greeted us respectfully'. The war provided him with a position that, under normal circumstances, he would not have reached before the age of 40.

As time went on, many combatants (especially the pro-governmental troops) became notorious for their primarily material interests.[56] Another reported that the *mujohid* groups had been able to provide regular food for their combatants, which was a motivating factor for many hungry young men. While some groups were very mobile, providing little opportunity for members to seize power in their native village, others managed to take local resources (most often relatively large tracts of land).[57] Thus, in addition to social and ideological factors, economic considerations also pushed young men to join combatant groups.

Generally speaking, as Jutta Bakonyi (2011: 65) claims, before civil violence erupts, specialists in violence (*Gewaltspezialisten*) are preceded by their 'professional' reputation. Some emerge from the state military apparatus, others from the criminal underworld, and both are accorded a cultural capital that marks them as experts in the use of violence. In times of conflict this cultural capital is overvalued, and provides a clear path to political and military titles. Hence specialists in the use of violence then become both locally embedded actors and political and economic players. While the teacher–student relation offers a nuanced view of the relation between a leader and his soldiers within the Islamic opposition, the cultural capital of those experienced in violence helps to explain why *ustod* Nuri turned out to be the more successful leader compared to the significantly more educated *qozi kalon** (supreme judge) Hoji Akbar Turajonzoda.[58]

Among the pro-government combatant groups, criminal leaders were the most successful. Many such leaders had already been active within their *mahal-la*s and bazaars during the Soviet period, enjoying the respect of young men who identified them with masculine values. Others – important leaders such as Khudoberdiev, Colonel Lunev (head of KGB soldiers) and Colonel Kvachkov (an explosives expert)[59] – had served in the Soviet army during the Soviet-Afghan war of the 1980s. Many of these *Afgantsy* retained their high-level connections and reorganized in the shadow economy or held position as bodyguards. They derived their cultural capital both from their perceived 'masculinity' and their successful entrepreneurship.

Yakub Salimov, another commander, was a leading underworld figure in Dushanbe with several years of prison experience; he rose to the position of Minister of Internal Affairs.[60] According to the political scientist Kılavuz (2009), Salimov had been a prominent militia leader on the streets of Dushanbe, engaged in the shadow economy. The recruitment of these underworld criminals by high-ranking politicians was not difficult, and considering that they already had a reputation – that is, cultural capital – among youth as successful specialists in violence, their being accorded official status by the government only upgraded their stature.

The successful mobilization of youth by these specialists in the use of violence – masculine icons who now also held military titles – was a dominant feature of the conflict in its early years. As mentioned above by Mirzokarim, to display masculinity meant to choose a side and participate in the conflict. This was not only true for young boys but for older men into their forties. It was only later that other motives, such as revenge, became increasingly relevant.

Youth as Troublemakers

Karim mentions, and at times emphasizes, the active participation of young men in the civil war as individual actors, which leads in the direction of portraying youth as a source of conflict, particularly in urban centres: 'Over a thousand young armed people made School No. 76 into a fortress and demanded that the opposition release their prisoners or else mullo Abdurahim would unleash terror' (Karim 1997: 452). In their account on the civil war, Bushkov and Mikul'skiy go even further in depicting youth as disruptive:

> The *criminal* situation in Dushanbe worsened. At around 3 PM on August 31, young people (probably from the neighbourhood [*mahalla*] groups and supporters of the Islamic-democratic opposition), together with refugees from the Qurgan Teppe and Kulob oblast, blocked the exit of the Presidential Palace and demanded a meeting with the president. The latter, who was warned by the security forces, managed to escape to the 201st Division. Since the occupiers could not find the president, they took people hostage. On the evening of September 1, they had 32 hostages from Leninobod and the Kulob oblasts. Their demands increased, and they wanted the people to be informed of the president's resignation. (Bushkov and Mikul'skiy 1995: 32)[61]

On April 29, in addition to opposition demonstrations in Shohidon Square and the pro-regime demonstration in Ozodī Square, a third demonstration organized by the 'youth of Dushanbe' took place in Sadriddin Aynī Square. Sources state that there were thirteen youth groups at the latter demonstration, predominantly of a criminal character. During the demonstration, they demanded participation in a conflict settlement by President Nabiev (ibid.: 63).

Similar statements have also been made by international commentators, reporting that on 3 September, 'the militants, from a Dushanbe youth group [who had occupied the presidential palace], refused to leave before the opening of the Supreme Soviet Session scheduled for September 4, for fear that their departure might allow President Nabiev to re-establish himself in power'.[62] Although the young people in all of the examples had clear political demands, they were criminalized by the authors (and politicians of the time) and declared to be sources of trouble, yet strong enough to force change.[63] Bushkov and Mikul'skiy attempted to link youth's engagement to traditional institutions (*gashtak**) and other customs, such as young people using public squares where they can demonstrate that they are 'strong men' (*molodcy**). Hence, these authors saw the youth groups as a continuation of violent, criminal traditions. They deny young people any political agency, reducing them to criminal urban youth gangs. Young people were considered troublemakers, and in the literature and interviews, doubt is expressed as to whether youth really had their own agenda or whether the young men were 'irresponsible children' or merely agents of political leaders under whose supervision they acted.

Broadening the scope of civil war analysis, the following excerpt suggests that the view of youth as a risk factor still persisted among the international community.

> Osh/Brussels, 31 Oct. 2003: Central Asian governments have all but abandoned an entire generation of young people. In a region where around half the population is under 30, such an approach can only bring increased risks of political instability and conflict. More international involvement is needed in all spheres of youth activity in Central Asia, where around half the population is under 30. In a world where many people expect progress with each generation, most of the young in this region are worse off than their parents. They have higher rates of illiteracy, unemployment, poor health, and drug use and are more likely to be victims or perpetrators of violence. Few regions have seen such sharp declines in the welfare of their youth, and the combination of declining living standards with a demographic bulge brings increased risks of political instability and conflict. Current trends must be reversed if the region is to avoid more serious economic and political problems . . . The Central Asian states need to confront grim realities in education and labor opportunities if they are to turn the next generation away from socially destructive alternatives.[64]

International organizations and their NGO partners typically base their actions on experiences and concepts developed in the Euro-American scientific world. This is particularly true in the case of youth approaches that only recently have begun to actively promote the role of youth as stakeholders in decision-making. Shepler (2005: 130), in an analysis of Sierra Leonean child combatants, emphasizes that young people sometimes use international discourses to construct themselves as rebellious fighters, unfortunate victims, schoolchildren and so on. She observes that NGOs use international standards and thereby help and support former child-soldiers to reintegrate them into their local community, which still tends to construct them as a source of insecurity. While 'children' can be framed as embedded, vulnerable members of communities and attract funds due to their assumed victim status, the word or category 'youth' becomes a dangerous label, especially when it is associated with the destruction of societal harmony. Hence, the youth category in international definitions remains linked to a risk group.

In short, youth has been identified as a risk group which is at the same time victim and perpetrator. According to Western concepts of youth, it is the economic marginalization of young people that inevitably compels them to look for 'destructive alternatives'. However, Hebdige (1988) argues that it is exactly because youth are given media and political attention only after using violence that this strategy has become a common means to claim rights.

Written and oral sources essentially present three versions of how the civil war constructed youth. The first version depicts youth as victims of leaders who avoided doing the 'dirty work' and left it to the sons of peasants. Here, recruitment was done legally under the assumption that every man is duty-bound to engage in the fight for his nation (which does not apply to women). Further, leaders used their regional power to recruit young men for their own combatant group.

The second version suggests that youth are responsible for their own lives and decide on their own to join combatant groups. Some young men also viewed their participation as an obligation, in that they needed to choose a side in order to demonstrate their masculinity. They acted out of and/or against structural pressure and formed emotional paternalistic bonds with their leaders. These leaders appeared to them as specialists in violence, parlaying their cultural capital and violent experiences into military and political positions. From both sides we learned that violent actors were awarded military titles, such as Sangak Safarov as leader of the presidential guard, and among the opposition a couple of men were made 'generals' in response to the emergence of the presidential guard.

Finally, the third version describes youth as troublemakers and poorly educated people who provoke conflicts. Here, youth are denied political relevance and are criminalized instead. Furthermore, young people as a general category are portrayed to be a risk factor to society. What appears most striking is the absence of neutrality in any of these three versions.[65] Young men, in their different conceptualizations, are potential combatants and cannot withdraw from this duty.

Conclusion

Before youth had become a distinct socio-demographic group, young people were gradually integrated into society through their master in a long period of apprenticeship. This form of domestication of youth was not the only one (there were men's houses, armies and so on, as we will see in the following chapter) but the most important one in terms of reproducing specialized groups (intellectual leadership, state workers, artisans and so forth). The traditional institutions of learning – *ustod* and *shogird*, *murshid* and *murid*, *muallim* and *talaba* and so on – were more the responsibility of the master and the community than the parents. While the reversing of knowledge transfer employed by the Komsomol – with youth taking the lead – challenged such forms of domestication, it never replaced this institution fully; however, today a similar reversal is becoming increasingly commonplace. Kikuta (2009), for example, describes how economic necessity causes *shogird*s to seek their independence quickly, driven by the pressing need to find a means of livelihood. Although traditional institutions have continued to maintain relevance in certain domains, such as among artisans, in religious education and even in secular schools, their overall impact has lessened. For example, respect for the work of masters in pottery has declined, and imitations have become more prevalent, Kikuta observes. Apprentices still go through a domestication process, but it appears that this domestication is not fully successful, in that the young person often fails to find a place within the hierarchy of the ceramic community.

Similarly, in religious education, with a multiplicity of possible paths, respect for the elderly village mullah has declined (especially those village mullahs educated during the Soviet period). Young men who study in other Muslim countries challenge their elders and openly question their knowledge and capacity to guide youth. In the business world, such as development projects, 'young specialists' are brought in to teach well-educated and experienced rural adults more efficient and effective ways to carry out their tasks, upending the traditional processes of adults teaching youth.[66]

I have organized this chapter in such a way as to explain how youth took on a central role in times of political twists and turns. Already by the end of the nineteenth century, young people were introducing reforms in Tajikistan and trying to bring about changes in teaching methods. They were later co-opted by the Bolsheviks, who installed an organization within the new socialist political frame: the Komsomol. In this way, youth were accorded the role of vanguards and defenders of the motherland. However, they also met with opposition from groups such as the *basmachi* and *mujohid*. In other words, the history of Tajikistan shows us that young men have been very active in shaping Central Asian history. Individual biographies, such as those of the *basmachi* Azam or members of the Komsomol, such as Mastibek Tashmukhammedov, provide a vivid illustration of how young men came to be integrated into the new system as vanguards. However, the ways and means by which they did so may greatly differ from place to place and time to time, and the situation in Bukhara can hardly be compared to the events occurring at the same time in the Qarotegin region.

In order to understand the relevance of youth movements with regard to socio-political development, it is useful to relate youth concepts to political ideologies. Through inclusion or exclusion strategies youth becomes a malleable concept from which demographic potential can be mobilized. The introduction of vanguard identities appears successful in redefining a subordinate youth status into a (politically) mature status that appears attractive to young people. These vanguard ideologies offer young people a group identity that promises action and social mobility in the future, such as through the *jadid*, Komsomol and *mujohid*. The historical examples, however, also demonstrate the change from a small vanguard identity to a majority ideology, which transforms vanguardism into an ideology experienced as oppression by the new young generation.

Whereas the *jadid*s were integrated into the new political system before gaining considerable political power, the Komsomol experienced the shift from being an exclusionist vanguard movement to a socio-political institution in the 1950s when they became a mass movement; however, by this time the Komsomol had already been subordinated to the Communist Party. Similarly, the Islamic identity offered by the Islamic opposition attracted many young men who enthusiastically engaged with it. Since the end of the war, however, many alternative Islamic groups have become active in Tajikistan, devaluing the vanguard status of the Islamic Revival Party of Tajikistan.

We have seen that young people played a central role in the political success of parties and have actively shaped Tajikistan's future (we will leave other aspects for discussion in later chapters). I have dedicated a large part of this chapter to describing the war and especially the role assigned to youth during the civil war. Competition among parties to recruit as many young people as possible – to maximize the demographic potential of youth for their own purposes – exemplifies how categories were shaped and used to this end. Arguing that youth had to defend their country, and in any event were obligated to perform their military service, was one way to objectify mass recruitment. The idea of choosing a side as a matter of honour and the concomitant absence of neutrality was another way to ensure that almost all men felt compelled to engage. But more general ideas such as youth as victims of elites or young men revenging relatives were also ways to conceptualize a fighting youth. Eventually, what is important for our discussion is the successful turn from conceptualizations and ideas to group formation, from an abstract youth bulge to the active participation of young people. We should not forget, however, that access to weapons and improved access to regular food and material goods when joining a combatant group were practical factors that transformed political discourses into violent actions.

This chapter has provided a historical perspective highlighting the periods in which youth categories were shaped and vanguard groups became important in restructuring society. The moments of crystallization of such vanguard groups vary by period and ideological background, but exhibit similarities insofar as youth's role within the imagined new social and political order is redefined. Young people are declared the constructor of this new order so as to maximize youthful engagement.

Notes

1. Brubaker (1994) has aptly described the (unintended) consequences of structuring the Soviet Union, first, along territorial models of nationhood and, second, as individual ethno-cultural nationalities. A large number of 'ethnic' groups came to live outside their newly defined national territory, a matter that seemed of lesser importance as long as the Soviet supra-state organized the inter-state relations of its satellites. See also Bergne (2007) for an excellent study of Tajik history.

2. Concerning the delayed mental acceptance of change, Assmann writes: 'Political acts . . . are rapid, punctual and irreversible, whereas mental attitudes and social behaviour change only slowly and may last for more than half a generation' (Assmann 1999: 13).
3. After the initial disturbances in 1990, the country continued to be more or less turbulent. These disturbances, however, are what remain foremost in people's minds, not the official date of the beginning of the war that is accepted by the international community. In memory of 12 February 1990, Karim's entire book on the Tajik civil war is constructed as moving from one 12 February to the next.
4. Sovietization was mainly conducted through the use of Turkic languages. Russians used Tatar translators, and the newspapers promoted Turkic while denouncing Farsi as the language of 'backwardness'. For an excellent description of the linguistic situation of Central Asia, with a focus on the Tajik language, see Rzehak (2001).
5. If we are to believe ethnographic accounts, the Tajiks retained this reputation as 'backward' people from the mountains throughout the Soviet era (Kisljakov 1972), and even now this perception continues to divide urban from rural residents.
6. For a description of the *maktab* in Central Asia and the way in which the Russian colonizers dealt with the institution, see Dudoignon (2004a); for the situation in Xinjiang, see Bellér-Hann (2008: 316–38).
7. For a discussion of religious education, see, e.g., Khalid (1998: 22–26) and Kemper, Motika and Reichmuth (2010); specifically on Tajikistan, see Stephan (2008: 60, 179–82) and Epkenhans (2010).
8. Dudoignon (1996, 2004a) mentions that the Russian strategy for destroying the influence of the *madrasa* and *maktab* system was to restrict the inflow of *waqf* (religious endowment), thus impoverishing the religious institutions.
9. Bellér-Hann (2008: 329–33) mentions that Uighurs needed almost twenty years of study before attaining the title of *damolla*. The local bureaucracy recruited among *madrasa* students. Although the *waqf* system was intended to allow poor students to study and achieve social mobility, it seems that sons of the elite received favourable treatment, while poor boys, as Aynī (1962) describes, had to perform chores for their schoolmaster or take up other jobs to earn their living.
10. (Stéphane Dudoignon, personal communication, 10 March 2009). I thank Professor Dudoignon for sharing his extensive knowledge of this period, which helped support an important argument of this book. He also mentions that while youth movements in Bukhara remained constrained, they developed much faster in other regions such as Volga-Ural: 'while (the youth movement) remained limited in Bukhara until the time of the Soviet period, in other regions of the Volga-Ural – with the return of the students from al-Azhar right up through the twentieth century and the rapid development of modern medias – personalities of a strong youth could quickly dominate the entire society, whereas in Central Asia their influence remained rather limited to their circles of confidants' (ibid.).
11. Among artisans, the apprentice becomes independent from his master through a ritual.
12. Kikuta (2009: 95) mentions that a *shogird* was an apprentice, usually a teenage boy.
13. Based on pottery production in an Uzbek town, Haruka Kikuta has described the system of apprenticeship in the Ferghana Valley. The relation between *usto* and *shogird* in the nineteenth century was only one of many hierarchical relations structuring the artisans of a town. Although 'child labour' came to be prohibited under Soviet law, even in the twentieth century many started as small boys in factories, and through the master–apprentice relationship acquired an education that was far more extensive than solely learning the skills of pottery making.

14. Khalid claims that, 'the new-method school, for instance, was much more than merely a reformed *maktab*: It was the site of a new cultural practice, that of schooling, which it marked off from everyday practice and objectified' (Khalid 1998: 13). Fedtke (1998) points to the fact that the *jadids* were a very heterogeneous group and that they didn't use the term to describe themselves, since it had a negative connotation and was ascribed to them by the *qadīmchī* (adherents of the 'old school').

15. For more aspects of *jadid* ideas concerning youth, see Fedtke (1998), Khalid (1998, 2007), Komatsu (2000) and Kamp (2006).

16. This point was used by the so-called traditionalist *qadīmchī* as an argument against the reforms, considering that Russia was to fight against the Ottoman Empire in the First World War. Although there was no mass movement of students towards Istanbul, their number was sufficient, when they returned, to provide the catalyst for supporting and accelerating reforms.

17. Aynī (1962: 206–8), Bellér-Hann (2008: 330) and many others have mentioned that there were three times more students attending during the winter than in the summer months.

18. I would like to thank Stéphane Dudoignon for advising caution when comparing examples from Bukhara with those elsewhere – scientific research tends to frame much of our knowledge; history writing is, however, based on phenomena, periods and areas for which documents are available, and therefore, generalizations would be inappropriate in this context.

19. For a more precise description of the collective farming system, see Humphrey (1983) and Creed (1998).

20. Interview with Bakhtigul, an elder woman, November 2006.

21. Several authors (e.g., Snesarev 1963; Rakhimov 1990) have documented the phenomenon of the 'men's house' (*muzhskie doma*, Russ.) in Central Asia. Rakhimov observes a great deal of variety among such institutions in terms of their internal organization. In my research area, male gatherings continue to take place throughout the five-month winter period (Roche 2009, 2010).

22. A slightly different institution, but one worth mentioning, is the *mäşräp*, described by Roberts (1998) and Bellér-Hann (2008: 213), a social institution for men in Xinjiang and young Uighur in Kazakhstan's Almaty oblast where they were taught the 'rules of communal behaviour'. Dudoignon (1996: 135) has mentioned this institution as an educational institution in which knowledge was passed from the elders or more experienced people (who were often one and the same) to the younger, less experienced members of the community in the *maktab*.

23. Roy (1999) draws interesting parallels between the *basmachi* bastions and recruitment into the Islamic movement in the early 1990s (from Kala-i Khum, Tahvil Dara, Khait and Gharm). Some villages such as Hoid have maintained their reputation for providing *mujohid* fighters. Moreover, the term *basmachi* is still used informally to refer to former *mujohid*.

24. In Lakhsh, the *basmachi* (*mujohid*) Azam is still remembered today. He originally worked for the Bolsheviks, but after having been falsely condemned of misusing his power, he escaped from prison and turned against the invaders and fought them. Many years later, in the mid 1930s, he was eventually killed, not far from his village. His *avlod* (kinship group) were persecuted, causing them to flee their village and ultimately settle among Kyrgyz in Lakhsh.

25. Komsomol cells were established within the army and navy (Juricic 1994: 36–56).

26. Juricic (1994) provides rich material on the early Komsomol and quotes relevant sources. While most English-language books on the Komsomol written before the early 1990s saw

primarily ideological motivations in the Komsomol's activities, some of them nevertheless provide a comprehensive look at the Komsomol based on documentary sources.

27. Penati (2008) mentions that youth as young as 17 to 20 years were sent out to implement water reforms, often facing ridicule and outright rejection by village elders. The Komsomol built bridges, irrigation systems, the Baikal-Amur railway line and so on (Olimova and Bosc 2003).

28. This changed when young people started to create their own 'subculture', prompting the state to redefine the Komsomol's task and adapt the organization to its own political needs.

29. To counter this resistance, the Komsomol sent to rural areas introduced scientifically based methods of soil cultivation, mechanization, machine tractor stations, and so on, to industrialize the lives of peasants and destroy the traditional means of production.

30. This is supported by other informants, who claimed that party membership was not easily attained and was offered only to people who demonstrated steadfast political activism and 'proper' conduct.

31. Harris (2006: 37–42) provides another look at an early socialist Tajik. The protagonist's father was enthusiastic about belonging to the vanguard communists in his youth and supported his wife's unveiling, but abandoned many secular and Russian values in old age after socialism had become the dominant system.

32. The Komsomol's military role was integral to the Young Communist League, with one of its rules being to 'activate participants in the work of sports associations and prepare youth for service in the ranks of the USSR armed forces' (Hahn 1969: 224). Kuebart (1989) mentions that the Komsomol, together with civil defence organizations, organized games during which youth were introduced to military skills and drilling. Later, when the military role of the Komsomol had diminished, the party went so far as to criticize the Soviet Union's emphasis on peace rather than on military heroism.

33. For an analysis of the categories of deviance, see Hahn (1971: 389–97) and Yurchak (2006: 102–8).

34. In a village near Gharm, as well as in Lakhsh, youth leaders still existed in 2002, but since most of them were working in Russia by then, nothing much had happened in their absence with regard to youth activities. In another village near Gharm, a group of men turned an old, unused teahouse into a youth club, where boys were taught wrestling (gushtin) and table tennis. Young men 17 years and older 'hung out' at this youth club, while younger boys went to the youth club only to learn something (but not to hang out).

35. This kind of dualism is a classic construction of war, in that it simplifies multifaceted activities. Moreover, the analyses of Tajikistan in the early 1990s by Nourzhanov (2005) and, more cogently, Hall (2005) have described how the dualistic view is only a superficial overview of the realities of a civil war. The fact that the main wing of the opposition group under Said Abdullo Nuri had but six thousand soldiers – according to one of the students in his inner circle – proves that this simplified dualistic reduction does not represent the complex nature of the conflict.

36. After Ramadan ended, fifty thousand people from rural areas joined the demonstrators in April 1992 (Bushkov 1995: 16).

37. For a detailed description of the political figures and motivations of the era, see Schoeberlein-Engel (1994), Bushkov (1995) and Atkin (1996).

38. *Central Asia Monitor*, No. 1, 1993 (p.12).

39. Karim (1997: 456–57) explains that *vovchik* derives from Wahhabi and was associated with 'some strange and interesting ideas' about Islam that were introduced by the KGB. The term Wahhabi was applied to all religious people who – or to all Islamic thought

which – came into conflict with authoritative religious personnel (official and independent scholars) or state authorities. Karim also writes about the case of two *mullo** in Kulob (Mullo Haydar and Mullo Abdurahim), who divided believers on the basis of religious matters, calling one faction *vovchik* and the other *yurchik*.

40. Nourzhanov (2005) claims that every warlord pursued his own interest in the conflict, leaving the government with no unified army of its own and creating numerous small, competing groups that fought against each other. See also Aliev (1997) and Zviagelskaya (1998: 167).

41. In this instance, a conflict arose between two parties: one wanted Lakhsh to become economically independent from Jirgatol, while the other did not. Although this difference of opinion did not apparently have an explicit ethnic basis, ethnicity did seem to have played a role in the way the conflict ended – the group, the majority of which was ethnic Tajik, and even though it was numerically weaker than the Kyrgyz-dominated group, was eventually the winner in this conflict, thanks to the newly elected government (1994) that promoted Tajikness over all other ethnicities.

42. The concept of *mahalgaroi* shows that place of origin is relevant, not the actual location of settlements. In this sense, the Gharmi included those who had settled in and around Gharm before relocating to the Vakhsh Valley in the 1950s (cf. Roy 1998). Heathershaw discusses how this regionalism is not as territorially bound as it seems at first glance, and claims that, 'Soviet legacies provide a unique historical basis for Central Asia's new regionalism – network elites across the region who share similar experiences, spaces, and discourses' (Heathershaw 2009: 133).

43. People remember this brief period because of the independent television station that kept them informed.

44. The written document signed on 27 June 1997 can be retrieved from: http://www.un.org/ Depts/DPKO/Missions/unmot/prst9757.htm.

45. The followers of Rahmon Gitler (Russian pronunciation of Hitler) were regarded as bandits and were well known for their brutality. Although I do not know the reason, they – like Rizvon's followers – were not included in the redistribution performed under the peace process. The group survived until 2003, when Gitler was killed in Dushanbe. According to records, in 2001 he twice ambushed people in what was known as the 'green bazaar' of the city and stole their goods. Previously, in 2000, he had risked open combat with another armed group in the centre of Dushanbe (see also Chapter 6 for the story of Rizvon).

46. In 2007, the president wanted to dissolve this special unit because he believed he no longer needed it to maintain law and order (Hamroboyeva 2008). The situation turned more serious in February 2008 when Colonel Oleg Zakharchenko, commander of the OMON (the Special Purpose Police Squad), visited Gharm (some sources claim that he was accompanied by two heavy trucks full of OMON servicemen). Mirzokhoja Ahmadov and other local commanders thought that they had come to arrest them and opened fire. As a result, Zakharchenko was killed and four OMON servicemen were seriously injured.

47. Nizomov fled the region during the Rasht events, which led people to assume that he had been one of the main informants for the state. He was denied refuge in Russia, and it is assumed that he went back to Dushanbe.

48. A young man once told me that he had been sent by his father, a local commander, to fight at the age of 14. In this way, his father sought to deflect the criticism that leaders save their own children but exploit those of other families.

49. It has become an unwritten rule that university entrance demands a bribe. This bribe depends on the student's capability to pass exams, the status of the father and his relation

to the director of the university, the subject and the kind of university. Universities in Tajikistan are managed like private enterprises in which teachers receive a minimal salary from the state and the rest through bribe management.

50. Interview with Muhiddin, aged 31, February 2007.

51. According to Halbach (1996: 17), youth groups emerged in the southern territories where people from Gharm had been relocated earlier on. They organized themselves and in 1983 started the newspaper *Hidojat* (Guidance).

52. The opposition provided training in numerous areas (in Qunduz and Jalalabad, in neighbouring Afghanistan, with Ahmed Shah Masud as Afghan Defence Minister at that time, and in remote mountain areas of Tajikistan such as Vakhio). Chatterjee (2002: 101) speaks of ten to twelve thousand fighters who were trained in Afghan camps.

53. Nuri's grandfather had been deported in the 1930s because of his religious devotion. As part of the resettlement campaigns, Nuri's family was relocated to Qurgan Teppe where they 'never saw a quiet day', because his father was also active in the fight for freedom. Nuri himself was arrested twice and even deported for engaging in religious affairs. Nuri's last public talk was in Gharm for the celebration of the June 2006 peace agreement; he died shortly afterwards. The Tajik media spared only a few minutes in his memory – my informant complained bitterly – but at least he was remembered in other countries. This certainly encouraged Nuri's biography to be constructed around the idea of martyrdom. I suggest viewing narratives of Nuri's life as a distillation of Muslim suffering during the Soviet and postwar eras. As such, his story has become a master narrative for former *mujohid*s.

54. Only limited information about individual members of this group is provided here, for the sake of their personal safety.

55. Interview with Mirzokarim, aged 41, February 2007.

56. People told me that these combatants would demand clothes from people whom they encountered on the street, steal the rings from women's fingers, and drive off with cars parked in front of houses.

57. In 2002, I accompanied the German aid group Deutsche Welthunger Hilfe (DWH) in Gharm during their distribution of potato seed. I conducted brief interviews with several farmers entitled to help. According to my assistant, most of the 'farmers' who came from various surrounding villages had been former *mujohid*s, which also explained the incredible tension the workers felt during this mission – threatened by the farmers at the time of the distribution, and blamed afterwards by the DWH for distributing seeds incorrectly.

58. The *qozi kalon* Hoji Akbar Turajonzoda was a controversial authority in the years of unrest. He sided with the Islamic Revival Party at a later stage but turned away from the party after the peace agreement and remained an independent political player (Epkenhans 2011: 85–87).

59. Colonel Kvachkov was the leader of the Fifteenth Brigade and responsible for the design and implementation of the entire military operation in Kughan Tepe.

60. Salimov was later appointed ambassador to Turkey by Rahmon, to remove him from the circles of power. Salimov, Safarov and Khudoberdiev were only the most known among many other commanders.

61. One of my informants was in the Parliament building at the time. For him, being part of such a group was extremely empowering; they felt able to take political action. In the past they had been controlled and often subjected to inequitable treatment, he claimed, so taking over the state symbol of power gave them a surge of confidence and satisfied their desire for revenge (often against more visible branches of state power, such as the police or directors).

62. 'Civil War in Tajikistan: Diary of Events', *Central Asia Monitor*, No. 5, 1992 (p.5).
63. Khudjibaeva (1999) has discussed the role of television in manipulating information so as to portray the opposition as 'barbarians and savages'.
64. International Crisis Group, *Youth in Central Asia: Losing the New Generation*, Asia Report No. 66, 31 October 2003 (available at: www.crisisweb.org). A later report states: 'The war is rapidly ceasing to be a living memory. The median age is 21; around 35 per cent of the population is under fourteen . . . Although there are no indications of either an external threat or any well-organized local insurgency, there are signs of cracks and fissures in the regime' (International Crisis Group, *Tajikistan: On the Road to Failure*, Asia Report No. 162, 12 February 2009, available at: www.crisisweb.org).
65. The absence of neutrality is problematic, as it puts every man in the role of a potential perpetrator. Combined with religious, ethnic or regional markers, every man is an enemy or partner, and individual neutrality thus becomes impossible. This is the dilemma I was told existed in Shahrigul, where many men hid from both sides but were persecuted anyway if they had served in the military sometime during Soviet rule. Although the fighter ethos does not say that every man likes to fight, it assumes that every man potentially could be a fighter; again, neutrality becomes impossible.
66. See the Zentrum Moderner Orient project by Jeanne Féaux de la Croix about development work and generational relations (available at: www.zmo.de/forschung/projekte_2008/de_la_croix_kirgisien.html).

Chapter 3

'Siblings Are as Different as the Five Fingers of a Hand'

The Developmental Cycle of Domestic Groups and Siblingship

Before discussing whether the domestication of youth can be seen as a conflict over the status of young people, let us consider two institutions that structure the process of domestication within the community and family: first, the developmental cycle of domestic groups, and second, siblingship. The picture presented in this chapter is rather static, not because traditions have been unchanging but because here the focus is on how people construct their community through rules. In order to understand the dynamic changes that have taken place – to which we will turn in the following chapter – it is necessary to explore these rules and traditions as they are intended to function. In this sense the chapter provides insight into how these two central institutions provide the structural base upon which domestication of young people becomes possible.

In contrast to kinship among neighbouring Turkic peoples, Tajik kinship does not know tribal or clan organization, which may serve to define the position of youths vis-à-vis relatives. However, seniority is one of the main principles of organization. In this context, it is useful to recall Bonte's (1985) observation that, in societies where kinship is underdeveloped structurally, the distinction between 'social juniors' (*cadets sociaux*) and 'social seniors' becomes the organizing principle.[1] Demographic size is also an important consideration, as are the ways, means and attempts of society to remould demographic size. Thus, the junior–senior relation (the weak majority against the strong minority – a reflection of social oligarchy) can be challenged through external resources, conflicts and alternative education (maturity).

The Developmental Cycle of Domestic Groups

Studying the developmental cycle of domestic groups we become aware of how families deal with several children. A central tenet of the communist ideology of modernization was the change in household developments towards an independent nuclear family model.[2] The following section takes a closer look at the developmental cycle of domestic groups.

The Household as an Indicator of Development

Kislyakov (1972: 11–14), who conducted fieldwork in mountainous Tajikistan from the 1950s to the 1970s, cited as one of the greatest gains of socialism that more people than ever before had been able to build their own home. Although his theoretical approach to Tajik society was heavily influenced by an evolutionary perspective – in line with Engels, Morgan and Maine – Kislyakov's observations have lost little of their importance.[3] Earlier on, Kislyakov writes, a family that decided to split into different households would be fined by the local authorities (*mir*). 'Every father who separated his sons from home had to pay 20 to 30 teneg and was considered *gunahkor* [guilty]' (ibid.: 12). This imposition of a fine was also supported by a social perception that such a family had failed in maintaining internal peace, and thus would find itself the unwelcome subject of neighbourhood talk.

> A family often split after the death of the old father because of quarrels among the brothers and especially their wives. In this process of splitting up, the inheritance was also divided between the members of the family. This responsibility devolved upon a *qozi* [religious legal authority] or a person who was sent from the *amlokdor* [landowner], together with two to three respected and experienced local men. (ibid.: 11)

Kislyakov's descriptions were supported by villagers' accounts, which confirmed that in the past people lived in very cramped spaces, with several families sharing one or two rooms. However, thanks to the communists' efforts in spreading (or imposing) 'Soviet modernity' in remote areas, a greater number of houses could be built due to improved incomes and access to building materials. These changes were ushered in by the introduction of the kolkhoz system, which provided every worker with an independent income. Thus, Kislyakov argues that the large patriarchal kinship group was perceived as a transitional state from the patriarchal 'clan' organization to a village-based (*mahalla*) organization (the aim of Sovietization being the destruction of the traditional kinship structure in favour of nuclear family patterns). The conjugal family became the new economic unit in villages (Holzwarth 1978). To this debate, Abashin (1999: 13) adds that the change from larger to smaller households was connected to taxation politics. Until the October Revolution of 1917, the authorities would collect an equal amount of tax from each compound, independent of the size of the family or its land. This changed in the 1920s, when the ownership of large tracts of land was targeted and became a reason for persecution; hence, smaller plots came to be preferred and many households split into smaller ones.

Abashin (ibid.) has criticized research that approaches the household on the basis of ideological assumptions, since such studies reduce the complexity of the concept to merely a monetary aspect and separate it from other forms of organization such as kinship.[4] Similarly, Nourzhanov (1998: 149) has argued that seven decades of Soviet politics have done little to change the 'patriarchal undivided family' that constitutes the main household unit (cf. Kislyakov 1976; Bushkov and Mikul'skiy 1996: 36). Moreover, Kandiyoti (1999) has corroborated this claim by providing different examples of the way in which households are run and differences between men's and women's access to wealth. Thus, the organization of a household extends far beyond the borders of its compound to acquire a temporal meaning, for example, in feasts. In most cases, the head of the household collects the income of the entire family and provides the family with every necessity (Kislyakov 1976).

> My husband's eldest brother would collect the income of all the household (*khojagī*) members. As long as we lived in their house, the money that my husband earned would remain in his eldest brother's hand – we were many people in this house (*havlī*), and everybody would give their money to him . . . If I needed something personally, I would go to my parents' house. After we moved into our own household (*khojagī*), he kept the money.[5]

Different terms are used for defining a household. In order to explain the various conceptions of the household, I refer to Goody's (1972) approach, which clearly differentiates among production, consumption, residential and reproduction units. First, he suggests that the size of the dwelling, or the 'houseful', should be differentiated from the consumption and production unit, the household, as from kinship relations. In Tajik terms, the compound that is surrounded by a mud wall – the *havlī* – refers to a dwelling unit, or a houseful. Usually within one *havlī* we find one 'roof' (*khona*, house) to which is attached a portion of agricultural land and a cowshed. This is also referred to as *mulk*, or private property (often referred to in pairs, for example *molu mulk*, which includes the whole private property). Members of the *khona* comprise the central production, consumption and residential unit and may comprise a single conjugal family or even three or four generations (grandparents, their unmarried daughters, sons and those sons' children), as well as other people, for example, divorced daughters or sisters and their children, and so on.

Another term that is used to describe a farming unit is *khojagī* (peasant family) – this refers to a production unit. In such units, the members' income is usually controlled and redistributed by the father; at times, this practice continues even after his sons move out and establish their own independent households (Nourzhanov 1998: 151). This term may also be used to describe the consumption unit; hence, its primary meaning is 'peasant family', in the sense of a joint production unit.[6] Finally, we find terms that refer to biological reproduction, such as the *oila* (wife or family, that is, wife and children). These units of reproduction exist independent of consumption, consisting basically of a mating pair and their young offspring.

Laslett (1969) has presented a demographic analysis of the household and family – two distinct entities that may overlap but are not congruent. Thus, families with very few children may call in other people to meet their working needs. From the statistical point of view then, the household that includes several generations may be the same size as a household that includes several *oila*s and other members (foster children and servants, for example, in eighteenth-century Europe). When Bakhtigul (quoted above) mentioned a family moving out, she meant, first, that a part of the family would move into a new *havlī*, thereby creating a new household; second, that this family would also form a new farming unit (*khojagī*); and third, the family would become independent (*oila*) (which they had already been within the *havlī* of her husband's brother). In this way, it is important to clarify the context of the houseful when discussing it – if the economic aspect is under consideration, then the compound is usually not a useful indication of what constitutes the household. If, however, we are looking at the reproductive aspect, the *oila* must be our focus of attention. In the same way, in an analysis of taxation politics, we take the *havlī* as the point of reference.

Domestic Developmental Cycles

Although the change in household patterns has been declared a radical achievement of socialism, in reality it simply signifies a practical response to earlier problems and not a change in the underlying pattern. The concept of the domestic developmental cycle may clarify whether this change equals a radically new form of residence or merely an acceleration of the process of the division of a family. No houseful can stay together over several generations – eventually, space constraints and social tension lead to divisions among its members. The moot question, therefore, is regarding the developmental cycle of domestic groups. If sons marry young and remain within the parental *havlī* for a while, the tendency to have larger units may temporarily apply, resulting in joint households (Hajnal 1982). However, sons will eventually split off from the household (*havlī*), and each *oila* will become an independent *havlī*, and most probably also an independent *khojagī* – or in simple terms, a household.

According to Kislyakov (1976), in the pre-Soviet era this splitting would take place after the father's death, and sons would probably inherit an equal share of the property. Goody (1972: 14–17) has suggested viewing the different 'types' of family – nuclear, extended (paternal) and expanded (fraternal) – not as distinct types but diachronically as phases in the developmental cycle of the typical family. Thus, in Lakhsh every family passes through the stage of nuclear family to extended family if the parents are still alive; and, if the sons do not move out during their parents' lifetime, they will certainly split from a fraternal household at a later stage. Yet, extended families are comparatively rare because they last only for a short period of time, until nuclear families move out.

With the idea of a developmental cycle, therefore, Goody has also introduced the time factor. Families go through developmental cycles just as individuals go through life cycles; therefore any study of family patterns needs to be done with respect to time. In fact, there seems to have been little fundamental change in the household developmental cycle during the Soviet period. What changed was the impartibility of the compound[7] and the age at which a son moves out of his parental home (they began moving out sooner). Generally the concept of the *havlī* as a 'houseful' has remained and economic units continue to exist beyond domestic units. A daughter-in-law (*kelin*) still 'has to perform her duty before her mother-in-law for at least a year'.[8] In this sense, the joint household (as a domestic and consumption unit) has been maintained as a system. Even economic patterns have remained, albeit with many variations. At least by the time the father is dead, the brothers would have established economically independent households.

Holzwarth (1978: 50) has suggested analysing the domestic developmental cycle in terms of pushing and pulling factors. In this sense, *taqsim* and *judo* (distribution and splitting) – that is, pulling factors – take place due to reasons associated with inheritance or the overcrowding of households, while pushing factors can be called *tirok*, which refers to demographic and economic increase, concentration and accumulation. My data show large variations in the time span between the marriage of a son and his splitting from the household. This reflects the different circumstances within and among villages. In Shahrigul, for instance, all of the agricultural land has been sold for the construction of houses (which, incidentally, is against state law). Therefore, young people wishing to set up their own home must vie for a piece of land further up the valley. There is no agricultural land around the village, apart from some steep mountain slopes. Most young men no longer regard themselves as farmers; instead, they aspire to the life of (migrant) workers. In Lakhsh, there is a great scarcity of suitable plots, and usually large sums of money need to change hands to ensure access to a piece of land or to buy a house vacated by Kyrgyz migrants. In Shahrituz, people are subject to state policies, since the state owns the cotton plantations and sporadically allocates or sells land to families with sons. Here, young men currently invest in rebuilding their parental homes (which had been destroyed during the civil war) rather than setting up their own households.

Generally, fathers avoid splitting up their property and instead try to buy or acquire new land. This impartible practice of inheritance, however, has been contested by some sons and brothers in urban centres, who have invoked Russian law against traditional practice (cf. Bushkov and Mikul'skiy 1996: 16; Cole and

Wolf 1999). However, while impartible inheritance in the Alpine regions of Tyrol means that only one son would inherit his father's property (Cole and Wolf 1999), in present-day Tajikistan this means that the father acquires new property for each son in the form of agricultural land – with an enormous, expansionist impact.

How do people solve the question of labour in these times of accelerated splitting? Tajik rural households not only tend to have many children but also avail themselves of kin, friends and the system of *hashar** until the children are old enough to work.[9] Further, hierarchical sibling relations ensure that younger siblings (and their children) always help their elder brothers. Thus, the entire community collectively solves the labour problem by activating multiple networks that interconnect households within a village.

Moving Out of the Parental Home

Full maturity is reached when a young family moves out of the parental compound. Although this act does not mean full economic independence, the family is integrated into the village community as a full member and the couple will be invited to meetings and gatherings as such. But how many years do sons, after marriage, stay with their parents before they move out? Statistical data provide little information on this question, since they range from a period of one year to more than twenty-seven years. Therefore, it appears that moving out of the parental home shows great variation.

For Shahrituz, I found that, on average, a couple would have had four children before moving out of the parental home, while the average size of a household was 8.5 persons.[10] Moving out after having four children is rather late and stems from the fact that the Shahrituz neighbourhood had been totally destroyed during the civil war. Hence, the delay is because children work for their parent's home rather than for their own. The results from Sasik Bulak indicate, on average, a couple having two children instead of four before moving out, which may be more representative of the wider society. Generally, children marry rather

Table 3.1: Number of years between marriage and moving out of the parental home.

	Total	Shahrituz	Sasik Bulak
n	114	29	85
Mean	7.37	11.10	6.09
Standard error of mean	0.5	1.34	0.41
Median	6	9	5
Mode	7	7	5
Standard deviation	5.30	7.20	3.75
Variance	28.09	51.88	14.04
Minimum	1	1	1
Maximum	27	27	17

early and remain with their family until they have a couple of children. This way, not only does the young couple confirm its ability to reproduce, but also in that time the parents begin to expect a certain level of maturity from their sons. If we assume that young men get married around the age of 22 or 23, this means that they are in their late twenties when they eventually become responsible for their own lives and that of their family.

However, moving out in practical terms means relocating to a different house in another compound, which is not the same as total economic independence. When talking to young couples who had serious economic problems, I learned that they would often secure a hot meal by each visiting his or her own parents' home. While the young men felt ashamed of asking their parents for help, it was common for the young women to be sent home to ask for support in kind – for example, food.[11] Facing the reality of being responsible for a family makes young men realize that having an independent household is a much greater burden than keeping a wife and children within the parental home, where all costs are shared among the members. Furthermore, they also realize that the more sons they have, the more secure is their own future.

Household studies can be broad and can strive to be comprehensive, but for present purposes I have concentrated on only a few aspects of the household. I have mentioned before that moving out of the parental home is one of the most important events for a young man in Lakhsh, because only then can he partici-pate in teahouse meetings. An exception to this norm is the youngest son, who inherits the parental compound and therefore never moves out of his father's household – he is eventually expected to take over from his father.

Let us look at the significance accorded to the establishment of one's own household. Although children finance their own houses, their parents supervise the construction work. The father contributes through his network and – most importantly – gives his blessing to the effort, which assures his son good fortune in the future as the head of a household. Thus, the house is much more than merely an independent production, consumption and reproduction unit – it is a symbol of social maturity and represents the son's successful domestication. Moving into one's individual household literally means to move into one's private room. With this act, a family gains full membership within the community. The 'hearth' (alov) is where the wife cooks, that is, produce and redistribute food. The redistribution of food is an essential aspect of community membership (Pétric 2002).

Gifts are exchanged on the basis of 'independent hearths' – not on the basis of a person's age or individual position. Thus, only married couples who can claim to have an independent house (independent hearth) are invited as guests, with the full right to bring and receive a gift. In other words, people can enter the game of reciprocity only after having split from the parental household.[12] Thus, even if siblings share a common budget in the form of the harvest, if they live in separate households they hold the status of full community membership.

In present-day Tajikistan, the duty of helping one's children to move out of the parental home has become a religious duty, like circumcision and marriage (cf. Stephan 2008: 149). It is through successfully ensuring this act that parental obligation towards domesticating children is fully accomplished – children are literally provided a *domus* and are therefore successfully civilized (that is, domesticated). Only when 'smoke comes out of the chimney' has the couple gained full membership of the community. In this way, an act that was regarded as deplorable a hundred years ago has become a fatherly duty in religious terms and a central rite of passage for young men. Considering the fact that current housing in Lakhsh is linked to local political representation, one of the primary aims of migrants is also to build a comfortable, impressive house, separate from that of their parents.

In Shahrigul, houses have undergone several changes in architecture and size and have become objects of displaying wealth. It is also interesting to note that some young men – even if they spent most of their time in Russia – decided to move out, provided their wife lived in the new house. It appears that moving out is a way to avoid inheritance conflicts and accumulate wealth for oneself rather than sharing it with one's brothers. However, in some cases wherein a systematic division of the household fails, conflicts do erupt between brothers.

The Diversification Strategy among Siblings

Studying the effects of a surplus of sons can provide a key perspective from which to view the 'youth bulge conflict' argument. This section is based on the idea that brothers compete for the same limited resources (such as inheritance and jobs) and therefore tend to look for alternative ways to attain social recognition – for example, through heroic warfare. According to Heinsohn (2006), those societies that have many sons (*Sohnreichtum*) gain an advantage in war.[13] In Europe or the United States today, a son is often the only male child within a family or even at times the only child, Heinsohn claims. Thus, this son becomes the focus of parental care and is restrained from entering lethal occupations. The situation, Heinsohn (ibid.: 15–16) argues, is different in countries where large families are the norm and competition for inheritance and status positions often erupt. Here parents can 'spare' sons for war while the family continues to function. After analysing the history of family life in Europe and the United States and surveying several of the current 'youth bulge' nations around the world, Heinsohn concludes that families in non-Western societies take into account the possibility of losing children in wars. Apart from the fact that a society's treatment of death is a cultural matter, the above quantity-based argument deserves a closer look. Therefore, in this chapter I will deal with the issue of Tajik families and multiple sons.

In Tajikistan, having many children not only increases a family's status within the community but is a strategy for increasing a family's social security. Parents place children in different sectors and thereby maximize family security by managing the siblings (especially brothers) as a unit, not as individuals. At the same time, parents promote individual siblings – especially boys – who show a special talent in any area, which encourages siblings to compete for this favoured treatment. Relying on Durkheim and Schlee,[14] I call this a diversification strategy. How do siblings in Tajikistan influence, manipulate or reject positions that are structurally defined for them? Do siblings cooperate, compete or even fight among themselves? This chapter tests the assumption that having many sons is a source of conflict in society. I will first present a basic structural description of relations among siblings. The developmental cycle of domestic groups is a path through which to study the dynamics of sibling relationships within the family context. The independent household has become the symbol of successful integration into the local community and, for parents, the last step in 'domesticating' their sons. We can observe an acceleration of the cycle of change within domestic groups, which occurs alongside socio-economic changes but is at odds with the severe land shortage. Today, houses are built everywhere, on agricultural land, along river banks and up against steep mountain slopes.

Often ignored in macro-political approaches to youth bulges, questions relating to siblings and households, I believe, are central to understanding the dynamics of youth. It is within the household and the family that youth is structurally bound and where young people rebel against those structures. Political movements that have successfully mobilized youth have also intensively engaged with the family institution (household, marriage, education and so on). This is not only true for Europe (Sternberg 1981) but also for the Soviet Union and Islamic parties in Tajikistan.

Introduction to the Study of Siblingship

S.R.: When do you go to your elder brother's (*aka*) house?

Murad: When I need something, I go there.

S.R.: If you do religious teaching (*amru ma'ruf**) there, does he listen?

Murad: If I do it, my younger brother (*dodar**) listens.

S.R.: What about your elder brother?

Murad: Hmm. I don't try to teach him – I just don't tell him things because he is older than me.

S.R.: Do you tell things to your friends?

Murad: I tell everything to my friends.

S.R.: Do you listen to your elder and younger brothers?

Murad: I listen to my elder brother, but not to my younger brother.

S.R.: What about your friends?

Murad: I listen to all my friends.

S.R.: Today which relations are more important: siblings or friends?

MURAD: Elder and younger brothers are more important.

S.R.: Did you get any help from your brothers this year?

MURAD: Yes; for example, my elder brother brought coal, other products, and clothes from Kyrgyzstan.

S.R.: Did you ask him for help?

MURAD: No, he brings those things voluntarily.

S.R.: From your younger brother, what help did you receive?

MURAD: None.

S.R.: Do you help your elder brother?

MURAD: Yes; for example, I help him to cut grass and harvest potatoes, and when he has a celebration (*tui*), we go to help him.

S.R.: If you didn't have an elder brother, would you have more freedom?

MURAD: No. It is good to have an elder brother – from the eldest brother, you can ask for anything.

S.R.: Why does a younger brother ask his elder brother's permission when leaving?

MURAD: He just does it as a mark of respect for his elder brother. If he doesn't show respect, he will not be respected by his younger brothers later on.[15]

The sibling relation is central to Tajik society, but scientific studies and approaches have usually neglected it and tended to dwell on the parent–child relation. Whereas I consider the parent–child relation a sacred one that is therefore assumed incapable of resulting in conflict (even if conflicts do exist, they are negated by both the parents and their children),[16] among a set of siblings family matters are negotiated and there is competition for the available positions from which they can choose. At the same time, the hierarchical organization of siblings turns them into a strong unit that cooperates to make strategic decisions.[17] Many parents in rural areas do not necessarily invest in each child's individual development equally; instead, they try to cultivate the different nature and abilities of each child in order to increase diversification and thereby to strengthen the family's social security (cf. Bushkov and Mikul'skiy 1996: 9–10; Schlee and Werner 1996: 16; Schlee 2001: 20). In light of such social diversification, children influence their roles through strategic behaviour.

There is a saying that 'children are as different as the five fingers of a hand – no two are the same', which nicely demonstrates this diversification strategy. The basic inheritance rules accord the eldest son all the rights of his deceased father, while the youngest son inherits the family compound and therefore remains in the parental household, with all the other siblings eventually moving out. Although sisters are part of the sibling group, they are accorded less attention in this process of diversification because it is believed that their future husband's family will take care of them. Moreover, daughters are not perceived as legal heirs under traditional law. Nevertheless, brothers and sisters do feel as if they are part of one group and assume duties and responsibilities with respect to one another.[18]

I have included a short review of the literature on siblingship in this chapter because I consider it important to understand how the contradictory ideas of competing brothers and cooperating brothers emerged and why these ideas can coexist. Although Lévi-Strauss (1958: 59) views brothers and sisters as one of the four basic kin relations, in his work on kinship he dedicated much less attention to this relation than to the other three (husband–wife, parent–child, and mother's brother–child). However, he briefly mentions that brothers and sisters are 'the strongest of all social relations' (ibid.: 59). Usually in anthropological approaches, siblings are structurally classified as occupying equal positions vis-à-vis their parents – also equal to parallel cousins but not to cross cousins (Lévi-Strauss 1993: 222).

The question of siblingship has been discussed in social anthropology, on the one hand, as a social relation of kinship, descent and affinity (Radcliffe-Brown 1958; Fortes 1962a, 1967, 1970),[19] and on the other hand as a problem of inheritance, conflict and economy, to name but a few. In the study of households and the domestic developmental cycle, the tension between brothers becomes more apparent (see below).

To understand the 'surplus sons' argument, one must look at how siblings have been portrayed in Europe, which in certain regards stands in sharp contrast to non-European ideas about siblingship. Sulloway argues that, in the West, the nature of siblingship has progressed in the following manner:

> Siblings compete with one another in an effort to secure physical, emotional, and intellectual resources from parents. Depending on differences in birth order, gender, physical traits, and aspects of temperament, siblings create differing roles for themselves within the family system. These differing roles in turn lead to disparate ways of currying parental favor. Oldest children, for example, are likely to seek parental favor by acting as surrogate parents towards their younger siblings. Younger siblings are not in a position to ingratiate themselves with parents in the same manner. Their niche is typically less parent identified, less driven by conscientious behavior, and more inclined toward sociability. (Sulloway 1997: 21)

Sulloway refers to the concept of niches to explain why siblings are so different from one another in their attempts and efforts. The Darwinian idea behind this model is obvious.

Kluckhohn asserts that in myths, 'the rivalry between brothers is portrayed far oftener than any other [theme], and usually in the form of fratricide' (Kluckhohn 1969: 52). This observation has made René Girard wonder why we regard the fraternal relationship as an affectionate one, while in mythology and history this relation is one of 'contagion' and accompanied by 'malevolent violence': 'in fact, the theme itself is a form of violence' (Girard 1979: 61). In addition, Kasten (1999: 110–11, 150), on the basis of multiple studies, suggests that siblings, in their youth, tend to fight continuously and have much more aggressive arguments than at any other age, until they leave their parental household. He links this to fighting over material belongings and rivalry problems. Looking at the complete life course of sibling relations, Pitt-Rivers has argued that siblings have identical interests at birth (competition for parental affection, food, inheritance and so on), but these change through the course of life, so that they have 'opposed interests by the time they are grandfathers' (Pitt-Rivers 1975: 101).

While Western mythological archetypes of brothers as rivals – such as the biblical Cain and Abel, and the Roman Amulius Silvius and his older brother Numitor Silvius, and Numitor's nephews Romulus and Remus – shape our perception of fraternal social and especially political relations as being characterized by conflict, in Central Asia we find other symbolic representations. I heard the following story from several inhabitants in a mountain village in Tajikistan, concerning a family that had eight sons and two daughters. The father of the ten children called all of them together; he had collected ten branches and gave one branch to each child, asking each to break their branch – which all did, without difficulty. Then the father bound ten branches together and asked each of them to try to break the bundle of branches, which proved impossible. Then he explained: 'Look, if you are on your own, you are easily broken. However, if you – all ten siblings – remain together, no one can ever do you any harm'. This story dates back to the 'secret history of the Mongols' of 1240 and is quite widespread in Central Asia.[20] The parable seems especially popular in Kyrgyzstan, where it appears in numerous proverbs as well as in the epics of Manas.[21]

To conclude, when it comes to social and political positions, siblings (most often brothers) are portrayed as rivals and enemies in the Western scholarly tradition, and as constituents of a strong social unit in Central Asian perception. In the Western portrayal, therefore, it is not surprising that the youth bulge argument depicts brothers competing against one another and thus becoming a source of social conflict – or as Heinsohn puts it, one brother means peace in the family, two brothers war in the country, and three brothers war in the world. In contrast, Central Asians identify sets of brothers as a source of stability and political success, and thus downplay their potential to become a cause of conflict. Even if the 'surplus sons' argument cannot be cleanly lifted from its European context and placed into a discussion of Tajikistan, it nevertheless reminds us to pay particular attention to the dynamic nature of the sibling relationship.

The Relevance of Birth Order among Tajik Brothers

The following terms are used to address brothers: *aka**, *dodar** and *barodar**. *Aka* means elder brother and is also used as a term of respect for any older man (though not necessarily an old man). *Dodar* – which means younger brother – is used less often, since a younger brother is usually addressed by name. The term is a categorical one, defining a kinship position, and to a certain extent it also denotes respect. *Barodar* (pl. *barodaron*) is seldom used as a kinship term, even though its primary meaning is 'brothers of one mother'; its more common use is to refer to a social relation based on shared ideas (Islam, communism). The term *biyor** stands for siblings from one mother and is solely reserved to describe a kin relation; thus, it cannot be used as a social term like *aka*, *dodar* or *barodar*. Further, it is not a term of address but solely one of reference.

A Case Study of Relations between Brothers

Mirzokhoja (b. 1949), Mirzokarim (b. 1965) and Mirzovali (b. 1972) are brothers.[22] Mirzokhoja studied but did not get the chance to pursue a higher degree (*kandidatura*) and even lost his job in the district (*rayon*) when he married another woman. As the eldest son, he was heir to inherit his father's titles. Since the latter did not feel confident enough to make decisions on educational matters, he passed on some of his authority to his eldest son (Mirzokhoja) even before his death. In this way, Mirzokhoja had to decide on his siblings' educational paths. This not only meant that he could decide which subjects they should study, but also if they were to be educated at all, and to what extent, depending on the workload at the family farm and the family's honour. Higher education in the 1980s was a matter of prestige for men, as well as a way toward improving the opportunity of earning an alternative income, so nothing should have stopped his younger brother, Mirzokarim, from pursuing higher studies.

When Mirzokarim asked to continue his studies (*kandidatura*), however, Mirzokhoja did not give him permission to do so, claiming that there was too much work on the family's farm. Mirzokhoja's eldest sister, whose teachers had recommended she pursue higher education, was rejected by the university due to her brother's objection (he requested that the commission not accept her application). At that time, very few women in the village had received their family's permission to pursue further studies. Educating girls was said to spoil not only the girl's personal honour but also that of her family.

Mirzokhoja managed the family by maintaining his position as the only competent decision-maker, and also as the most highly qualified member. All of his brothers proceeded to create a place for themselves, although the youngest brother could only train as a teacher after his parents had died.

Mirzokhoja built a house next to his father's compound, and the youngest brother remained in the parental home. Mirzokarim bought a house a little further away in the village – just far enough, he told me, to allow him to stay out of the daily activities of his eldest brother, who has the right to make regular use of his younger brothers' physical help.

This family is typical in Lakhsh with regard to how the brothers found their place in society. The eldest – heir to his father's title, an authority figure in relation to his siblings, and in many ways the most conventional in lifestyle – remained in residential proximity to his parents – even though he had lived in the district (*rayon*) centre for a while. The youngest son did not leave the parental home for a longer period of time (for studies or migration) and was responsible for looking after his parents in their old age, and thereafter inherited the compound, including the livestock. The middle son, who in terms of parental obligation was the least bound, finished his studies, spent some time as a seasonal worker with his relatives in Shahrituz, and is today involved in the activities of the Islamic Revival Party (IRP) in Tajikistan. He is also the only one who chose his own wife – an educated teacher.[23]

Mirzokhoja is consulted for any major event that concerns the family's honour, such as marriage, education and so on. Mirzokhoja informed me that he was the favourite child of his parents and that his mother chose to die in his house (not in her own house, which is to say her youngest son's house).

Turning our attention to the next generation of Mirzokhoja's family, we see that Mirzokhoja married his first wife in 1973 and with her he had three surviving sons – Abdullo (b. 1974), Jamshed (b. 1976) and Bakhtullo (b. 1980). He divorced this wife to marry Sharifmoh in 1983, who then gave birth to eight children, one of whom died. Her sons are Aziz (b. 1984), Rahmatullo (b. 1991) and Amir (b. 1993). What did these young men do during the civil war of the 1990s? I have already mentioned Mirzokarim's membership of the IRP – his house was used for the recruitment of young men (*generalni stab*), and Abdullo was their commander. Although Mirzokarim refused to fight, his peers and other young men were recruited in his house, where they swore allegiance to the party with their hand on the Koran: *man kafoi tu meravam* ('I will be following your message'). From there, they went to the regional leader in Tavildara, where they received their official registration and weapons to take to their regional cell.

Abdullo, Jamshed and Bakhtullo – the sons of Mirzokhoja's first wife – all actively participated in the civil war, each in his own way. Their maternal uncle (MB) had been an important local *mujohid* leader in their mother's village, and the three brothers joined his group. However, while Abdullo became a commander and managed to take a state post immediately after the war, Bakhtullo continued to run in the company of an unruly group of boys and get into fights. After killing a state soldier, he escaped to Russia, where he remains in hiding. In addition, his eldest brother Abdullo also had to flee when the government started a systematic persecution of the opposition. Jamshed accompanied *mujohid* groups, providing them with the necessary information about local people.[24] In this way, all three brothers were involved in civil war action, although in different ways – hence, they were brothers by kinship and *barodaron* (brothers within an Islamic fighting group) at the same time.[25]

For Aziz – eldest son of Mirzokhoja's second wife – his elder brothers are heroes, and he continues to be enamoured with their ideas and to admire their activities during the war. As the eldest son in his mother's household, he bears the maximum workload, although he does try to escape it whenever possible. His younger brother, Rahmatullo, wants to study further and therefore follows the strategy of resisting physical work, which will ultimately make him useless for agricultural work, after which he is very likely to be sent to study. The youngest brother, Amir, is always compelled to do the husbandry work, based on the argument that the livestock are his anyway. Throughout the year I resided with this family, I witnessed daily fights – sometimes in words and often involving violence. The brothers did not compete for parental affection at all, but they seemed to resist their prescribed positions within the family as much as possible. In this way, they appear to be challenging the established hierarchy.

Mirzokhoja had not actively participated in the civil war; however, he did not desert his siblings. As the eldest brother, he takes his duty very seriously and carefully tries to balance all the interests of his children, siblings and his siblings' children. He continues to do whatever he can to protect his younger activist brother.[26] He is careful not to provoke state institutions because in his position as the coordinator of projects by international organizations, he depends on the goodwill of many political figures. To this end, he spends a lot of time and money with various authorities of the state and personnel of NGOs and international organizations. He sent his eldest daughter to study further, thus taking a step forward regarding female education, and is one of very few Tajik fathers to do so in his village. For him, balancing traditional judgements, international demands, state political power and his brother's oppositional activities is anything but easy. Only in rare instances, when he knew he was safely out of earshot of judgemental parties, did he express his personal opinion on matters.

Birth Order

Birth order in many societies influences succession practices. This has been discussed by many studies and is also true for Tajikistan (Barrera-González 1992; Lévi-Strauss 1993: 350, 372). Birth order in a Tajik family, for example, determines succession and inheritance patterns, and also the other obligations of siblings. However, succession and inheritance rights differ from one another and are given neither at the same time nor to the same person. By rule, the eldest son inherits the father's titles while the youngest inherits the parental wealth and belongings.

As in many other countries, areas of duties are strictly divided between men and women, boys and girls. This can result in a difficult predicament for a family that has either no sons or no daughters. Performing the work of the opposite sex is usually met with much teasing from peers. (Teasing is the most common way to punish non-conformist behaviour.) Biological determinants also make it necessary to introduce some flexibility in this matter; hence, a family that has only sons or only daughters will usually have to transgress certain gender rules. Further, in some areas during the summer, entire villages are emptied of young men – who go to work in Russia – leaving the whole panoply of agricultural work to the remaining women and elders.

THE ELDEST BROTHER

The eldest brother among a set of siblings is usually addressed by a special term that distinguishes him from the other brothers. In Lakhsh, all of his nephews and nieces would refer to him using the honourable title of *avo* kata* or *avo kalon* (great father), while they would call their own father *avo* (father), *bobo** (grand-father, father) or *aka* (elder brother, father).

The position of the eldest brother lies on the continuum of parental author-ity; hence, he occupies a special position in a Tajik family. This practice has been observed in many other societies as well, and Radcliffe-Brown (1958: 73) has explained it as follows: it is through the first-born son that the woman transforms her status, which is extremely essential in a society where there is no initiation ritual into adulthood for young, unmarried girls. Marriage constitutes merely the first step to full social status, the epitome of which is motherhood – which in turn can only be achieved by giving birth to a (male) child. This is the reason, according to Radcliffe-Brown, that the first-born son is often accorded a kind of parental status by his siblings. In Lakhsh society, the eldest son is not only the first one to physically contribute to the agricultural work of his family but also the one who will inherit the status of his father – for his other siblings, he is the continuation of the father. Hence, in practice, this sometimes entails that a very young man assumes the position of head of the household in the event of his father's death, which includes fulfilling all duties and responsibilities towards his brothers, sisters, mother and the community. In other circumstances, the eldest son takes over his father's rights and duties only very late, at a much older age, after his elderly father's death, or when the father reaches around the age of 60 if he feels unable to continue to fulfil his role as the one who decides all family matters.[27] Thus, how and when the eldest son is allocated his rights and duties as the head of the family depends on the family in question.

As head of the household, the father is responsible for the distribution of work among his children. While in some Tajik families the father directly assigns various duties to the siblings who are his children, in other families the father gives orders only to his eldest son, who then delegates the work to his younger siblings. If they shirk their duties, however, the eldest son has no choice but to finish the work himself, since he is the one held responsible for completing the task.

The eldest brother, as the inheritor of his father's authority, remains the head of his sibling group throughout his lifetime. This principle fits into the more general seniority-based system that accords older generations more power than younger ones. Unlike in a gerontocracy, where power accumulates along with age, and older men hold the greatest power, in the seniority system, power is always relative to one's position within the corporate group. Thus, a father might hold a fixed, predetermined position within his set of siblings, but he always exerts the highest authority over his children.[28] Apart from the responsibility of managing his siblings and his own children, the eldest brother also takes over the responsibility of marrying off his siblings if his parents have not been able to do so during their lifetimes.

The importance of the position of eldest son is demonstrated through the following example. In Shahrigul, a first-born son had left for Russia long ago, where he had several relationships and had even got married and had children. He only returned home after many years; by then his younger brothers were already married. In order to restore his social position as the eldest brother, he then decided to marry another woman in the village, who would remain with his parents and thereby represent his interests within his set of siblings.

It is important to perceive and analyse siblings as a group – for instance, an eldest brother who had been unable to study due to the war or the family's economic situation would insist on educating one of his younger brothers in order 'to have at least one educated person in the family'. Thus, in many families the eldest brother would finance a younger or youngest brother's education, while receiving such an education would remain an unfulfilled dream for him. In other families, the eldest brother continued to be the formal head of the set of siblings, although he might be financially far worse off than his younger brothers and therefore unable to perform a part of his duties (that is, the duty of generosity towards his younger siblings). In modern times, social diversification also makes it difficult for the eldest brother to maintain his dominant position economically as well as educationally. According to the norms of Tajik society, brothers move out of their parental home (*judo kardan*) by birth order, while sisters relocate to their husbands' home (marriage is virilocal).[29] From what I observed, parents try to keep their eldest son in geographic proximity: the eldest and youngest brothers live closest to their parents, while the other brothers tend to stay wherever they happen to buy a house or wherever they find land for building their house.

Some eldest brothers perceived their position as an extremely difficult one because of the great responsibility it entails – any brother or sister can come to them at any time and ask for help, which they cannot easily refuse. Generosity is an important marker of high social status; however, it can be extremely difficult to be generous in times of economic crisis.[30] Gifts are considered public transfers and therefore come under public scrutiny, especially if they come from a person or family with a high status (Pétric 2002). Thus, eldest brothers perceive their social obligation as being a difficult one – they tend to complain that it is much easier for their younger siblings to accumulate wealth than it is for them.

KENJA: THE YOUNGEST BROTHER

In the case of Mirzokhoja's family (above), Amir is the *kenja** (youngest brother) who is always delegated the husbandry work by his older siblings. However, he often manages to either escape his duties or resist performing them in the hope that his elder brothers will relieve him of them. Even in the case of twins, the one who is born second holds a different status from the first born, represented by the choice of names, which indicate birth order (for example, if twin boys are born traditionally, the older twin will be called Hassan, while the younger one will have the name Hussein). A boy can also be named *kenja* when his parents hope to have no more children after him.[31] With this name, they hope to end child production. In this sense, the word is said to have the power to prevent fertility.

I met and talked with three *kenja*s, all of whom were in their twenties. All three told me that they disliked their position despite its material security, because it considerably constrained their freedom of movement. The *kenja* is perceived as the son who will ensure parental old-age security; he will inherit the compound (*havlī**) after their death and is therefore expected to look after his parents in their old age. Although some parents emphasized the fact that they reserved the power to decide who would inherit their compound, most of the time it was the youngest son who inherited it. Nevertheless, in one family, the parents' questioning of this practice led to a kind of competition among the daughters-in-law (*kelins**) for the favour of their mother-in-law. (Girls prefer to marry a *kenja* because of the material security they can expect.) Moreover, at times I also heard parents questioning this practice, which according to them might encourage 'laziness' in the *kenjas*.

According to the older siblings, the term *kenja* is often a synonym for *erka* (spoiled child). Older siblings are generally of the opinion that they have to do all the work, while the youngest one faces the least hardship in day-to-day work as well as the least difficulty in acquiring wealth, because eventually he will inherit all of his parents' holdings without much effort. This discourse does not hold true everywhere, but it is widespread and is also accorded relevance in marriage strategies.

From the point of view of the youngest brother, however, things are different. Being at the bottom of the ladder when it comes to delegated work, the youngest brother is always at hand to help out his older siblings. Thus, the material security of the youngest brother is only obtained by giving up all prospects of relative freedom and individual choice. Since youngest brothers are looked after by their elder brothers, somehow they never seem to grow up – they always remain in a subordinate position.

THE MIDDLE BROTHERS

Some men who are born into the middle position believe that life is more difficult for them because they have to make a living for themselves. They tend to complain that since their parents spent all their wealth on establishing the eldest son(s), they were hardly able to meet the financial requirements of their younger son(s). Generally, however, they agree with the other siblings' opinions that the advantage of being the middle son is the relative freedom he is accorded for managing his own family and personal life, with few parental obligations. The extract from an interview with Murad, a middle son (quoted above), shows how material help is reciprocated with physical help.

Two aspects characterize the position of the middle brother: showing respect towards elder brothers and receiving respect from younger brothers. While middle brothers receive material help from their elder brothers, they can expect physical help from the younger ones. Moreover, although they do have some responsibilities towards their parents, their help is perceived as additional rather than obligatory. I have already mentioned the case of Rahmatullo, who used a specific strategy to make himself appear as a surplus son/brother within the farming household, which increased his chances of being sent away to pursue higher education. He knew that unlike his eldest brother, who takes care of the major agricultural workload and has no interest in studies, as the middle brother he had a good chance of receiving an education – and in his case he succeeded in being sent to study in September 2009. The obstacle for him, however, was his youngest brother – Rahmatullo's father had once mentioned his intention to send his youngest son to Dushanbe for further studies. Although nobody would question Rahmatullo going to Dushanbe for higher education, he knew that his father would hardly be able to finance several children's university education; furthermore, the family did not hide their regret over having sent their daughter for such an education without understanding beforehand the extent of the financial burden and at the same time realizing how little they would benefit from her education since all rights over her and her earnings would go to her husband.

Middle brothers, in this way, seem to have the most options; however, this does not mean that all middle brothers make use of those options. Many envy their eldest or youngest brother for their structural position and the advantages that accompany it. In terms of youth bulge theory, this position is the most interesting because of the possible options and strategies and the relative freedom that middle brothers enjoy as compared to eldest and youngest brothers. Mirzokarim's example certainly represents the active use of this freedom.

The study of siblings in Tajikistan thus reveals a very structured relationship. Based on the idea that siblingship is primarily predefined biologically, individuals may choose to react against this position or enforce it through their claims. Hence, my point in this regard is that by structuring sibling relations, parents are freed from much educational responsibility, while at the same time, they can strategically place their children in different sectors – this is best described as a diversification strategy – by thinking of them as a unit, not as competing individuals.

Subversion and Competition among Siblings

Brothers are the social security of the family. Sisters also depend on their help and support and therefore create social ties with individual brothers, upon whom they lavish special care during their childhood and thus secure their protection later in life, but at the same time they are subjected to male dominance and have to accept their brothers' control over them (Joseph 1994).[32] In many families, the brothers were the ones who decided the extent of any freedoms that their sisters should enjoy and whether or not their sisters could attend school, go to a wedding, stay at home, and so on, until the girls were married. While the husband–wife relation is quite well formalized in Tajik society and mutual rights are culturally defined, the relationship between siblings appears to be much less formalized, even though it is institutionalized. Unlike marriage, which affects two families and thus two parties, sibling relations occur within one family and therefore might appear to be less structured or organized. However, this is generally not the case. In particular, societies with large families such as Tajik society develop sibling-specific rules and institutions.

Rites of passage such as circumcision, marriage and funerals are a heavy financial burden to a family. In order to ease this burden, brothers tend to share the costs and divide duties among themselves – this includes the rites of passage concerning their parents as well as their children. For example, for a boy's marriage, the groom's father's brothers offer economic help by providing animals for the feast (cows or sheep). For a girl's marriage, the bride's father's brothers divide the expense of the furniture that is part of her dowry. In the event of funerals, relatives bring sheep or calves for the feast, while the dead person's sons organize the ritual by either sharing the costs equally or by agreeing to contribute to the different parts of the ritual according to each brother's capacity. The mourning period stretches over a year; therefore, the brothers split the costs for the different feasts according to their economic means.

> Everyone, for instance, assumes a particular duty after a parent's death. For example, one takes on the responsibility of *se begohī* [the ritual for cleaning the house during the first three days]; another, of *sari sol* [the largest feast to mark the end of the mourning period of one year]; a third, of *shash moha* [the feast after six months] – I took care of the *chilla* [the feast after forty days], for example, because it is less expensive and I don't have much.[33]

The importance of the brother group also emerges in the field of education, as revealed by the following example. An elderly man and former teacher complained about the fact that brothers have the power to make decisions regarding their sisters' education; even the parents, it seems, are unable to prevent this. Young people assume their authority from new interpretations of Islam, which grant them power independent of their age, and then seek to implement these rules with regard to their siblings.

S.R.: Why don't they let the girls learn?

BAKHTIGUL: This is all useless talk; it is meaningless talk between people that girls should not learn – this talk is between people who are uneducated and religious. There are two kinds of religious people: those who lack learning and those who are educated. There are believers who do not know their own religion – those Muslims don't know the basic principles of Islam. For example, in the Koran it is written that learning is not forbidden; in contrast, the Koran states that human beings should learn. . . .

S.R.: Do elder and younger brothers have the right to decide whether their sister should be educated or not?

BAKHTIGUL: Exactly. Some brothers don't allow their sisters to study.

S.R.: Why is it like this?

BAKHTIGUL: For example, Shiringul's elder brother does not let her learn – her parents have nothing against her education – but her brother just doesn't let her.

S.R.: Is the word of an elder brother more important than the wishes of the parents?

BAKHTIGUL: Yes. It happened like this. Her brother said, 'If she goes to school, I will not return home'. Now her brother works in Russia and says that if she is educated any further, he will not return from Russia.[34]

It is not clear whether parents are reluctant to assert their authority in this matter because in recent times they have become increasingly dependent financially on their sons, or whether brothers have always played a central role in deciding their sisters' lives. It is my view that rather than a change in the structural institution of the sibling relation, this control results from the increasing power and influence of individual brothers over their siblings. I believe that these observations are not unique to the post-civil war period, as there seem to have been similar arguments when secular education was introduced during the Soviet era (see the example regarding Mirzokhoja and his siblings, above). Education is perceived as a generation-specific matter, and parents can feel unqualified to make all of the decisions regarding which of their children should be educated and to what extent. This is not always the case, of course, but it seems to be rather common, especially in the case of older parents.

Higher education is not seen as something that has the potential to advance society, as such (in which the connection between the individual and society is emphasized); rather, education is considered a family matter and is related to the family's honour. Although parents initiate much of their children's activities – for instance, they decide which child will be allowed to study further and which will be married and when – and constitute the ultimate authority in their children's lives, thus influencing individual careers, they leave much of children's educational development to negotiations with their siblings and with external specialists (such as teachers, state and religious authorities and so on). This may be one reason why youngest siblings are today so often pushed to study further by their older siblings in order to make up for the older siblings' failure in this matter due to the civil war and economic difficulties.

Any discussion of Tajik siblings must also include a key development in the aftermath of the fall of the Soviet Union – the resurrection of Islam in Tajik society. While the older generation (*mūisafed**) claims a certain level of religious knowledge (though very limited), the majority of the parental generation is ambivalent towards the new Islamic movements and interpretations of Islam, and most parents do not interfere in their children's attempts to learn about Islam. Nevertheless, they often refuse to be proselytized by their children, as the following incident reveals.

One day, I was conducting an interview with a middle-aged woman when another woman rushed in and sat down, heaved a sigh of relief, and then laughed. On being asked what was the matter, the woman explained that she had sneaked out of her home, because of her son. He had become a strict practitioner of Islam, forbidding his sisters from attending school, watching Indian soap operas (the girls' favourite television programmes) and attending public parts of weddings. He had also tried to convert his mother, but she had refused, saying that she was too old to change her habits now; he should go on praying and leave her in peace. However, he was eager to change his sisters and was successful in that attempt.

In this way, social change results from a kind of bargaining strategy among siblings, especially younger siblings. Whereas the parent–child relation appears to have little room for change, it is among siblings that various tensions often play out through negotiation. This is true mainly for large rural families who live within various networks, and may be less true for urban families who place the parent–child relation above any other relation, whether that of kin or friend (Harris 2004). While brothers in rural areas often compete intensely against one another, they also cooperate and socialize in accordance with seniority principles. A brother who lacks other brothers experiences life on his own as very difficult when compared to families that have many brothers and where brothers can rely on each other's support.

In Shahrigul and Sari Kenja, I recorded some families with eight to ten sons. In both villages, these families were regarded as the richest because each family member could accumulate wealth according to his ability and redistribute it fairly so that none of the brothers was left behind, even though each brother was very different in character – for instance, some were hardworking while others tended to avoid work. Brothers are a source of wealth because they are different from one another; even if one of them goes 'wrong', he will not disturb the system, provided that there are enough brothers. Therefore, to draw on Heinsohn's (2006) idea of surplus sons, families do not think in terms of an equivalent position for their children – that is, children competing for an equal inheritance. Instead, they structure the positions of siblings in such a way as to reduce brotherly competition and create a strong social group through the strategy of diversification. Returning to the youth bulge argument, we therefore must be cautious about linking multiple siblings intrinsically with competition and conflict; however, we can connect siblings to a dynamic process of social change that at times can be adversarial.

Cooperating, Competing, Fighting

Do brothers tend to cooperate or compete in times of civil crisis? Brothers typically do both – they compete as well as cooperate – and this was also true during the civil war. At the war's onset, some young men took advantage of the opportunity to empower themselves through Islamic knowledge and/or through weapons. In other words, they left their position within the family in order to look for positions in other groups. In some cases, entire sets of brothers went and joined combatant groups together, while in others only one or two brothers from a family did so. I was unable to identify any fixed pattern in these decisions, since every possible combination occurred. Age appeared to be the main criterion – younger people were more eager to join combatant groups for no specific reason, while older people were more likely to join to enact revenge on those who had killed their relatives.

> S.R.: So they became *mujohid** of their own free will?
>
> SAFARMOH: They went of their own free will and became *mujohid*; if you wanted to fight, you would leave the family and go to war. In one family, four people from one household had joined the war. For example, if the eldest son was killed in the war, his siblings would want revenge, so they too would leave the family and go into the mountains.
>
> S.R.: Can you give me other examples?
>
> SAFARMOH: One young man came to join a combatant group along with his son and two younger brothers.
>
> S.R.: How old was the man?
>
> SAFARMOH: I think he was about 45 years old.[35]
>
> S.R.: And his son?
>
> SAFARMOH: His son was *hamghul* (peer) to me, I think.
>
> S.R.: And his two other brothers?
>
> SAFARMOH: I think they were around 35 and 37 years old.[36]

The different life histories that I collected indicated that sets of siblings tended to support each other – I did not come across any incident in which brothers fought against each other, although this does not preclude that it happened, as some people contend. I have mentioned that Mirzokhoja, the eldest of three brothers, had a moderate position in the war. His strategy was to mediate between his brother, who was active in the opposition, and the state authorities. His two younger brothers had left to perform their youthful duties by participating in the war (they were out on the streets during conflicts in order to show which group they belonged to and their determination to fight), while he played a mediating role without having to directly oppose either of them.

Another such story concerns the political figure Sodirov Rizvon Mardon, who entered the civil war arena as a religiously motivated fighter. He had three brothers helping and supporting him, and they were his only adherents at the war's end. Rizvon joined the conflict after it had started; his group was generally regarded as a bunch of thugs with little ideological commitment, and they were extremely mobile (for some time, they had even joined up with Ahmed Shah Masud in Afghanistan). Eventually, Rizvon's claims were not regarded seriously in the peace negotiation process, and apart from his brothers, no one remained with him. According to some accounts, the four brothers played the central role within the group, which gives rise to the presumption that Rizvon's outfit was, in reality, merely a concern of the brothers, and only temporarily attracted other young fighters (Tutubalina 2006: 6).

Thus far I have discussed brothers cooperating with one another. However, despite the fact that brothers cooperate for specific events, they tend to avoid each other in daily life. Each brother is traditionally placed in a hierarchical relation to their other brother(s), which is why they cannot be close friends. Brothers – particularly elder brothers – carefully avoid revealing details about their life to their younger brother(s), who might discover some non-conformist behaviour, knowledge which is perceived as a dangerous tool in the hands of a younger brother.

This hierarchical distance helps to explain why, when the community was forced to divide into two groups due to lack of sufficient mosque space, Mirzokarim chose to attend a different mosque from the one his elder and younger brothers attended. He is not the only example of this – many sets of brothers chose to be divided. Mirzokarim stated that he enjoyed more freedom by attending a different mosque than the one his elder brother attended, because he always felt inhibited in his elder brother's presence. The seniority principle demands submission in any immediate contact. Thus, men tend to separate their personal environment from that of their brothers and avoid contact.

I witnessed an interesting case of fraternal conflict that could not be reconciled in the urban context of Dushanbe, in which traditional ideas of siblingship clashed with socialist (Western) legal concepts. While the younger brother – who according to traditional law is the legal heir to the parental home – had left his mother's compound during the Soviet era to live in a 'modern' city flat, the elder brother had taken care of the mother and maintained the compound. Towards the end of the 1990s, the younger brother decided to return to his mother's compound and claim his legal inheritance. The elder brother, however, refused to hand over the compound because he had invested a lot in its upkeep. The case was brought to court and resolved according to state law (which is very similar to former Soviet law). The court ruled that the compound be divided, in terms of its value, among all of the children – including the four daughters. Each daughter returned her share to their mother, claiming that she did not need it, and the mother then accorded all these shares, including the younger brother's (and thus five-sixths of the compound), to her younger son. Thus, the elder son basically lost the compound and all of his rights over it. The brothers are as yet not reconciled.[37]

The above example shows how a sibling conflict erupted when traditional law, based on the seniority system, was made ineffective and was replaced by state law, which treats all siblings equally. Anton Blok (2000) has stated that equalizing relations leads to an increased potential for conflict. His argument pertains to the husband–wife relationship, but also seems to apply to Tajik siblingship.

In many societies, siblings are expected to be different – not only do they hold very different kinship positions but their grade of social obligation also varies considerably, according some siblings more freedom, while other siblings are more strictly bound. Social security is achieved by having strategic positions, not equal positions. This seems to be reflected in the way Tajik families manage their children. For example, they place one child in state education, support another's religious education, and invest in sending the others to Russia; in this way, it is clear that the family supports a diversification strategy in order to form a close social unit. To return to the symbol of the hand, children's characters are as different as five fingers – which, however, still function as parts of a single hand.[38] The institution of siblingship frees middle sons from an obligation towards the parents but does not push them out of the fraternal unit. Fraternal harmony is, however, constantly at risk of collapse due to the simultaneous competition of brothers for special treatment and familial resources. If we consider that a new household takes about fifteen years (so young men claimed) to achieve the same level of material wealth as the parental household, we can understand this competition better.

Conclusion

In contrast to the assumption of Heinsohn (2006) that second, third and more sons are a 'surplus' within their families in high-parity societies, in Tajikistan siblings are perceived as the strongest social unit and ensure a family's social security through diversification. This diversification strategy depends not (only) on individual nature but also on family management and a child's birth order position.

The concept of diversification has been suggested by Schlee (2001: 20), who observes that distance between elements is important for successful integration (integration through diversification). This also applies to siblings who, as we have seen, maintain a distance from one another in their daily activities but form a strong social unit, consisting of members with very different characteristics. This model integrates the elements of both competing and united individuals, and is therefore appropriate for describing siblingship in Tajikistan.

Differences in the social position of siblings are even reflected in the fertility history of particular communities. Hence, as the following graph shows, eldest and youngest sons tend to have fewer children than middle siblings; but their average family size has remained more stable over the decades. In other words, socio-political change and the politics of fertility in the Soviet Union have mostly affected the families of middle sons, while the eldest and the youngest sons seem to have been protected from these external influences. Both the eldest and especially the youngest sons remain under close supervision of their parents, which results in fewer children.

Rather than assuming that competition for resources (parental investment, housing, land and so on) may increase the potential for conflict among siblings, it is worth reflecting on how sets of siblings are handled in a particular society, especially in relation to the developmental cycle of domestic groups. Fertility history is a direct outcome of the institution of siblingship and the position accorded to siblings within the family. The strong emphasis on unity and stability through diversification is, however, not a guarantee for stability in society. More important than the number of siblings a young man has or lacks, I believe, is the actual age of the young man and the backing of his siblings in his political engagement. As mentioned above, age – and to some extent his position as middle son – were the determining factors that led Mirzokarim to join the Islamic opposition, supported by attributes of youth that urged young men to join combatant groups and demonstrate their determination, courage and honour. His choice led neither to the splitting of the set of siblings nor to all of his siblings conforming to a single ideology.

The potential for conflict has re-emerged due to unequal opportunities for brothers to accumulate wealth. The proper education of an eldest brother is no longer a guarantee for a good income, which is needed for meeting his social obligations vis-à-vis his parents and siblings. His position nowadays has become more difficult than that of his middle siblings, who enjoy much more freedom and social security. In fact, today we may find the eldest, middle, or youngest siblings working in Russia; however, this is more of an economic choice than a structural result. Sets of siblings have proven capable of adapting to socio-political

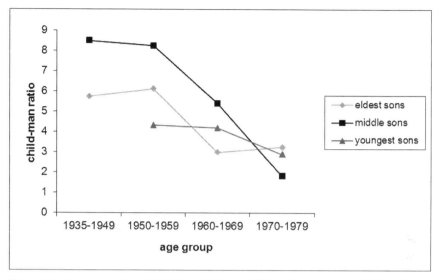

Figure 3.1: Average number of children of eldest, middle and youngest sons (Shahrituz).

and economic changes, and thus keeping the family going through crises and changes.

They are not only victims of change but also actors in crises and conflicts. In this role they receive the backing of the family even if siblings do not agree politically and ideologically. Although people in Tajikistan claim that siblings have radically different opinions about politics, fraternal splitting based on such disagreement appears to be rare.

At this point, it is helpful to reflect on the idea of seniority, mentioned in the opening of this chapter. This word refers to the relation between juniors and seniors that exists as an organizing principle far beyond the scope of the father–son relation.[39] This age-related principle of social organization has been discussed by Bonte (1985) in his study of East Africa. Bonte argues that societies organized on the basis of age tend to attach less importance to kinship and more importance to gender. His generational concept, based on the father–son relation, may also be extended to the Tajik society as a whole. At the most, three or four generations are considered to be relevant, while the others are 'forgotten': 'This forgetting is necessary in order to allow the society the social reproduction in terms of an equivalence of alternating generations' (ibid.: 62). Further, Bonte argues that the female counterpart is important as an intermediary, for domestic regulation, and is constructed in opposition to the duties of the male. Although the gender-based duties found in East African societies are reversed in Lakhsh – where women (and children) are responsible for husbandry, while men are responsible for agriculture – the principal idea of a seniority-centric society based on generational and gender oppositions allows us to understand that, within a seniority society, kinship acquires a different relevance. Although kinship is certainly not unimportant, its political use is restricted in favour of a generalized junior–senior relation.

Unfortunately, Bonte does not consider the question of size. I contend it is significant that, in a seniority-centric society, a minority of elders hold sway over the (marginalized) majority, and moreover that this can become a source of volatility when the minority, which controls access to resources and the path to social maturity, is deprived of these resources and challenged by alternative methods of education (that is, alternative concepts of social maturity). Economic independence and alternative concepts of maturation can call into question existing traditional institutions such as the developmental cycle of domestic groups and sibling hierarchy, as will be shown in subsequent chapters. The consequences of mass migration and the dependency of elders on their sons in Tajikistan is a case in point.

The institution of siblingship offers the most effective means of exerting control over the majority of youth within families and communities. In this sense, the seniority-centric society of Tajiks emphasizes not only gender oppositions but also sibling hierarchy. Siblingship is at the base of family efforts to increase social security and to secure reproduction. The way in which this organizing principle has been challenged in the civil war and thereafter will be discussed in the next chapter. Today, people refer to rules of siblingship, but they often feel unable to follow them because of political and economic insecurity.

Notes

1. While seniority does not exclude tribal or clan organization, it is a principle that, in the absence of the latter, can become the basis of social structure.
2. 'With the passage of the means of production into common property, the individual family ceases to be the economic unity of society. Private housekeeping is transformed into a social industry. The care and education of the children becomes a public matter. Society takes care of all children equally, irrespective of whether they are born in wedlock or not' (Engels 2004: 81).
3. I would like to thank Wolfgang Holzwarth, a respected expert on the Pamir Tajiks, for sharing his material with me and providing very helpful suggestions in his review of the concept of the household in Central Asian societies. Holzwarth (1978) discusses the problem of Kislyakov's evolutionary *Stufenmodel* ('step model') and the influence of a Marxist approach on later interpretations of what is nonetheless extraordinary ethnographic material.
4. This criticism seems to apply equally within the context of international organizations that insist on household surveys as a primary tool for generating policy-relevant information but fail to capture transitions and changes in gender roles (Kandiyoti 1999: 500).
5. Interview with Bakhtigul, elder woman, October 2006.
6. For example, in the course of privatization, the 'new' units of private farms that were formed out of the former sovkhoz or kolkhoz have been labelled *khojagii dehqonī* – translated as a juridical unit of a private family farm.

7. Although in Shahrituz brothers in several families rebuilt their parental house as a fraternal house after the war, i.e., a house within which several brothers have their own rooms after the death of the father. The reason is the increasingly limited and costly access to land.

8. Shukrona, aged 22, April 2007.

9. In Tajikistan, as in other countries of Central Asia, the system of *hashar** (pl. *hasharho*) is widely used. *Hashar* means a group of people who agree to perform some task together without payment (collective work). Usually, this system is embedded in a certain circulatory form of *hashar*, which means the work is not voluntary but rather a reciprocal system of 'work for work' (in the case of brothers, this would be 'work for help'). *Hashar* can exist in different domains, and it is commonly used in agriculture to complete labour-intensive tasks (such as cropping and harvesting or preparing feasts for marriages, funerals or circumcisions). A *hashar* is usually called for seasonal work, which makes participation useful only to those families who can expect the same workload within the same season. Thus, if a person is spared by one's own family to take part in somebody else's *hashar*, this record is carefully balanced against later reciprocations of the work. Usually, the repayment of work is only through work – there is no system for compensating a failed attempt at completing some task with any other form of work or help. Even more common, though not necessarily so, the type of work performed is repaid with the same type of work within the same working season – for example, hay harvesting and potato planting. This is associated with the perception that different tasks have differing degrees of difficulty, so one should reciprocate with work of a similar degree or 'grade' of difficulty. (Binding hay into bundles is seen as a very difficult task, while potato harvesting is ranked as an easy task.) These *hashar*s end with a meal for all participants – the meal is obligatory but is not considered as payment.

   The term *hashar*, however, is also used when a chief employs his subordinates to perform a private task; common examples of this are teachers employing students, military chiefs employing soldiers – e.g., to work in the fields. These services are perceived as reciprocal insofar as the chief is seen as an elder brother caring for his subordinates.

   To conclude, *hashar* work exists at the community level. It helps the community get work done from which the entire community is likely to benefit, e.g., the construction of roads and water channels. Hence, *hashar* is never perceived as 'voluntary work' in the European sense of the term, but always retains a reciprocal aspect in which the person benefits from their service in one way or another.

10. The data for Sasik Bulak and Shahrigul indicate an average of 9.3 and 9.4 persons per household, respectively. This is almost the same as that calculated by Faroughi (1999: 16) through a socio-economic survey of households in 1998.

11. This situation becomes even more serious if those who have migrated send all their money to their parents instead of sending some to their wife. She then has to depend on the help of others, which is not always available and can put women in very vulnerable positions.

12. I once spoke with a young woman who had recently separated her household from her mother-in-law's. She was very proud of receiving an individual invitation for the first time and for being able to bring her own gift – it gave her the feeling of being a complete woman with a social position within the community of women. She could claim money for buying the gift from her husband, decide what to bring, and assume responsibility for her family's honour in the game of gift exchange.

13. The belief that in traditional society youth were always integrated into family life has long been discredited in the European world. Various social and political institutions – such as knighthood (knights were classically younger sons without inheritance), apprenticeship

and servitude – absorbed surplus offspring, leading to the postponing of marriage and 'generally eased the strains which inheritance systems were undergoing in reproducing these class positions in the later Middle Ages' (Cohen 1999: 188–89).

14. In this regard, I am referring to a model suggested by Durkheim and developed by Schlee and Werner (1996: 16; Schlee 2001: 20) indicating that interpersonal differences do not necessarily create conflict and may even have integrative potential, thus increasing family security.

15. Interview with Murad, aged 30, February 2007. Murad was born in 1976; he is married and has two sons and one daughter. He has studied at a *madrasa** in Kyrgyzstan and is a farmer in Lakhsh. Murad is the second of three living sons (he has five sisters). His elder brother was born in 1960, while the younger was born in 1981.

16. During my research in Tajikistan, I had a chance to observe the parent–child relation in various situations. While parents and children alike would deny ever having argued with one another, I saw many young people listen politely to their parents' orders only to do whatever they wanted afterwards. And, occasionally, they did argue aloud with them. From this and many other observations, I conclude that the parent–child relation, which is highly valued and formulated in religious terms (e.g., paradise lies under the feet of the mother), is an ideal that is not affected by the daily reality of interactions, which can be and often are highly contentious.

17. I believe that this argument is more applicable to boys than girls, who de facto spend most of their time in the domestic sphere, always under their parents' eye. In contrast, young men are expected to spend most of the day outside their home, which allows them a life-style characterized by much more freedom than young women can ever hope to experience.

18. The importance of brothers within Tajik kinship has been stressed by numerous Russian ethnographers, such as Andreev (1953), Kislyakov (1969), Monogarova (1992), Monogarova and Mukhiddinov (1992) and Bushkov and Mikul'skiy (1996).

19. Meyer Fortes claimed that, 'Siblingship implies equality of status among like-sex siblings in contraposition to the inequality of status that characterizes other relations of kinship, descent, and affinity' (Fortes 1970: 77).

20. For the specific passages, see Rachewiltz (2006: 4–5 and 21–22).

21. I am thankful to my colleague Aksana Ismailbekova for her remark that this story exists in Kyrgyzstan as well, in the form of numerous proverbs as well as in the famous epics of Manas: 'No one can destroy you if you are together [brothers and sisters]'. However, this is not limited to Central Asia: Günther Schlee knows this story from the Rendille in East Africa. It is possible that this story represents one kind of master narrative for a widespread perception of siblings' relations.

22. Although I have renamed the brothers, I have also adhered to the widespread practice of giving brothers similar-sounding names. Six sisters and one brother were born in between the brothers; of these, three sisters and the brother died.

23. For their story, see Chapter 5. There is a similar story of another middle son who lives with his three daughters in Dushanbe, while his youngest half-brother was forced to marry a second wife because he only had two daughters with his first wife, and no other children.

24. In one such instance, which later proved calamitous for him, Jamshed helped the *mujo-hid*s to find the house of a former Soviet leader, whom they robbed and abused. In 2006, Jamshed came back to visit his father but was soon arrested, because his father was unable to pay high bribes to the victim, the police and the secret service.

25. This is not a unique case; it is very similar to the relation between Commander Rizvon, who is better known in the political field, and his brothers. More details on Rizvon are provided below.

26. For example, during the election in 2006, he was forced to host one of the secret service representatives in his own house at his own expense – they had come to represent the state authorities at the local level. The village was known for its support of the IRP, so with this preventive strategy, the state hoped to make sure that the villagers would vote in favour of the then president, Emomali Rahmonov. The secret service representative spent much of his time inquiring about this younger brother.

27. In northern Afghanistan the practice whereby an elderly father hands over responsibility to the eldest son once he reaches the age of 60 continues to be applied and may also have been systematically applied in Tajikistan in the past.

28. What I have described here is the system prevalent in Lakhsh and Shahrigul; in urban centres, however, the kin group is often smaller, or other relations are often absent, which leads to a much stronger parent–child relation (Harris 2006; Stephan 2008).

29. There is an important exception to this norm: If the eldest brother had functioned as the head of the household for a long period of time, residing in the parental home and occupying the place of his father, he generally does not set up his own household. Instead, he marries off all of his siblings, including the youngest brother – who usually relinquishes his right of inheritance and accepts moving out as well.

30. I was living with a family where the head of the household and eldest of three brothers was also the head of an international organization. For this reason, people believed him to be very rich. However, during my stay I witnessed how he spent the scarce resources he owned (occasionally he would even borrow money from me) on maintaining his social status and existing network, while his own family, at times, did not even get one proper meal a day.

31. Only in Jirgatol did I come across the use of the term *kiz* ('girl' in Kyrgyz) for the youngest daughter in Tajik families.

32. The brother–sister relation has been discussed for the Middle East by Meeker (1976), El-Shamy (1981) and Joseph (1994). Meeker notes that, for Turks as for Arabs, the brother–sister relation contrasts with the husband–wife relation 'just as "control" through conventions contrasts with "love"' (Meeker 1976: 388). This has implications for the way in which the husband, father, brother and, generally, agnates respond to an attack on honour. Meeker compares Arab and Turkic ways of dealing with the brother–sister bond and claims that Turks cultivate this relationship less intensely and do not keep honour (*nomus*) after their sister's marriage (it passes to the husband's agnates). Among Arabs, on the other hand, the 'love' for the sister remains with the brother and his agnates – and with it the honour. Tajiks seem to follow an Arab pattern in which the brother–sister relationship remains a central one throughout the siblings' lives. After her parents' death, a rural woman's security depends entirely on her brother, at least until her own sons are old enough to help her.

33. Interview with Miroj, a middle-aged man, December 2006.

34. Interview with Bakhtigul, an older woman, September 2006.

35. Note that Safarmoh refers to the 'young man' as a man of 45 years in the war context.

36. Interview with Safarmoh, aged 28, November 2006.

37. For a detailed analysis of this case, see Roche (2005). Bushkov and Mikul'skiy (1996: 16) also provide a similar example.

38. Herzfeld mentions a similar proverb in Greek that, 'describes just this tension between any kind of internal differentiation and the need to display unity before outsiders' (Herzfeld 1980: 341).

39. I would like to thank Martine Guichard for encouraging me to take up this topic in order to capture the dynamic processes between the social construction of youth (juniors) and elders (seniors).

Chapter 4
'The Gift of Youth'
Workers, Religious Actors and Migrants

The terms and constructions that refer to 'youth' are far from standardized, not easily agreed upon, and vary according to intention and situation. Different aspects, concepts and points of view can be emphasized or downplayed, depending on whether one wants to portray a more or less homogeneous social group or provide a more complex situation. It is this susceptibility to various constructions that makes the term 'youth' so interesting and popular in approaches to conflicts. But it is the concept's inherent imprecision that causes confusion over terms in theoretical debates on youth bulges – for example, the discussions of youth bulges based on psychological definitions that fail to reflect the local context. As the previous chapter has shown, youth concepts have remained fluid and flexible – not only in historical moments of political change but also as a way to continuously adapt and readapt to local and global developments.

Youth is an abstract category, sometimes legal, social or demographic but most often related to a census (Anderson 1999: 164–65). In this study, I do not intend to create a new census category but rather wish to investigate the dynamics of various existing categories and concepts. The Tajik state, for instance, conceptualizes youth in a manner similar to that of the Soviets (progressive, deviant, uncivilized). In contrast to these external conceptualizations are local concepts of youth, which are often ignored (such as siblingship). Yet, it is through the interaction of these very different youth concepts (roles, expectations and so on) that dynamics develop.

Some youth concepts produce clear-cut cohorts or groups, while others are linked to status (social juniors versus social seniors) and processes of maturation; yet, in the youth bulge discussion, all of the various nuances of these concepts are essential to understanding the formation of categories and groups in the context of cultural dynamics. Categories can initiate group identities but need not do so. The development of Islamic youth concepts shows that global notions of youth are an important resource for negotiating local (submissive) notions of youth and transforming them into status positions. In the case of combatant groups, we have an example of how Islamic concepts of belonging (brotherhood) turned a demographic category into groups. The discrepancy between categories and groups is, however, best shown in migration from Tajikistan to the north in search of employment, which, while affecting and shaping the youth bulge, has yet to coalesce into a collective identity or movement. In fact, migration is responsible for a demographic paradox – that is, a statistical youth bulge which turns into an empirical 'youth indentation'.

In the Introduction I provided a set of basic terms referring to youth, such as *bacha** (young boy, young man; pl. *bachaho* or *bacho*, lads, guys) and *javonon** (youth as a social category). In the historical outline given in Chapter 2 we have seen that youth as a distinct social category emerged in Central Asia through Bolshevik politics. In Chapter 3, meanwhile, we looked at the role of the household and siblingship in regulating maturation processes. Domestication in this context refers to the rules of gradual integration of young people into the community and the household as full members.

In this chapter I will concentrate on the period of youth and maturation (*davrai javonon** and *davrai kamolod**), looking first at how religious concepts recast youth as the vanguard of the Muslim world, and second at how migration has changed young people's position within the family and the community. While Chapter 3, on the household and siblingship, provided a static picture of how society imagines domestication to occur, this chapter will challenge many of these static assumptions and show that domestication is the result of the negotiation of status involving family, community and politics. This will be further explored in the subsequent two chapters, focusing first on a specific ritual (marriage) and then on the impact of politics in shaping youth categories and domestication efforts.

Work and Maturity

What do people in Tajikistan associate with youth above all? To a rural family, youth represents physical strength, which allows them to work for the benefit of family and society; the wealth of the family depends on them. In other words, work and maturity are directly linked. Of course, learning is also part of this maturation process, and yet learning is seen as independent from the family's economic needs – at least for most rural people. In Tajikistan, the construction of the life course is thus closely connected to perceptions of work.[1] This observation has already been made by numerous authors researching youth as a social group in society (e.g., Mead 1970: 84–86; Eisenstadt 1988). Hard physical work is considered to be the task of young people. Tohir, a young man of 24 from Jirgatol, expressed this widespread perception: 'Men's work is always difficult; women's work is easy' (cf. Jum'aev 2001: 28). Referring to agricultural work in particular, he expressed a wish that is often shared by young men: to escape such work and leave the village for a completely different life. Tohir left to pursue his studies in Dushanbe but never found a job afterwards. He refused to engage in agricultural work and eventually left for Russia, where he was arrested for criminal activities.

Another young man, Aziz, also disparaged agricultural work as difficult. He is the eldest of the six children of his father's second wife.[2] He currently manages most of the agricultural work, which his father orders him to do every morning. Aziz had previously run away to Dushanbe in search of another life. Upon returning, he claimed to love the city because it offers more alternatives than his village. He wants to leave for Russia, but his father cannot spare him from agricultural work. His father is employed by an international organization and has little time to do the work himself. Living with Aziz's family for many months, I observed the siblings fighting over how work was divided up and the different strategies used by them to avoid doing it. Agricultural work was particularly seen in a negative light, despite being the most productive resource in the area and for Aziz's family – potatoes are dubbed the 'gold of Jirgatol'. For Aziz, men's status increases as they increase their leisure time and consumption capacity, a goal that he believes can only be reached through education: 'If only I had gone to school, if only I had studied, I would drive a car today . . . The others work less; I do all the work'.[3] Aziz missed out on an education because of the civil war and feels that this is why he now has to work so hard. Being the eldest son of the family, Aziz shares the same responsibilities with Asad, who also dreams of going to Russia (see below).[4] Even the work done by migrants in Russia is considered easier than the work back home. Therefore, young men aspire to leave their village and agricultural work to accumulate wealth abroad and return with a new status.

I spent a lot of time with Asad's family, helping to water the fields, plant and harvest potatoes, herd animals, cut grass, cook for feasts and so on. Every now and then, his father would order me to relax in the shade, explaining that work was a matter of status, and therefore, the youth should be working. Asad's father also informed me of his status change, which brings new duties and expectations. Since his two daughters already had children and his eldest son was able to manage most of the agricultural work, he was expected to dedicate his life to community matters and religious duties. Almost painfully, he rose from a pleasant family gathering and explained how he was now expected to show up for prayer in the mosque five times a day. Providing a contrasting perspective, his son Asad often complained that his father 'rested' in the cool house while he did all the hard work, sweating in the sun, and that his younger brothers escaped work whenever possible.

The examples of Aziz and Asad demonstrate the importance of work in defining status among young people and among siblings. The broad term for work (and generally being engaged in something) is *kor* kardan*, but when work is related to young people's duties (that is, moral obligations), the terms *mehnat** and *amal kardan* are used. These terms capture the concept of youth working hard, even suffering physical pain, for the sake of society (cf. Qodirov 1995).

These terms are sometimes not much different from *khizmat**, which describes the work that one is indebted to do (such as a son for his parents, a groom for his parents-in-law, a soldier serving in the military, even a slave for his master). The status of a person is determined by workload and the delegation of labour. In this sense, being young implies holding the status of a servant. Therefore, ageing signals a retreat from physical work and the ability to delegate labour to younger people. Umar's description of the division of labour in the Introduction ('My father says, "My son, do this work, go there, and say that"; then, he prays his *namoz** and sits at home') is in this sense representative of how life-course constructions of the Tajik connect work and age. As people grow older, they delegate hard physical work to younger (that is, subordinate) people.

It is expected that young men leave the house in the morning and only return in the evening (or briefly for lunch). Although being outside the house does not necessarily imply hard work, it strongly contributes to the young man's public role as a hardworking, highly responsible individual. As they grow older, young men begin to dominate the public sphere of their villages, which usually involves socializing in central places. Hanging out in the streets becomes symbolic of their ability to enjoy free time and demonstrate consumption without compulsorily engaging in hard, physical, agricultural work.[5] In the rural context, only when a man has sons of working age can he delegate work to them; he then rests to compensate for the hardships that he endured earlier in life. As Kobil, a young man said, 'It is better to marry early so that once your son is 15 you may lay back and rest while he does the work'.[6] In other words, Kobil suggests accelerating the developmental cycle of domestic groups so as to gain maturity and the status of a social senior as early as possible.[7] Therefore, the concept of youth is perceived as a time when an individual invests all his physical power in fulfilling public and family expectations and has minimal social rights while making decisions.

The above quotes indicate the great complexity involved when attempting to plot out the life course of young people. There are terms that overlap and others that draw boundaries between one status and another, between one stage and the next. As a matter of convenience, different authors have used different numbers of life stages – usually between four and seven. Similar to the way Uzbeks divide society into four age groups, Tajiks accord men three to five stages in life (Dor 2007: 126).[8] The age in which we are most interested here is referred to in the literature variously as 'the age of full physical power', 'the beautiful age', 'the eternal age in paradise' and so on, a period that can embrace ages anywhere from about 14 to as old as 40.

There are very different approaches to the life course regarding psychological condition and social and political maturity. Umar married recently and regrets the end of his life as a young, unmarried boy. His complaint about a young husband's hardships should be viewed in light of the constant reminders he receives by older generations of his responsibilities. He is supposed to pass through a painful domestication process,[9] against which many young people struggle. This implies that young men need sound guidance and education from the older generation; yet, it does not take into account how young people view their own actions. In other words, young men are not considered fully responsible, even after their marriage; they remain youth who need domestication by older, experienced people, including in their relationship with their spouse. Hence, Olcott refers to Tajik men as 'infantilized males' who are not responsible for their mistakes (Olcott 1992: xxi; cf. Wyn and White 1997: 53). The consequence of such a view has been shown in the conceptualization of young combatants in the Tajik civil war as victims of authoritative leaders who misused young people's enthusiasm and physical power (Chapter 3).

Except in the educational system (especially universities), 'youth' in Tajikistan applies to young males only and not to girls or young women. Several times I visited a 'youth club' and enquired about the absence of girls participating in the club's activities. One response was that it was the duty of the female representative to organize activities for them. The gender bias in youth studies has been criticized by numerous authors (Wyn and White 1997: 78; Cohen 1999: 202). Often youth has been equated to young men because they are the more visible, their activities more impressive and extraordinary than those girls are capable of in their 'bedroom culture'. Although the gender difference of youth has received some scientific attention and young women have been included in the youth category, some societies do not recognize women as youth on equal terms.

In Tajikistan, girls are regarded first as females and then as youths. A girl is expected to move from the status of girl/daughter (*dukhtar**) to that of daughter-in-law (*kelin**) as quickly as possible,[10] whereas boys are allowed broader parameters within which to experiment. A girl, having completed school, enters the marriage market. Maturity for girls is measured by biological determinants and physical appearance (breast development, body size, birth order, menstruation and so on). In contrast, a young man's maturation is judged by his psychological and social stage, not his biological development.

To summarize the discussion of youth terms and local concepts of youth, we can distinguish three ways of conceptualizing youth. First, there are the actual linguistic terms themselves, with the masculine designations – *bacha** and *mardak** – within the broader (gendered) definition *javonon**. Second, youth is related to physical work, which in the rural context has a negative connotation. This also refers to the perception that youth need to be 'domesticated' (such as through work), since by nature they tend to be undisciplined and irresponsible (the 'infantilized male'). Third, youth is a stage in the life cycle of a Tajik male structured by rituals and communal rights. Based on these terms and concepts, I wish to extend the discussion in two directions: religion and migration. Both phenomena have become relevant more recently (since perestroika), and have affected notions and concepts of youth, young people's duties within the family, community and country, and young people's self-perception of the period of youth.

The Concept of Youth in Islam

Here, I wish to consider youth within the Tajik concept of Islam, based on my observations in the field. To this end, I will examine how different movements – or, rather, different ideas of Islam – frame youth and its roles. I will also discuss the implications of these movements for young people in their social environment. Here, I would like to further develop this idea and discuss the concepts offered by Islamic movements that have been introduced and localized in recent times, resulting in a 'new Islam' (Mandaville 2001: 86).[11] These concepts contrast with the traditional and state-supported idea of submissive youth, because according to the concepts of 'new Islam' youth should be submissive only to God, and perhaps to one of his mediators. Before God, each individual has to answer for their acts by themselves (and not through one's parents or siblings, whom one must respect and honour but not necessarily obey). In this sense, studying the conceptualization of youth in Islam opens up a new sphere of reflection on youth in Tajikistan. However, in this study I will neither provide an exhaustive review of the existing literature on Islam in Central Asia nor discuss all of the nuances and interpretations of Islam that exist in Tajikistan. Rather, I will solely analyse my own ethnographic material in terms of the conceptualization of youth and what young people themselves have revealed to me regarding their individual interests in certain interpretations of Islam that are available to them.

Saodat Olimova (2002, 2006) has provided detailed descriptions of the kind of interest that young Tajik people have in new Islamic interpretations, not only as a source of social status in the face of communist authoritarianism but also as a way to emancipate themselves from local structural and parental domestication.[12] She discusses young people's disagreement with their elders' interpretations of Islam, which young people see as using Islam as a pretext to exert control over others rather than living it as a faith or in direct relation to God.[13] Young people want to be informed about Islam; they want to understand their religion and perform their duties correctly (Roy 2004: 148–200; Olimova 2006).

I mentioned earlier that religiosity is not only a family matter but also a parental strategy for the diversification of siblings. Thus, it would be difficult to estimate whether there are more or fewer young men interested in Islam today than there were, let us say, five years ago; rather, we should take a look at when and how Islam becomes important as a spiritual resource. Observing how young people react when they watch the numerous Islamic videos that circulate gave me some idea of their degree of receptiveness to new interpretations (see below). However, the imported (new) forms of Islam are not the only ones that are regarded as attractive. Local religious authorities also compete for the attention of young people, drawing upon different sources and discourses to establish their legitimacy.

The Gift of Youth

How does Tajik Islam define youth? Is there any such definition of youth in Tajik Islam, or do purportedly Islamic interpretations merely reflect local perceptions? These are questions that I will address in this section. A recent dissertation by Manja Stephan (2008) has presented a more distinctive view of the maturation of youth through Islam from the perspective of Tajik parents. Stephan (ibid.: 147–48) refers to the concept of *gunohdor* (being sinful, committing sins that will become relevant before God) and the idea of *aql giriftan/rasidan* (gaining reason, maturing) as part of religious maturity, which according to the prophet Muhammad's biography and religious interpretations is set at the age of 9 for girls and 12 for boys (Jum'aev 2001: 27). From this age onward, children are considered full members of Muslim society and expected to perform religious duties such as fasting. Moreover, they can also get married after reaching this level of maturity, and their death, if it occurs after this age, is regarded as the death of an adult and will be judged by God according to adult standards.

In this context, Olimova has mentioned the importance of Islam in socialization processes: 'the masses of Muslims in Tajikistan are socialized as Muslims in the process of transition to adulthood . . . through the influence of the family, through educational means, through marriage and the creation of a family. The adaptation of youth and their inclusion in social life in modern Tajikistan also means their integration into the main structure of society' (Olimova 2006: 166). According to her informants, gaining maturity implies becoming a practising Muslim: 'young people believe that the realizing of rituals and norms form the transition to the adult class. They are of the opinion that in the process of becoming an adult one would have to become stricter in observing religious norms and should extend and intensify their participation in rituals and religious feasts' (ibid.: 166–67). This nicely reflects the idea that religious practice comes with age, whereas basic concepts can be transmitted during childhood by a local mullah. However, in the course of her analysis, it turns out that instead of moving passively through this stage of the life cycle, many young people today actively engage in religious practices, thus accelerating their maturity. Young people, she claims, can be as religious as people in their forties, and are much more religious than their parents were at a similar age.

Emancipation through Islam

During my investigations, I chanced upon a blog that condemned the view of adolescence as a phase between childhood and adulthood as a Western invention, contrasting this view with Islam, which accorded young people maturity from puberty onwards, as soon as they reached the 'age of awareness'.[14] This reflects much of what has been discussed as individualization and modernity in Islam in recent years (e.g., Eickelman and Piscatori 1996, Eickelman and Anderson 1999; Jacobson 1998; Roy 2004; Olimova 2006; Kakpo 2007). Young people increasingly see religion as an individual connection with God, independent of their parents' claims regarding traditions. Islam allows them to emancipate themselves from tradition without necessarily confronting their parents directly. This aspect of Islam also emerges in religious teachings (see below), where mullahs exhort young people to take responsibility for their own lives. In this manner, what other studies approach as a generational conflict appears to be more a redefinition of youth within Islam. This may not necessarily lead to intergenerational conflicts, as the Tajik examples show, but provides young people with the necessary resources to find individual solutions for their situation within the larger society, allowing them to free themselves of parental control – regardless of whether this pertains to masculine crises in France or the stunted future of youth in Tajikistan (Dudoignon 2004c; Olimova 2006).

We have seen that *javonon* is a term referring to young men, who dedicate their physical energy and abilities in the service of family and community. Being closely aligned with concepts of work, youth in the local context refers to a period of (political) immaturity but maximal physical strength. Many religious authorities draw on similar ideas in the context of religious performance. They see the physical act of praying *namoz* (bending down and getting up) as the actual work of religion, and here youth have the physical advantage over their elders. This may sound like an odd way of looking at it, but in Tajikistan it makes sense when seen as a reaction to previous constructions of religiosity that were associated with ageing. Especially during the Soviet era, when religious activities were strictly controlled by the state, only older people could seriously engage in religious life, with the goal of purifying their past sins. Against this background, the conceptualization of youth in Islam as a physical advantage seems less strange. Thus, Eshon Nuriddinjon, one of the most popular religious authorities in contemporary Tajikistan, emphasizes that youth's advantage in Islam is their physical advantage when observing religious rules. According to him, youth means having the ability to (physically) serve God, one's parents and the community:

> Young Muslims – youth who honour the Koran – you must know the value of youth before old age comes. Youth means hardship . . . The duties of youth lie in obedience to God, in being bound to God, in serving the parents, in serving the society before old age draws near . . . While you are young, you can do all this, but once you are old, you will no longer have the power to show obedience to God, no strength to work, no strength to serve anybody . . . The Prophet has said that youth means a person from the age of 16 to 33 years . . . Dear young people, the Prophet has said that the young man who is clean, well-mannered

and well-educated, and who serves God, his parents and society – this young man is dear to his parents, dear to the neighbourhood (*mahalla**), dear to the Prophet and dear to God.[15]

Eshon Nuriddinjon, in his speeches, encourages young people to live in accordance with Islam, and preaches that Islam calls for a young person's submission to parents and community (cf. Andreev 1953: 190). This concept of Islam as a submissive practice, however, sometimes clashes with other interpretations of Islam that accord young people independence from parental and community authority.[16]

Eshon Nuriddinjon still follows a rather traditional interpretation of youth – that the aim of youth, first and foremost, is to serve society and one's parents – and underscores this interpretation using religious arguments. This view is reinforced by Mullah Sirojiddin, who dedicated an entire meeting (the *mavludi nabi* celebration in honour of the Prophet's birthday) to the problem of youth.[17] 'Dear youth (*javononi aziz*)', he said, 'today young men do not respect their father anymore and daughters do not respect their mother. You have gone far from Islam . . . [M]*ardi benamoz* [a man who is not a praying, practising believer], God is fed up with you'. Throughout the meeting (which lasted about an hour) he spoke to youth directly, without addressing them in the third person or as a general category. He sees youth as a product of political and social degradation and seeks to remind them of their duty before God. At this meeting he also condemned those elder mullahs who would use Islam for their own interests and exhorted youth to engage with Islam, to take responsibility for their own faith and not postpone it until old age. In this sense, he demands from youth a serious engagement with Islam which would simultaneously lead to a respectful attitude towards parents.

Such concepts can be found in Islamic interpretations that have been removed from their cultural contexts and travel globally by way of religious students. Although global Islamic concepts have repeatedly arisen out of an Arab cultural context, they can still appear to be culturally neutral as they are linked to an imagined global (culturally independent) Islam rather than to Arab traditions. One of the scholars who has integrated these global Islamic concepts into Tajik religious debates is Sulaimon, of the Islamic University in Dushanbe. In an interview he spoke of a youth (*al-shubab*) concept that is analogous to the Prophet Muhammad's life. Having studied in other Muslim countries, he framed his understanding as a culturally independent concept of youth to which Tajik young people could subscribe. He explained it to me:

> SULAIMON: Youth is the most important period from the point of view of Islam . . . A person will be asked three things: One, where did you get your wealth from and how did you spend it? Two, how did you spend

your period of youth? Did you pass it well or not? Three, what did you do with your knowledge?

The period of youth, if you look at Islam, gives youth the highest responsibility . . . The requirement of Islam is that youth must be most active in spreading Islam, in practising Islam, in looking for and learning about Islam. The requirement is that youth must be very active.

S.R.: Is there any specific age?

SULAIMON: You see, our Prophet says, you have to encourage our children to worship and pray from an early age; not by force – just say, 'My son, you should pray'. And when they are 10 years old you use some kind of pressure on them. From the age of 10 you have to distinguish between a girl and a boy.

. . . Women become responsible with their menstruation before God . . . For boys the matter is different, a boy has a sexual dream as a symbol of maturity, for the first time. If he doesn't have any, then with 16 years he will be declared mature.

. . .

Youth – this is the end of a period (*holat*) that is called *al-kuhūla*. Islam does not give a specific point of ending, sometimes this starts around 40 years. *Al-kuhūla* means that he has gained experiences and has become mature . . .

In the *shariat* [Islamic law], *kuhūla* starts at the age of 40. Because at this age our Prophet became a prophet and was ordered by God to start his *da'va* (calling people to Islam) . . . From 40 years until 60 years it is *kuhūla*; over 65 it is already old age.

Youth means *al-shabāb*, and the age before that is *al-murāhiq* (teenager).[18]

In the interview, Sulaimon argued that this Arab terminology applies equally to men and women. This account provides insight into how Sulaimon has identified the life of the Prophet with a more generalized concept of maturation. Noteworthy is the absence of ritual structuring from the life course of the Prophet; for example, marriage, which culturally is an important step in social maturation, is not mentioned. Furthermore, he does not provide a period of adulthood or parenthood; rather, the maturation process depends on the intellectual ability to gain, spread and apply knowledge, and on an age-related (biological) structuring of life. Youth is related to the companions of the Prophet who helped spread Islam, such as Ali, who was a child when he embraced Islam. When the Prophet died, Ali was just 25 years old, but he had been the Prophet's right-hand man at times. Also, Musabi ibn Umair was chosen to be the first ambassador for Islam when he was only aged 20. Sulaimon offered up other examples of famous people who had been rather young but highly appreciated by the Prophet. In contrast to how Eshon Nuriddinjon has conceptualized the youth period as submissive and duty-bound to serve, Sulaimon refers to an Islamic youth concept that suggests a heightened responsibility to one's society. Although physical strength is mentioned as well (the ability to spread Islam), mental capacity is regarded as central to the maturation process.

Comparing the youth concept introduced by Islamic scholars to local youth concepts, the former appears to be an emancipation from the latter. Islam, Sulaimon claims, provides youth with responsibility and special tasks. This has even been extended to declare that the status of a Muslim in paradise is an 'eternal youth'.[19] The rhetoric of subordinate youth is replaced here for the most part with a youth concept that seems suspiciously similar to globalized Western youth concepts, as promoted for instance by the United Nations.[20] The responsibility towards society accorded to youth in Islam parallels the demand of the UN to delegate more rights to young people and encourage them to engage in their communities. Hence, we see a concept of 'youth' that is evolving today in various parts of the world. Although often used to emphasize an opposition between Islam and the West – for instance, to contrast moral, hardworking Muslim youth with amoral, leisure-obsessed Western youth – the Islamic concept appears to share with the Western concept many ideas, namely, those of success, agency and independence from parental and political domination.

Brothers in God

Whereas the global notion of Islamic youth is a resource for youth, the formation of movements and groups is a process of crystallization around identities based on, for instance, specific political agendas. Let us go back to the Tajik civil war of the 1990s to analyse examples of communitas in Turner's (1995) sense. Bonding in groups and among similar groups (such as the subgroups of the United Tajik Opposition) was done on the basis of a common notion of brotherhood.[21] Cancelling out the strict age hierarchy that exists among siblings, 'youth' became the core ideology of a shared identity. Brotherhood in combatant groups was less a specific 'youth' term than a term imbued with youthful qualities, namely, physical power and a fighter ethos.

Let us consider the way in which 'brother' (*barodar**), as a non-kinship term, is conceptualized in Tajikistan: 'Brother is the one who helps you in times of hardship', explains Nosiri Khisrav, a poet and philosopher (and Ismaili leader) of the eleventh century (quoted in Shukurov et al. 1969: 149). The general view is that a brother is somebody you can rely on and trust – this completely contradicts the idea of a brother as a potential enemy and competitor and suggests that the word 'brother', at its very essence, is a term with positive connotations.

During one of my field trips I was given several little books that had been initially distributed among refugees in Afghanistan, especially those who lived in the refugee camp at Qunduz, which was the camp supported by 'Arabistan' (Arab countries). Later, when the refugees returned to Tajikistan, these booklets were brought en masse and distributed, which is how one of my informants received many of them. One is titled 'Islamic brotherhood' (Alavon 1997). The booklet explains the rules and advantages of brotherhood, and provides many historical examples from Muslim history. Brotherhood in God is said to be more than kinship – it is asserted as the basis of Muslim society. While it is not explicitly reserved to men, all but one example refer to men. Brotherhood is a sacred relation; thus 'from the seven groups of those who on the Day of Last Judgement will rest in the shadow of the throne of God, one refers to two men (*mard*), that have made friendship (*dusti*) in the name of God' (ibid.: 14).

Towards the end of the booklet, the author elucidates the purpose of the book: 'Ai, youth joining the call, brave soldiers of Islam! Today you are the only hope of bright Islam! The hopeful eye of Islam rests upon you, and wishes to see you reviving the honour, the state and the unity of this religion' (ibid.: 110). The booklet directly addresses youth as the vanguards of a future Muslim nation (*millati musulmoni*) under one banner (*bairaqi Islom*). It is a call to understand brotherhood as the necessary strength that links youth beyond kinship (*khesh*) and tribal affiliations (*qavm*). The ideas put forward in this booklet are similar to the notion of a young person living independent of their relatives, in this instance for the greater goal of establishing a larger Muslim community.

How were the terms 'brother' and 'youth' used during the Tajik civil war, and how were they applied among combatant groups? Did the idea of vanguard and its potential use to maximize youth under a common concept apply to the Tajik conflict? The civil war, especially the involvement of the Islamic opposition, is often referred to as *jangi* barodarkushī*, 'the war between brothers'.[22] The idea that underlies the concept of *barodar* (brother) is unity and sharing the same set of ideas regarding life, which are expressed in group-specific practices. A female informant who lived in a combatant group during the war told me:

SAFARMOH: The first day after I was caught, I started learning all the *suras**, and already by the second day I was praying with them. Then we had training most of the time – how to shoot, where, and when. When the commander offered to marry me to any one of the men, I refused, and he said, 'Okay, keep up your prayers and don't talk to the men for any reason'. If anyone had troubled me, he would have killed the man – they knew this . . .

S.R.: How many girls were you?

SAFARMOH: Six or seven.

S.R.: From among these seven girls, how many got married?

SAFARMOH: Five of them took a husband, but another girl and I – we did not marry. When they captured me I was 14 years old, and the commander himself said, 'If you had been a little older I would have married you, but since you are young, I will look after you like my daughter . . .

One *azatin* [Ossetian?] took a Tajik wife; the commander forced him to
marry even when [he] didn't want to. He would say, 'In these mountains,
what should I do with a wife?' However, the commander forced him
to marry in order to prevent him from running away, because the two
azatin [in our group] were snipers.

. . . [Our commander] was . . . really good . . . So far, he has helped
us; if I need money I ask him, and if I need work he finds me a job. He
told me, 'I will give you whatever job you want, because you suffered so
much – you beat people and you fought in the war, so we will give you
an important job.[23]

Safarmoh perceives her commander as a psychological specialist, who managed
the group skilfully despite all the different personalities and expectations of its
members. Their group comprised about sixty people – it was one of the larger
combatant groups. Within the group, they regarded each other as brothers and
sisters, as different as siblings are and as united as a family is imagined to be. The
account of Safarmoh goes on to show that the civil war alliances were long-term
alliances that did not end when the fighting ended. The creation of a family-like
institution with a strong, fatherly commander appeared to have been effective as
a collective concept.

Another young man – let us call him Muhiddin – was captured in the mountains while attempting to escape the fighting in Dushanbe. He was taken to a
training camp in Afghanistan, where he learned the basic principles of Islam and
certain skills, such as 'how to fly a plane, to throw bombs and fight', as he told me.
He further quoted his kidnappers: "After you cross the border (to Afghanistan),
you are free", they had told us, "and then you may go to Iran, Pakistan, America –
wherever you want". We joined the camp, and the people there were good people
– they were within Islam. They were not with girls and thieves'.

Muhiddin did not learn the Koran by heart, but he was taught enough to
spend a large part of the interview reciting specific passages, which he then interpreted for me. After his return from Afghanistan, he entered the state military
service, together with twenty-two other fellow fighters, but he did not stay in
it after the peace agreement had been signed in 1997 and some order had been
installed: 'I remained until our homeland (*vatan**) had calmed down (*tenji*)'.
Then he returned to his village. Some of his co-fighter brothers (*barodaron*),
however, remained within the military; others went to Iran, Russia, or returned
to their villages. He has some contact with them, but he lacks the financial means
to visit them regularly.

When questioned about the age of his fellow fighters, Muhiddin told me, 'We
had older ones and younger ones. I told you, once you became a brother (*barodar*),
it did not matter – your age did not matter anymore'. For him, the perception of
barodar was that hierarchies had been eliminated; these brothers had equal status

and were therefore very different from his brothers within his own family, with whom he had hierarchical relations. Any question regarding his fellow fighters' age was rebuffed with the argument that once brotherhood (based on Islamic principles) had been established, these differences – referring to the Tajik seniority system – were eliminated and everyone was equal before God. This status was apparently only achieved within a group – again an exclusive distinction.

Muhiddin discussed the concepts of siblingship under Islam, and he argued for a construction of friendship that aims at guiding others along the right path (Roche 2010). In this sense, relations between brothers in Islam are not structured in terms of hierarchy; rather, each encourages the other to follow the right path according to the principles of Islam. Instead of a man waiting for religiosity to arrive with age, there is a youthful engagement with Islam, a way to bring together traditional concepts of youth that relate to physical work and social emancipation.

Schlee (2008: 37–53) has argued that exclusion practices serve to maintain a group at a certain size. When the group becomes too large and risks the depletion of its capacities (resources), exclusion practices are intensified in order to reduce the number of members. This also holds true for combatant groups, which were rather small in size but numerous in kind. Within Muhiddin's brotherhood group, too, certain cultural boundaries were erected while others were abolished, such as the marriage ritual (high costs, social networks, birth order); the intent of these practices was to ensure that the group retained an optimal size. Earlier I emphasized that it is groups that act, not categories; the example of an abstract global Islamic youth category and the concrete combatant groups demonstrates this opposition well.

While among many elderly people Islam is seen as a way to domesticate youth as they are absorbed into the religious community, youth sees Islam as a domestication of the self and a way to oppose local traditions that they find restrictive. Brotherhood becomes the bond among youth, who are called to lead Muslims toward a single, united Muslim nation. This redefinition of Islam as a vanguard concept is not restricted to Tajikistan, but its beginnings can be seen in the Islamic Revival movement organized by Said Abdullo Nuri in the 1970s (Chapter 3). At that time, Islam became a strong concept which many young people used to confront communism. That a civil war resulted, however, had less to do with the concept of Islam and vanguardism than it did with the political situation of the time. More important is the fact that these youthful concepts have grown in popularity since the civil war ended, turning Tajikistan into a dynamic place in which youth in particular are engaging with various movements of Islam.

The Impact of Migration on Youth Concepts

Migration in Tajikistan has classically been linked to high population growth and a lack of resources (over 90 per cent of the country consists of mountainous areas that are agriculturally unproductive). For many people, migration is the only alternative to poverty, the only way to increase their standard of life, or the only solution to escape from a vicious cycle of indebtedness. Statistical data provide a rough sense of the dimensions of the migration issue, and consequently the extent of the impact that it has had on Tajik society.

In 2005, migrants sent back home, according to official data, as much as 600 million dollars through bank transfers. Umarov claims that remittances from migrants outside the country 'exceed governmental budgetary expenditures by a third' (Umarov 2006: 97–99; see also Mughal 2007). If we add informal transfers of remittances, which comprise 40 per cent of the total figure, Umarov estimates an inflow of about 1.5 billion dollars in 2005 – an amount that is 3.4 times governmental budgetary expenditures. Nor are the official data reliable when it comes to the number of migrants. Estimates range from 600,000 – which is definitely too low – to 1.5 million and as high as 2 million people (out of a population of about 7 million). While the most recent studies concentrate on seasonal or temporary economic migration, I learned during my experiences in Qarotegin that many former combatants have settled in Russia, awaiting a change of regime. Since any attempt to return would mean a risk of imprisonment, these men continue to live in Russia, while their children and wives remain in a difficult economic and political situation back home.[24]

As in other countries, migration is classically linked to unemployment rates: Olimova and Bosc (2003) state that the highest unemployment rate exists for young people aged 18 to 29.[25] For many young people, migration gives them their first opportunity for legitimate employment – often, the only alternative back home is to enter the drug trade. 'Anxiety about the future is common, and many young people are resentful of adults whom they hold responsible for creating a society in which the youth feel unwanted. The appearance of this new group of socially excluded youth with no job experience and dim employment prospects has spurred labour migration' (ibid.: 15). Those who remain at home continue to be dependent on their parents and have few opportunities to develop their own career and earn their own living. Even those who do find jobs are often so underpaid that they remain dependent on their extended family for their basic needs.

The majority of young people travel to Russia (and Kazakhstan) in search of work and a decent income. In Qarotegin, I observed that almost only men migrate in search of work; however, this strong gender bias does not exist everywhere. Although I found only one instance where a woman had migrated in search of work, many women accompany their husbands when they migrate, temporarily or for good. (The most common reason why women are sent to Russia is to undergo infertility treatment.)

My statistical analysis of Shahrigul – an area that is highly affected by migration – shows that in some age cohorts up to 50 per cent of the men leave or

Table 4.1: Cohort-specific percentages of men who opted for migration (Shahrigul).

	Number of Men Who Migrate	Size of Age Cohort	Cohort-specific Percentages
16–19	7	64	10.94
20–23	25	58	43.10
24–27	30	62	48.39
28–31	16	36	44.44
32–35	13	26	50.00
36–39	18	36	50.00
40–43	12	26	46.15
44–47	14	31	45.16
48–51	2	20	10.00
52–55	4	18	22.22
Total	141	377	37.40

have left home for seasonal or long-term migration. Table 4.1 shows that approximately half of the male population stays abroad temporarily or for a longer period of time, with a sharp drop between the age groups 44 to 47 and 48 to 51. It is around this age that men usually start getting some support from a son who is old enough to take over the difficult task of migration, thus allowing his father to retire from physical work – that is, to enter a new stage of life.

Against this statistical background we can understand the possible impact that migration has in various cultural fields outside the economic sector. Since my interest in this study is youth, I will restrict the following analysis to the way in which migration has contributed to negotiations concerning youth status and youth concepts. Before discussing youth bulge and migration in the chapter's conclusion, I will focus next on the cultural dimension of migration.

Migration: Dream and Nightmare

The burden of responsibility on young men in Tajikistan is enormous and surpasses any previous duty that young people in the nation have had to shoulder. Challenging working conditions in Russia have made labour migration increasingly difficult. This is why the local discourse on youth and migration includes the belief that young men are being asked to do more than they are capable of. Although physical effort is central to the concept of youth, the expectation that young men should assume full responsibility for their family – including their parents – leads many parents to imagine migration as a nightmare, while young men themselves have accepted it as a way of life. The dominant discourse that leaving one's country is difficult and unpleasant, and done solely out of economic necessity, is based on the assumption that Tajikistan is, after all, the homeland (*vatan**) and central to Tajik identity. This is, however, a distorted perception, as is evident in the responses of migrants to a survey conducted by Olimova and Bosc (2003: 35). They asked people who, before leaving for Russia, had held positions in Tajikistan (for instance, as teachers) whether they would return to their old jobs if they became available again. Only 20 per cent said 'yes', while 57 per cent said 'no' – thus indicating that they had chosen migration as a basic life strategy. But most young men found their very first job in Russia.

Let us now take a look at some narratives that exemplify different discourses regarding migration. To these, I shall add my own analysis to show how migrants' narratives have shaped the meaning of the journey in a way that makes it highly attractive to young people.

> ASAD: What is a nice way of life for youth? To go to Russia, saying, 'Let's earn lots of money, let's become rich, let's build a house in town, buy a foreign car' – this is what our boys like, and I like it too. Then they like wearing a tie, their hair nicely cut, black trousers, and they like a white wife from town.
> S.R.: Would you like to go to Russia?
> ASAD: I would definitely like to go there, but I am still too young. Many have gone to Russia from our Lakhsh – the majority of our youth have gone to Russia.
> S.R.: And what do they say about Russia?
> ASAD: They go there, then they call up and say, 'Come here, I have earned so much money – take this money, but I will stay here a while longer' – this is what they say when they telephone home. A young man continues working in Russia because his father allows him to, since he is also interested in the money. Then he comes back home and improves his family's living conditions. His father, so that his son should not suffer at home, does all the [agricultural] work himself. The young man sends home money, and he even manages to save some of it for himself over there. If he ends up saving lots of money, he puts it in a bank there, and here they can take it from the Tajik bank. At times, when a young man returns home, his mother asks, 'My son, how much money have you earned?' And he replies, 'Mother, I worked hard and earned $10,000 or $3,000'.[26]

> S.R.: What is your opinion – how was life when you were young, and how is it today for youth?
> ANON.: Today, the living conditions seem to matter to everybody [not only to the parents or the father]. In the past, living conditions were excellent, but today there are no jobs, and the unemployed young men are forced (*majbur*) to go to Russia.
> S.R.: Are today's young people different from those during the civil war?

ANON.: Earlier on, boys would study, but today they only walk around on the streets. Today's generation is different. The young people after the war do not study anymore; they are brainless (*be savod*, lit. 'uneducated'). Today only a few of them want to learn or study.[27]

S.R.: How was it for youth during the Soviet times and how is it today?
HABIBULLO: Life has become more difficult today; there were no problems during the Soviet times – we had work at that time, but today there is no work. There is only one factory in Shahrituz – that's all! This is why young men are forced to go [to Russia] and work; they go there looking for a better life, but they have no time to study in colleges.[28]

S.R.: How long did you stay in Russia?
SAIFIDDIN: For six years.
S.R.: During those six years, how much money did you send back home and how much did you bring back with you when you returned?
SAIFIDDIN: I did send money. For example, I sent money home once in two years.
S.R.: How much, for example?
SAIFIDDIN: First I sent $600, and then a year later I sent $1,000 to my father, then I sent $100 to $150 every month to my younger brother who studies in Dushanbe.
S.R.: Why didn't your younger brother go to work in Russia?
SAIFIDDIN: I didn't want him to go to Russia – firstly, because he doesn't know the language well, and secondly, because life is difficult there. If you don't know the rules, the militia harass you a lot. I have gone through these experiences – I know how difficult it is. That is why I don't want my younger brother to go to Russia.
S.R.: Are you the eldest brother?
SAIFIDDIN: Yes . . .
S.R.: Did you get married because your parents needed a *kelin* (daughter-in-law), or will you take your wife to Russia?
SAIFIDDIN: I have no wish to live in Tajikistan – the mountains squeeze in from all four sides. If you get used to living there, then you want to stay there – it is a different kind of freedom that you can experience in Russia. About my wife – until I find a good job there, she will stay with my father and mother. After finding a good job, I will rent a flat and take her with me to Russia – only if my parents agree, I'll take her.[29]

These interview excerpts are arranged to reveal varying views on migration, which differ according to the person's gender and, particularly, age.[30] For parents who grew up during the Soviet era, migration, while necessary, is not viewed as an appropriate or desirable way for their young sons to be forced to make a living, while the sons perceive migration as an opportunity to emancipate themselves from parental control. The young migrant's description of how 'the mountains squeeze in from all four sides' is a wonderful image that explains how communities place pressure on young men and how they find release from it in Russia. As the young pupil (Asad) explains, migration entails liberation from agricultural work.[31] My observation that migrant young people tended to mature more quickly than their village peers was confirmed by Rahmat (aged 26), who declared, 'Yes! Our views, beliefs and ideas soon become like those of adults'. This is another reason why migrating to Russia becomes the dream of most young men who long for a more respected position within the village. Similar to, though less intense than, the observations of Rousseau et al. (1998: 385) regarding young Somalis eagerly waiting for their turn to leave home, Tajik value travel as a way of reaching maturity – an idea that is strongly embedded in their imaginations. In many societies in which migration is common, young people imagine lifestyles in a world that offers a limited set of options but a large repertoire of possible interpretations; and, on this basis, they reimagine their native place as something very different from what it is (Appadurai 1998). It is in such 'ethnoscapes' that dynamics develop and imagined lives are produced, based on information spread by various channels (media, rumours, stories and so on).

This is why many pupils are eager to leave for work – sooner rather than later.[32] For Asad, it is not merely migration but the general idea of leaving the village in order to 'become somebody' that is important. As the eldest son, Asad does most of the agricultural work, which he perceives as a heavy burden. For him, an increase in social status goes hand in hand with not having to do agricultural work. His description of status is linked to ideas of 'walking around in clean and nice clothes, with one's hair brushed neatly, or leaning on one's own car'. Asad's dream is reinforced through the migrants' narratives of Russia as a place where they experience total freedom and independence from parental and communal control, paired with the flow of pictures transmitted by television and returnees' demonstrations of material success.

Against this image of freedom and increased status stands parents' fear that their sons might become alienated from their homeland (*vatan*). Although young migrants certainly do retain a strong sense of attachment to their *vatan*, those who have decent jobs in Russia are ready to do anything to stay there, or at least return to Russia as soon as possible once having gone back home to Tajikistan. Their village appears 'backward' and 'underdeveloped' to them when compared to the cosmopolitan life in Russia. (The migration discourse in Russia itself varies from this, as migrants are constantly confronted with everyday problems.) Hence, this sense of double belonging – to Russia and to their own *vatan* – is an inherent part of migrants' worlds.

One final incident serves to emphasize this dual picture of Russia (as a dream and a nightmare). Once I witnessed a phone call during which a young man shouted at his cousin in Russia, telling him that he should never complain to his parents again about hardship – if he was too weak to bear the hardship, he should just come back. If he complained again, the young man warned him that he would have him evicted from his flat, where he was living with two of his cousins. Just before this telephone call, the father of the caller's cousin had come to the caller's house and had shared news of his son's suffering in Russia with his elder brother, the caller's father.

This brief anecdote represents much more than the relevance of kinship in migration – it shows how migrants consciously control and manipulate information. Parents are left with an ambivalent picture about migrant life in Russia: on the one hand it involves hardship and risk, while on the other it is a source of wealth and success. I argue that young men consciously maintain this ambivalent picture because it allows them to exploit the status change they expect to receive in their local community. This status change works in two ways: In Russia, young men exploit their youthful freedom and experience, and copy and follow European ways of being a 'youth' (premarital sexual relations, consumption of goods and so on).[33] Back home, due to their enormous responsibility towards their family, they experience the respect accorded an adult. By controlling the information flow regarding their experiences, nourished by fantasies about life in the destination country, migrants manage to separate the two geographical areas into two distinct worlds between which they switch – a phenomenon that Boris Nieswand (2007) has called the 'status paradox of migration'.

Through selective and interpretative narratives, migrants create the necessary discourses that allow them to separate their lives in the village from their experiences of migration. Local interpretations of the narratives and the approval of the visible results of migration (behaviour, economic success) are the response to migrants' strategies. As a consequence, migrants are compensated with a status change. This interpretation also implies that a concept such as youth does not travel as a fixed concept but is redefined, localized, adapted and thereby 'translated' into local meanings.

Asad (see above) has mentioned that migrants are treated differently once they return home – if possible, they are spared hard work. Thus, instead of having to tackle agricultural work, they spend much of their time with friends. This is certainly not true for all migrants, but my observation supports the view that migrants receive a lot of respect from their parents and the community, and are reported to behave respectfully and helpfully towards their own family and community members; they display their social role as sons in a demonstrative way. As Weyland writes of an Egyptian village, migrants first break with patriarchal hegemony, and once having 'realized household separation they gradually come closer to their father's households again by complying in a demonstrative way with a son's obligations towards his parents' (Weyland 1993: 206). Parents try to make migrants' lives easier back home until they leave again – for the unknown country of hardship. In other words, migrants behave like adults and not like youth in the local context, but enjoy an extension of youthful independence from their family and freer access to cash.

Migration as a Rite of Passage

During the Soviet era military service certified that a young man was healthy and sound; if he did not opt for military service, he was suspected of having some physical or mental deficiency and therefore was not considered a good candidate in the marriage market. Migration has replaced military service as a rite of passage. Today, a young man who has been to Russia is said to be clever enough to 'find money anywhere', girls claim; working in Russia has become synonymous with 'seeing the world' (*duniyo didagī*) and gaining knowledge. Travel increases a young man's social status because it is believed to completely transform him. This is demonstrated by the migrant's attitude of respect and honour towards his elders, points illustrated in the following interview extract:

> MAHMUD: Having seen the world (*duniyo didagī*) has an impact on the character. A person who has never gone out of the village differs from one who has seen the world.
> S.R.: How does he differ, for example?
> MAHMUD: In the way he deals with people, for example, in the way he receives guests; then his manners and conduct improve, and he treats his relatives well. Because after having seen the world and come back, he sees what travel means, and he honours his brothers, his grandfather and the *mŭisafed**.[34]

I have mentioned before that social status is gained by a person's generosity and ability to redistribute goods. A migrant not only comes back with money and goods but also knowledge and mature behaviour. In return, he is treated with respect by his family and community. Rousseau et al. have shown how travel is integrated into local concepts among Somalis. Their contention is that, 'travel, regardless of its reason or purpose, is considered to be a learning process and a source of wisdom in itself' (Rousseau et al. 1998: 136). Along similar lines, Helms (1988) has discussed the importance of travel in increasing one's power and knowledge. It is in this sense that Tajik society recognizes the significance of travel, but with a slight difference concerning the importance of the homeland (*vatan*). Undertaking travel in order to gain knowledge is an ancient motif for the Tajik, and Tajik constructions of migration fit into this idea.[35] Although most of the migration patterns today are said to be driven by economic necessity, the idea of 'seeing the world' and gaining knowledge and experience in this way still persists in the Tajik notion of migration (*muhojiri*).[36] Integral to the idea of travel is the notion of being separated from one's (beloved) homeland (*vatan*) and being deprived of daily commodities. In another sense, travel for the sake of learning and travel out of economic necessity may complement each other. Girls of a marriageable age considered migration (or at least education) an essential feature in a young man, similar to the view of military service in earlier times. 'If a man manages to survive or even earn money in Russia, he will manage life', they explained to me; his experiences will serve as a guarantee of future security for his family. Boys who had never left the village were considered by those girls as childish, immature and unable to provide security.

Migration is so drastically different from any other kind of employment that it has been integrated into leaving-home and returning-home rituals. Thus, a young man who is going to Russia for the first time has farewell parties thrown in his honour and is invited to the home of his relatives. Those who can spare the money contribute financially to the migrant's trip which, when the migrant returns, is reciprocated in the form of gifts. I observed this in Lakhsh, but I am not sure whether this holds true everywhere. In Shahrigul, for instance, the emphasis was on the migrant's return. After spending a long time abroad, the migrant would be reintegrated into the community and accorded a high status only after generously sharing his wealth with the community (by sponsoring a meal in the local teahouse/mosque, for example).

In another village, migrants made monetary donations to the teahouse/mosque, which the community used to buy television sets and other equipment. In fact, in one village, the migrant community financed a mosque the size of a small cathedral (while the international organization that was locally active financed and ran a health clinic in a small trailer due to the lack of medical services in the entire area). This shows that migration in many villages in Qarotegin is closely connected to religious life and the (male) community's well-being. Whether we should see migrants' investment as a kind of payment made by young men to retain their place in the male community or as a way to increase their individual social status by obtaining the collective respect of the religious male community is a matter of perception. I believe that both aspects play a role, because young men are primarily constructed as subordinate subjects who need to develop slowly into full members of the local community. Moreover, children's status also reflects on that of their parents, which is principally determined by the male community of the teahouse and mosque.

The enormous economic importance of migrants' earnings, on the other hand, has increased young men's actual power. They find themselves raised to a higher status within their society. This change in status, however, can be temporary and depends to a large extent on their continued success in supporting their families. Status that is acquired in this way can also rapidly plummet. Therefore, we can assume that the status that is acquired through migration is temporary and needs to be renewed on a regular basis, since savings tend to be used up rather quickly.

Based on van Gennep's (1999) concept of rites of passage, Turner (1995) sees modern youth movements as the continuation of traditional rites of passage associated with adolescence. Migration can be perceived as a Turnerian liminal phase in which young people experience humiliation and create solidarities in communitas (yet remain reluctant to organize into groups). They come back transformed and their behaviour is perceived as that of an adult – the migrant differs from those of his peers who do not leave the village and therefore remain 'young'. In migration, it is the 'world' – and not the state nor the family or community – that domesticates youth. The difficulties experienced during the journey and the harsh conditions under which migrants live are said to domesticate a young man. If travel is successful, the migrant is accorded a new status back home. Success depends on the aim of travel – if it is to visit relatives, then stories and knowledge are the proof of success; if it is for economic gain, then bringing back cash or goods evinces a young man's ability to master life. This can also be demonstrated by the opposite. A young man in his late twenties in Lakhsh had to return home due to ill health. He was accorded no respect in his village because his travels were unsuccessful and he failed to navigate the rite of passage into a new status. (He also had not married, despite his 30 years.) The majority of migrants, however, succeed abroad, thus motivating an increasing number of young men to leave in search of similar success.

From an adult perspective, travel is said to domesticate young people. The task of domestication, in this way, has been handed over to Russia – who in turn employs young Tajik men, humbles them, and offers them positions in its society, transforming the 'wild, infantile' young men into mature adults. Here, adult perception diverges from that of those young men who make migration a life strategy rather than perceiving it as a limited period in one's life course.

I have contended that domestication is an authoritative process, but only to a certain degree – eventually negotiation occurs. In the next chapter I will show the changes that have taken place in marriage as a result of mass migration. However, the extent of migration has also caused deep changes on other levels. For example, Shahrigul, which has been entirely dependent on its migrants and their remittances for more than ten years, has been completely transformed. In the village, men are gradually replacing small wooden fences with 2-metre-high stone walls around their property to prevent outsiders from seeing their wives and daughters. These stone walls, men argue, have been erected because the women are often on their own in summer, while their husbands and sons are in Russia. In order to 'protect' the women from the glances of outsiders, men are currently reducing female mobility to a minimum. Likewise, a mother in Shahrigul once told me that her son, who worked in Russia, had threatened never to return if his sister was sent to school. Dependent on their son's financial support, the parents were afraid to refuse his demand. In an interview with me he justified his stand on the basis of Islamic concepts that support the strategy of keeping women from the public gaze while their husbands, brothers and sons are away in other lands.

It was impressive to witness how communication among migrants occurred faster than within the village itself – the presence of the stone wall is a good example of this. Once I was sitting with a woman when her son called from Russia and asked whether it was true that a woman from the neighbourhood (*mahalla*) had delivered a child. The woman answered that she did not know, but some days ago it had not yet been born. Afterwards she told me, laughing: 'You see, migrants are better informed about village life than we are within the village!'[37] Women are even afraid to go to the local shop along the main road more than once every second or third day. Only feasts give them the right to move around the village and spend long hours in the company of other women. Although many women take over much of the responsibility of running their household while their husband is away, every step is controlled by local young men in the community, who communicate any behavioural changes immediately to migrant relatives.

Youth Indentation and Migrant Mobilization

Tajikistan is primarily a country of old people, women and children. Needless to say, neither of these first two demographic cohorts (elders and children) form the core of militant movements; furthermore, the parents and the older generation experienced the war as victims and are said to reject any activity that would harm social harmony (Bichsel 2005; Stephan 2008; Heathershaw 2009), no matter how difficult life becomes. For them, Russia is domesticating their sons, who return from migration economically successful and socially mature.

Figure 4.1 demonstrates that age pyramids must be considered from a social as well as a biological perspective. If we note the number of migrants who leave the village, we can identify a 'youth indentation' that represents social reality, in contrast to a biological 'youth bulge' as a theoretical construct. The darker segments represent migrants; to this we must add students and young men on military service, which further reduces the youth cohort. In other words, a statistical youth bulge may be in truth a 'youth indentation', which demands a rephrasing of questions regarding youth bulges and conflict.

It is beyond the scope of this chapter to engage in detail with the world of Tajik migrants in Russia; however, I can provide an illustration of how groups that are politically engaged must be able to appeal to these migrant youth. The following example demonstrates concrete efforts to turn youth as a category (migrant workers) into a political movement. Between 2010 and 2012 I followed one of the groups that has emerged in Russia and intends to promote youth as a political power. This specific group concentrates on training young people (so far only men) to understand political and legal procedures and structures. The leader

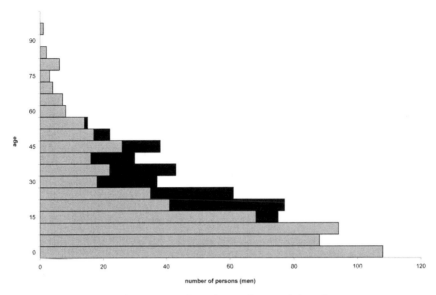

Figure 4.1: Percentage of migrants in the male population (Shahrigul).

of the group motivates participants to attend weekly meetings by telling them that they can be the ministers and other important political leaders of the future. In other words, he imparts to them the belief that they will be the vanguard of a new regime. He also has established a virtual parliament on Facebook, in which politics is discussed. But while democratic structures are at the base of the group's political interest, Islam is the moral glue. Collective prayer hence accompanies all of the group's meetings, and an Islamic centre long served as host to the group. In a private conversation, the group leader explained to me that any political change in Tajikistan today must necessarily regard Islam as a key element. While he believes that the masses will rise only for Islam, he acknowledges that there must exist a political party outside Islam because religious belief does not offer the political system necessary to organize a nation-state.

This group leader is currently engaged in the next step – founding a party – and has a very clear idea of how the masses can be mobilized to participate. He maintains good contacts with other youth groups in Tajikistan and abroad, even though they do not submit to his authority; on the contrary, these youth groups compete and have different ideas, while agreeing on the necessity of working towards political change. As we saw in the Introduction, in the discussion of the flash mob, these groups make use of Russian as an intellectual language, and therefore the leader of the group in Russia uses both Russian and Tajik to close the gap between ordinary Tajiks and russified intellectuals. He uses mosques and religious events (Koran recitation competitions) to engage ordinary Tajik

Muslims, knowing that they will provide the necessary numbers in order to make his party viable. Unsurprisingly, he is not the only leader who is aware that the youth indentation in Tajikistan has led to a concentration of Tajik youth in Russia. The Islamic Revival Party has established offices in some major Russian cities, and independent religious authorities, such as the Turajonzoda brothers, Salafi leaders and others,[38] have also invested time and resources in furthering their popularity among Tajik youth in Russia. Their meetings are filmed and the videos disseminated among migrants.

Religiously motivated movements also succeed in Russia because many young Tajiks turn to Islam there. According to my research, they turn to faith because it gives meaning to their suffering, because prayer and feasts structure their days and year without the need for elaborate celebrations, and because it separates them from the Russian population which they feel dominates them, but which at the same time they consider 'dirty' and *harom** (taboo, forbidden by Islamic law, not pure). Islamic rituals can be conducted with minimal resources and still reinforce a sense of collective belonging. Consequently, many mosques in Moscow where I conducted research are visited by Tajiks on Fridays and religious holidays. Many Tajiks also hold the position of prayer leader in Russian mosques, and religious dedication has become a marker of the trustworthy Tajik worker.

We now can understand the role that migration has played in maintaining the peace in post-civil war Tajikistan despite young people's increasing political and economic marginalization. Dividing their lives between two countries, many migrants come to exist in a kind of fantasy that is somewhere between the reality of Russia and an imagined future in Tajikistan. Tajikistan's peace is highly dependent upon migrants' faith in Russia, a fact of which the Tajik government is well aware.

Conclusion

In this chapter I have discussed notions of youth in contemporary Tajikistan. We have seen that the concepts of work are at the base of life-course constructions, and that they differ from the constructions of the life cycle based on rites of passage.

Young people seek to increase their social status. Status is first of all a cultural matter, and despite its relative stability in the history of a community, it constantly readapts to socio-political changes. Consequently, much of the ethnographic description in this chapter deals with negotiations of status. But status also affects categories, and 'youth' is a very important category within every society. Affected by the global circulation of concepts of youth – that have become the core of the idea of a cosmopolitan man (who is above all young in his outlook and behaviour, and also dynamic, independent, healthy, wealthy and successful) – local youth concepts that emphasize young people's dependency and immaturity have been challenged. Sulaiman's global Islamic youth concept is very similar to the United Nations' idea of youth, but with the advantage of being rooted in an Islamic historical narrative.

But the greatest impact today certainly comes from migration. With Russia becoming 'the West' for Tajik young men and 'the world' for Tajik women, much of the cultural transformation in Tajikistan enters via Russia, whether related to fashion, food, housing, youth leisure activities or whatever. Turning from a dream into an economic necessity, migration has developed an enormous influence on all aspects of Tajik life.

Whether for military service, study, work and migration, one generation (those young people who finished school and have not yet married) is predominantly absent from villages. This seems to have been true earlier as well (Beisembijev 1987; Bushkov 1993).[39] The 'missing generation' is the one said to cause trouble because of the liminal status it holds (cf. Turner 1995; van Gennep 1999). In other words, the villagers remove the critical social group from the village. Therefore, the young men who could possibly become 'the troublesome majority in the community' are sent out of the village or leave the village by themselves and return as youth, but now ready to negotiate the more formal aspects of life (marriage, peer meetings, teahouse meetings and so on). Young men who have finished school often try to leave the village to study, travel or work. From the 1990s until 2010, many young people travelled to various Muslim countries to get a religious education.[40] Parents support this if the household can manage without the migrant's labour. Thus, a large segment of young men are temporarily absent from the village after finishing school and before marriage. Therefore, when the civil war broke out, many young people were not at home but elsewhere. In fact, when I tried to investigate which young people of the village served in combat units, it was usually 'the others' who fought. Those young men who were with their families were often, but not always, prevented by their parents from joining the militant groups. Hence, this aspect is highly relevant to concepts that declare youth as the source of conflicts.

The farther away a youth is from home, the less relevant is their obedience to elders, Poliakov argues:

> The much-acclaimed idea of respect for one's elders may serve to confirm that behaviour depends on one's surroundings, since observations from various parts of Central Asia and other regions of the USSR attest uniformly that such behaviour is selective. The nearer a person is to home, the more the number of Muslims surrounding him, and the more he respects his elders. (Poliakov 1992: 81–82)

Poliakov states that the change from a non-Muslim to a Muslim environment helps to guide the behaviour of young people. To declare youth as wild and dangerous outside their controlling Muslim environment is a bit far fetched; however, Poliakov is right in saying that youth follow contextual demands of behaviour in performing certain roles (submission to parents, close kin and co-village elders), and that the performance of this role decreases with physical distance from kin and co-villagers. It can also be argued that this absence does not make them 'wilder', since 'the world' is said to domesticate youth as well, in that they experience the hardships of life while away from home.

We have seen that 'youth' denotes public subordination; in other words, a youth is subordinate to every person who is older than them, and this subordination takes place in public because it is performative. Second, youth means utilizing one's physical power in the service of family and community. This is also how the religious figure Eshon Nuriddinjon qualified 'youth'. According to him, youth means having the ability to (physically) serve God, one's parents and the community, and spans the ages 16 to 33 years. In fact, I observed that in front of their parents, young people bow their heads and listen, appearing to agree with everything their parents say. It is this performative subordination that has led so many (adult) scientists to perceive Tajik youth as totally controlled by older generations. Consequently, Poliakov believes that there exists no 'youth problem' in Central Asia. He writes, 'Young people are always controllable' (ibid.: 91). Harris's (2004, 2006) conclusions about youth in Tajikistan were similar; hence, her work concentrates on the domestic domain and particularly on women, a sphere in which control seems far more obvious, visible and applicable. Harris (2004: 92–113; 2006: 69–74) argues that young men may dominate same-aged and younger females but remain subordinate to older ones (cf. Kandiyoti 2007). Fairly recently, Stephan (2008) captured the rhetoric of parents and educational authorities concerning domestication strategies and concepts. I would suggest greater differentiation in this matter.

Emancipation from parental and community domestication is found through economic independence, migration experiences and religious concepts. Although the Islamic opposition acted locally and never relied on global concepts in their political agenda, the booklet on brotherhood in Islam, as well as many other ideas that have entered Tajikistan, conceptualize Muslim youth as a vanguard of the *umma* – the community of Muslims that transcends national borders – and not of individual countries. Thus, domestication as a process of integrating youth into the community is increasingly being challenged.

As migration has increased over the years, the position of young people within families, communities and society has been redefined. Migration provides an alternative route of maturation within the community and also an alternative path to political maturity. Slowly, the migrant community in Russia has been forming groups that seek to challenge political power in Tajikistan. Thus, despite a de facto 'youth indentation' in Tajikistan, the demographic 'youth bulge' (of which a large part is in Russia and in the Muslim world) is a potential resource for political parties.

Notes

1. The notion of work is culture specific. I will not engage in a theoretical discussion here, and instead will accept emic concepts of work that are related to physical effort and duties. In this sense, female work per se is easy, and men's work is difficult. However, women see their workload differently. Older women regard female suffering as 'fate', and younger women, especially the newly married ones, serve (*khizmat**) their in-laws quietly and often far above their capacities and physical ability.
2. See also Chapter 4 for more details on Aziz and his family.
3. Aziz, aged 22 years, May 2006.
4. Interview with Asad, aged 17, May 2006.
5. Several authors have argued that the term youth was initially reserved for the new social class of young people (working-class males) who had a considerable income to dispose of in leisure activities (cf. Wyn and White 1997: 18–21; Liechty 2002).
6. Interview with Kobil, aged 31, July 2006.
7. Harris (2004: 35 n.29, 184) has made a similar observation, stating that a mature man is one who has a child of marriageable age.
8. Snesarev (1963: 158) identifies five to seven age groups in Khorezm; cf. Bikzhanova, Zadykhina and Sukhareva (1974: 243).
9. This does not mean that being a young husband is necessarily painful; the discourse, however, reinforces a perception that maturation is a painful process.
10. The word *kelin** (daughter-in-law) is more than a kinship term; it is a concept related to work (*khizmat**), which has been described in numerous studies of Central Asia (e.g., Tett 1995; Harris 2004).
11. In this study, I have not made use of the various labels, such as Wahhabi, Salafi and so on, which have political connotations that are often rejected by local people (Stephan 2006). By using the neutral term 'new Islam', I seek to avoid judgments about the various real, false and invented forms of Islam, and merely refer to the active redefinition, translation and localization of Islam that has occurred on a large scale over the last two decades, which at the same time remains replete with pre-Soviet memories, Soviet classifications, and external sources of reference. For an excellent study on the subjectivities of being Muslim and the role of community in defining these, see Rasanayagam (2010).
12. Olimova (2002: esp. 65–70); cf. Hetmanek (1993: 370). Stephan (2008) provides an illuminating discussion about the discursive dimension of Islam for the parental generation in Tajikistan. Beyond Tajikistan, McBrien (2008) and Kirmse (2009) provide good descriptions of youth's controversial interests in Islam.
13. Jacobson (1998) has made similar observations: since their parents' lives no longer serve as the desired ideal for British Pakistani youth, they turn to Islamic ideals, hoping to find guidance in them.
14. In a little booklet titled 'The Gift of Youth', Shaykh Muhammad Saleem Dhorat (2007) criticizes Western conceptualizations that, he contends, allow youth to be irresponsible for far too long. See also: http://www.youthofislam.com/.
15. This quote is taken from a religious speech (*amru ma'ruf**) made during a wedding, and was videotaped and subsequently sold as a DVD that also included other teachings of

Eshon Nuriddinjon. The DVD is dated 2010, but the various video pieces are from as early as 2004, and some are not individually dated.

16. I remember that one of the many cassettes listened to by young men dealt with the question of loyalty: Whom should a believer listen to – his parents or his religious duties? As the story goes, it is time to pray *namoz*, but a parent asks the son to go to the bazaar to buy medicine. 'Should I go and miss *namoz* or perform *namoz* first and then go for the medicine?' the young man asks the mullah. The mullah advises him to consider whether the medicine is urgently needed. If it is urgently needed, then *namoz* should wait; if the need is not urgent, there is no reason to postpone prayer.

17. Mullah Sirojiddin is a controversial figure within the varied religious landscape of Tajikistan. For example, in June 2009, accused of being a Salafi, he was arrested along with approximately forty other so-called Salafi. He has been most successful among students in Dushanbe. These young men prioritize religious obligations and nuclear family life, but they are less interested in community and political discussions. ('Salafi cleric detained in Tajikistan', *Radio Free Europe/Radio Liberty*. Retrieved 25 June 2009 from: http://www.unhcr.org/refworld/docid/4a49fd482d.html)

18. Interview with Sulaimon, Islamic University, Dushanbe, October 2010.

19. 'I asked him: "O Messenger of Allah! Of what was the creation made?" He replied: "Of water." We asked: "[As for] Paradise, what is its foundation?" He said: "One brick of gold and one brick of silver. Its mortars are of musk of strong scent, its stones are pearls and emeralds, and its soil is of saffron. Whoever enters it will be in bliss and not in want, live in bliss and not die, their clothes will not get old, and their youth will not end"' (Hadith collected by Ahmad and Tirmidhi: see, http://www.harunyahya.com/paradise04.php).

20. Youth and the United Nations promoting 'International Year of Youth: Dialogue and Mutual Understanding', 12 August 2010 to 11 August 2011 (www.un.org/youth).

21. For a discussion on 'brotherhood' in social anthropology, consider Eisenstadt (1956: 90) and Pitt-Rivers (1975). Pitt-Rivers (ibid.: 89–101) points out the paradox that 'blood brothers' are like brothers – 'in fact, they are closer than real brothers'. He is troubled by the suggestion that true fraternity is found in freely chosen relations and not in biological 'real brothers'.

22. Būri Karim speaks of *jangi barodarkushii Tojikiston* (Karim 1997: 587, cited from the newspaper *Sadoi Mardum*, 25 February 1993). However, in the preface to his book, Karim calls the people '*hamvatan*', which is a reference to 'you, people from the same country/place of origin (*vatan**) as I'. Another term used is *jangi shahrvandī* ('the war among citizens').

23. Interview with Safarmoh, aged 28, November 2006.

24. I have witnessed the case of a former *mujohid* who failed to register as an official fighter of the opposition, and who therefore did not get any political protection. Instead of migrating to escape persecution, he had been living underground for more than ten years. As soon as he turned up in his native village (2007), however, he was arrested and imprisoned, despite many efforts to release him by bribing the authorities, claiming sympathy for his health, and citing his responsibility towards his family.

25. See Olimova and Bosc (2003) on labour migration from Tajikistan. For another report on migration in southern Tajikistan, see Mughal (2007). Navrūzshoh (2009) claims that the age group 20 to 39 is the most affected by unemployment.

26. Interview with Asad, aged 17, May 2006. Asad, born in 1989, was in the tenth grade at the time of this interview. Unskilled migrants, such as the majority of those from Tajikistan, earn around $200 to $500 a month. If they live within their workplace (for instance in containers within the bazaar or from the (building) company), accommodation costs are

not too high ($50 to $100); if they rent a flat in an urban centre, they usually share it with ten to thirty other migrants to reduce costs. Big cities are particularly expensive. Skilled migrants who are able to fill more desirable positions can earn much more and organize their living situation independently.

27. Interview with an elderly woman, January 2007.
28. Interview with Habibullo, an elderly man, January 2007.
29. Interview with Saifiddin, aged 26, November 2007. Saifiddin is a young man born in 1981, who works in Russia but had returned to Tajikistan for his marriage.
30. Nieswand (2007) discusses the difference between migration discourses in the destination country and those back home. My accounts in this study solely represent the discourse 'back home'; however, it is to be expected that the discourse in Russia greatly differs from the one at home, just as Nieswand observed in the case of Ghanaian migrants.
31. Similarly, Weyland (1993: 182) in an Egyptian context writes of a feminization of agriculture, observing that there are not necessarily more women engaging in agriculture than before migration, but that they spend more time at it. However, unlike her observation that migrants coming back to their village re-engage with agricultural work, young Tajik migrants do anything to avoid reintegration into the agricultural sector, which would imply the acceptance of the village social structure and the hierarchical division of labour.
32. Rousseau et al. (1998) provide an interesting example involving Somali refugees to show how young people may pursue the dream of leaving home to the brink of being driven mad by it.
33. Although in fact few migrants reach the point where they can participate in consumption – most live in terrible conditions, with not enough income to live comfortably (since much of the income is being saved to send home), and are not allowed to move freely due to registration regimes – they nonetheless have become symbols of success and examples to follow.
34. Interview with Mahmud, aged 39, September 2006.
35. In the Sufi tradition, the idea of travel is best represented as a lifelong path of learning.
36. A traveller (*muhojir*) allows the host to perform good deeds. Therefore, travellers are privileged guests according to the rules of hospitality. Thus, one may break the Ramadan fast in order to share food with a traveller. The traveller enjoys immunity from any harm while she stays with the host. By sharing bread and salt (*nonu namak*), they (travellers) are integrated into the family (and through it, the community) as a friend (as opposed to an enemy, who would refuse to accept such offers from the host). Elderly people told me about a previous tradition in which young women would rush out and bring offerings of bread to any traveller who happened to pass by the village.
37. Rukhshona, an elderly woman, October 2006.
38. Ozodi (Tajik Radio Free Europe) regularly reports on these religious authorities' activities in Russia (e.g., Kayumzoda 2012).
39. Here, Beisembijev (1987) talks of young people 'offered' to the emir as soldiers, and Bushkov (1993) speaks of a young generation (before the coming of the Russians at the beginning of the twentieth century) so caught up in feuds and fights that the number of reproductive young men was reduced.
40. In 2010, the government placed heavy restrictions on religious education abroad, and, in the spring of 2011, a law was passed to restrict religious education at home as well. Students who had been enrolled in various Muslim countries were called back to Tajikistan. The impact of these measures on young people has yet to be studied.

Chapter 5

'The Only Thing in Life that Makes You Feel Like a King'

Marriage as an Indicator of Social and Demographic Change

M arriage has often been constructed by anthropologists as the primary ritual marking the transition from childhood or youth to adulthood, especially in the absence of other youth-specific rituals such as those observed in age-system societies. In this chapter I will discuss the transition from *bacha** to *mardak** through marriage, which also represents a change in status from unmarried man to married man. The marriage ritual is essential in the sense that it regulates reproductive responsibilities. Moreover, while this ritual aptly demonstrates ideas of domestication by communities, the case of the Tajik civil war shows how these domestication attempts have been contested by young men.

I have included statistical data in order to identify changes through this central life-cycle event, particularly by taking a closer look at changes in age at first marriage. My analysis has revealed that the Tajik life course was much more homogeneous during the Soviet era than it is today. The situation appears to have changed considerably during the civil war and afterwards. Thus, marriage has become an event through which the period of youth is negotiated between parents and their children, and between the community and its youth. I will look at marriage as a 'barometer of cultural [and demographic] change' for youth (Şen 2007: 257).

Although marriage is part of a highly formalized system, in this chapter, instead of emphasizing its structural importance, I will examine the way in which marriage, as a central life-cycle ritual, is exposed to social change. In my view, the various forms of marriage are extremely sensitive to change and thus represent an excellent way to observe domestication processes. In fact, marriage practices are the best indicators of generational conflicts between social juniors and seniors over social and reproductive rights. The topic of marriage is a huge field of research, but here I will limit my focus to examining how young people used the civil war to appropriate the right to marry – and as a means to emancipate themselves from parental domination.

Control over Maturation through Marriage

Within social anthropology, marriage has long been a core theme, particularly in the study of alliances and as a ritual practice. In contrast, demographers have tended to reduce marriage to an increased exposure to intercourse. More recent demographers, however, including Meekers (1992), Hammel and Friou (1997: 188–89) and Eloundou-Enyegue, Stokes and Cornwell (2000: 56), have suggested that marriage is much more than an increase in exposure to intercourse; it is necessary to approach the topic by respecting the local traditions associated with it, especially cohabitation rules. They suggest that marriage should be viewed not merely as an institution or relation but as a process, an idea suggested decades earlier by Radcliffe-Brown (1958: 54) and which relates to discussions about the role of marriage in maturation processes.

Let us first consider the role of marriage in the process of (social) maturation and then marriage as a ritual practice. Often, marriage is perceived as a necessary step towards attaining maturity and full membership in the community. Some societies, however, construct maturity as a gradual process, and it may only be in more formal societies that marriage or other rituals are a central step in gaining full membership in the community (see Malinowski 1927: 66; 1929: 80; Fortes 1962a: 7).[1]

Maturity is defined, firstly, as the legal transfer of reproductive rights from parents to children. As Fortes explains: 'The rights and claims pertain to socially responsible procreative sexuality as opposed to the irresponsible juvenile and adolescent sexual indulgence which is often condoned, if not freely allowed, pre-maritally' (Fortes 1962b: 8). Secondly, maturity is defined as an indicator of a young man's ability to secure the survival of his family in line with community expectations. Malinowski (1927: 204; 1929: 179–202) argued in this context that marriage is a necessary social institution for regulating the behaviour of men who, by 'nature', refuse to take responsibility for the children they produce. To rephrase it differently, marriage is one of the most effective tools of society for domesticating youth's sexual and reproductive behaviour. In this sense, Lévi-Strauss (1993: 368) has identified that most societies possess severe punishments for adultery, which implies that marriage represents a communal matter and not purely a domestic one (cf. Fortes 1962b: 9). Maturity here is the ability to conform to communal rules and expectations.

Leaving aside for a moment the role of marriage in the process of maturation, I wish to take a look at marriage within alliance theory and the study of rituals. Marriage holds a central position as a strategic event that influences relationships between people, and not infrequently enforces political ties. Hence, marriage becomes a contract between two social groups within a wider system of the transfer of goods, rights and women or men. In this sense, Lévi-Strauss (1993: 333–34) situates marriage at the foundation of society and sees a direct correlation between the rules of marriage and social structure.

Among Tajiks, marriage is the result of various exchanges of goods and visits through which two parties engage in a contract. Transactions take place between the two parties within the jural and moral tenets of the social group, and the social status of both the young couple and the parents changes. However, unlike in many other societies, among Tajiks the bride never becomes a member of her husband's corporate group – she remains a member of her own *avlod**. It is only her reproductive capacities and labour that now belong less to her husband than to his *avlod*, who refer to her as 'our daughter-in-law (*kelin**)' (cf. ibid.: 348).

The important relation between rituals and demography has been pointed out by Patrick Heady:

> It is simply not credible to assume that the vast expenditures of time and resources that accompany life-cycle rituals have no effect on the events they purport to deal with. This seems to me a theoretical priority for demographic anthropology, and one which calls for a combination of detailed description and analysis of local data with the development of a robust body of general theory. (Heady 2007: 558)

I agree with Heady that the analysis of rituals provides important data for the analysis of demographic processes. Following his lead, in this chapter I will relate data on age at first marriage to changes in ritual practice due to socio-political change in Tajikistan.

Based on these two aspects of marriage (as a step within the maturation process and as a ritual practice) let us take a look at the engagement of conflict studies with marriage as a ritual practice and demographic event. With regard to the impact of civil conflicts on nuptial processes, some authors assume that marriage is delayed in times of war (Agadjanian and Prata 2002: 217) – this being the main reason for conflict-related fertility decline. Other authors have challenged this idea; for example, Randal (2005) claims that there was no considerable change in marriage patterns among Tuareg during the civil crisis in Mali. In this sense, Randal has questioned the classic view in anthropology that marriage is a strategy to secure alliances. She does not assert that more marriages took place during the civil conflict because people wanted to increase their alliances; rather, she sees an increase in the incidence of marriage among younger and older women (who in normal circumstance would have remained unmarried) in the context of refugee camps, where parents tended to lose control over their children and therefore married their daughters off quickly in order to secure their protection and avoid (unacceptable) premarital pregnancies (ibid.: 309).

With regard to Central Asia, the argument that in times of crisis marriage tends to be postponed has been questioned, particularly in the case of civil-war Tajikistan (Shemyakina 2007; Clifford 2009; Hohmann, Roche and

Garenne 2010). After the emergence of perestroika, people began to feel insecure about their future; this might have prompted Agadjanian and Makarova (2003) to suggest that parents sought to marry off their daughters at a young age before unforeseen circumstances might make marriages more difficult to arrange.

Cruise O'Brien has remarked that one should not write off the family as a social unit, despite the social conflicts in West Africa: 'It can indeed be argued that the family is the most durable of political institutions in such a context, perhaps with a shifting balance of power between the generations' (Cruise O'Brien 1996: 70). Keeping in mind the extent to which the institution of the family has been shaken due to the social conflict in Tajikistan, the re-enactment of life-cycle rituals seems to have a stabilizing effect. The Tajik perceive the family as a sacred unit, and the recent civil war has done little to change this perception. Parents' efforts to marry off their children goes back to the belief that it is a parental duty before God to marry off one's children – along with organizing the circumcision feast (*khatna tüy*) and providing housing.

In general, Agadjanian's thesis – namely, that in times of social changes and uncertainty, 'people do not change all components of their demographic behaviour equally and uniformly' (Agadjanian 1999: 426) – may be taken as a guideline to encourage further research into different correlations. The Tajik civil war is an excellent example of variations in marriage patterns and ritual practice due to conflict.[2] Comparing nuptial behaviour in Tajikistan during the Soviet period, the civil war period and the postwar period, we can see that marriage adapted to socio-political changes (Roche and Hohmann 2011) but also reflected intergenerational tensions. In my view, various forms of marriage are extremely sensitive to change and thus represent an excellent lens through which socio-demographic processes can be observed. In fact, marriage practices are the best indicators of generational conflicts between social juniors and seniors over social and reproductive rights. The topic of marriage is admittedly a huge field of research, but in this study I will limit my focus to two aspects: first, how maturity is negotiated intergenerationally through marriage; and second, the socio-political changes that shape marriage in its ritual and demographic dimensions. The statistical examination of changes in age at first marriage during three time periods will be used to discuss these aspects.

The chapter starts with a historical overview of marriage and continues with a socio-economic analysis of rituals and, more precisely, marriage. The reason for the latter analysis is that the socio-economic factor is highly relevant in the negotiation of maturity and youth status, and much of the tension arising from marriage is reflected in socio-economic dependencies. After presenting ethnographic examples I will then engage with the question of age at first marriage as an indicator of social change.

A History of Marriage in Tajikistan

In Tajik society, which takes its value system from Islam, conjugal life is perceived as the aim of every human being, or, to be more precise, it is supposed to be the aim of every Muslim. Living without a partner is regarded as abnormal, while social life is highly valued. Marianne Kamp, in a detailed analysis of Uzbek women, not only states that marriage was the expected status for males and females but also provides data from the 1897 census showing that: 'the majority of girls were first married between the ages of fifteen and nineteen, and that 99 per cent of all adult Turkestani women were married at least once. By contrast, while men also attained a 98 per cent rate of marriage, the majority were married for the first time when they were between thirty and thirty-nine' (Kamp 2006: 43). Although Kamp does record her doubts regarding the accuracy of these statistics, the stories that I collected mainly in rural Tajikistan concerning this period (the pre-Soviet era) appear to verify her findings. Some of the reasons for this large age gap between couples seem to have been due to economic problems, lack of resources, and dependence on rich landowners.[3]

> ALIMARDON: Only rich people would marry – those who had wealth could have weddings, but the one who didn't have resources could not marry. In earlier times, weddings would last for two to three days.
> S.R.: Would they pay the bridewealth (*qalin**)?
> ALIMARDON: They would not give money. The rich people, during their weddings, would give a bridewealth of fifteen to twenty cows, horses and camels.[4]

In 1917, the Bolsheviks promulgated a decree to regulate marriage within society. Only marriages performed through a civil ceremony would be considered legal, and both partners had to be present and give their consent. The minimum age for marriage was set at 16 for girls and 18 for boys (ibid.: 69).

If we want to look at marriage in the context of youth, we have to go back to pre-Soviet times in order to understand the connection between marriage and youth. I will draw from Kamp's historical analysis of Turkestan and her discussion of changes in marriage brought about by the *jadid* (reformers). The *jadid* were a group of Muslim reformers in Russia at the turn of the nineteenth century (see Chapter 3). While they generally agreed on the importance of marriage, they sought to address problems associated with age at first marriage. Apparently, the large age gap between a man and his wife posed a problem, which was mainly discussed as a health and an economic problem. Kamp (ibid.: 47 n.57, 252) found documents in which Behbudi, a *jadid*, referred to certain European research (though the sources were not identified) and argued that unmarried men were more likely to commit criminal acts. Thus, delaying marriage was held responsible for an increase in criminality. Unfortunately, Behbudi has left no indication of how he related this observation to Turkestani society. In addition, the *jadid*'s discussions on reforming marriage in Central Asia dealt with the issue of marriage expenses rather than marriage itself, asserting that if such expenses were curbed, it would allow the poor as well as the rich access to women.

Until 1927, Turkestan's family law was still in place. Based on Russian imperial traditions, under this law, Muslims would be judged by Muslim 'people's judges' according to sharia and customary law, while non-native people would be judged according to Russian law. In 1928, however, it became obligatory to register marriages under the Record of Civil Status Act (ZAGS) in order for them to be recognized as legal.[5] Barbieri et al. (1996: 72–74) have argued that between the 1920s and the 1930s, age at first marriage of women in Uzbekistan increased considerably, eventually stabilizing at approximately 19 years in the 1950s.[6] Their contention is that changes in marriage are the consequence of secularization; however, they do not provide any evidence indicating that religion (Islam) had any influence on fertility changes. Religious marriages were still allowed after the communist reforms, though they were not legally recognized. Similar to the Turkish civil code, the modernization of family law under Soviet rule in Central Asia 'banned polygyny, established seventeen as the lowest marriageable age for women and eighteen for men, gave women the right to civil divorce, ended the Islamic freedom of unilateral divorce for men, and equalized inheritance for sons and daughters' (Kamp 2006: 70). However, laws do not necessarily achieve their intended outcome; widespread manipulation practices in the Soviet era helped the authorities to produce data that conformed to their ideology but did not hinder the persistence of various traditional practices.[7] I would like to argue that the nationwide introduction of the education system was the main reason for some standardization in marriage (and certainly also fertility) practices.

The marriage ceremony in Tajikistan today extends over several days and can be divided into three parts: the religious marriage (*nikoh**), the traditional marriage (*tŭy**)[8] and the state registration (ZAGS).[9] Although couples do have to officially register their marriage, many avoid this step until it becomes absolutely necessary – for example, when their children begin school. In particular, migrants who live in Russia and only come back to visit their family after a few months, a year, or maybe even a few years, avoid registering their marriage in order to leave open the option of marrying a Russian woman, which allows them access to a permanent residence permit in Russia. Thus, marriage registration in Tajikistan is also affected by changes in Russian law, and unless collected through a legitimate survey, the official data are unreliable.[10] The problem continues with the arrival of children, who may be registered under any relative's name if the parents are not married according to state law – this is especially true for children of second, third and more wives, and for women who are separated but not divorced.[11]

A religious marriage (*nikoh*) is the most important type in Tajik society, in the sense that it actually legitimizes the couple to rear *halol** (here, lawful) children. (I was told that a child born without his parents having had a *nikoh* can never be a prayer leader – he will always have to stand behind a prayer leader.) The traditional marriage (*tūy*) is the most sensitive to social change and shows extremely dynamic changes over time and region. This type of marriage constitutes a public performance of the groom's and his family's ideological orientation (whether they are strictly Islamic or comparatively modern, in Tajik terms).[12] I will return to this point later.

Marriage is not only of symbolic importance in Tajik society; it has been and continues to be a political issue, both during the Soviet era and today. While the Soviet regime's political concerns focused on a girl's minimum age at marriage and sought to implement laws to regulate it, in recent times political interference has been driven by economic interests. Thus, in May 2007, the Tajik government passed a law to regulate marriage expenses and the number of people participating in the festivities (in terms of number of dresses purchased and so on).[13] This law was based on the assumption that people's expenditure on feasts and celebrations far exceeded their means, and they preferred to take out loans rather than reduce the scale of the celebration. For once, the clerics agreed with the state, but with an aim to promote Islam rather than reinforce state control. In cities, security services may be present throughout the ceremony in order to keep an eye on the number of people attending and the expenditure incurred by the parties; nevertheless, in order to meet cultural expectations, and because the vagueness of the law leaves plenty of room for individual interpretation, people are often able to use bribery to overcome bureaucratic obstacles and interference.

The above historical outline has demonstrated that marriage and age at first marriage remained a central concern of politics throughout the Soviet period and within independent Tajikistan. Through marriage politics, the state remained directly involved in the private life of its citizens. Even today the police employ a special unit (the 4th *adel*) to patrol Dushanbe's streets at night in order to arrest prostitutes and – if unable to identify them to their satisfaction – to issue fines to mixed unmarried couples for 'criminal behaviour'. The idea that marriage successfully 'domesticates' youth is best expressed in Behbudi's concern that men who cannot afford marrying may be at a higher risk of engaging in criminal activities, and therefore marriage has to be affordable for poor and rich equally.[14] This idea – that marriage is a tool for domesticating sons – still exists today and leads parents to favour early marriage for their sons to bind them to family and community.

The Socio-economic Role of Marriage

Another aspect that concerns not only marriage but also numerous other life-cycle rituals is the socio-economic aspect. Rites of passage are the doorway to certain rights and status, and are thus desirable to the people who have not yet passed through them. The wedding, in this sense, allows a man to have legitimate sexual intercourse, start a separate family and thereafter a separate household, gain full membership in the local community, and eventually obtain access to land and other resources.[15] Humphrey (1983: 373–432) has argued that life-cycle rituals have become ritually simpler and materially more complex and extravagant in Buryatia only in the last century, that is, under socialist policies. Due to economic constraints resulting from a socialist economy, people were forced to accumulate goods through private channels.[16] Hence, the display of consumer goods in rituals turned into an important sign of social status reflecting the large social network of the groom's or the bride's father. People who did not enjoy such a social network chose to deprive themselves of the most basic goods rather than reduce the size of the rituals (Ro'i 2000: 458). In this context, Agadjanian and Makarova (2003) argue that marriage was elevated to the central ritual – as compared to other life-cycle rituals during the Soviet era – demonstrating social status. However, it is not so much accumulation as the successful and generous redistribution of goods through ritual exchange that elevates marriage to its position as such an important ritual for young people.

In Tajik villages, people accept the display of conspicuous consumption in rituals as a way to acquire social status. However, if a family accumulates goods only for private consumption and does not generously distribute them in life-cycle rituals, it risks social exclusion. This was the case for the family of a teacher: A neighbour in Lakhsh – a teacher who was considered to be well off but stingy – arranged for the marriage of his eldest son (who was working as a freelance filmmaker). His wife had often complained to me about the traditions that required such expensive rituals, and that it would make much more sense to invest in improving their own living conditions (*ozod kardan*). During the wedding, some women complained that they had not received meat according to their status – that is, the share of meat they deserved (*haq*). Among the general discontent and jealousy surrounding this family, young people disturbed the public festivities of the wedding by cutting off the electric supply for the music, which came from a generator. All this led to the marriage being talked of as a disaster.

Improving one's lifestyle (or one's house) is said to be a selfish act and is frowned upon because this process excludes the collective. Without doubt, during the Soviet era investment in one's home and lifestyle was suspiciously regarded as a sign of corruption, while the 'conspicuous giving' of gifts in rituals during the 'shortage economy' that characterized the Soviet era was a legal way to display one's economic success and maintain one's social network (Creed 1998: 119, 202–4).

To understand access to goods within a shortage economy, let us take a look at Murod. Murod, father of three children, used to work in a beer factory in Dushanbe, providing a friend who was working in the meat factory (*kombinat*) in Dushanbe with easy access to beer, and therefore receiving meat when needed. He had another friend working in a company that produced ceramics who would exchange dishes (needed as bridewealth and as gifts in ritual exchange) for beer. He also had various other friends working at other factories. In addition, he was a very skilled labourer and able to install electrical lines by diverting electricity from public lines to neighbours, relatives and friends. This social and economic network allowed his family to live comfortably despite the constant shortage of goods in shops, and to participate in conspicuous consumption during rituals. Upon the collapse of the Soviet Union, however, his socio-economic network broke down, as did his easy access to various goods. Today he must buy everything with cash, but no job allows him to accumulate enough cash to live as easily as he did during the Soviet period. Being in conflict with his relatives, even his kinship network has been reduced to a minimum.

Murod is not an exception; many people experienced the breakdown of the socialist system as a shrinking of their social network. Wealth today is a matter of individual effort that requires strategic friendships to secure (not accumulate) one's individual wealth (for example, business, political position). Poor kin are perceived as a burden, and numerous individuals have withdrawn from the practice of supporting kin members in order to concentrate on friendships that are economically and politically more profitable. For the majority today, migration is the only way out of poverty.

Approximately 1.5 million Tajiks work abroad, most often in Russia. In Shahrigul, sons (or fathers) would usually go abroad and earn money first and celebrate a costly marriage only afterwards.[17] Conspicuous consumption in rituals stands in stark contrast to migratory hardship, and is seen as a legitimate way to spend and enjoy the money earned under harsh conditions. Marriages are central events in which migrants can convert their savings into an increase in status. This occasional spending, however, makes them ignorant about daily difficulties in the village that the family who stays behind must face. This importance of rituals for migrants is also the reason why the wedding period has been adapted to migratory patterns and today takes place in winter, when migrants return home, rather than in autumn, which was previously considered to be the appropriate season (when the weather is pleasant and the recent harvest suggests wealth at hand). This kind of ostentatious celebration not only increases the social capital of the 'owner of the wedding' (*sohibi tūy*, usually the father of the groom) but also that of all those who were invited. This sharing of status within a defined group legitimates (and even requires) conspicuous consumption in rituals.

Rituals, Creed argues, cannot be used as 'simply a barometer of economic and political difficulty'; instead, they constitute the process as well as the result of socio-cultural changes (Creed 2002: 70). Creed has observed that 'ritual decline is not a universal phenomenon in rural Bulgaria but a pervasive one that correlates closely with economic difficulty' (ibid.: 65–66). In Tajikistan as well, rituals are closely related to social and economic changes, yet rituals have proven to reach the highest point of economic excess in times of great economic hardship.

To conclude, in this section I have discussed some aspects of the socio-economic context of marriage, with a focus on changes that are relevant to the marriage ritual and consequently to youth's social status. In order to be able to meet ritual requirements, parents engage in socio-economic network activities or seriously stint on other needs, creating a sense of dependency between children and parents. Recent mass migration, in contrast, has pushed young men to become the main breadwinners in their families and financers of life-cycle rituals. This affects parent–child relations considerably, placing many parents in a vulnerable position. Although the majority of young male migrants agree with their parents that they should marry in their native land, most migrants in Russia wish to postpone marriage. Young men running away, divorcing right after marriage, or cutting off communication with home while in Russia are not an exception, contributing to a sharp increase in age at first marriage during the last decade (see below). Yet, marriage as such has remained a pivotal event in young people's lives. The transformation of marriage into a central ritual of conspicuous consumption is not only the result of political and economic changes – it has become a compromise between parents and young men, the former seeing marriage as an important tool to domesticate their children, and the latter viewing the ritual as a way to demonstrate their ability to earn money and show generosity, which increases their social status.

Ethnographic Examples

Before engaging in a statistical analysis I will present ethnographic examples of marriages across several time periods. When compared to the widespread assumption that parents have total control over their children's marital life, these examples offer a much more finely grained view of the parent–child dynamic with respect to marriage. Only if we understand this subtle relationship of parents and their children, as well as the role of friends, neighbours and relatives, with respect to marriage can the changes in age at first marriage make sense as an indicator of demographic dynamics and social change. It is through the negotiation of power and status in marriage that youth are able to contest their subordinate position.

A Marriage in the 1980s

I begin with a lengthy extract from an interview with Mirzokarim, born in the mid 1960s and one of the set of brothers described in some detail in Chapter 3.

> S.R.: Who married you off?
> MIRZOKARIM: My father and my mother – my wife is from Regar. I found her myself. It was my turn to get married (*zangirī* budam*), then

my father and mother also agreed to the match, and we got married. The thing is that my parents wanted me to get married to a relative's daughter, but I refused. Once, my elder brother came at night to tell me, 'We are to marry you off to a certain person' (*turo khonador* kardani hastem*). I told him then that I already had somebody in mind and that I wouldn't get married to anyone else.

S.R.: Did you tell them yourself or via another person?

MIRZOKARIM: Well, it was like this. I had first met the girl when I was studying. After I was promoted to the second course [second year], the girl – she is my wife now – was one year junior to me and had enrolled in the first course. After that, when I was helping the girls in their studies – I was a tutor at the institute by then – I got to know this girl, and affection and love grew between us (*meheru muhabbat*). We got to know each other better and became friends; we spent some time together, went for walks together. Then four years later, when I was in the fifth course and my wife was in the fourth course, my elder brother came to Dushanbe along with my brother's wife (*yanga**) in order to visit me. They told me, 'We are planning to get you married off, and our mother keeps saying that they will go to a certain place and dress the girl' [which means that the couple will thenceforth be regarded as engaged]. I replied, 'I know a girl that I like; I will marry her'. Then they said, 'We have to see your girl. Introduce us to her'. After that, I told them to go to the Hotel Dushanbe and wait there in the restaurant, and I would walk around in front of them, talking to the girl – I didn't tell my wife; if she had known, she would have refused to come for that walk. I only told her that we would go to the cinema, walk around, and then go to Sadbarg, and that's how I tricked her – if I had told her the truth, it would have lost the effect. Then, talking and laughing, we passed them. My elder brother and my *yanga* had informed me beforehand, 'If this girl is to please us, she shouldn't wear European clothes'. That's why I told her to wear a traditional dress, and in that manner, we slowly walked past them. After that, I left her at Sadbarg and went with them to the hotel. My *yanga* said, 'Okay, she's okay. Give us her address, and we will go to her house straight from here and negotiate'. They had decided to go there immediately by car – my brother had just bought a new blue Neva. Then I wrote down her parents' address and gave it to my brother. My *yanga* had told me, 'I will buy three or four kilogrammes of sweets and other such things and we'll visit them'.

S.R.: Didn't your father and mother go?

MIRZOKARIM: No, my elder brother and my *yanga* went – my parents were already quite old (*müisafedu kampir*), and they didn't know the city.

S.R.: Is your brother very much older than you? By how many years?

MIRZOKARIM: He is much older – he is ten, no, fourteen years older than me. After that, according to their plan, they went. Her father and mother told them, 'Jirgatol is far away in the mountains; we will not give our daughter there'.[18] But my brother said, 'We don't give daughters anymore, because the times have changed for youth'. Her parents said, 'Maybe our daughter has met a boy that she likes, but our daughter hasn't told us – we haven't investigated the matter'. Then my brother and *yanga* assured them, 'Don't worry; we come in the name of the girl and the boy, and they agree to this match – they both said that they wanted to marry each other'. Did you understand? I mean, when my elder brother and *yanga* went to see them, they first said, 'We won't give her to people from the mountains'. But my brother and *yanga* convinced them, saying, 'You don't need to give her – they have already decided it between themselves, because they know each other (*shino*s). They both agree to marry each other, they consulted each other, and they both sent us'. Then the parents replied, 'If they say so, and if the girl agrees, then we will agree'; however, they didn't take the chocolates and sweets my elder brother and *yanga* had brought for them. And so they returned, with the things still in the back of their car. They came back to Dushanbe and told me that the stuff should stay in Dushanbe.

S.R.: Why so?

MIRZOKARIM: If the girl suddenly changed her mind, the people [back home in the village] would not know. Then the second time that they went to ask for the girl's hand in marriage, her parents said that they had planned to give her to another boy, but the girl had said, 'No, I will marry this boy, or I will not marry anyone else'. After that, they had felt compelled to agree. In order to get married I came here [to Lakhsh]. Here there was a music ensemble. We took a bus, climbed in and went.

S.R.: Who gave you the money for the wedding?

MIRZOKARIM: Two thousand Soviet money [roubles] it cost – equivalent to 2,500 dollars – my elder brother provided this.

S.R.: By himself?

MIRZOKARIM: Yes, he himself gave it.

S.R.: At that time, would the sovkhoz give anything?

MIRZOKARIM: No, we only took musicians from the sovkhoz – we asked their permission and took them – they were all our people anyway. There were seven or eight of us who went there, and we had a concert that lasted a whole night – it was a fine wedding. In the morning, we climbed aboard the bus again and returned home.

S.R.: Who organized your wedding?

MIRZOKARIM: My elder brother – he played the role of both my father and my mother. This was with my parents' consent, of course, and we took my father's blessing. He said, 'Go ahead'. This old man, my father, he did not interfere in our work. My elder brother Mirzokhoja was the one who knew the city [an educated man], and everything was on his head [he shouldered the entire responsibility]. And the money for the wedding – thanks to my mother and father – they gave it to him.[19]

A Marriage during the Civil War

Firuza represents a good example of a young girl who was full of dreams for the future before the war, dreams which she never managed to realize because she was married at a young age to a village boy.

I had other ideas, when I was small – to become somebody . . . During the war I wrote [a diary] because I thought one day I might need it – I wrote it so that the events would stay in my mind. After the war, they opened the school for a while. By then, the other girls in the village had stopped going. I went for one year; I ignored their talk and went to school – completed grade nine. Then they would not allow me to study anymore.

One day, we walked to Gharm on foot – my father was with me, and we reached the venue after the poetry competition had already begun. When I took first place, everybody was wondering how a girl from a village could make it to first place. If it had been possible, I would have gone to town for studies and never returned. Then they married me off, because they did not have the means to support me – it was difficult here. My father was a teacher and worked in the *jamoat**, lots of people came to meet him to ask him for me [i.e., to marry her]. He was afraid of having an unmarried girl (*dukhtari* kholi*) at home, and I had several sisters younger than me; it was a very hard time – he didn't have a choice . . . We didn't know if the world would ever be peaceful again. If I had known that everything would change in a few years, I would have resisted for a while. I was married in 1996, then she [her first daughter] was born in 1998; I worked in the school for a year, and then she [her second daughter] was born in 2000. Now I have four girls.[20]

Her mother reports the following:

When the soldiers came [and occupied the village], they were looking for him [her husband] again – this time because he had been an official [director of a school], so he had to go into hiding again. We were hiding our eldest daughter as well, and one day we told her, 'Okay, come into the house for some time'. Then suddenly, a soldier walked by – my heart was exploding out of fear. If the soldiers saw a girl they would take her, but they did not enter the house this [time]. They came to our house now and again because they had killed his brother [the speaker's husband's brother], but usually, they remained outside. One day they saw her, and a young lad asked me to give my daughter to him, so we hid her. They came again with gifts, asking us to give them our daughter. We were so scared, and she remained in hiding – at my mother's place in the mountains, in a cave . . . Afterwards they left. It took several months for things to improve.[21]

The above account suggests that they had resisted marrying her off, hiding her in a cave and cellar, but eventually they had to give in because of uncertainty regarding if and when the country would emerge from civil war.

A Marriage in 2006
On a day in June 2006, the friends and classmates of the bride and four more girls from the groom's side came for a *shabnishin* (here, a gathering of girls in the evening)[22] in the *mekhmonkhona** (guestroom) and spend the whole night together, eating and dancing in the room where the dowry – comprising clothes and furniture – of the future bride were on display.[23] The girl had just finished school and did not seem very happy to be getting married. Most of the girls remained there for the whole night and went back home at 5.00 in the morning, leaving the room free to be prepared for the upcoming religious marriage. The mullah arrived by 7.30 in the morning, while the groom turned up much later, accompanied by a friend and a male relative – they all sat together in the *mekhmonkhona*. (The bride saw her future husband for the first time through the window of this room.)

While the mullah discoursed (*amru ma'ruf**) on the ideals of Islamic family life to the audience, the groom quietly listened, with his close friend beside him. In the adjacent rooms, the bride was getting ready and her girlfriends were bustling around. Then the bride was taken to another room and sat down in a corner, while some women sat in front of her. A curtain (*chodar*) was put up in front of her (cf. Andreev 1953: 159). Now everybody was waiting for her to agree to the marriage, by saying, 'yes'. At the beginning, the girls had been sitting next to the bride in order to cheer her up, but later on they were sent out and only a *yanga* (sister-in-law) was left. The bride's maternal brother came in twice, requesting the bride say 'yes' and begging her not to bring shame on their family. The bride, however, sat behind the curtain with the scarf over her face and cried constantly. Some of her friends came and sat with her again, giggling and laughing. Then the mullah himself approached the bride and ordered her uncle (MB) to sit next to the curtain.[24] He suggested that a small 'ho' (okay) would be enough to approve the marriage.[25] After he had left, the girlfriends announced that the bride had said 'yes'. After that, the room fell silent – nobody was smiling, and the bride was crying openly. Then the mullah passed around a cup of water from which the groom and the witnesses had taken a sip, and passed it over, first to the bride and then to all the women sitting in the room. After that, all the men, including the groom, left the house without having seen the bride. Then the bride was made ready for the state registration of the marriage under ZAGS. Again, life came back into the girls and women – they tried out their new dresses and poured out a stream of comments on the new husband. Instead of the rented ('dirty') traditional Russian dress, the bride opted for a traditional (Tajik) rose-coloured one, on top of which she wore a coat with silver embroidery.

In the early afternoon, a caravan of ten cars (driven by the groom's peers and young relatives) arrived in order to pick up the bride – there were only young people in the group. The groom took his wife and seated her in the marriage car – this was their first meeting. The young people sat wherever they found some space and the group drove to the office of the local administration (*jamoat**). The person in charge of marriage registration then married the couple according to state law. After that, the whole company squeezed themselves into one car or another, and the convoy drove to the next village, eventually arriving at a *dacha* (garden house). Accompanied by music, all of the bride's closest friends and young relatives, and all of the groom's *hamsinf*s (peers, from *hamsol**) and young male relatives sat, ate, danced and made merry – curiously watched by a crowd of children. After several hours of dancing, the bride was brought back to her home.

The next day, I went to the bride's house, where many women arrived (four-fifths were from the bride's side and one-fifth was from the groom's side), bringing their *tavaq* (or *tabaq* – a large plate filled with baked sweets, covered by a cloth); they went and sat in one of the five rooms. All the gifts were registered in a booklet, after which the *tavaq* was emptied and then refilled with other sweets and a gift, depending on the status of the person.[26] The bride was sitting in a neighbour's house (her father's brother's son's house).

The men (from both sides) were seated in the garden in long rows and received their 'share' (*haq*). They left as soon as they had finished eating. Only the groom remained behind with his friends, until he was 'dressed' (with a *chalpon*) by one of the bride's relatives. After the groom's family had distributed all their presents, which they brought in a chest, to the nearest relatives of the future bride, the bride met her mother-in-law for the first time. After the women had left, the mother of the bride repacked the *sanduk*s (chests), after which all of the dowry was loaded onto a truck.

The actual leaving of the parental home seemed to be the hardest event for the whole family, including the bride. She was accompanied by an uncle (FB), her *yanga* (sister-in-law) and one of her friends. At the groom's house, the groom's relatives had to give a sheep and a piece of cloth to the bride's side before they were allowed access to the truck carrying the dowry, and again, the same to the uncle in order to get the bride out of the car. The bride was then guided to a room which contained girls and young women from the groom's side. The groom's entire house was packed with women guests, while the groom, his *hamsinf*s, and young male relatives were seated in the new couple's room.

In the evening, they organized a big party, with music and dancing. This event is very important for young people and has a semi-public character. Often, the party takes place in the middle of the street; since it starts after sunset, most of its participants comprise the youth of the *mahalla** (neighbourhood). Girls put on their best clothes and fear neither cold nor discomfort while joining the festivities along with their girlfriends. Boys and young men come from areas that are much farther off. In marriages between famous families, even people from other villages come to watch the event and – which is more important – to look for girls from the *mahalla* concerned and continue fights of rivalry that had started on other occasions (such as weddings or at school) with boys from other neighbourhoods or villages.

At the end of this party, after everybody had left, only two *yanga*s remained behind – one from the bride's side and one from the groom's side – and waited for the proof of virginity. This is important because if the girl fails to prove her virginity, it is said that the marriage will end in divorce within a year.

A Religious Marriage in 2007

This last example is of a religious marriage. The brother of the groom's father was a mullah and had decided that the marriage should be in accordance with Islam, in memory of his pious deceased father (the grandfather of the groom). This implied that the whole event was to be cleansed of 'un-Islamic' elements.[27] This was a meticulous and detailed procedure, with constant deliberation on whether an action, tradition or habit was in accordance with Islam, all under the watchful eyes of the mullah.

The women began to cook early in the morning, just as they did for other weddings, but no man other than those belonging to the groom's family was allowed to enter the backyard. Men and women entered the house through separate doors and sat separately. In the evening, the mullah gave a *mavlud** (religious feast) in the mosque, exclusively for the men.

The greatest restrictions were imposed on the festivities of the young – for example, meetings between peers and friends was without music or alcohol – and in many other small details, such as the absence of the bunch of flowers that the groom is traditionally supposed to present to the bride while picking her up. Before going to the bride's house in this village, they would traditionally perform *sartarosh* (a haircut for the groom). The groom sits on a table, while the guests dance around him and people give him money. An old man combs the groom's hair. For this ritual, instead of calling a professional artist to perform at this ceremony, the mullah himself sang the old songs while the others recited poems. Women were forbidden to attend the celebration. Meanwhile, the bride was dressed at her home, and her girlfriends were dancing to songs played on a tape-player. Only the *shah* (groom), the mullah and one of the groom's friends came to the bride's house for the *nikoh** (wedding ceremony) accompanied by an elder sister of the *shah* and two daughters of the *shah*'s paternal uncles (FBs). The bride was represented by her brother (*vakil*) and two witnesses (*amak** and *taghoi**). The girl said 'yes' immediately and the visitors were served a meal, after which they took the bride to her husband's home.

Nine *yanga*s from the bride's side accompanied the bride to her husband's home, and they remained at the groom's house in the same room as the bride until the next day. There they danced and enjoyed the feast, while the few men (all family members) watched movies in the neighbouring room. The bride, sitting in a corner, could hide behind a curtain (*chodar*) and relax, but as soon as the curtain was lifted, she performed her role as a submissive, newly married girl perfectly. In the afternoon, the mullah came over to the room where the women were gathering and held an *amru ma'ruf** (religious teaching) for the women. After that, a group of elder village women prayed together in a private home.[28]

The nine *yanga*s spent the night at the groom's house, and the next day, after exchanging presents, they left with the bride. The *shah* had planned to pick her up from her parents' home after a couple of days. In this village, they do not check a girl's virginity, so the couple is left with plenty of time to get to know each other. They did not perform a civil marriage, however, which the mullah regarded as unnecessary for a proper marital life before God.

Discussion

Marriages vary by social and ethnic group, by village, by religion, and even by family. The above examples thus only provide a small sample of actual marriages and how different they can be. Unlike many other descriptions of marriage in Central Asia (e.g., Andreev 1953; Pétric 2002; Harris 2004; Kehl-Bodrogi 2008), the first example (and it is not exceptional) accords the young man a degree of agency, which is however often subtle (see Jum'aev 2001; Harris 2006).[29] Parents perform the role of initiators – for example, they decide whether or not it is time for their children to get married – but their authority extends only as far as their children are willing to accept it.

The example of Mirzokarim is a case in point. The young man was proud to emphasize how he managed to marry the girl he loved against his parents' will. Nonetheless, he still conformed to the traditional life-cycle construction: a young man marries in the last years of his education or after completing his studies or military service, when it is his turn to do so, according to birth order. The initiative might be taken by the parents, but the process of finding a suitable partner involves the whole family. The second example shows a change in strategy during the civil war. Instead of making marriage a collective endeavour, parents married off their daughter in haste, in order to prevent her from falling into the hands of the soldiers occupying their village. The girl's parents were afraid to keep a young, unmarried daughter at home and recognized a young man's relatively advantageous position during the insecurity of the civil war. In this instance, we also see an example of a power shift from older generations to younger ones. How this is seen from the young man's point of view will be discussed at length below. For now, the example serves to show how domestication through marriage is a collective process and that, in times of crisis, rituals cannot be performed in the same way anymore, which disrupts the domestication abilities of the older generation.

The two post-war marriages show a renewed emphasis on the ritualistic aspect. More generally, young men use their weddings to display the wealth they have accumulated by working abroad. Through the display of conspicuous consumption at their weddings, they increase their social status – for many men, their marriage is, 'the only thing in life that makes you feel like a king', as Aziz (aged 22) expressed it. The fact that parents and elders are absent from many rituals demonstrates the importance of the wedding as a youthful event.

In the marriage observed in 2006, the girl had never seen (or noticed in school) her future husband; her marriage was arranged in order to forge a strong bond between her parents and the most powerful authority in the village (the chief of the sovkhoz). Although his father could have married him off earlier, the young man ended up marrying rather late, after spending some time in Russia. Neither he nor his *hamsinf*s (peers) were particularly Islamic – instead, they favoured the kind of 'modernity' that they believed could be demonstrated through conspicuous consumption.[30] He eventually left his wife to his mother's care and authority. He is an example of a young man who manages to retain his autonomy while happily delegating much of his marital responsibility, including his wife, to the extended family.[31] He has accepted domestication by the family and community, which will gradually guide him to become the head of an independent domestic unit and thereafter accord him full (community) membership.[32] Concerning the role of his peers (*hamsinf*s), his status change from *bacha* to *mardak* becomes a topic of much teasing and jesting, while allowing him to retain a youthful position within the group with which he has progressed into adulthood, and with which he will eventually join teahouse meetings as a full adult.[33]

In the example of the religious wedding in 2007, it can be argued that Islam has become an alternative to a display of conspicuous consumption, provided that the groom accepts the numerous restrictions imposed and possibly even the social exclusion of village youth. In the case of youth, some use this alternative as a 'cheap' way to get married, while others perform it with religious conviction.[34] Note that in the religious marriage, the bride and the groom never appear together before the audience; in the traditional wedding, however, they do so on many occasions. The *mavlud* (here: religious wedding feast) emphasizes the young man's submission to God as a member of the religious community. The choice of a religious marriage is thus also a chance to be accepted into the religious community before old age.

However, not everyone can opt for a religious marriage because it demands the public demonstration of religiosity and restrictions in many domains (abstinence from alcohol, regular prayers, 'mature' behaviour and so on). Furthermore, religious weddings can also lead to the social exclusion of the groom by the majority of his peers, who do not want any restriction imposed on their consumption of alcohol, dancing, music and so on, or any restraints on the display of conspicuous consumption at the marriage. This happened in the case of the religious wedding described above, when the majority of the groom's peers did not show up, since this wedding did not give young people a chance to dance and celebrate the occasion or to become 'the only thing in youth that makes you feel like a king'. In other words, the religious wedding was already a mature ritual in itself in which 'youthfulness' was unwelcome.

Marriage as an Indicator of Change: Age at First Marriage

Thus far we have dealt with concepts of marriage in social anthropology and demography and with marriage as a ritual that is sensitive to socio-political and economic change. In this section I wish to provide statistical data on age at first marriage. The analysis of age at first marriage is a way to turn observations into statistics in order to check the actual impact of the observed phenomenon on demographic development. For the study of youth bulges, changes in marriage are probably the most important measurable proof evidencing the dynamic of youth as a socio-demographic group. Furthermore, age at first marriage is at the core of the tension between parents and their children and parents and the state in Tajikistan. Generational tensions about responsibilities and independence become apparent in discussions of the maturity of youth, and age at first marriage is often a central focus of such discussions. After several ethnographic accounts of discussions about age at first marriage in Tajikistan, I will provide statistics and a discussion about observable marriage patterns.

In the 1930s and 1940s, when the Soviet state had penetrated even the remotest villages through the system of collectivization, doctors were given the responsibility of estimating the age of young girls and deciding whether or not they were mature enough to marry. By law, the minimum age for marriage was 17 years. Shortly after, it became compulsory to register births, and the law became a bureaucratic hurdle that could only be bypassed by changing the girl's birth certificate.[35] The discourse at that time was more concerned with a girl's physical maturity than with her real age.[36] Manipulating young people's ages was therefore a common practice – the state itself did so during the Second World War. In order to recruit more soldiers into the army, the authorities changed the birth records of boys in order to qualify them for recruitment. Thus, the law was bent to accommodate social or political practices.

A case in point is that of Bakhtigul, who was married off to her teacher when she was below the minimum age required by the state for a woman to marry:

> BAKHTIGUL: They brought me to this man – I was very young. Earlier on, one had to go to the doctor and get a certificate [giving proof of age, if they wanted to marry]. The doctor kept staring at me and then said, 'You are not of age yet'. After that they paid him a lot of honey as a bribe, and only then did he give me the certificate.
> S.R.: How old were you?
> BAKHTIGUL: I was 15 years old. Before marriage, we had to go to the doctor to get his certificate because we did not have any documents – he would then estimate the girl's age. When we left, he said, 'She is still a girl'. Earlier on, girls were given away in marriage at a very young age . . . I lived with my husband for three years, and then they recruited him into the army. I didn't have children at that time.[37]

Earlier I mentioned the importance of the introduction of the Soviet educational system in creating a more standardized life course, and thus more standardized marriage cohorts.[38] After completing their schooling, the girls enter the marriage market, which is clearly defined and encompasses three to four years after schooling. While I was conducting research in 2006 and 2007, girls born between 1985 and 1988/89 were in the marriage market. This does not mean that older or younger girls could not marry, but generally, when searching for a partner (when a man was *zangirī**), he would be looking for a girl in this age group. The girls who remained unmarried after this age were treated as if they were inferior in some way. This is why some agreed to bride abduction – a controversial practice that still exists in Jirgatol. While this is a traditional practice among Kyrgyz, Tajik do not consider it an appropriate way to get married, and even now, fathers occasionally repudiate their daughters if they have been abducted. It must, however, be mentioned that state laws have become stricter in recent times, so the girl must sign a paper before the mullah can marry the couple. This is why a young man usually discusses the matter with a girl he is interested in and obtains some kind of agreement from her before 'abducting' her with his friends.

Once, Salomat overheard a neighbour's remark that 22-year-old girls (born in 1984) were already too old for marriage. Although the discussion was not about her, she was troubled by it and agreed to elope with a man from another village. One day, in the bazaar, a man approached her and offered to marry her. Since he was 'good looking', she accepted. For her family, she fabricated the story that she had been forcibly abducted (which after all was the case), but her girlfriends knew that she had given her consent beforehand. When they came and abducted her, however, she discovered that she had been cheated: it was not the man who had talked to her who she was to marry, but a 'short and ugly man from a poor family'. She had no choice and married him anyway, because returning home would have been seen as an even bigger shame – a girl who has been abducted once is perceived as spoiled forever. Her husband is two years older than her. The husband's family made an effort to mollify the girl's family's anger through gifts. They even organized a conventional marriage in their village, but none of these efforts appeared to appease Salomat's family. When Salomat came back home for the first time after her 'abduction', she first fell into her mother's arms, crying, then she repeated this performance with each household member, in order to show her strong sense of discontent with what had happened to her. While all the female family members accepted this request for forgiveness, she was very afraid of the reaction of her male relatives. In particular, her father's reaction would be decisive for her future life.[39] She met her father in the evening, and he forgave her. Her youngest brother, however, did not forgive her and denied her siblingship with him.

Salomat did everything possible to avoid being an 'old maid' – a status accorded little respect and actively avoided by girls themselves, as well as by their parents and the community (cf. Harris 2004: 86). For men, however, the situation is somewhat different. Men are deemed old enough to marry around the age of 22 (after completing their higher studies), but they are not regarded as unfit for the market after attaining a certain age. Rather, they are expected to marry an older girl if they marry later in life, so that there will not be too much of an age difference between the partners.

Following the break-up of the Soviet Union, it is possible to observe a radical change in the practice of marriage during the civil war and considerable changes in age at first marriage in post-civil war Tajikistan. A civil war affects the entire population that is involved in the conflict, and people usually have to reorganize their lives in an intense and unpredictable environment. While combatant groups develop clear rules and organizational patterns, for the non-fighting population – and especially for women, who are responsible for their families – survival becomes a daily struggle. A state of general insecurity leads to many changes in the decision-making processes of daily life, including decisions pertaining to marriage. For young men, the civil war provided a sudden opportunity to gain access to women outside the control of older generations and the long and costly ritual procedures of marriage. Their first reaction, therefore, was to appropriate this ritual. They were also able to do so because they were exposed to interpretations of Islam that favoured their attempts.

Islam is a just (*odilona*) religion and never forces hard work on anyone. When, for example, a young person (*javon*) likes a girl and loves her, he does not have to ask his father and mother for permission [to marry], because it is he who will be living with this girl in the future. And if the father and mother decide on [a girl] for the boy, and if this girl is not to the boy's liking, he should not take her. It is true that here [in Tajikistan] parents appear to choose. However, since this is the right of children and the duty of their father and mother, it is good to let the children select. A man should choose a partner corresponding to himself – a partner who respects and likes him.[40]

In this way, young men rejected parental domestication and chose to assume responsibility for their own lives. At the onset of the civil war, this meant a drop in age at first marriage; but it appears that, once those who wanted to marry had taken a wife, the age at first marriage increased rapidly. It was only after the war that parents regained some control over the institution of marriage, with the argument that it was their duty before God and that parental blessings were essential for a successful married life. However, parents have so far not regained full control over their children marriages, as is demonstrated in the amount of effort parents have to put into persuading their sons to marry.

To get an idea of the way in which migration affects marriage, let us refer to the account of Saifiddin, whom I introduced in Chapter 4. Saifiddin is a young man, born in 1981, who had been in Russia for six years before marrying in his native village. He had repeatedly refused to marry, but eventually agreed to save his parents' honour. Still, he announced that he would leave again, because in his village, 'mountains squeeze in from all four sides'.

> S.R.: When your parents chose a wife for you, what did you tell them about your wish to marry?
> SAIFIDDIN: I said I won't marry – I am not yet ready to get married. But then my grandmother and my grandfather told me, 'Son, you are getting older; what will people say?' I am already 26 years old. If I don't take a wife, people will spread all kinds of bad rumours – that is why I agreed.[41]

Here the community as well as the parents perceive marriage as a means to curb the unbridled power of youth and gradually 'domesticate' young people into leading a proper adult life, as is expected in rural areas. Saifiddin was not even sure that he would be allowed to take his wife to Russia, because she had to serve his parents first of all. 'After finding a good job, I will rent a flat and take her with me to Russia – only if my parents agree', he told me.

Marriage has become a core event for negotiating generational tensions. The study of the civil war and post-civil war periods shows that marriage was not and has not been abolished or rejected in either period, but negotiations about maturity and marriage revolve around questions of when, whom and how to marry, focusing on the age of those marrying, their choice of partner, and whether to follow a simple religious ceremony or one involving conspicuous consumption.

A Statistical Analysis of Age at First Marriage

If social changes can be observed, they must also be measurable. Also, if the civil war disrupted cultural practices, it must have had numerous repercussions. With these hypotheses in mind, I will look at marriage from a statistical point of view and thereby determine whether it is possible to measure the changes that have been observed and described in personal accounts. In the following analysis, I will concentrate on only one aspect pertaining to this issue: changes in age at first marriage, which will allow me to use quantitative as well as qualitative methods. Through measurement of this single issue, I intend to capture change in marriage practices, and hence in domestication more generally, in order to complement the discursive intentions and arguments of this study.

Marital Data from Three Villages

All the data presented in this chapter have been extrapolated from the genealogies collected in 2006 and 2007. I have presented each village separately because each of the three field sites – Shahrituz, Shahrigul and Sasik Bulak – experienced the civil war differently. While in Shahrituz the entire population in question fled during the civil war, only returning in the second half of the 1990s, in Shahrigul people fled to the mountains for a while and experienced the social stress that accompanies unsettled living conditions, but they were able to return to their villages sooner, with the exception of combatants. Sasik Bulak was involved in the war only briefly and towards the end of the conflict, but people had to deal with numerous local tensions and a large number of refugees. The data have been divided into three time periods: the first period extending from 1983 to 1990; the second (the civil war) from 1991 to 1998; the third (the postwar period) from 1999 to 2006.[42]

A comparison of the data in Figure 5.1 shows a peak in the absolute number of marriages during the civil war, with one exception – the data for Sasik Bulak – where the figures peak in the postwar period and therefore correspond to demographic growth. In general, it can be said that there was a marriage boom at the beginning of the civil war; however, the incidence of marriage decreased sharply with the continuation of the conflict, and there has been little recovery in the postwar period.[43] The period around 1996 was marked by relative peace, the occurrence of famine in many parts of the country, and a political tug-of-war among those in power. The first wave of violent conflict had passed. The figures therefore suggest that the outbreak of the war was perceived with shock by most families, who reacted to it by maximizing their security and reducing their risk (marrying off their unmarried daughters in order to avert danger). Here, we recall

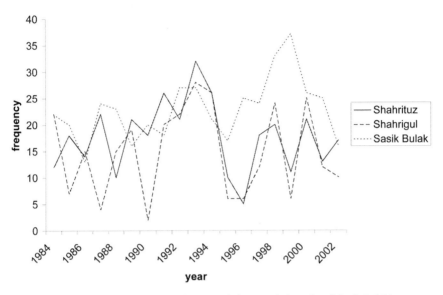

Figure 5.1: Number of marriages, both sexes (Shahrituz, Shahrigul and Sasik Bulak).

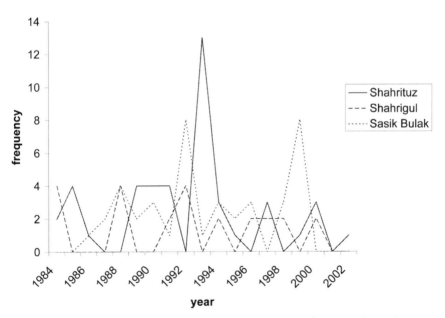

Figure 5.2: Number of divorces, both sexes, including cessation of marriage due to the death of a partner (Shahrituz, Shahrigul and Sasik Bulak).

Firuza's description of the civil war situation in 1996, when several attempts to sign a peace agreement had failed and the overall situation was perceived as extremely dangerous by Tajik families: 'We didn't know if the world would ever be peaceful again'.[44]

Some parents condemned marriages made during the civil war as impulsive, emotion-driven events lacking collective approval. Therefore, many believed that those marriages would eventually end up in divorce. The statistics presented in Figure 5.2 support this assumption for Shahrituz and Sasik Bulak, but not for Shahrigul. If we consider the divorce rates for men in Shahrituz, then the risk of divorce is high for the 25 to 39 age group, with a crude divorce rate of 12.5 per cent for the 30 to 34 age group. In other words, the probability of experiencing a divorce in this age group is higher than the probability of getting married. The data of course show a bias due to the small sample size. Nevertheless, the results do reflect the generational tension that becomes visible in marital behaviour, whether in age at first marriage or in divorce rate. Divorce, as young men see it, is a way to escape from an economic burden when they would rather spend their money on consumer goods (buying mobile phones, cars and so on), because the men are solely responsible for feeding their families. Whereas for men divorce has become rather easy since the break-up of the Soviet Union, for women divorce leaves them in a precarious position due to their restricted access to social assistance.

Let us now take a closer look at changes in age at first marriage over the three periods defined above, looking in turn at the villages of Shahrituz, Shahrigul and Sasik Bulak.

SHAHRITUZ

The data from Shahrituz for age at first marriage for women (see Figure 5.3) show changing patterns throughout the three periods: The pyramid of the prewar period has a clear peak at age 18 and a concentration between ages 17 and 21. In the second period, the age at first marriage drops during the civil war, with a much larger percentage of women being married between ages 14 and 20. For the postwar period, the age at first marriage peaks one year later than previously, and we can see that a somewhat larger percentage of women are married off at a later age, especially in comparison to the wartime data.

The figures clearly articulate the general insecurity associated with having girls of a marriageable age during wartime. They were married off in order to protect them from what is the riskiest status for girls in Tajik society: being an unmarried young woman. Girls entering puberty become a great concern to their families, since they are the focus of honour for the men who are responsible for ensuring their security: their brothers and fathers. Note that many of these brothers and fathers were spread throughout the country during the war – some in refugee camps in Afghanistan, others in Dushanbe or farther away in the mountainous

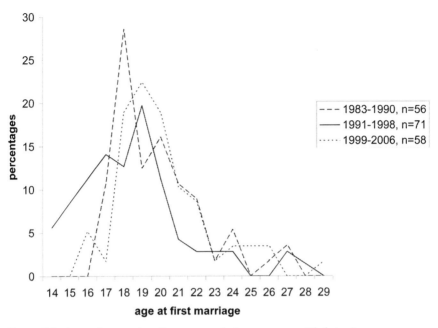

Figure 5.3: Age at first marriage for women, relative percentages (Shahrituz).

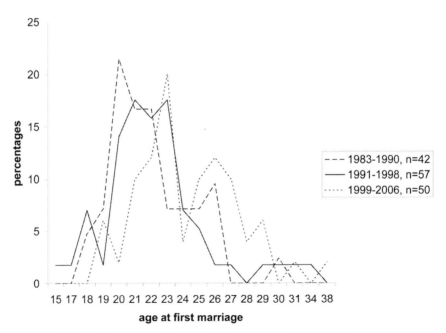

Figure 5.4: Age at first marriage for men, relative percentages (Shahrituz).

regions, and some even in their neighbours' houses. Refugees experienced even greater insecurity regarding their daughters' safety, because they had to cross borders with them.

The data form a different pattern for men (see Figure 5.4). Rather than age at first marriage forming a distinct peak as it did with young women, there is a much wider range during the civil war period, dispersed more generally from as young as 15 up to 34 years.[45] The reason for this change has been mentioned: it is an essential feature of a civil war. During the Tajik civil war, not only did state law become ineffective but the traditions of marriage were also jettisoned, and men could get married with no regard to birth order or the performance of long and costly premarital rituals. Men got 'a wife for free', as they explained to me, due to the minimal transfer of goods. Thus, we can observe that this period, which was devoid of traditional rules, allowed men a different kind of access to women, whereas in times of peace a large number of them would have been restricted by tradition and/or state law.

The shift in marriage trends – towards a later age at first marriage in the postwar period – reflects the growing economic difficulties and, to a lesser degree, the re-establishment of traditional rules (control by parents) that again restrict a young man's access to women through the requirement of a proper marriage. Moreover, many men are bent on migration and therefore postpone marriage – not only for economic reasons but also because they get to experience an alternative way of life in Russia.

SHAHRIGUL

The data from Shahrigul for women (see Figure 5.5) reveal slightly different patterns. This small village did experience a regime change, but its people were not forced to flee their village for a very long period (although they left the village many times during the day to escape fights and forced recruitment). Thus, the basic shape of the pyramid of the data pertaining to women shows little change throughout the three periods (yet with slightly more marriages above 23 years during the civil war period), with a peak between 19 and 20 years, which is the traditional optimum.

The pattern is different for men (see Figure 5.6). Here, there is no clear pyramid, and instead we can identify a core cohort aged from 19 to 24/25 – this is especially true for the wartime and postwar data. We can also see the statistical dispersion for men during wartime, though not very clearly. This again hints at the changing rules of marriage. In this village, in fact, some men used arms and weapons to forcibly marry women. The high percentage of marriages involving men over 25 in the postwar period is the result of increasing economic responsibility taken up by the younger men. Most men in this village today must raise money for their own wedding, which they accumulate by working in Russia for a couple of years. Many boys leave or are sent to Russia at age 17. The optimum age

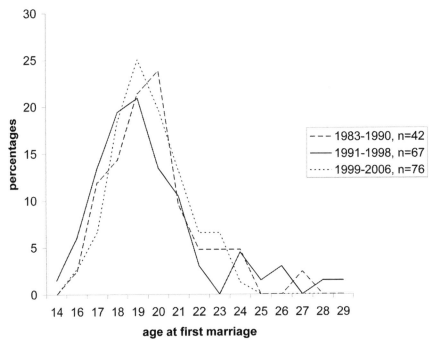

Figure 5.5: Age at first marriage for women, relative percentages (Shahrigul).

Figure 5.6: Age at first marriage for men, relative percentages (Shahrigul).

for marriage that had developed since the introduction of the education system and military service has become less relevant in recent times, and a young man's capacity to earn money and the social pressure he experiences back home become the decisive factors.

SASIK BULAK

Sasik Bulak, which was situated on the periphery of the conflict, was controlled by *mujohids** but experienced less lethal fighting; therefore, it became a primary area of retreat for refugees. The data for women from Sasik Bulak (Figure 5.7) show little change for the prewar and civil war periods, but there is a shift in the postwar period towards a later age at first marriage. This again has to do with economic change; hence, many girls are promised (*fotiha**) to a particular boy at a younger age, which severely restricts their freedom of movement, but the actual marriage only takes place when the groom's family is economically able to pay for the wedding ceremony. The persistence of the pyramid structure also reflects the strong perception that there is a marriage market for women, which starts when the woman attains 17 to 18 years of age and lasts till she is 22 (today, closer to 24).

The data for the postwar period pertaining to men (Figure 5.8) are basically marked by an almost totally flattened pyramid with no peak and a wider dispersion. The civil war seems to have had comparatively less effect on marriage in this village. Another interesting aspect is the high incidence of marriage among those over 30. I met some men who had left for Russia many years ago and become comfortably settled there. Some had even married or at least had a girlfriend there, and only came back to marry when they were in their mid 30s in order to re-establish a link and reinforce their position within the village.

Discussion: Marriage Patterns

Comparing the three sample data sets, it is clear that the intensity of the civil war had a significant impact on marital behaviour – yet in very different ways for men and women. Whereas men experienced the civil war as a time in which their power increased and their access to women, goods and social positions improved, the rising level of insecurity surrounding young women became the primary concern for families. The more the villages experienced lethal risk, the more radical the changes in patterns of age at first marriage. The postwar period does not show the same pattern as marital behaviour during the Soviet era. Instead, age at first marriage has steadily increased, again more for men than for women, the former having become the main breadwinners in their families, forced to earn their living through migration. Generational tension between parents and their children and negotiation over maturity become visible in changes of age at first marriage. The path to social maturity still involves marriage, even if economic ambitions compensate for some of the immaturity accorded to unmarried boys in rural Tajikistan.

Figure 5.7: Age at first marriage for women, relative percentages (Sasik Bulak).

Figure 5.8: Age at first marriage for men, relative percentages (Sasik Bulak).

To better understand the changes in marriage patterns presented above, they can be analysed against those from a different period, such as the Soviet era, when an easily distinguishable age pyramid indicated traditional patterns of marriage. Depending on the intensity and experience of the civil war in a particular area, this Soviet marriage pattern changed both during and after the war. The most distinctive pattern represented in the data pertains to men in Shahrigul, men and women in Sasik Bulak, and very strongly to women in Shahrituz. I will call this pattern the war-related 'one- or two-directional shift in age at first marriage'. The main characteristic of this pattern is that it first indicates a shift towards a younger age (at first marriage) during the civil war, with age at first marriage clearly increasing in the postwar period, thus moving in opposing directions at different times in relation to the conflict.

Another characteristic of marriage in Tajikistan is the 'dispersed marriage pattern'. In this case, what is immediately apparent to the observer is the wide dispersion of age at first marriage. In some cases this seems to be true only for civil war marriages, while in others it is characteristic of postwar marriages. In other words, during the civil war, and to a lesser degree after the war, men and women married far beyond and below the traditional optimum. In several cases this produced a flattened pyramid – the more obvious pyramid that was typical of Soviet-era marriage patterns widens out in favour of a much larger age cohort experiencing first marriages. The pattern is clearly shown in the incidence of postwar marriages among men in Shahrigul. In Shahrigul this pattern began in the civil war period and has continued into the postwar period. Since the same can also be observed in the data pertaining to men's marriage in Sasik Bulak, it seems to mark a change in a trend that appears to have started during the civil war and persisted afterwards. This pattern resembles accounts of pre-Soviet marriage habits, when men marrying at a later age were common for the majority of the poor population. With this in mind, we can assume that the clear-cut marital age cohort that appeared during the Soviet period is historically more the exception than the rule; hence, a dispersed marriage pattern reflects social insecurity and economic inequality, in addition to liberation from Soviet influence and control.

Conclusion

During a civil war, people tend to lose their sense of long-term planning in personal matters. Parents married their daughters off as young as 14 during the civil war in Tajikistan because they were afraid that their daughters would fall into the hands of their enemies. In the absence of dependable local agencies and a stable political system, young women during the civil war became one of the most vulnerable social groups. This is why parents hid their daughters in caves, cellars and even in trees, or married them off to relatives or young men from the village. In doing so, they passed on the responsibility of taking care of their girls and ensured their safety to the younger generation, which seemed more capable of protecting a family at a time of violent conflict. Thus, it becomes clear that marriage strategies are subject to change in times of social conflict. In other words, marriage as a central rite of passage is affected by violent conflicts and radical political changes.

For men, the civil war provided easier access to women through force of arms, without having to navigate tradition (such as marriage according to birth order and exchange rules) and state rules (such as minimum age restriction, ZAGS registration and monogamy). However, even if to some young men this was an opportunity to display their masculinity, I do not believe that easier access to marriage was the main motive behind joining combatant groups. Although it became rather difficult to quantify matters due to the lack of data, it can be said that from the twenty-seven (first) marriages in Shahrituz that involved girls aged 14 to 16, nineteen took place during the civil war period.

Let us now look at the aforementioned three periods in political history: the Soviet period (1955 to 1991), the civil war period (1992 to 1997) and the postwar period (1998 to 2006). Distinguishing these three periods allows me to assess the effects of political developments. Before 1991, only few girls were married below 18 years, with an average of 19.3 years for the prewar period of 1955 to 1991 (there is a possibility that the data may have been biased due to age manipulations). During the civil war, this suddenly dropped to an average age at first marriage of 18.4 years, after which it has risen to 20 years, on average, as of 2006. The same tendency can be observed for males – the age-related changes are even more obvious in their case. For men, the age at first marriage went down, from an average of 22.3 years during the Soviet period (1955 to 1991) to an average of 21 years during the second period (1992 to 1997); in the postwar period (1998 to 2006), however, the average has gone up to 24.8 years.

Men in Tajikistan are traditionally restricted from marriage due to their place in the birth order, their family's economic situation and their social status. Marriage thus domesticates men in a very controlling manner. Although men may have access to single women, they cannot establish a family without the approval of the collective group.[46] The examples of civil war marriages support the view that cultural rules as well as state laws lost their power during the conflict, and young men could disregard restrictions in order to marry the girl they wanted. New restrictions, however, were set by another kind of control: limiting physical access to girls, as many families hid their daughters in order to protect them from marriage. Hence, marriage came to be redefined under a new set of rights: the rights of the stronger.

The age dispersion of marriage during the civil war period supports very different narratives, wherein some enjoyed the fact that they would not have to marry immediately, while others were glad to be able to skip birth-order considerations and get their girl of choice right away. In other words, young men contested their parents' exclusive right in this matter and took advantage of Islamic propaganda that stated marriage was a right for everybody, independent of other restrictions. In order to show respect for their parents, young people claimed that even in the case of an Islamic marriage, it is important to inform the parents and receive their blessings, but parents were denied much of their previous domestication rights concerning the marriage of their sons. However, these marriage strategies, which lay outside traditional rules, invited criticism that the bond was less stable and more easily broken, because it lacked the involvement of the collective. Having married a wife 'for free', a civil war marriage meant that the groom had invested little in his wife, which would affect his respect towards her. In contrast to this stands the argument that many of these marriages were due to love, at least on the boy's part, and thus I met happy couples who got married at this time as well.

The study of marriage has shown that marriage, in itself, was not a ritual that defined youth absolutely; instead, it was one step within a larger 'domestication project' that was meant to 'civilize' men. This was possible because elder generations controlled access to women and resources. But the project failed for men during the civil war when marriage was made easier due to force of arms. Since then it has remained a contested ritual over which parents and their children negotiate. While parents wish to bind their sons as soon as possible, the latter try to postpone marriage and extend the period of relative independence in Russia,[47] while still wishing to remain integrated into their local village.

The manipulation of life-cycle rituals appears to be the strongest tool available for reshaping the junior–senior relation. Seniority is based on the control of resources and status, which is eventually contested by young people. In other words, juniors today do not need the elders' resources anymore (apart from the blessing of their parents) since they have multiple options open to them for manipulating their social status in other ways.

This analysis of marriage reveals the tension between parents and their children with regard to definitions and behaviour of youth and maturity, where marriage is a central, though not the only, step. During the war, however, marriage became a matter between two people and a mullah, which need not interfere with the continuation of youthful behaviour. It is only in the postwar period that marriage has once again become a tool trough which parents attempt to gain control, and they implement this tool to bind their sons to their native village, despite their awareness that many young men prefer life in Russia to that in a remote mountain village in Tajikistan. However, Islamic concepts also offer young men a way to escape the tradition of gradual maturation by offering them the possibility of an alternative masculine role, the primary aim of which is to submit to God and assume social responsibility for oneself (Chapter 4).

In this chapter I have addressed the question of marriage in relation to the youth bulge issue. The struggle over marriage between generations has been presented as a struggle over the domestication of youth. This struggle over marriage is, demographically speaking, highly relevant as it regulates future reproductive behaviour and consequently the population pyramid. Looked at from another angle, it is the struggle over youthfulness and maturity that shapes the youth bulge and a changing perception of youth's social status. Marriage is a way to view this struggle in relation to its various dimensions and dynamics.

Chapter 2 discussed the dependency ratio as a marker of youth bulge societies and the chance to accumulate wealth under such circumstances. The study of marriage relates to this argument as well. Young people contest maturity definitions (linked to the ability to produce children) and social status by contesting existing marriage patterns. In the process, young people (especially male migrants) have been able to accumulate wealth and develop (*obod kardan*) outside their native land before engaging in rearing children. However, this relative independence from family bonds due to the postponement of marriage also leads to a rather undomesticated and undomesticatable youth bulge. This may be a reason why the state itself is so strongly interested in regulating and controlling marriage and access to women (recall the special unit of the police that is out every night to catch unmarried couples). Yet, I argue, it is not the strict control of the state nor of parents that has caused the postponement of marriage and the decline in fertility; rather, it is the alternative avenues to gaining social status via economic success and religious education.

Notes

1. Only after attaining full maturity can a man marry, so that he is better able to carry out all of his marital duties as well as enjoy marital privileges; in other words, maturity is a precondition for marriage. Furthermore, marriage is an event that not only affects the careers of individuals but also regulates the developmental cycle of the family and kin group (Fortes 1962b: 4).
2. Clifford (2009), in an analysis of Tajik demographic developments since 1989, has provided similar results to those discussed by Agadjanian (1999). However, in a supplement, he includes food shortages as in important factor influencing demographic processes.
3. During an interview in 2003 with a 97-year-old man from the Gharm district, he affirmed that the leading *mir* would allow their sons to have several wives, while they – the poor peasant population working in the service of the *mir* – could barely feed themselves. They would only be able to marry very late after overcoming such difficulties. Many would migrate to find work in other places, for instance in the Ferghana Valley, where they would also marry, or they would return to their village after many years and then get married there. See also Beisembijev (1987) and Bushkov (2000).
4. Interview with Alimardon, an elderly man, December 2006.
5. Soviet sources claim that by 1923 a network of offices for civil registration under the Record of Civil Status Act (*Zapis Aktov Grazhdanskogo Sostoyaniya*, ZAGS) had been set up in most areas with the exception of the Central Asian republics and other outlying areas (Jones and Grupp 1987: 38).
6. Although the authors raise many interesting points and provide an excellent introduction to the demographic history of the southern regions of the former Soviet Union, they ignore cultural specificities, thus repeating the mistake of regarding Islam as a pro-natalist variable, discussing women's access to contraception without including the male population in the discussion, and using Soviet censuses indiscriminately.
7. I assume that the above-mentioned practices continued throughout the Soviet era since they can still be found today. For further information on these and other such practices,

see Kamp (2006: 116–18). Even anthropologists have sometimes changed their informants' age at marriage in order to protect them.

8. By traditional marriage I do not mean static rituals that persist over generations but the
   emic perception with regard to those elements of marriage that display the community's
   commonly accepted practices for the ceremony (such as those pertaining to clothing, food
   and music). The socialist state produced a cultural context and allowed for the generation
   of traditions, just as the state does today. Because the *tüy* is susceptible to cultural and
   social changes, it differs in character from the *nikoh*, which consists of a rather fixed set of
   rituals.

9. For Tajik, the main distinction lies between a Soviet marriage (*tüy komsomoli*) and a religious wedding (*tüy islomi*) (Ato 2011). Civil registration (ZAGS) is a matter of negotiation
   between people and the state (Roche and Hohmann 2011). For a description of marriage in Uzbekistan, see Pétric (2002: 98) and Kehl-Bodrogi (2008: 105–14). A detailed
   description of the Tajik kinship system can be found in Jum'aev (2001) and Roche (2009).

10. The data recently extrapolated by Sophie Hohmann are interesting: due to the new 2007
    law, implemented rather strictly in urban and semi-urban settings, the data increase by
    more than 100 per cent in some areas (Roche and Hohmann 2011). This represents less
    the sudden wish to marry than the effectiveness of the law, as well as the many marriages
    made under *nikoh* that were also registered under ZAGS.

11. To my knowledge, this problem has thus far been totally neglected, despite its tremendous
    implication for women and its rather common practice. Men refuse to divorce their wives
    in order to escape the legal consequences (providing financial support to the wife and
    children), and women have little power to initiate divorce if their brothers do not support
    them; hence, such women are prevented from remarrying as well as claiming any legal
    rights, such as alimony and child support from their husband.

12. I use 'modern' here in the Tajik sense of the description of marriage – namely, to describe
    a feast in which status is displayed through wealth.

13. Jumhuri Todjikiston (2007). For similar developments in Uzbekistan since 2002, see
    Kehl-Bodrogi (2008: 100).

14. Abbink (2001: 132) describes marriage among south-western Ethiopian groups as signi-
    fying the end of youth. This construction of marriage induces young men to postpone
    their initiation, and with it their domestic responsibilities, and choose instead to spend
    more time at the 'warrior' grade, which allows them to partake in violence in the form of
    raiding, ambushing and killing their enemies. In contrast, Heald (2000: 114) shows that
    the Kuria, unlike their Masai neighbours, marry very young but still go on raids.

15. In most Tajik rural areas, land for construction is distributed only according to how many
    sons a family has.

16. Similarly, Creed (2002: 63), discussing the practice of conspicuous giving in Bulgaria,
    mentions the informal sector's importance in financing these rituals.

17. In 2006, an average marriage cost between $2,000 and $4,000; in comparison, a teacher's
    income was about $40 per month. People claim that a wedding is equally expensive for
    both sides, because the bride provides the furniture and basic household equipment, and
    there is no limit to these expenses, as per tradition. Further, the bride's family is often less
    prepared financially for the wedding, while the groom would have had a chance to save
    money. Thus, the bride's family has to gather the requisite financial resources in a very
    short time (even if parents have been saving for their daughter's dowry since she finished
    school), which is perceived as the main burden of having a daughter.

18. This is a reflection of communist ideology, according to which the mountainous regions
    were backward by definition, while the city was the centre of modernity – the belief being

that the deeper one went into the mountains, the less developed was the area and its people.

19. Interview with Mirzokarim, aged 41, September 2006.

20. Interview with Firuza, aged 27, October 2006.

21. Comments from a conversation with Bakhtigul, an elder woman, October 2006.

22. This word is also used to refer to school gatherings where boys and girls meet for a common meal; it is not used exclusively for men's or women's meetings.

23. Since this was a marriage between two rich families, the dowry was quite extensive, comprising several coats, five jumpers of the best quality, thirteen dresses of all manner of quality, numerous scarves, towels, cloths, bedsheets and so on, and about four *sanduq*s (chests); in addition, there were heaps of *kurpacha* (mattresses and bedcovers) of all kinds, which reached right up to the ceiling of the room.

24. Similar to the Islamic wedding, the *eshon** (a respected religious person) played the role of 'purifying' the ceremony of un-Islamic elements and behaviours by teaching and constantly repeating the rules to the congregation.

25. In fact, the mullah said this to remind the group that it was possible for someone to hear this 'ho' without the bride actually saying it, and since he considered the bride's girlfriends to be a negative influence on her, he had asked them to leave the bride. Whereas in this village the bride is supposed to postpone the agreement as long as possible (several hours) to demonstrate that she does not want to leave her parents whom she loves most, in other villages postponing the agreement is perceived as shameful.

26. Although this process of receiving and redistributing gifts is complex and quickly performed, each gesture is founded on an extensive set of cultural rules. It is in such processes that relations are negotiated and status defined. In this particular process, the women in-laws of the family – such as the *kelin** (daughters-in-law) and *yanga** (brother's wife, father's brother's wife, mother's brother's wife) – play a central role. Due to their affinal status, they are expected to respect status before emotional ties. They are entrusted with redistributing gifts among the relatives. Young *yanga*s also perform the role of mediating between parents and their children in matters of trust (marriage arrangements, choice of partner and so on) and often accompany the couple to receive the proof of virginity (cf. Jum'aev 2001: 54; Kehl-Bodrogi 2008: 109).

27. This appears to have been a central point in the agenda of Islamic movements in Tajikistan (Hetmanek 1993: 369).

28. This was the first time I had seen such an event during all my stays in Tajikistan.

29. The problem of choice of marriage partner has received considerable attention because of the visibly contentious relation between a *kelin* and her mother-in-law. It is perhaps also the most discussed relation in Tajik society itself (in informal talks, newspapers and at NGOs), leading to the view that marriage is the actual problem and not the organization and distribution of responsibility within the domestic sphere of an extended family.

30. There is one orthodox Muslim in their age group, but he does not participate in the *hamsinf* institution. Although the reason he cites for staying out of the peer group is that his peers (*hamsinf*s) are not religious enough, the economic aspect seems to play a role as well – he lives with his poor mother. For an ethnographic description of various friendship relations in Tajikistan, see Roche (2010).

31. He even invited me to record their nightly conversations, which apparently did not appear to him to be that private. Among friends, topics such as the first night with one's wife are openly discussed and joked about.

32. Marriage changes the life of young men and women in very different ways. While young men can continue to have an active social life with their peers even after marriage, only

gradually assuming a position of responsibility, young women have little option but to obey their new in-laws.

33. For the first forty days after marriage, he is always accompanied by a friend if he has to leave his house at night for any reason, for example, to meet with his peers. As in the case of newborns, the newly married are said to be sensitive to negative influences (such as the evil eye), which are especially threatening at night, for forty days. Therefore, they need special protection.

34. Julie McBrien (2008), presenting an account of similar weddings in southern Kyrgyzstan, describes the great attraction such weddings have for youth, while the older generations are rather sceptical and wish to separate tradition from religion.

35. My source here is an interview with Bakhtigul, an older woman, November 2006.

36. This discourse continues to this day. Thus, I witnessed the marriage of a girl who had not yet attained the age of 17, but since she looked much older than her classmates, she was considered 'mature' enough for marriage.

37. Interview with Bakhtigul, married in the 1970s, October 2006. Today Bakhtigul and her husband have four daughters.

38. The school continues to serve as a reference related to age, regardless of whether the girl currently attends school or not. She belongs to a particular class (*sinf*) and is promoted along with the class – even if she misses a year, she will still rejoin her classmates (*hamsinf*). In this sense, attending school is not necessarily synonymous with belonging to a class. The peer group is a lifelong connection, while school might be a very temporary aspect of it.

39. In winter 2006, young men from a village that was about an hour's drive from Lakhsh decided to get their brides from Lakhsh. Within one month, they had abducted five girls, and they made plans to abduct many others. After this, all girls of marriageable age – typically whose duty included fetching water – had to stay at home for a few weeks, and did not step out in public unless in the company of another person.

40. Comments from a discussion with young men in the Haji Yakoub Mosque, Dushanbe, April 2006.

41. Interview with Saifiddin, aged 26, November 2007.

42. Refer to Chapter 3 for an explanation of these three periods. Based on people's cognitive perceptions of civil conflict, I have chosen to extend the civil war period from 1991 to 1998.

43. Since I used absolute figures, the number of marriages should have increased after 2000, in accordance with the increase in population. The fact that the number of marriages has not increased in line with population means that there are fewer marriages in recent times when compared to the past.

44. Interview with Firuza, aged 27, October 2006.

45. I have some reservations concerning the accuracy of the lower end of this range, considering the possibility of false registration. Nonetheless, this neither diminishes the general argument nor seriously affects the data.

46. While girls are very unlikely to have any premarital sexual experiences (Harris 2006), men do have other options. In many villages, I was introduced to the so-called 'village prostitute' (in only some of these cases was she actually working for money; hence, it is often impossible to differentiate between a real prostitute and a pejorative description of a girlfriend). Eventually, the majority of men had gone to cities in Tajikistan or Russia and gained sexual experience there.

47. We have to understand that this independence is relative. Young migrant men remain highly dependent on their families, but many perceive having a wife and children as representing a much greater obligation than remaining unmarried.

Chapter 6

'Youth Are Our Future'

Categories, Groups and the State

A central feature of discussions of youth bulges is how young people are viewed by the state. Rather than pursuing a political analysis, I will present concrete examples to demonstrate how the state[1] constructs 'youth' in a specific way and how young people deal with these ascriptions (internalize, challenge, reject, negotiate). I intend to argue that a domestication of youth through conceptualizations and classifications must be preceded by an understanding of how young people are categorized and which values they are accorded by the state. The state's constructions of youth reflect its interest in youth – in terms of both the role that youth are expected to play and the categories that are applied to them. This chapter's purpose, then, is to show youth categories less as abstract concepts than as practical solutions by the state to dealing with young people. Specific events help to reveal such practices, especially in cases where young people clash with state security services.

The state, Brubaker and Cooper note, 'is a powerful "identifier," not because it can create "identities" in the strong sense – in general, it cannot – but because it has the material and symbolic resources to impose the categories, classificatory schemes, and modes of social counting and accounting' (Brubaker and Cooper 2000: 16). The state imposes its categories to which teachers, doctors, judges, bureaucrats etc. have to refer. Shepler argues, in a discussion of youth in postwar Sierra Leone, that 'struggles over youth are political struggles over *futures*, and especially about national futures' (Shepler 2005: 131, original emphasis). That is to say, the state is not only interested in controlling and socializing young people but also contributes considerably to the creation of specific constructions of youth.

What is important in our case is less a discussion of the nature of the post-Soviet Tajik state than on the inherited institutions that survived the Soviet Union.[2] I refer, for instance, to the fundamental principle of defining categories and classifications. Ethnicity is only one example (Brubaker 1994); youth is another category that persisted beyond the Soviet Union's collapse and has been taken over (though with changes) by newly independent states. Within the Soviet Union, youth politics were less a matter of national policy than of supra-national or Soviet interest. The Komsomol, for example, was the institution of youth within this wider framework. Unlike gender policies that bore much more of a regional imprint (such as Islam in the southern states exerting a restraining influence on women), the Soviet concept of youth was meant to be universal. This certainly relates to the centralized education system and to military service that served to link otherwise more localized nation-states of the Soviet Union. Regarded as a demographic element by the state (a future workforce, military potential and so on), young men were the subject of direct interest in the sphere of Soviet politics. In previous chapters I have referred to the Soviet concept that assigned to youth the role of vanguard and builder of communism, as successfully structured within the Komsomol organization. With the end of the Soviet Union, the Komsomol ceased to exist, but the idea that youth are the future of the country remains, albeit within the framework of national ideologies.

In this sense, this chapter extends the historical overview of youth and vanguard groups by focusing on contemporary concepts and practices of the state towards young people. An ethnographic analysis shows the extent to which young men (and women) remain central to post-Soviet Tajik policies not only as the bearers of ethno-national values, and not necessarily as a future elite, but as a demographic potential. Whereas the nationalizing project of the post-Soviet state appears to be rather successful, young people's living conditions have in many cases worsened over the last two decades. In this way, the Tajik case is very similar to the observations of Clifford Geertz (1973) regarding postcolonial states in the mid twentieth century. Geertz argues that nationalism was the common denominator when uniting against a colonial power, and that it lay at the core of a belief that the 'we' of a national sentiment – which is first of all an anti-colonial sentiment – would logically translate into a functioning state, but this proved problematic because nationalism lacks the ability to guide structural changes within new states (cf. Elwert 1989).

We cannot discuss the post-Soviet period without discussing Soviet institutions, since many of these institutions, despite having been reshaped, have survived in certain fundamental ways. With these ideas in mind, this chapter engages with various institutions through which categories and classifications are produced and applied to young people. Understanding the creation and implementation of such categories is fundamental to understanding how young people behave towards, and are treated when finding themselves in conflict with, state institutions. The scope of possible behaviours from which young people choose are influenced by the roles they are accorded, and the categories that are applied to them, by the state, society and the international community.

To this day, the Tajik state still maintains the rhetorical claim that youth are 'its future', but this is done in a paternalistic manner, as if the state were a caring father who possesses the right to reward and punish young people. In practice, this attitude takes the form of repressive measures that seek to force young people to conform to a state-defined life course, which includes controlling how young people express themselves culturally.[3] The average age of members of the Tajik government is 54, which means that it has the oldest body of government employees among the Central Asian states (Gulzoda 2011: 8). In the 1990s, Tajik politicians were part of the new post-Soviet generation, but today, twenty years later, their regime is unable to incorporate young people who are not directly related to the ruling family.

Tajik state representatives continue to assert the incontestable right to domesticate youth and do so by controlling central educational institutions (such as schools, universities and the military). In this manner, the state creates categories and groups of people that are framed and shaped along ideological lines. State policies towards youth outside the field of education also seek to control and shape, a process that I include under the rubric of domestication. The following incident provides an example of how everyday practices are aimed at 'domesticating' youth.

In June 2006, while I was travelling by bus, I witnessed an interaction between a man from the secret police and a conductor on the bus who was no more than a boy. The state agent complained about the conductor's shabby clothes, urging him to wear 'proper' clothes during work (white shirt, tie and dark trousers). The conductor replied that he had no money and tried to ignore his comment, but the man became angry and, claiming to be from the secret police, made him understand that this was an order: young people must wear proper clothes when working in public services. To lend added power to his words, the man showed the conductor his ID card, which identified him as a member of the secret police. This was only one of many daily occurrences in which state representatives actively engage with young people in public in order to 'educate' them and eventually make them conform to the state's standards.

Harris (2004: 24, 35) finds parallels in the ways in which the family and the state are constructed. Gender roles form the basic framework for both the society and the state.[4] In fact, people think of the president as the 'father' of the country, and some even regard oppositional thinking as an insult to the nation itself. Similar to the above incident, the state has recently introduced clothing rules in universities, directing that women wear 'female clothes' (a skirt or a dress) without the Muslim headscarf (which is banned), and men wear a white shirt and tie (cf. Heathershaw 2009: 84). However, authoritative domestication practices by the authorities are not always successful, as several subsequent examples will show.

The following sections explore the Tajik state's approach towards domesticating youth and how it seeks to shape categories and classifications through its representatives, such as the president, the police, the military, the secret services, teachers, and chiefs of collective state farms. Most examples provided here occurred in the urban context, because it is in the capital Dushanbe that confrontations between young people and state authorities reveal the use of categories and concepts.

From Komsomol to Somoniyon

From the very beginning of the Soviet Union's existence, youth were central to Soviet state formation and Soviet politics. They were seen as the vanguards of the revolution. In Chapter 3, I described how young people were organized through the Komsomol*. In rural areas of Tajikistan, the introduction of the Komsomol went hand in hand with military education. This began with the *pioners** (pupils attending grades 4 to 8), who were prescribed a substantial amount of outdoor training, which continued throughout their school years. Thus, the state interfered significantly in the socialization of youth by introducing a military-patriotic education through the Compulsory Military Service Law of 1967 (Kuebart 1989: 105). (Interestingly, this kind of military-patriotic education is still practised in some schools in Tajikistan.) This contributed to the establishment of a nationwide (masculine) fighter ethos, which still exists today. Although it cannot be said that all young people joined the Komsomol, it was through this youth vanguard that massive projects – as part of the industrialization of the USSR – could be completed. I have discussed in earlier chapters how vanguard concepts are used in exclusionary and inclusive ways. Many other historical periods stand witness to similar uses of youth as political vanguards, as in the Hitler Youth (Hitler-Jugend, or HJ) of Nazi Germany (Sternberg 1981: 310–15). Founded in 1922, the initially voluntary Hitler Youth was an auxiliary to the National Socialist Party and, supposedly, a vanguard of the Nazi movement, one which would supply the Third Reich with its future political elite. By 1936, membership became mandatory, and the Hitler Youth had increased its membership to 8 million by 1940.

According to Soviet ideology, youth were expected to progress gradually through the different stages of political maturity: *oktyabryat**, *pioner**, Komsomol, communist. The status of Komsomol was more than merely prestigious – it was the 'passport' to higher education and esteemed positions.

Although the Komsomol ceased to exist in its Soviet form with the end of the Soviet Union, young people continued to be viewed along the Komsomol's concept. During the civil war, that is, until 1997, there was no other (nationwide) organizing institution. According to Faridun Hodiboev, the leader of Youth, Sports and Tourism of the Sughd region and director of the Youth Union of Tajikistan in Sughd, 'there are two kinds of organizations today: the organization within the civil society and the Committee for Youth, Sports and Tourism of the *hukumat* . . . they both work differently. The Youth Union of Tajikistan (*Ittifoqi Javononi Tojikiston*) depends on grants and projects (financed by international donors). . . From 1997 on, after the president of the country, His Holiness, the revered Emomali Rahmon (president of Tajikistan), established relation with the youths of the country, the Committee for the Youth of Tajikistan started to work.'

In 2007 the Committee for the Youth of Tajikistan was merged with the Committee for Tourism into the Committee for Youth, Sports and Tourism. In 1998, the 23 May was made the Day of Youth. According to Hodiboev, the Day of Youth is meant to bring the state and youth closer through 'ideological work'. For this purpose the government redefined the political life course of young people by renaming the stages of political maturity listed below with symbols taken from the life of the newly independent state's national hero, Ismoil Somoni, a Persian ruler of the Samanid Empire (819–999), who is said to have created the 'first Tajik state'. While the Soviet system applied to both men and women, the new system focuses more exclusively on men. Hence, the terms of the system allude to the fighter ethos, which in Tajikistan is a masculine identity, and grades are awarded every 23 February, national 'Day of Military Forces of the Republic of Tajikistan' (*Rūzi Quvvahoi Musallahi Jumhurii Tojikiston*). While the Soviet institutions were effective – I met young men who had been denied membership to the Komsomol, and thereby denied access to universities and higher education, because of their religious family background – the new institution has little or no power; moreover, the symbols of progression (tie, star, neck scarf) have to be acquired on a voluntary basis at the family's own expense. Nor do these symbols influence the student's future life in any way – they merely represent a symbolic act of patriotism that is promoted in schools together with numerous other symbolic gestures to influence youth (banners, songs, history and so on).

When the Komsomol system disintegrated along with the Soviet Union, there were at most a few youth groups scattered throughout Tajikistan. However, even though the political structure was shaken, the idea of youth as it had been propagated through the Komsomol had already been internalized by former members of the Komsomol as well as by state authorities. During Tajikistan's civil war, the recruitment of young men and boys aged 17 and above (although in actuality often younger) was seen as a legal practice by all parties, in the belief that every

Table 6.1: State definitions and symbols of youth.

Communist Definitions and Symbols	Tajik Definitions and Symbols
oktyabryat (symbol: medal with the picture of Lenin as a child in the middle of a star, given to students in grades 1–4)	*akhtaron* [stars] (symbol: a star)
pioner (symbol: red neck scarf, students in grades 4–8)	*vorisoni somonī* [heirs, adherents of Somoni] (symbol: a neck scarf in the colours of the Tajik flag)
Komsomol (a booklet and medal, students in grades 9 and 10)	*Somoniyon** (symbol: tie in the colour of the Tajik flag) membership in the People's Democratic Party of Tajikistan
communist (party book)	

young man is duty-bound to do military service and engage in combat for the sake of his country. The idea that young people should volunteer their physical strength in the service of the state continues to exist; however, the current state is incapable of providing these young people with adequate work to compensate for such loyalty.

State Control of Youth

Harwin (1996) provides a detailed description of the Soviet state's interest in children and young people. Under the Soviet system, the state could take children away from their parents, or single mothers could bring their child to a state-run boarding school.[5] Under Brezhnev, the Commission for the Affairs of Minors dealt with young offenders, truants and families that had neglected or abused their children. This commission constituted 'the main body to coordinate the work of state and social organizations in child welfare and protection' (ibid.: 48) and had a multidisciplinary character, usually including doctors, experts on drug- or alcohol-induced problems, lawyers, police, children's inspectors and school directors. Teachers held a central position in schools, and in many villages, they were feared by parents. In some villages in Tajikistan, such as Shahrigul, for instance, the school director continues to retain some of this authority (while nonetheless complaining about his loss of authority over parents). Usually, the school is the most obvious and central place representing state authority in remote rural villages. Complaints against male pupils in Shahrigul are not directed to their parents but to the school director, who not only investigates the matter but also assumes responsibility for punishing the child.[6] Even if boys fight each other after school hours, the director remains responsible for punishing (beating) them in order to steer them back to the 'right path'. To a certain degree, the school director is responsible for the overall education of his male pupils in the public (village) sphere.[7]

The Tajik state defines youth as the period roughly between the ages of 14 and 30.[8] This time span is rather wide because the term 'youth' is mainly used to refer to men, particularly young men who are eligible for entering military service. It is possible to recruit young men up to nine years after the completion of their schooling, although usually only those who have been out of school for three or four years are targeted (that is, after grade 11, when boys are 17 years old, until they are in their early 20s). Twice every year, in spring and autumn, the military commence their nationwide campaign to 'catch' young men. Each district has a fixed quota to fill; thus, the game of cat-and-mouse begins on a specific date. Since young men and their families usually make a great effort to avoid this duty, it becomes a serious, difficult and sometimes even lethal game that officially ends once the quota has been met.[9] However, meeting the regional quota does not necessarily mean that the game is over. Authorities continue to recruit young men and then demand that they buy their freedom – a practice that increases the income of some military staff.[10] Apart from this cat-and-mouse game, all families registered as having a son in this age category are asked to send him voluntarily.

> During the Soviet times, if a man could not go to serve in the military, earlier on, nobody would marry his daughter to him. They would think that he might be handicapped or foolish. Today it is the opposite – if one goes to the army he tends to become foolish, which is why young men marry early and try to have children fast.[11]

As this quote shows, military service was not always perceived in such a negative light by parents; during the Soviet era, it was considered a rite of passage. Those who were unable to finish military service, in fact, were suspected of having some kind of mental or physical deficiency. Today most parents prefer to send their children to Russia or to continue their studies rather than allowing them to be recruited.

However, even if the majority of parents in the Qarotegin area try to keep their sons safe from recruitment, some young men see military service as a viable option – apart from migration and the pursuit of higher studies – for gaining experience outside the local sphere of the village, and at the same time increase their social status back home (if they succeed in climbing the military hierarchy).[12] I cannot provide numbers here, but I can state that such young men are definitely a small minority; nonetheless, many young men told me that if the army could reliably supply them with good living arrangements and food, they would join. In other words, they were less fearful of the prospect of violence (which was the main concern of mothers) than they were of the possibility of unsanitary conditions and the lack of proper food.

It should be noted that after a man has two children, the state is no longer allowed to recruit him into military service, as he is considered the primary breadwinner of his family. This usually also applies to widows – they are allowed to keep one son at home, even if he is old enough to join the military. However, these laws exist only on paper and are rarely applied when the recruitment drive starts and it is time to fill the regional quota.

Despite this, there certainly have been cases where young men used the system of forced recruitment to leave the village against their parents' wishes. Thus, at times it was not clear whether it was the parents who were stopping their sons from joining the military – 'it is a waste of time: they'd be better off going to Russia where life is hard as well, but at least they will earn some money' – or it was the young men who refused to enrol due to 'the risk of being beaten, mutilated, starved, or catching diseases'.[13] The widespread fear of military service and villagers' efforts to protect their sons from recruitment stem from the innumerable cases wherein young men ruined their health due to violence (such as bullying),[14] malnutrition and disease. The matter has worsened since 2008, with the introduction of new international passports for every migrant who wishes to enter Russia. These are only given to young men once they have performed the required two years of military service.[15] Interviews also revealed, however, that it is very important for young men to leave the village for any activity so that they can return as mature men (Chapter 4). In this way, military service remains an option, especially for boys who cannot afford to study or whose parents refuse to send them to Russia.

Having looked at schools and military service as domestication strategies of the state, we should not lose sight of the fact that such practices do not exclude celebrating youth as the nation's future,[16] as is the case currently in Tajikistan (*javonon* oyandai most*: 'youth are our future'). The project of building a national (youth) identity has been rather successful despite widespread discontent with the political regime. The state today attempts to exert direct control over young people through concentrating on the category of students.[17] The main reason, I assume, is the lack of a functioning Tajikistan-wide institution such as the Komsomol that would allow the state greater influence in rural communities. Furthermore, universities are not only economically linked to the state but directly managed by it. This includes the curriculum,[18] the dress code, state-run projects such as the Roghun power station,[19] students' obligatory participation in yearly festivities (such as Independence Day), and their involvement in television discussions or meetings with the president on the national Day of Youth in Tajikistan (*Rūzi Javononi Tojikiston*), celebrated on 23 May each year. Navrūzshoh, commenting on the Day of Youth celebrations in 2009, has aptly described how the state conceptualizes youth as its future, while at the same time young people feel alienated from these symbolic gestures and demand concrete solutions to their problems:

> Abdurahmon Khonov, one member of the preparation committee, says about youth: . . . 'luckily, every year the celebration for the week of youth (*haftai javonon*) increases in splendour and this also proves that the state and the regime pay special attention to the generation of youth (*nasli* javon*), because the future of the nation and homeland will be organized by exactly these youth'. (Navrūzshoh 2009)

However, Navrūzshoh claims that all this has little relevance for the majority of the other youth (non-students), who depend on television and the national press to inform them about these events. These young people prefer to see discussions of youth unemployment (*bekorī va nabudi joyi kori munosib az rūi ikhtisosashon*, 'unemployed and unable to find a job worthy of their educational level') and housing problems (*bemanzilī*, lit. 'without home'). In fact, Navrūzshoh's protagonist claims, 'If they built houses, or at least accorded a piece of land to those young people concerned, this would be a great help to the generation of youth' (ibid.).

However, the ruling party's political propaganda does not extend much beyond the capital and perhaps the Kulob area. The newspaper *Javononi Tojikiston* is quite unremarkable and provides few answers to young people's real questions; it is a relic of the Soviet Union.[20] Just like the other governmental efforts, the newspaper aims at shaping youth as active, patriotic participants in the future of the country.

The 'Arash Rebellion': From Youth Categories to Youth Groups

In the Introduction I opened with a brief account of a protest in Dushanbe against the state-run energy company by some of the country's educated youth. The protest, focused on the inability of the company to provide a reliable electricity supply, was meant to represent a more generalized frustration with the regime. The following example – the reaction of young people to a cancelled concert – bears the same political signature of frustration, but in this case it is the spontaneous expression of a group rather than of an organized group.

In the following, I intend to show how the state, confident in its paternalistic power, initiated an event that was meant to be a 'presidential gift' but which instead turned into an outpouring of political dissent. This example is an apt demonstration of the dynamic process of youth in their roles as members of a group and as belonging to a category. The example shows how a category crystallized into a group at a particular moment in time on the basis of shared experiences, and an accumulation of similar experiences over a long period. It was the development of a group identity based on the systematic exclusion of a whole social category: 'youth'. The example demonstrates that spontaneous events can offer the necessary environment for the development of a group identity. It is the transformation of latent grievances and negative experiences accumulated over years that crystallized in this specific event, producing a collective expression of anger. The lack of organized groups that could harness the spontaneous collective power into an organized protest, however, restricted the event to one of many similar desperate outbursts of anger by youth. On the one hand, it explicates the role of leadership in channelling and translating dynamic processes into political group claims. On the other, it reflects the role of size in social processes, in other words, the emerging group was neither large enough nor powerful enough to mobilize enough young people with similar experiences for common protest. However, these young people acted as group members (yet without a leader) but were treated as belonging to a category, namely (uneducated, wild, rural) youth.

The event in question began when government authorities announced that a concert by the Iranian-Swedish singer Arash was to take place on 10 September 2006 in Dushanbe's stadium, a venue often used for important political events. It was promoted as a free concert, and had been widely advertised on television; hence, many people anticipated the event with excitement. The concert was proclaimed by the government-controlled newspaper *Tojikiston* as, 'the president's gift to the youth on Independence Day [9 September] and to celebrate 2,700 years of the city of Kulob'. (The main festivities for the Independence Day, however, were scheduled to take place in Kulob, the capital of the president's home region.)[21] It should be noted here that *Tojikiston* also claimed that it had been Arash's wish to give a concert to his 'Tajik brothers for free'.[22] Nonetheless, whether it was initially Arash's idea or the government's, the important point is that in the minds of Tajik youth, the concert was considered to be a presentation of the state.

On 10 September, a steady stream of people began to arrive as early as 11 AM, as one student told me. Young people arrived from distant rural areas hoping to enjoy the concert in the capital. By late afternoon, the stadium was packed, but people continued to jam into the areas around the stadium. The concert was scheduled to start at 6 PM, but the doors to the stadium had to be closed around 5 PM.

> When we arrived around 4 PM, it was already full. We waited for one hour or so. At 5 PM they closed [the doors], then they started beating the crowd with policemen's truncheons and the young people threw back stones. When it was almost 6 PM, the presenter came out and said that first there would be some songs by Tajik singers. Arash, however, didn't come, or rather, Arash came but without his orchestra and instruments. Then some singers like Zikriyo, Shabnam and Sukhrob sang. Then the people – how should I say this – with him [Arash] not turning up, they became impatient. Then all began to shout for Arash: '*Gum shav, Orash*' ('Get lost, we want Arash'). They [some youth from the audience] threw bottles at the public and fights started. Many were schoolboys and girls from the ninth grade upwards. Then there were those who had just finished their military service, and also the recruiters – who had a free day because of the festivities – I recognized them by their shoes . . .
>
> Then the presenter came on stage again to say that Arash was unable to sing because his orchestra had not yet arrived. He called Arash on stage to say a few words to the public. Everybody became quiet and sat down. Arash, however, said '*salom alaikum*' to the crowd and spoke for only two to three minutes. He declared that he couldn't sing and asked the crowd to forgive him, then he left – this was about 8 PM. When he was leaving the stage, some young toughs (*buzbala*) climbed onto the stage and ran to catch him in order to beat him up. The militia came immediately and separated them . . . Then the fights started, and since Arash was not going to sing, everybody went out. Outside, people were already fighting because they had not been let in. There were so many people. Of course people had paid bribes – the stadium was full, so the security was not allowing anyone in.[23]

... The older boys began to throw stones. Inside, it was the young boys who started fighting, while outside, men maybe about 20 to 25 years old – and also as young as 18 or 19 years – fought and beat up the militia. The authorities caught many people and arrested them ... Both sides were fighting.[24] Whoever happened to fall into their hands was beaten up ... People had come from everywhere, from Leninobod, Pomir, Kulob ... They destroyed cars, buses, bus stops, trolley-buses, shops, whatever was in front of them.

... The crowd started to proceed towards Profsoyuz [a city neighbourhood]; then someone suggested going to the presidential palace, so they started marching and rioting at the same time. ... One of my friends [born in 1984] who had just finished military service did not break anything; he was with the crowd, though – he didn't follow the orders of the militia, he resisted them – then the militia knocked him down, pulled him into the *marshrutka** and took him into custody.

When asked if there was any leader present on the scene who might have roused the angry crowd for his own political purpose, my informant said,

No, when you are in action you don't need a leader; when one starts throwing stones, they all throw stones, and when one stops, all stop. I mean, within the crowd there were leaders, but in that entire crowd, whom will you declare to be a leader while arresting them?[25]

On the internet there were uncensored discussions, in which the following grievances were articulated:

haha ... WTF did u expect from Government??!
weren't they the ones who brought arash?
BUT ... being angry doeznt justify pucking up ... although i dont get it ...
we hardly stand up to our government's corruption and 2 all the puck faces out there for just raping us ... and stealing from us ... man ... if it takes one cancelled concert to bring ppl together to protest government we should do lotz more ... peace.[26]

No more shame than this is possible. Shame on you, shame. Tajikistan holds independent for 15 years but everything is still wild.[27]

Officials complained that young people had behaved in an uneducated manner (*betarbiya*) and labelled the rebels 'hooligans' (*khuligans**). However, a hidden political message was also making the rounds: 'A group of young people took the initiative and started to riot, which brought to mind memories of the years 1991–1992'.[28] The journalist drew analogies to unrest at the beginning of the 1990s, and thus reawakened a civil war memory that was still fresh in the minds of most people. As a result of this clash, approximately twenty people ended up in hospital with serious injuries, while many more were arrested. Many urban residents condemned the event as an act of hooliganism, complaining that the activists had 'spoiled the Tajik name abroad'. Urban residents blamed 'those who came down from the mountains' (*hamin az kūh khambidagiho*) for their wild, uncivilized and shameful behaviour.[29]

Similar explanations (wild rural youth rioting in the city) had been used to describe the turmoil in 1990, when young people had demonstrated their griev-ances by rioting: 'The Dushanbe population, both Russian and Central Asian, claimed that young men had been brought into the city on buses and given money, drugs, and alcohol to encourage them to riot' (Schoeberlein-Engel 1994: 23). Young people's rioting after the 1992 demonstrations (see Chapter 2) had also been imputed to the failure of institutions meant to control and educate youth (such as the family, communities and state institutions). Rural young men were portrayed as uneducated and unruly, as opposed to city people, who were portrayed as educated and civilized. The colleague who spoke enthusiasti-cally about the flash mob of 2011 (see Introduction) had looked on dismissively during the Arash unrest, regarding it as little more than acts of vandalism by rural youth. He became more excited when the event began to be referred to as a 'rebellion', but by then of course it was over.

There are more recent examples to show how challenges by youth to the state have been constructed as a failure of societal control and the result of educational inadequacies. In June 2006, several bombs exploded in Dushanbe in a single night. In order to dispel rumours of terrorist or political acts, the authorities pre-sented ten young boys to journalists; the boys were accused of being improperly educated, which was 'why they had come to the city centre during the night, carrying homemade bombs' (Gaijsina 2008). The boys – if in fact they were the ones responsible for planting the bombs – were presented as simple uneducated young people who lacked paternal guidance, and it was expressly denied that their actions were politically motivated.

If we consider what happened at the concert, however, we can see that some young people turned their disappointment into a political grievance and framed their acts as a political message.[30] Some began to call the failed concert *bunti Orash* ('the Arash rebellion'), but their claims were neither heard nor met with any response aside from a physical one. As might be expected, there was little information and much imprecise reporting on this event by the official press, which referred to the rioters as *khuligans*.

The Role of the Street

In order to understand the state's use of categories in dealing with young people, it is useful to discuss the place where direct confrontations between young people and the state have been most likely to occur: the street. The above-mentioned criminalization of young people's outbursts seems to be rooted in a Soviet discourse about young people and their presence on the street.[31] The street, as a geographical space within the restructuring of urban space in the 1970s and 1980s, was 'considered to be leading young people into delinquency . . . First, the street was the collecting ground for people with criminal records, and second, the street was controlled by "group mentality" which often leads "normal" youngsters to act uncharacteristically' (Pilkington 1994: 82).

The street is where people congregate if they have nothing better to do – here, it is important to differentiate between streets in a neighbourhood as part of the private sphere and streets as a state-controlled space. The term for 'street' (*guzar*) in Tajikistan was originally used to refer to a small village inhabited by a sedentary population, in contrast to the *qishlok*, rural (nomadic) settlements (Schiewek 1998; Geiss 2001). In today's urban context, *guzar* may be used simply to describe a street or a neighbourhood, similar to the term *mahalla**. An important point in this context is the relative privacy of the *guzar* and *mahalla*, as contrasted with main streets (*roh*), which are more public. This qualitative difference between the terms used to describe streets is very important because each of these terms implies specific rules of conduct. For example, young girls and women may move freely within their own *mahalla* and *guzar*; however, their movements are restricted as soon as they leave their own *mahalla*.

The street also plays a central role for young men. Being out on the street means being part of the public sphere, which is generally the area reserved for men in Tajik society. The importance of the street for youth has been discussed in numerous studies. For example, Koehler regards the street as, 'an intermediate social space through which most Georgian youth have to pass and which is also today a central point of reference for the prestige status of many boys and men' (Koehler 2000: 46).[32]

Protests in the street provoke an immediate contact with the state security sector, and conquering the street en masse is a means of political expression. In this sense, the street became the continuum of the stadium and reflected young people's response to the state's failure to take their grievances seriously. Koehler argues that the concept of the street as a socially recognized space emerged during the Soviet era in reaction to the state's monopoly over power, which was resented by citizens. The street is also a part of the criminal world, and thus can be understood in this sense as well as a place for contesting the state's power. Stephan (2008: 199), in her study on moral education, mentions that religious courses (*sabaq*) were a generally accepted means (even by state authorities, who have no alternatives to suggest) for getting young men off the street, which is blamed for having a negative influence on them.

Dealing with a Youth Bulge

Tajikistan has a large proportion of young people. The state is fully aware of the inherent potential of this demographic imbalance and attempts to control youth, albeit without any demonstrable investment in young people. Thus, a large portion of youth-centred state activities do not rise above the level of propaganda, such as activities that aim at awakening a nationalist sentiment in young people through television programmes and public meetings, as well as the regularly repainted slogans that line the roads, declaring 'youth are our future' and similar optimistic proclamations. However, the state does not provide youth with a feeling of security about the future. Corruption and the appropriation of scarce resources by a small elite ensure that it is almost impossible for young people to experience social mobility. For many, even higher education is blocked because their parents are unable to pay the legal and illegal entrance fees, which may amount to several thousand dollars.

With regard to the Arash concert, there is no evidence that the crowd's reaction was a planned provocation; however, the intensity of the spontaneous outburst shows how easily widespread latent discontent can be transformed into an expression of political unrest.[33] It can be argued that this is the result of the systematic and repeated exclusion of youth from social and political developments since the end of the civil war. The sudden decision to march towards the presidential palace in order to start a demonstration (*miting*) suggests that historical events and places, particularly with regard to the civil war, remain at the forefront of collective memory – as the discussion among Dushanbe residents the next day indicated.[34] The police, however, dispersed the crowd before it could reach the critical place – the presidential palace – and critical mass (with more young people joining in).

Youth are treated as people who are not yet fully responsible for their actions. By publicly claiming such an interpretation of youth, the state devalues young people's attempts to demand rights. The above example reveals how a group of young people collectively interpreted the organizational failure of the concert as a form of cheating perpetrated by the state, to which some of the young men responded with anger. However, only very few opted for violence; the majority expressed their anger non-violently. While the state had touted the free concert as a gift for youth,[35] when the plan went awry, instead of attempting to understand the pervasive level of anger among young people, the regime took recourse to its classic means of 'domestication': violent repression and the criminalization of young people in the face of non-conformist behaviour.

The state's strategy of domestication finds expression in an authoritarian, paternalistic role allocation (Harris 2004). For example, the category *bujetnī* refers to students who receive a grant (about the equivalent of $15 per month) from the state throughout their studies. Students whose parents do not have the means to pay for their education can apply for *bujetnī* status. In this way, they receive a monthly grant of about 40 to 80 somoni (about 10 Euro) and in theory are spared extra costs during their studies. (In practice, everyone must spend huge amounts of money in order to pass examinations, and *bujetnī* have to work off their grants by being constantly available to the professors and university staff, even during holidays).

Once they finish their studies, the *bujetnī* students obtain their diplomas only after they have worked off their debts from the state. To this end, the students are sent back to their respective native areas to offer their services as teachers for three years. By making these teachers work compulsorily for very low wages, the state also attempts to overcome the shortage of teachers throughout the country. Usually young people cannot circumvent this order and have to pay the price for their education. In 2008, however, students protested against this practice, claiming that the salary offered was not even enough for one person, let alone for a family (following university, young men are expected to marry). Following this protest, the students – apparently as many as four thousand students – were brought to trial (Mirzobekova 2008).[36]

This expectation of the state can be seen as part of its promotion of the idea that youth should serve the nation through labour (*mehnat**). Qodirov, redefined this concept during the civil war: 'The one who seeks realization through work may be transformed, and in the form of concrete work he will find satisfaction' (Qodirov 1995: 37). Moreover, relying on Soviet literature, he argues that, 'the best education of people is through *mehnat*', which is also of the greatest benefit to society (ibid.: 46). Qodirov thus justifies obligatory work in the cotton fields for pupils as part of their regular curriculum. In this way, the state's approach to youth is less centred on individual development than on domesticating youth so as to create good workers for the advancement of society.

The above-mentioned protest by students, however, reveals that the state's attempts to domesticate youth through control and reward have not succeeded, in that young people see themselves as reduced to 'cheap labour' rather than being given a sense of security for their future. Apparently the state expected a minimal investment (the grant) to be sufficient for obtaining young people's obedience and national support in return. It is in such cases that the difference between individual and collective domestication is most visible. This kind of state oppression might have worked in the absence of mass protest, and the state might have been able to control youth if interactions were limited to dual relations, such as in the courtroom. However, turning individual controlling methods into collective practices risks the formation of a stronger shared identity among the victims, who may then react as a group. Even if young people are not collectively organized, through their shared experiences they can become a dynamic group during specific events that act as crystallization points, thereby creating a sense of shared identity. However, in the case of the four thousand students, international organizations rushed to the young people's defence, thus averting any possible escalation of the dispute.

The examples provided above shall suffice for further developing the theoretical argument of this study. Being an important demographic factor, the youth cohort cannot be ignored by the state. The state has attempted to deal with young people along the lines of the concepts of youth developed during the Soviet era. Based upon conceptualizations that frame young people as immature and naturally 'undomesticated', the state, through its employees in various sectors (such as schools, the military and the government) behaves like an educator. This is not limited to the space of schools and the military but extends into the public sphere. Under such repressive conditions, young people have few avenues through which to express non-conformist ideas (as they are more or less constantly being 'educated'). Recourse to mass protest is one way (one of the most effective ways) to voice discontent. Within these categorizations, as we have seen, it is assumed that young people need constant educational guidance until they are transformed into mature political persons loyal to the national idea and the state. Deviating from such a course is not viewed, at least not publicly, by the state as political opposition but rather as misbehaviour and a failure of education.

The resort to violence by young people to express anger is more problematic for the state, in that it cannot be overlooked and it catches the attention of the media, even though the state attempts to reduce the significance of such behaviour by classifying it as 'immature'. Hebdige has succinctly formulated how young people can become what they have been described to be – people who can attract attention only by stirring up trouble:

I shall begin with a proposition – one that is so commonplace that its significance is often overlooked – that in our society, youth is presented only when its presence is a problem, or is regarded as a problem. More precisely, the category 'youth' gets mobilized in official documentary discourse, in concerned or outraged editorials and features, or in the supposedly disinterested tracts emanating from the social sciences at those times when young people make their presence felt by going 'out of bounds' . . . When young people do these things, when they adopt these strategies, they get talked about, taken seriously; their grievances are acted upon. They get arrested, harassed, admonished, disciplined, incarcerated, applauded, vilified, emulated, listened to. They get defended by social workers and other concerned philanthropists. They get explained by sociologists, social psychologists, by pundits of every political complexion. In other words, there is a logic to transgression. (Hebdige 1988: 17–18)

The example of the four thousand students (and similarly the 'Arash rebellion') suggests that the real power of youth lies in its demographic size. Sommers describes this paradox of youth bulge as follows: 'They are a demographic majority that sees itself as an outcast minority' (Sommers 2006: 155). Youth is a stage in the human life course as well as a social category for the state; however, it is only as a concrete group that youth become strong and dynamic. As a social category, youth are a majority, but as a social group, young people hold minority rights.

It is rather unlikely that the youth of a country will ever raise its voice collectively against older generations or a government; instead, individual youth groups claim to speak in the name of 'the youth' or even 'the people', and in this way they seek to mobilize the critical mass necessary to force change. Such a critical mass was not reached during the aborted concert. The response to the student protest demonstrated that the state is prepared to deal with relatively large groups of young people, and that four thousand young people do not represent a group large enough to make the state reconsider its laws. A feeling of grievance alone was not enough to lead to the crystallization of groups and, subsequently, masses of young people. Although it was enough to prompt a confrontational event, it lacked the ideological backing, a vanguard group and/or a (charismatic) leader around which a general grievance could be transformed into a shared group identity with the potential to serve as the basis for organized protest.

Conclusion

The concept of youth bulge accords the state a central role. Greed and grievances are said to result from the political and economic isolation of youth. From this experience, youth violence is believed to emerge. The causal relation between policies, economic marginalization and young people as a source of violence ignores the empirical difference between categories of exclusiveness and group formation processes. This chapter set out to examine this interdependence by focusing on the way that the state as a powerful 'identifier' shapes youth categories, and how this influences young people's range of behaviour and identifications. The example of the aborted concert and the collective court case of the four thousand students show that young people are treated as belonging to a category that holds minority rights but that reacts in groups, which crystallize around specific events that capture, in the particular moment, general shared experiences such as suppression, inferiority and grievance.

Unlike the analysis of the civil war, this chapter has looked at contemporary events, with an aim towards showing that, within Tajikistan, oppositional activities do take place but have not yet grown into larger protests.[37] This failure to galvanize discontented individuals into greater action is not because the state has provided democratic avenues that allow for smaller protests and the integration of changes to its laws to appease anger (any demonstration is dissolved no matter how small); rather, such failure speaks to the reality that, in order to mobilize a demographic potential, more than a general sense of grievance is needed.

The state deals with youth as a social category, and in the Tajik case, as a problematic category due to the lack of employment and its size in relation to the population. Until the break-up of the Soviet Union, the state through military service was central in turning a young man not only into an expected loyal soldier but into a mature man. Unemployment was less of a problem during the Soviet period but has become an uncontrollable problem since independence. The Russian economy is today the largest employer of Tajiks, and in this way the solution to the demographic unemployment problem has been temporarily solved by the northern migration of young workers. Moving back and forth between two states, the Tajik youth bulge becomes best described as a 'levitating' entity. I refer to it as a 'free pending' entity because Tajik youth are considered a problem in Russia, which refuses to seriously engage with its huge transient population of migrants from the countries of the Commonwealth of Independent States (CIS), of whom only comparatively few integrate and settle; and a problem in Tajikistan, because the country is unable to integrate youth by providing adequate employment opportunities within its borders.

The de-escalation of the potential risk of such a free pending youth bulge lies in the continual movement of individuals between the two states. This enables the Tajik state to deal with a de facto population pyramid that is much less of a problem to its security sector. The Tajik migrant population has basically no wider structural organization than the support of their native villages. In other words, these young people remain a category, namely migrants, which in its content is similar to youth. The lack of effective group formation among migrants in Tajikistan shows that migration in itself has not yet had the necessary crystallizing effect (although a strong migrant group is currently forming and may in the near future become a political party). Instead, events that led to temporary crystallization were based on events within Tajikistan. Some people blame a lack of leadership for the inability to initiate mass protests, while others believe that the majority of the nation remains paralysed by civil war memories.

A central tension between youth and the state arises from the clash between the state's concept of youth and global discourses of youth. This discourse derives from Western experiences and political standards set, for instance, by international bodies such as the United Nations. Having declared 12 August 2010 to 11 August 2011 as the Year of Youth, the UN has clearly articulated and framed a Western notion of youth that seeks ideas, such as: 'How can youth participation and representation be made more effective in your community? In other words, what are the ways to make sure that young people's voices are heard in your community?'[38] Within this set of ideas young people are called on to participate in the political process as actors with individual ideas. Such a political understanding of youth stands in sharp contrast to the perception of youth among Central Asian political elites, who assert that the political integration of youth is accomplished through an educational process controlled by the state.[39]

An example of a successful youth struggle is the revolution in Egypt in early 2011, as a result of which the sitting president, Husni Mubarak, was deposed. While the state treated the demonstrators as immature rioters, denying them political relevance, young people claimed that they must be allowed political rights to pursue peace, maturity and progress. This is even more impressive if we consider that the state sent armed former criminals among the demonstrators to provoke violence, but still failed to draw the youth into counter-violence that would have turned them from political actors into rioters.

Categories do not act, and this also applies to youth bulges as a demographic phenomenon. It is in the form of groups (whether spontaneous or organized), not as a category (however representative of that category groups may be), that young people have found ways to express their general, cumulative discontent. These concrete incidents are necessary for the crystallization of a common identity of youth, and thereby bring together enough young people who share the same emotions. Whether such incidents will turn into an organized political movement or remain unstructured local incidents depends on the level of organization among youth, whether there is a leader or not and the historical moment in which it happens.

Notes

1. Heathershaw discusses the missing distinction between the 'state' and the 'regime' in Central Asian discourses: 'In elite public transcripts, "the state" and "state officials" are inscribed as being synonymous. As neither opposition nor popular discourses clearly distinguish between "state" and "regime", this implies that an unambiguous divide is not socially and politically meaningful, and thus not analytically valuable' (Heathershaw 2009: 81).

2. It is beyond the scope of this study to engage in a discussion of the nature of postcolonial states and the question of nationalism inherent in such a discussion. For recent valuable discussions, see Knörr (2007) and Kohl (2010), as well as classic authors such as Geertz (1973), Gellner (1990), Hobsbawm (1999) and Anderson (1999). I will treat the state as a powerful denominator and state officials as agents of this state.

3. The life choices of young people are carefully observed and controlled by the state security forces. This applies to clothing (traditional clothing is encouraged but not religious attire), to religious expression (banning prayer for people aged under 18) and to the production of music (inviting bands from the United States but monitoring the content of songs composed by local groups).

4. Harris, whose research deals mainly with family matters, claims that, 'Tajik tend to draw an analogy between the family and the state, insisting that a family needs the same kind

of firm hand in its leader as a state, and that democracy is out of place in both' (Harris 2004: 35).

5. For more details, see Harwin (1996: 28–30). Even today, children with only one parent are classified as 'orphans'.

6. I was told the following story: A truck driver arriving in the village late at night spotted two bodies wrapped in white cloth lying on the street (two boys pretending to be dead). The driver was so rattled by the sight that he complained to the director, who punished the boys.

7. This was different for girls, who remain under the control of the family. Whereas boys would be fined for not showing up at school, girls were often discouraged from attending school at all.

8. In 2011, youth as a biological and psychological category was redefined by the government. Until the age of 18, young people are forbidden by law to visit mosques for prayer or to get a religious education outside the parental home. This is based on the idea that, until this age, young people can easily be manipulated by teachers and absorb all kinds of 'radical' ideas (whether religious and/or political).

9. Numerous stories circulate about the 'game' of military recruitment. Some schoolboys join in for fun, but every year the recruitment drive ends fatally for some young men, who either are beaten to death or who, in fear, jump off bridges or commit suicide by other means. The military enters mosques as well as houses in order to look for young men; hence, many of them – if they do not manage to leave the country before the campaign opens – hide in the mountains or in a neighbour's house.

10. The practices are multiple: while some pay to have their recruitment orders 'hidden' under a pile of orders (i.e., to postpone recruitment), others pay for a certificate from the Military Recruiting Office. As long as a young man walks about without such proof, he may be 'caught' any time during the recruitment period and face other legal restrictions, such as rejection of an application for an international passport.

11. Remark from a conversation with an anonymous mother, 2006.

12. Interestingly, in Lakhsh, while Tajiks were known to avoid military service, Kyrgyz would occasionally send their sons to do what they perceived as a duty. However, I have also met Tajik young men who 'ran away' from their parents by allowing themselves to be caught by military recruitment drives.

13. Quotes from conversations with an anonymous mother, 2006.

14. The problem of bullying within the army seems to have cropped up in other countries as well. For example, Pilkington writes about Russia: 'In its crudest form this was the subjugation of conscripts in their first six months by those in the fourth and last stage of service. Its most common manifestations it included forcing young soldiers to do the domestic chores of the older ones, the uneven distribution of food rations, and the deprivation of young conscripts of their personal possessions' (Pilkington 1994: 190).

15. Naimov (2005) describes the problems created for Tajik youth by the new passport rules.

16. As much as most young men devote their energies to avoiding military service, many of these same young men agree that they would be willing to take up arms in defence of the 'great Tajik nation' that they imagine to have existed for many centuries in the past and that they hope will arise again.

17. This is not specific to Tajikistan; it also appears to be true for Uzbekistan (Brick Mustazashvili 1999).

18. The state not only defines obligatory curricula but also controls scientific production. Since 2011, every dissertation has to be approved by the Ministry of Education. One

doctoral student told me that she had to rewrite her dissertation on civil war migrants by removing any reference that cast the opposition in a positive light.

19. In early 2010, the entire population of Tajikistan was called upon to buy shares in the future Roghun power station. This created an enormous economic drain on many households already struggling with poverty. Students had to buy a share in their university (and at their workplace if they had one) and pay an additional rather large sum if they were to pass exams. These forced payments stopped when the revolution in Kyrgyzstan in April 2010 acted as a warning sign to neighbouring regimes.

20. *Javononi Tojikiston* is a small weekly newspaper, usually not exceeding eight pages, which comes out rather irregularly. According to Kislyakov (1976: 22), it was a mouthpiece of Soviet ideology in the 1970s.

21. *Tojikiston*, 14 September 2006. The main festivities for Independence Day, however, were scheduled to take place in Kulob, the capital of the president's home region. Hence, most high-level government officials and security forces had gone to Kulob, leaving 'only' the lower levels of administrative and security staff in Dushanbe.

22. *Tojikiston*, 14 September 2006.

23. According to another informant, there were two rings of security forces, and when the stadium was starting to fill up, the security staff began to charge admission (10 to 20 somonī) – even though the concert had been advertised as 'free for all' – to any person who wanted to get into the stadium. When those who had paid found out that the concert had been cancelled, they turned their anger against the security forces.

24. My informant also said that further down, among the spectators, there were no fights; however, in another place he claims that some girls had been beaten with stones, while the newspaper carried an account of a girl who claimed that young men had torn her jewellery off.

25. This and the previous quotation are taken from an interview with an anonymous student, aged 22, September 2006.

26. Quote retrieved 16 and 18 September 2006 from VatanWeb, http:/rupor.info/. I have left the text as it appears in English on the blog.

27. Quotation retrieved 18 September 2006 from: VatanWeb, http:/rupor.info/.

28. *Tojikiston*, 14 September 2006 (p.5).

29. Remarks retrieved 16 and 18 September 2006 from: VatanWeb, http:/rupor.info/. This deprecation of people from rural areas is not new, as it was integral to Soviet ideology; in Marx's words, urban centres are an alternative to the 'idiotism of rural life' (quoted in Pilkington 1994: 77).

30. In a brief report on VatanWeb, it was written that young people had started marching in order to start a demonstration at a square (*miting**) in front of the parliament building (retrieved 11 September 2006 from: http:/rupor.info/).

31. With regard to deviant behaviour, Hahn (1971: 396–97) describes 'hooligan' as the classic juvenile delinquent who can be found in any country, thus framing this phenomenon as a universal one rather than treating it as a popular Soviet label for non-conformist youth.

32. Koehler's study is in line with Park's Chicago School brand of sociology, and that of all researchers who have subsequently followed his approach to urban subculture.

33. Many more such incidents (e.g., demonstrations because of constant problems with energy supplies, because of economic problems, or because of the introduction of highway tolls) started to take place in 2011, encouraged by the events in the Arab world. However, so far these have not developed into a mass movement.

34. Tajikistan still lives in the shadow of its civil war. This can be seen in how the state security services deal with the slightest social uprising, how adults comment on any effort

by youth to gain attention, and the manner in which newspapers report such events (if they are reported at all). Even foreign personnel from the UN viewed the Arash concert disturbance with alarm, as I learned when I visited them some time after the event.

35. Political festivities, typically held to honour the president, are usually not celebrated in the villages (which are not enlisted as participants in such centralized events). For ordinary villagers, the extent of their awareness of such celebrations is a day of guaranteed access to electricity.

36. Of the approximately four thousand graduate students brought to trial by the Ministry of Education, all were *bujetni*, which means that they had all received a grant from the government for continuing their studies.

37. Since the summer of 2010, a number of youth groups have emerged, especially in urban centres, which engage in small protests and organize themselves 'underground'. These groups recruit from the small educated elite that communicates primarily in Russian (and also on the internet), thus excluding the large majority of poorly educated rural youth.

38. Quotation retrieved from United Nations, International Year of Youth. Dialogue and Mutual Understanding, 10 August 2010, from http:/.un.org/youth.

39. The nature of such a clash could be observed in Kyrgyzstan during the April 'Rose' revolution of 2010 (Roche and Ismailbekova 2010). After the successful overthrow of the Bakiyev regime, new elections were to be held. A youth party, centred around students who had been studying in the West, demanded a level of political participation suited to mature members of society, while the political elite offered them no more than the opportunity to participate in an apprenticeship role. Eventually the group did not participate in the election; according to the group's self-assessment afterward, they had not managed to gain a widespread following, or at least an adequately significant presence, to succeed in playing a greater role.

Conclusion

The Dynamics of Youth Bulges as a Question of Domestication

I opened this book with two examples: one showing youth participation in protest and the other youth participation in mass events (religious events). Both appear unrelated but in fact highlight two of the main preconditions necessary for the participation of youth in violent conflicts. On the one hand, we find vanguard groups who protest against the current order and claim to represent a larger category (youth, an ethnic group, the whole population and so on); on the other hand, we have young people who engage in mass activities (in this case, religious gatherings) only if these activities make sense to them. In other words, there is no natural correlation between youth as a large subordinated category (such as believers) and as vanguard groups (such as political actors who aim to assert or acquire power).

In 2012, Eshon Nuriddinjon was banned from leading prayers in his village mosque and his brothers were placed under close surveillance by the secret services, which has led to less open discussions and more direct confrontations between the Islamic board (the official institution in charge of regulating religious affairs) and religious authorities such as Eshon Nuriddinjon. Since, as we have seen, a significant segment of Tajik youth are now found in Russia, consequently the religious opposition has turned to these migrant youths. There, they find not only the frustrated youth who toil in humiliating conditions and see in Islam a way to regain their dignity, but also the politicized and intellectual elite. The youth indentation is the result of this mass migration, and it is this indentation that becomes the focus for political actors who are well aware of the potential of these young people that form the bulge in Tajikistan.

In order to understand how demographic categories and groups concretely affect young people, I have suggested looking at domestication strategies. In this way one can approach the question of demographic size and group action from a social anthropological perspective. Tajik society includes various institutions and rules that claim to exert domestication over youth. Not only families and communities but also the state uses categories to domesticate young people and guide the course of their maturation. Examples of domestication strategies by families and communities are sibling hierarchies and marriage rules; those of the state are military service and control over education (such as who gets into university, how students should dress, and what can be taught). Hence domestication through categories and rules allows adults and elders as well as the government – all, demographically speaking, minorities – to wield control over youth. In other words, domestication makes sure that the demographic imbalance does not disrupt the power balance.

This is how traditions, institutions and rules are meant to work. But we have seen throughout this study that pressure from youth challenges such domestication strategies. While young people do not act as a category, and hence demographic size is not directly linked to youth activities, youth movements crystallize in direct opposition to existing domestication practices and structures. In a seniority-centric society such as Tajikistan, 'juniority' (*cadets sociaux*) may be similar to 'youthfulness'. Through disruptive events that affect the social relation between juniority and seniority, the actual vulnerability of elders becomes obvious when they are challenged by youth. Consequently, the size imbalance between those exerting domestication (parents, government authorities, elders, teachers, etc.) and youth creates disturbances between social juniors and social seniors.

I have explored in particular the question of demographic size (youth bulges) and its relevance to conflict. It appears that youth categories – that include a large section of a given population – increase in size proportional to the controlled distribution of (scarce) resources. This takes place through the allocation of social maturity, as in the right to biological reproduction (having a family) and access to resources (housing, money, work, fields, social status and so on). Such large youth categories are prerequisites for the creation of vanguard groups, which, although consisting of relatively few young people, act in the name of the (deprived) category that is numerically a majority. It is through challenging and negotiating categories by concrete youth groups that youth bulges become successfully mobilized.

Young people are involved in various relations (kinship- or community-based, religious, political) that have 'domesticating' effects; thus, the move from the presence of a youth bulge to social conflict is anything but linear. To strengthen the argument, I have also discussed how rituals that are used to exert control over youth become contested and can change – in the case of Tajikistan, during the civil war and in the postwar period.

Reconstructing the Life Course

In any discussion of youth, it is important to first clarify whether we wish to approach the issue from the viewpoint of a Euro-American or a local construction of the life course. In other words, we have to carefully distinguish between categories of analysis and categories of practice. If some interpretations of Islam claim that a 12-year-old boy is socially mature, this view may influence his social position within the family and community and have consequences on the young man's political responsibility. How much sense would it make, in that case, to discuss youth only in terms of Western constructions? Various youth concepts appear to be travelling concepts translated into local contexts; hence we need to avoid assuming that one youth concept is universal. At the same time, we need to take into considerations global concepts of youth as sources of inspiration. Certainly, educational systems have provided more unified principles for structuring the life cycle, and many a revolution has been led successfully by students. Their success lies, however, in their ability to formulate 'vanguard' ideas and claims to representativeness that serve to promote the highest possible youth participation. This is done by replacing a prevailing understanding of youth as submissive with a view that ascribes to youth a constructive and responsible role in society and politics.

In local perceptions, people differentiate between a life course that is, firstly, divided into identifiable rites of passage: circumcision, marriage, the establishment of an independent household, parenthood, grandparenthood, death (*bacha, mardak, miyonsol/mard, müisafed*). Secondly, that life course involves the gradual acquisition of maturity: full physical power and naturalized behaviour, social maturity (*javon, kamolod*). Within the web of kin relations, the local community and the state, young people are constructed as subordinate and dependent individuals – they are regarded as social juniors within a society that is organized in terms of principles of seniority. While this makes them a social minority, they are, at the same time, a numerical majority. The minority status allocated to young people stems from elders' control of access to social and material resources (which is linked to the acquisition of social and political maturity), a process that I have called domestication.

Marriage is classically framed as a turning point in the life course of a young person. During the civil war in Tajikistan, young men usurped elders' control over marriage and thereby forced a revision of the domesticating power of elders. Although in recent times parents have regained much of the prewar control they once exerted over marriage, young people influence the choices, finance the rituals, and many even try to delay their marriage if they work in Russia. Through their experiences in Russia, they gain maturity independent of marriage, yet their parents' status within the community remains dependent on their children's marital status.

In opposition to these structuring attempts and the public performance of successful domestication are the strategies employed by young men to find their own individual spaces and realize their own dreams. For example, migration has allowed them to redefine their subordinate position by controlling the flow of information and overemphasizing their rhetorical and performative subordinate positions vis-à-vis their parents, resulting in a real increase in their social status and independence. Islam provides another means by which to emancipate oneself from a subordinate role in society and assume the position of a respected member of the community. In this regard, the situation in Tajikistan is not an exception but conforms to that in many other countries where young people have achieved similar emancipation from parental and community domestication through the reinterpretation of Islamic sources, through access to new or alternative knowledge (such as in development work), and through economic channels that allow them to engage in businesses independent of a master and craft guilds.

Social Status and Unemployment

This brings us to a central question: How are social status and work related? The concept of youth in Tajikistan is a social construction of a status that is related to specific expectations of work. In this sense, the role of youth in rural Tajikistan is associated with physical work that includes serving the community, the family, the state and more recently God, and does not generate individual wealth but contributes to the well-being of the family and community. Except for the latter religious element, this idea seems to be related to socialist ideas about youth as they were promoted within the Komsomol; however, these ideas are also rooted in local constructions of youth.

I would argue that the chief impetus behind young people engaging in rebellious activities is not merely the result of difficult economic conditions but is also caused by restricted access to a respected social status.[1] In that case, work (and this refers to emic concepts) can be seen from two perspectives: on the one hand, physical hardship is inherent to the definition of youth and thus should be overcome as soon as possible; on the other hand, work can be a means of controlling resources and claiming consumption rights – both factors that are pathways to a higher status.

For this reason, I advocate a closer look at social status in relation to work, because the correlation between 'unemployed youth and civil conflict' is only partly correct (Urdal 2004, 2007). Rather than limiting a discussion of status to issues of employment and unemployment, it is the social status connected to specific types of work that defines whether or not young people perceive themselves as successful. Farm work has long been considered inferior to other occupations, and this view continues to persist in many modern states – just as it was applied within the Soviet state, which overemphasized industrialization and urbanization as development goals. Within this context, we need not wonder that young men in rural Tajikistan – regardless of how lucrative farming may be – continue to dream of non-agricultural positions, preferably in urban centres. The main reason for this longing is that visibly non-physical work increases social status: it allows a person to spend his leisure time being seen on the streets, organizing feasts and distributing gifts (not to be confused with 'being lazy').

Migrants work hard in Russia, but many are spared the heaviest agricultural work upon their return to Tajikistan, which makes migratory life attractive for young men who are desirous of the migrants' increase in status back home. Furthermore, migration allows young men access to cash, which university education apparently does not – an important factor, since the redistribution of wealth is so essential for an increase in status. Boris Nieswand (2007) refers to this status difference between the receptive country and the migrant's home country as the 'status paradox' (a low status in the migrant's destination country is converted into high status back home). However, it is currently increasingly possible that a migrant will not be successful in Russia. Thus, young men who can no longer find work in Russia or have been refused entry, because they were involved in illegal activities or for other reasons, continue to remain without an occupation in Dushanbe or their village and refuse to perform (or resume) agricultural work, since it appears as a status loss to them. In this way, the situation results in a truly unemployed youth cultivating a grievance against a system that appears to block young people in all of their capacities (cf. Niyazi 1994, 1999, 2000; Collier and Hoeffler 2001; Urdal 2007). This specific situation of unemployment causes young adults to once again rely on their families, thus prolonging the period of emotional and economic dependency. The change in the use of terms – from young man (*mardak*) to boy (*bacha*) after migratory unemployment – supports Cohen's (1999: 200) argument that unemployment has an 'infantilizing' effect on youth.

Why are non-agricultural jobs so attractive? A government job, for example, secures much more than a good income – it secures a position of high status that can also be used for many other transaction and relations such as bribes, and access to various other resources; thus, government jobs are even more attractive in Tajikistan than they might be in a less corrupt system. However, since state representatives are basically recruited only from one region, the majority of young men find themselves excluded from social mobility. In addition to this, the state forces all stipend holders (*bujetni**) into teaching for three years in their home village. The work of a teacher is one of the worst-paid government jobs and it is of little relevance within the corrupt system (it is only lucrative for a farmer-teacher who earns supplementary cash by teaching and is allowed to employ pupils on his farm). Moreover, employment in international organizations is largely closed to young people who do not have the appropriate network. Thus, the political grievances of young men may be understood as a collective experience of social, political and economic exclusion.

Instead of discussing economic factors in a separate chapter, I have incorporated the economic aspects of situations whenever possible, and in doing so have shown that economic activities are closely connected to definitions of youth. Nevertheless, in this study I have also tried to show that it is not necessarily economic independence that is important but rather access to cash and opportunities to share, demonstrate and redistribute wealth. Migrants return home in winter for the wedding season. For their own wedding young men display their wealth through conspicuous consumption and thereby raise their own and their parents' social status. Those young men have not only taken control over their choice of marriage partner but often are the main breadwinners of their family, which reverses the access to resources between parents and children and consequently reshapes the youth concept (a migrant is said to gain maturity faster than his peers who have not left the village). What we can see is a constant revaluation and adaptation of youth categories, which becomes visible during concrete events (such as marriage or conflicts).

There are also many non-materialistic ways to increase one's social status. Group belonging is one such important way; for instance, belonging to combatant groups that redefine Islam as an active fight or struggle for a better and fairer world. 'Fighting' fits perfectly into local perceptions of appropriate work for (male) youth as it is physical, masculine and usually goal-oriented. Whether seen as a duty (military service) or as a chance to experience adventure, combatant groups appear attractive to many young people – for economic, opportunistic or emotional reasons. However, religion is also an inviting pursuit for young people in peaceful times because of the social recognition it accords, even if it demands abstinence from many habits typically seen as 'youthful', such as drinking alcohol, playing cards and flirting.

In Chapter 5 I discussed how contemporary concepts of youth in Islam and within international (Western) discourses (represented by the UN) offer young people alternative youth identities. The concepts suggest a youth category organized on the basis of groups that actively engage with their social and political environments. In other words, they challenge existing youth categories and push for group formation processes so as to redefine the demographic and political order. It is in this instance that we can see how domestication is challenged through demographic size. Muslim youth is called upon to act as the vanguard of a future Muslim nation, and to this end to relegate to a secondary level of importance their relations to kin, tribe and country.

Collective Power

In the Introduction, I discussed literature dealing with the issue of population density and reasons for youth violence (concepts such as delinquent youth, lumpen youth and youth bulge). In these discussions, we saw that the presence of unemployed youth in urban areas was declared the main source of social unrest. In this context, Tiger and Fox (1992: 227) have mentioned that those in 'positions of dominance' matter the most, and not merely the space they occupy (the density of population per square kilometre). In other words, density is not the main factor that provokes social conflict; rather, it is the distribution of power relative to cohort sizes. In this sense, we should take a closer look at the identities demanded by and offered to youth, which lay at the base of groups and categories. While most definitions of youth imply a low status position, these perceptions do appear open to manipulation. Thus, the minority position is also a powerful concept that allows the attribution of exclusion identities to youth, such as the Komsomol or *mujohid*. Without a doubt, being part of the Komsomol or the *mujohid*s did seem attractive, if not generally, at least to some young people (Pilkington 1994; Roy 2004). It is through vanguard groups that young people exert demographic pressure and agitate for change; it is the (silent) belief that a youth group may potentially be able to mobilize the whole cohort of youth – that is, a category may turn into a group of uncontrollable size. Therefore, demographic pressure is not the immediate source of unrest, but rather it is the belief that a small group of active young people can mobilize the suppressed majority and, in doing so, reverse the power structure. The potential power that is available in many 'youth bulge' societies is restricted to a limited period of time (the period of demographic transition). In this sense, it provides the societies in question with the opportunity to push through changes and promote creative developments. However, in the majority of 'youth bulge' societies, domestication strategies have restricted youth from developing its potential. Remaining unused, it has created enormous pressure that youth groups have been able, increasingly, to mobilize (such as in the 'Arab spring'). When young people marry relatively late and lack employment that would allow them to make a serious contribution to the family budget, to the community and, more generally, to social development, the potential power of youth becomes free for political purposes.

Through several historical examples, we can see that youth have been repeatedly reorganized and their traditional potential maximized so as to mobilize a substantial number of people for political purposes. Such examples have also been cited by many authors regarding the situation in Turkey, Kenya, Russia, China and, more recently, in Tunisia and Egypt, among others. However, what occurred in these countries was not only an increase in the demographic pressure of young people vying for positions, but also, more importantly, the operationalization of the term 'youth' to develop a mobilizing capacity – which played an essential role in concentrating and channelling individual and collective qualities and talents into a rational and radical concept of youth, as against the existing traditions or political parties that had been declared antiquated. Here, local values ascribed to youth – wild, enthusiastic and determined – were of great value for making use of youth's potential in the name of a political or ideological idea. If we look at youth as a liminal phase, young people hold an 'in-between' status, and excessive violence becomes a logical or justified option.[2] Hence, a group may declare itself to be a vanguard group (that regulates inclusion and exclusion), but if it is rejected by the majority, or even it is accepted to such an extent as to eventually absorb the majority, the vanguard identity must either turn into a majority identity or fail to become of wider relevance.

Central Asian history is a case in point. The restructuring of the emirate of Bukhara at the turn of the previous century may be taken as an example of such a change. Through the introduction of Russian schools, young people were strictly organized into groups on the basis of their age. These classes became very strong units, as I have discussed elsewhere (Roche 2010). Youth were no longer single individuals bound to their parents or teachers; instead, the young people who had been declared the vanguards of socialism became a collective force, bound to each other through solidarity and friendship ties. The creation of a category of youth made it possible to mobilize masses of young people within a concretely defined concept of youth not only by according them full social maturity and high societal responsibilities (temporarily) but also by allocating to them concrete goals worth fighting for and future leading positions within the vanguard group.

The study of the Arash incident (Chapter 6) has shown that instead of forming a coherent socio-demographic solidarity group, young people tend to gather in smaller units around ideas or ideologies (communism, Islam, democracy) or political situations (the Arash incident). Nevertheless, they are attributed a common identity through politically motivated discourses such as the propagandist slogan, 'Youth is our future'. However, young people complain that such declarations of collectivities do not help individuals, since everyday problems, such as lack of housing and unemployment, are not solved through such discourses. The president's call for collective identities is internalized, if at all, by pupils and students who are compelled to identify with national values (*vatan*) as a common denominator. However, the discourse falls short of being strong enough to unite young people into collectivities or provide them with vanguard identities; it only demonstrates that interaction between authorities or institutions and young people takes on the character of authoritative and structural 'domestication'.

Demographic pressure leads to a variety of identities that are based on collective ideologies and offer attractive positions for young people. In this sense, young people are domesticated by appropriation, redefinition and the adaptation of the concept of youth and the suggestion of an emancipated status. These new concepts of domestication appear acceptable to young men because they seem to redefine existing social relations and status. This process is only partly authoritative, as successful concepts need at least to be adapted, if not negotiated, according to young peoples' needs and demands. The fact that many of these ideologies are transformed from exclusive vanguard concepts into controlling institutions over a period of time only reinforces the problematic relation between categories and groups. There is no revolution if young people do not want it to happen, and there can be a huge youth bulge without unrest. Thus, whether or not youth becomes a source of conflict is largely a matter of how categories are valued and accepted.

Günther Schlee has repeatedly advocated the significance of group size and identity. Hence, I conclude by relating the youth bulge question to Schlee's theoretical discussion of size. In order to create groups, social categories associated with identities need to be manipulated, restructured and negotiated. In that case, subordination is reversed by the use of inclusionist concepts that are meant to mobilize masses but which eventually become caught up in a process that Schlee, drawing from economic models, has called 'crowding' (Schlee 2008: 26). When a youth concept reaches its limits by becoming unable to provide any further advantage to its members, new concepts emerge, which seem attractive and start competing with that youth concept. Hence, politically motivated youth categorizations are always rooted in local or traditional concepts of youth, which are much more difficult to change and thereby provide something like a set of values that are included or rejected in the face of other challenging concepts. Thus, while political youth identities can change quickly, traditional life-cycle constructions typically tend to lag behind in terms of change, though they are not resistant to change.

Demographic size changes with cultural change, and demographic dynamics are rooted in social, political and cultural dynamics. In order to make precise use of the concept of youth bulges and their relation to conflicts, it is therefore advisable to consider local domestication processes (such as structures, institutions, rules and youth categories) and relate those to movements that manipulate youth concepts in an exclusive and inclusive way (vanguard groups). In fact, many traditional concepts frame youth as a rather large group, denying them certain rights and controlling the path to social maturity. Also, state definitions vary depending on the obligations and rights tied to the concept of youth. At the beginning of an analysis, these two concepts must be minimally defined, providing relevant youth sizes based on cultural and political categories. Whether youth then internalize those concepts that continue to exist, or whether society itself becomes unable to provide status change and with it social maturity, remains an empirical matter. Here, I have suggested the use of the concept of structural and authoritative domestication due to the asymmetric relationship between young people and socializing institutions or authorities.

Only on the basis of existing conceptualizations and interaction processes are we able to understand counter-concepts as real alternatives to escape the existing definitions that appear restrictive, uninspired and even irresponsible. Instead of assuming that youth groups are identical to youth categories and that the claims of a group are the claims of all youth (even when it may appear to be the case, such as during periods of socio-political unrest), we need to pay attention to the formation of groups and their often skilful formulation of 'vanguard' ideas, as well as the various groups that join a conflict with very pragmatic claims. Political incidents are important events in which youth groups demonstrate the authenticity of their contention that they speak in the name of a category of deprived persons. During such incidents, enough young people may be mobilized to establish a legitimate demand for change. Demography matters not because of its absolute numerical size but because demography links real people to socio-political dynamics. Youth bulges in this context are resources that can be utilized and have an effect upon socio-political changes, yet as a constructed category they are not actors in violent conflicts.

Notes

1. I have addressed the concept of social status in a structural-functionalist manner, insofar as the Tajik define status in terms of age, economic success, gender and education. However, status consistency as a normative standard does not exclude the reshaping of status through individual efforts. In this sense, status inconsistency is inherent in the way that young people frame success and failure. For a summary of the theoretical discussion of the concept of status in the social sciences, see Nieswand (2007: 190–94).

2. It is worth mentioning that, during the revolutions in Tunisia and Egypt, youth rejected the use of violence, hence belying traditional concepts of 'infantilized, immature, wild' youth and, at the same time, making the governments' own violent responses to rational and mature calls for social justice appear to be blatantly disproportionate.

Appendix

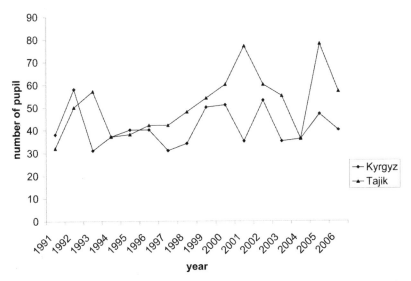

Figure A.1: Number of pupils in class one, Kyrgyz and Tajik classes. Source: local school in Lakhsh, 2006.

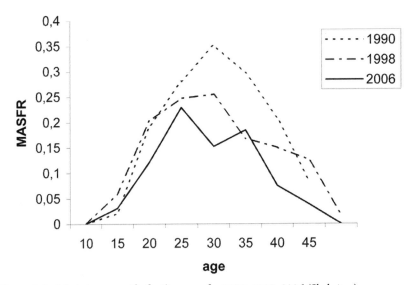

Figure A.2: Marital age-specific fertility rates for 1990, 1998, 2006 (Shahrituz).

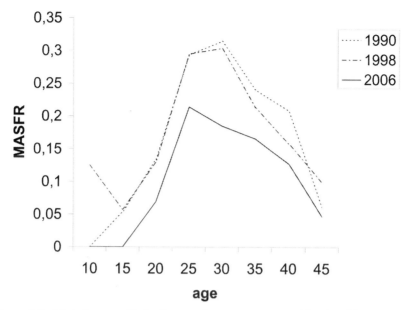

Figure A.3: Marital age-specific fertility rates for 1990, 1998, 2006 (Sasik Bulak).

Table A.1 Parity of women under 47 years of age (Shahrituz).

parity	number of women in party x	number of years in party x	average number of years in parity x
0	74	0	0
1	74	119	1.61
2	74	199	2.69
3	73	185	2.53
4	68	190	2.79
5	57	134	2.35
6	56	147	2.63
7	46	98	2.13
8	29	65	2.24
9	23	48	2.09
10	14	29	2.07
11	6	14	2.33
12	3	8	2.67
13	2	4	2
		average	2.32
		std	0.34

Maximal Reproduction

According to the estimated birth intervals, the average years between one birth and the next is 2.32 and the average reproductive period is twenty years for Shahrituz. With this information we can estimate the average number of children a woman would have if she kept to the exact birth interval for twenty years.

$$\frac{20}{2.32} = 8.62 \text{ children per woman}$$

Following Livi-Bacci (2001: 11), we can assume that a woman would only respect the smallest birth interval and the maximal fertility period (which for Shahrituz was twenty-eight years). Thus we can estimate the maximal reproduction for this population as a theoretical exercise.

The maximal fertility period (28 years) and the minimal birth interval (1.61 years):

$$\frac{28}{1.61} = 17.39 \text{ children per woman}$$

This is a much higher rate. This number shows that a woman could theoretically bear seventeen children, assuming that all conditions were favourable. But it also demonstrates that the average is not even half of the maximum, and thus even if it seems that women do bear children without break, social factors nonetheless impact upon their fertility.

Table A.2: Dependency ratio (Shahrituz).

population under age 15	642
population over age 64	30
population aged 15–64	796
dependency ratio	84.42

Glossary

The following glossary provides a selection of terms that have been used in this study. Although I have indicated word origins, it should be noted that the Tajik use of certain terms may differ from their original semantic use, pronunciation and notation. 'Turk.' refers to any Turkic language of Central Asia. Whereas much of the Turkic influence in Tajik derives from the Uzbek language, it is also true that various terms may have entered via Kyrgyz, Tatar or other Turkic languages to which Tajik people have been exposed.

Abbreviations

Arab.	Arabic
abbr.	abbreviation
cf.	compare
coll.	colloquial
Eng.	English
Kyr.	Kyrgyz
pl.	plural
Russ.	Russian
syn.	synonym
Taj.	Tajik
Turk.	Turkic
Uz.	Uzbek

Selected Terms

ailok (Taj.), *jailoo* (Kyr.): summer pastures in the mountains.

aka (Turk.): elder brother; in Tajik also used for father.

amak, from *am* (Arab.): father: father's brother.

amma (Arab.): father's sister.

amru ma'ruf (Arab.): religious teaching; *amr-e beh ma'ruf* (in Arabic).

avlod (Arab.): 'children of . . .', usually referring to lineage (patrilineage), corporate group, clan.

avo (Taj. dialect): father, grandfather; *avo kata*, *avo kalon*: eldest father's brother; syn. *padar* (Taj.), *bobo* (Taj.), *volid* (Arab.).

ayb (Arab.): shame, codes of decency; syn. *sharm* (Taj.), *nang* (Taj.), *sharmu hayo* (Taj.): shame.

bacha, pl. *bachaho* (Taj.): young man, pl. youth, young people, coll.: pl. *bacho*; often referring to an immature, unmarried, unreasonable and even 'naturally' wild young man.

barodar, pl. *barodaron* (Taj.): brother of one mother, brothers of faith.

basmachi (Russ.): bandit, pejorative term for fighters involved in the uprising against the Russian Empire and Soviet Russian rule in Central Asia in the 1930s; the emic term is *mujohid*.

beg, bey (Turk.): local leader.

biyor (Taj. dialect): siblings of one mother.

bobo (Taj.): father, father's father; cf. *avo*.

bujetnī (Taj.) from *byudzhetny* (Russ.): person who studies at university for free with a small stipend depending on the student's grades.

dodar (Taj.): younger brother.

dukhtar (Taj.): girl, unmarried woman, virgin; syn. *dukhtari khona, dukhtari kholī*: woman who has not married and remains with her parents.

egit (Turk.), *jigit* (Taj., from Kyr.): young men, strong young men, young lads.

eshon, ishon (Arab.): religious title.

fotiha (Arab.): short prayer (first sura in the Koran); a girl who has been engaged through *fotiha*.

gashtak (Taj.): peer-group meeting, male meeting, rotating evening meetings of peer groups or men's groups; verb *gashtan*: walking, moving.

halol (Arab.): according to Islamic law, clean.

hamsol (Taj.): companion, peer, classmate; syn. *hamsinf, hamghul.*

harom (Arab.): taboo, forbidden by Islamic law; coll.: not pure, not clean.

hashar (Taj.): a group of people who agree to perform some task together without payment (collective work).

havlī (Taj.): yard, house with a yard, compound.

hukumat (Arab.): district government, national government, people working in the district or national government, district officer.

jadid (Arab.): new, clean; reformers at the turn of the twentieth century.

jamoat (Arab.): meeting of people, first level of local administration, congregation, community.

jang (Taj.): war, battle, fight, conflict, quarrel, dispute; cf. *jangi barodarkushī, jangi shahrvandī*: civil war.

janoza (Arab.): funeral; syn. *maraka* (Arab.).

javon, pl. *javonon* (Taj.): young, pl. youth, young people; cf. *davrai javonon*: time of youth; *davrai kamolod*: period of having gained maturity.

kampir (Taj.): elder women.

kelin (Turk.): daughter-in-law.

kenja (Turk.): youngest son.

khizmat (Taj.) from *khizlon* (Arab.): service, work, aid; cf. *khizmatgor*: servant.

khonador (Taj.): to have a house; cf. *kase khonador kardan*: to marry someone off.

khuligan (Russ.), from 'hooligan' (Eng.): referring to young people rioting, meeting, rebelling or any other collective activity on public ground; also used to mean roguish little boy.

kuhūla (Arab.): middle age; cf. *kāhil*: middle aged person. (Not common or not frequent in Tajik).

Komsomol (Russ.): abbreviation of *Soyuz Kommunisticheskoy Molodyozhi*; the Young Communist League.

kor (Taj.): to work, to do something.

lengi (Taj. dialect): cloth that men use to tie their traditional coat; veil, women's headscarf; for women also syn. *faranji, farangi, faragi* (Taj.).

madrasa (Arab.): Islamic college.

mahalla (Arab.): place, neighbourhood, usually referring to a local community within a village or town; cf. *guzar, kūcha*: street, road, neighbourhood; the term is also used to designate regionalism, *mahalgaroi*.

maktab (Arab.): school; previously, local village school for boys.

mard (Taj.): man, brave, honest, hot blooded.

mardak (Taj.): young married man; not yet fully mature man.

marshrutka (Russ.): minibus taxi

mavlud (Arab.): celebration for the Prophet's birthday; in Tajikistan, it is also used to denote an Islamic-based feast, e.g., a religious wedding or funeral feast in which religious authorities deliver a sermon lasting several hours.

mehnat (Arab.): to work hard, to help, to serve; syn. *amal kardan*.

mekhmonkhona (Taj.): guesthouse, guestroom, central room in a Tajik house.

miting (Russ.), from 'meeting' (Eng.): mass meeting, rally, non-mobile demonstration.

miyonsol (Taj.): middle-aged man.

molodcy (Russ.): playing the strong man; cf. *molodoi* (Russ.): young.

muallim (Arab.): teacher.

mūisafed (Taj.): old man; white-haired, elderly man; syn. *oqsakol*.

mujohid (Taj.), from *mujahedin* (Arab.): fighter in the name of Islam.

mullo (Taj.), from *mullah* (Arab.): mullah, religious leader, elder person praying five times a day; after a long education in a *madrasa*, the religious scholar gains the title *domullo*.

mullobacha pl. *mullobachaho* (Taj.): boy who is educated in Islam.

namoz (Arab.): religious prayer.

nasl (Arab.): generation, sometimes also used for lineage; cf. *nasli javonon*: the young generation.

nikoh (Arab.): religious wedding ceremony.

nomus (Taj.): honour, dignity; syn. *nang* (Taj.), *oru nomus* (Taj.): honour.

oktyabryat (Russ.): Little (boy) Octoberist, child aged 7 to 10 or 11, preparing for entry into *pioners*.

oqsakol (Taj.), from *aksakal* (Turk.): elderly man, white-haired, in Tajik often referring to a position within the community' cf. *müisafed.*

pioner (Russ.): member of former children's organization, aged approximately 10 to 14.

qalin (Turk.): according to sharia law, the gift/money given by the groom to the bride; syn. *kobin* (Taj.), *mahr* (Arab.).

qavm (Arab.): lineage, corporate group based on common territory, often used for a loose concept of tribe.

qozi (Arab.): judge; *qozi kalon*: supreme judge.

rayon (Russ.), *viloyat* (Arab.): district, ruled by a *hokim* or *mir* chief; today, sub-district of the country.

shogird (Taj.): apprentice, person who learns a profession or a craft through a teacher; religious student of a personal teacher (*ustod*).

Somoniyon (Taj.): Samanids, full Tajik citizen and member of the ruling party; parallel to Komsomol during the Soviet Union.

sumanak (Taj.): traditional dish made from wheat sprouts for the Persian New Year Navrūz (21 March).

sura (Arab.): verse of the Qur'an.

talaba (Arab.): pupil, student.

tagho(ı̄) (Turk.): mother's brother.

tūy (Turk.): feast, happy event, wedding.

usto, ustod (Taj.): teacher, knowing person, artisan, craftsman, term of respect.

vatan (Arab.): place of birth, homeland, home country.

yanga (Turk.): brother's wife, father's brother's wife, mother's brother's wife.

yoshlar (Uz.): young people, emic term used by *jadid* reformer at the turn of the twentieth century.

ZAGS (Russ.): abbreviation of *Zapis Aktov Graždanskogo Sostoyaniya*, Record of Act of Civil Status.

zangirı̄ (Taj.): about to marry, having arrived at one's turn to be married, which implies looking for a partner or accepting one's parents' choice of partner.

Bibliography

Abashin, S.N. 1999. 'Statistika kak instrument etnograficheskogo issledovaniya. Uzbekskaya sem'ya v XX v' [Statistics as a mean of ethnographic research: The Uzbek family in the twentieth century], *Etnograficheskoe Obozrenie* 1: 3–16.

——— 2007. *Die Sartenproblematik in der russischen Geschichtsschreibung des 19. und des ersten Viertels des 20. Jahrhunderts.* Berlin: Klaus Schwarz.

Abbink, J. 2000. 'Restoring the Balance: Violence and Culture among the Suri of Southern Ethiopia', in G. Aijmer and J. Abbink (eds), *Meanings of Violence: A Cross-cultural Perspective.* Oxford: Berg, pp.77–100.

——— 2001. 'Violence and Culture: Anthropological and Evolutionary-psychological Reflections on Inter-ethnic Conflict in Southern Ethiopia', in B. Schmidt and I.W. Schröder (eds), *Anthropology of Violence and Conflict.* London: Routledge, pp.123–42.

——— 2005. 'Being Young in Africa: The Politics of Despair and Renewal', in J. Abbink and I. van Kessel (eds), *Vanguard or Vandals: Youth, Politics and Conflict in Africa.* Leiden: Brill, pp.1–34.

Abbink, J., and I. van Kessel (eds). 2005. *Vanguard or Vandals: Youth, Politics and Conflict in Africa.* Leiden: Brill.

Abdullah, I. 1998. 'Bush Path to Destruction: The Origin and Character of the Revolutionary United Front/Sierra Leone', *Journal of Modern African Studies* 36(2): 203–35.

Abélès, M., and C. Collard (eds). 1985. *Age, pouvoir et société en Afrique noire.* Paris: Karthala.

Agadjanian, V. 1999. 'Post-Soviet Demographic Paradoxes: Ethnic Differences in Marriage and Fertility in Kazakhstan', *Sociological Forum* 14(3): 425–46.

Agadjanian, V., and E. Makarova. 2003. 'Former Soviet Modernization to Post-Soviet Transformation: Understanding Marriage and Fertility Dynamics in Uzbekistan', *Development and Change* 34(3): 447–73.

Agadjanian, V., and N. Prata. 2002. 'War, Peace, and Fertility in Angola', *Demography* 29(2): 215–31.

Alavon, A.N. 1997. *Barodarii Islomī.* Translation Centre Islam Heritage.

Alber, E., S. von de Geest and S.R. Whyte (eds). 2008. *Generations in Africa: Connections and Conflicts.* Berlin: Lit.

Aliev, I. 1997. 'Tajikistan. Warlords – A Country's Scourge', *Radio Free Europe, Dushanbe.* Retrieved 25 February 2003 from: http://www.rferl.org/nca/features/1997/03/F.RU.970307154757.html.

Allworth, E.A. (ed.). 1971. *Nationalities of the Soviet East: Publications and Writing Systems*. New York: Columbia University.

———— 2000. *The Preoccupations of Abdalrauf Fitrat, Bukharan Nonconformist: An Analysis and List of his Writings*. Berlin: Das Arabische Buch.

Amit-Talai, V., and H. Wulff (eds). 1995. *Youth Cultures: A Cross-Cultural Perspective*. London: Routledge.

Anderson, B.O. 1999[1983]. *Imagined Communities: Reflections on the Origin and Spread of Nationalism*, rev. edn. London: Verso.

Andreev, M.C. 1953. *Tazhiki doliny khuf (verkhov'ya amu-dar'i)* [The Tajik region Khuf (The upper part of Amu-Darja)]. Bipusk I. Akademiya Nauk Tadzhikskoy SSR, Moscow: Institut Istorii, Arkheologii i Etnografii.

Anon. 1950. *Young Communists in the USSR: A Soviet Monograph Describing the Demands Made Upon Members of the Komsomol Organization*, trans. V. Rhine. Washington, DC: Public Affairs Press.

Appadurai, A. 1998. *Modernity at Large: Cultural Dimensions of Globalization*. Minneapolis: University of Minnesota.

Ariès, P. 1962. *Centuries of Childhood: A Social History of Family Life*. New York: Vintage.

Assmann, A. 1999. *Zeit und Tradition: Kulturelle Strategien der Dauer*. Cologne: Böhlau.

Atkin, M. 1996. 'The Politics of Polarization in Tajikistan', in H. Malik (ed.), *Central Asia: Its Strategic Importance and Future Prospects*. London: Macmillan, pp.211–32.

Ato, K. 2011. 'Az tūyhoi "komsomolī" ba tūyhoi "islamī"?' [From Komsomol weddings to Islamic weddings?] Retrieved 27 February 2011 from: http://www.ozodi.org.

Aynī, S. 1955. *Maktabi kūhna* [The old school]. Stalinobod: Nashriyoti Davlatii Tojikiston.

———— 1962. *Yoddoshtho* [Memories]. *Kulliyot* [Complete works], Vol. 6. Dushanbe: Nashriyoti Davlatii Tojikiston.

Baldauf, I. 1988. 'Die Knabenliebe in Mittelasien. Bacabozlik. Ethnizität und Gesellschaft'. *Occasional Paper 17*. Berlin: Das Arabische Buch.

Baltabaev, M. 2006. 'Viloyati Qarotegin' [The Qarotegin district], in M.M. Abdusattorov (ed.), *Diyori oshnoī va rūshnoī. Jashnovarai 75-solagii nohiyai Jirgatol* [Land of friendship and luminosity: For the 75 year anniversary of the Jirgatol district]. Dushanbe: AVA.

Bakonyi, J. 2011. *Land ohne Staat. Wirtschaft und Gesellschaft im Krieg am Beispiel Somalias*. Frankfurt am Main: Campus.

Barbieri, M., A. Blum, E. Dolkigh and A. Ergashev. 1996. 'Nuptiality, Fertility, Use of Contraception, and Family Policies in Uzbekistan', *Population Studies* 50: 69–88.

Barrera-González, A. 1992. 'Eldest and Younger Siblings in a Stem-family System: The Case of Rural Catalonia', *Continuity and Change* 7(3): 335–55.

Bashiri, I. 2003. 'Muslims and Communists Vie for Power in Tajikistan'. Retrieved 25 February 2003 from: http://www.angelfire.com/rnb/bashiri/muscom/Muslims.html.

Basu, A.M. (ed.). 2004[1998]. *The Methods and Uses of Anthropological Demography*. Oxford: Clarendon.

Beisembijev, T.K. 1987. *'Ta'rikhii Shakhrukhi' kak istoricheskiy istochnik* ['The history of Shakhrukhi' as historical source]. Alma-Ata: Akademija Nauk Kazaxskoj SSR.

Bellér-Hann, I. 2008. *Community Matters in Xinjian 1880–1949. Towards a Historical Anthropology of the Uyghur*. Leiden: Brill.

Benda-Beckmann, K. von. 2004. 'Law, Violence and Peace Making on the Island of Ambon', in T. von Trotha and M.-C. Foblets (eds), *Healing the Wounds: Essays on the Reconstruction of Societies after War*. Oxford: Hart, pp.221–39.

Bengtsson, T., O. Saito, D. Reher and C. Campbell. 1998. 'Population and the Economy: From Hunger to Modern Economic Growth', in C.-E. Nuñez (ed.), *Debates and Controversies in Economic History*. Madrid: Fundación Ramón Areces, pp.69–144.

Bennett, A. (ed.). 2004. *After Subculture: Critical Studies in Contemporary Youth Culture*. Basingstoke: Palgrave Macmillan.

Bergne, P. 2007. *The Birth of Tajikistan: National Identity and the Origins of the Republic*. London: Tauris.

Bernardi, L. 2003. 'Channels of Social Influence on Reproduction', Max Planck Institute for Demographic Research, *Working Paper 19*. Rostock: Max Planck Institute for Demographic Research.

Bernardi, L., and I. Hutter. 2007. 'The Anthropological Demography of Europe', *Demographic Research* 17(18): 541–66.

Bichsel, C. 2005. 'In Search of Harmony: Repairing Infrastructure and Social Relations in the Ferghana Valley', *Central Asian Survey* 24(1): 53–66.

Bikzhanova, M.A., K.L. Zadykhina and O.A. Sukhareva. 1974. 'Social and Family Life of the Uzbeks', in S. Dunn and E. Dunn (eds), *Introduction to Soviet Ethnography*. Berkley: Highgate Road Social Science Research Station, pp.239–71.

Bjerg, H., and C. Lenz. 2008. '"If Only Grandfather Was Were to Tell Us": Gender as a Category in the Culture of Memory of the Occupation in Denmark and Norway', in S. Palatschek and S. Schraut (eds), *The Gender of Memory. Cultures of Remembrance in Nineteenth- and Twentieth-century Europe*. Frankfurt: Campus, pp.221–36.

Blok, A. 2000. 'Relatives and Rivals: The Narcissism of Minor Differences', in H. Driessen and T. Otto (eds), *Perplexities of Identification*. Aarhus: Aarhus University Press, pp.27–55.

Bonte, P. 1985. 'Structure d'âge, organisation familiale et système de parenté en Afrique de l'Est', in M. Abélès and C. Collard (eds), *Age pouvoir et société en Afrique noire*. Paris: Karthala, pp. 57–90.

Boserup, E. 1965. *The Conditions of Agricultural Growth: The Economics of Agrarian Change under Population Pressure*. London: Allen and Unwin.

Bourdieu, P. 1993. *Soziologische Fragen*. Frankfurt am Main: Suhrkamp.

Bouthoul, G. 1968. 'De certains complexes et de la pyramide des ages', *Guerre et Paix* 4: 10–22.

Bräunlein, P.J., and A. Lauser. 1996. 'Fließende Übergänge … Kindheit, Jugend, Erwachsenwerden in einer ritualarmen Gesellschaft (Mangyan/ Mindoro/ Philippinen)', in D. Dracklé (ed.), *Jung und wild: Zur kulturellen Konstruktion von Kindheit und Jugend*. Berlin: Reimer, pp.152–82.

Brick Mustazashvili, J. 1999. 'Report from Samarkand: Uzbekistan through the Eyes of its Youth', *Central Asia Monitor* 3: 20–24.

Brubaker, R. 1994. 'Nationhood and the National Question in the Soviet Union and Post-Soviet Eurasia: An Institutionalist Account', *Theory and Society* 23(1): 47–78.

Brubaker, R., and F. Cooper. 2000. 'Beyond "Identity"', *Theory and Society* 29: 1–47.

Bucholtz, M. 2002. 'Youth and Cultural Practice', *Annual Review Anthropology* 31: 525–52.

Burkart, G., and J. Wolf (eds). 2002. *Lebenszeiten: Erkundung der Soziologie der Generationen*. Opladen: Leske and Buderich.

Bushkov, V.I. 1993. 'Tadschikistan vor dem Bürgerkrieg. Eine traditionelle Gesellschaft in der Krise', *Berichte des Bundesinstituts für Ostwissenschaftliche und Internationale Studien. Tadschikistan vor dem Bürgerkrieg: Eine traditionelle Gesellschaft in der Krise, Band* 26. Cologne: Bundesinstitut für Ostwissenschaftliche und Internationale Studien.

――― 1995. 'Politische Entwicklung im nachsowjetischen Mittelasien: der Machtkampf in Tadschikistan 1989–1994', *Berichte des Bundesinstituts für Ostwissenschaftliche und Internationale Studien*, Band 4. Cologne: Bundesinstitut für Ostwissenschaftliche und Internationale Studien.

――― 2000. 'Population Migration in Tajikistan: Past and Present', in K. Hisao, O. Chika and J.S. Schoeberlein (eds), *Migration in Central Asia: Its History and Current Problems*. Osaka: Japan Center for Area Studies, National Museum of Ethnoglogy, pp.147–56.

Bushkov, V.I., and D.V. Mikul'skiy. 1995. *Tadzhikskaya revolyutsiya i grazhdanskaya voyni (1989–1994 gg.)* [The Tajik revolution and the civil war (the years 1998–1994)]. Moscow: Institut etnologii i antropologii.

――― 1996. *Anatomiya grazhdanskoy voyni v Tadzhikistane (ethno-sotsial'nie Protsessi i politicheskaya bor'ba 1992–1995)* [Anatomy of the civil war in

Tajikistan (ethno-social processes and political struggle 1992–1995)]. Moscow: Institut etnologii i antropologii RAN; Institute prakticheskogo vostokvedeniya.

Chatterjee, S. 2002. *Politics and Society in Tajikistan: In the Aftermath of the Civil War*. Gurgaon: Hope India Publisher.

Chibnik, M. 1985. 'The Use of Statistics in Sociocultural Anthropology', *Annual Review of Anthropology* 14: 135–57.

Christiansen, C., M. Utas and H.E. Vigh. 2006. 'Introduction', in C. Christiansen, M. Utas and H.E. Vigh (eds), *Navigating Youth, Generating Adulthood: Social Becoming in an African Context*. Uppsala: Nordiska Afrikainstitutet, pp.9–28.

Cincotta, R.P., R. Engelman and D. Anastasion. 2003. *The Security Demographic: Population and Civil Conflict after the Cold War*. Washington, DC: Population Action International.

Clifford, D.M. 2009. 'Marriage and Fertility Change in Post-Soviet Tajikistan', Ph.D. diss. Southampton: University of Southampton.

Coal, A., and S. Watkins. 1986. *The Decline of Fertility in Europe*. Princeton: Princeton University Press.

Cohen, P. 1999[1997]. *Rethinking the Youth Question: Education, Labour and Cultural Studies*. Durham, NC: Duke University Press.

Cohen, S. 1973. *Folk Devils and Moral Panics*. St Albans: Paladin.

Cole, J.W., and E.R. Wolf. 1999[1974]. *The Hidden Frontier: Ecology and Ethnicity in an Alpine Valley*. Berkeley: University of California Press.

Collier, P., and A. Hoeffler. 2001. 'Greed and Grievance in Civil War', *World Bank*. Retrieved 26 June 2009 from: http://econ.worldbank.org/files/12205_greedgrievan, and from http://citeseerx.ist.psu.edu/viewdoc/summary?doi=10.1.1.17.7530.

Collier, P., and N. Sambanis (eds). 2005. *Understanding Civil War: Evidence and Analysis*. Washington, DC: World Bank.

Collins, R. 2008. *Violence: A Micro-sociological Theory*. Princeton: Princeton University Press.

Comaroff, J., and J. Comaroff. 2000. 'Réfléxions sur la jeunesse: Du passé à la postcolonie', *Politique Africaine* 80: 90–110.

——— 2005. 'Reflection on Youth: From the Past to the Postcolony', in A. Honwana and F. de Boeck (eds), *Makers and Breakers: Children and Youth in Postcolonial Africa*. Oxford: Currey, pp.19–30.

Creed, G.W. 1998. *Domesticating Revolution: From Socialist Reform to Ambivalent Transition in a Bulgarian Village*. Philadelphia: Pennsylvania State University Press.

——— 2002. 'Economic Crisis and Ritual Decline in Eastern Europe', in C.M. Hann (ed.), *Postsocialism: Ideals, Ideologies and Practices in Eurasia*. London: Routledge, pp.57–73.

Cruise O'Brien, D. 1996. 'A Lost Generation: Youth Identity and State Decay in West Africa', in R. Werbner and T. Ranger (eds), *Postcolonial Identities in Africa*. London: Zed Books, pp.55–74.

Dağyeli, J.E. 2008. 'Der Handwerker ist ein Freund Gottes. Zu Inhalten und Rezeption der mittelasiatischen Handwerker-*risāla*', Ph.D. diss. Berlin: Humboldt-Universität zu Berlin, Philosophische Fakultät III.

D'Almeida-Topor, H., C. Coquery-Vidrovitch and O. Goerg (eds). 1992. *Les jeunes en Afrique*, 2 vols. Paris: L'Harmattan.

De Boer, A., and V.M. Hudson. 2004. 'The Security Threat of Asia's Sex Ratios', *SAIS Review* 24(2): 27–43.

Dereje Feyissa. 2011. *Playing Different Games: The Paradox of Anywaa and Nuer Identification Strategies in the Gambella Region, Ethiopia*. Oxford: Berghahn.

Dhillon, N., and T. Yousef. 2007. 'Inclusion. Meeting the 100 Million Youth Challenge', *Middle East Youth Initiative*. Retrieved 12 February 2009 from: http://www.shababinclusion.org/.

Dhorat, M.S. 2007. *The Gift of Youth*. Leicester: Islāmic Da'wah Academy.

Dor, R. 2007. 'Les âges-de-vie (yaş) dans le chant populaire turc', in F. Georgean and K. Kreise (eds), *Enfance et jeunesse dans le monde musulman*. Paris: Maisonneuve et Larose, pp.123–46.

Dorman, S.R. 2005. 'Past the Kalashnikov: Youth, Politics and the State in Eritrea', in J. Abbink and I. van Kessel (eds), *Vanguard or Vandals: Youth, Politics and Conflict in Africa*. Leiden: Brill, pp.189–204.

Dracklé, D. 1996. 'Kulturelle Repräsentationen von Jugend in der Ethnologie', in D. Dracklé (ed.), *Jung und wild: Zur kulturellen Konstruktion von Kindheit und Jugend*. Berlin: Reimer, pp.14–53.

Dudoignon, S.A. 1994. 'Une segmentation peut en cacher une autre: Régionalismes et clivage politico-économiques au Tadjikistan', *Cahier d'Etudes sur la Méditerranée Orientale et le Monde Turco-Iranien* 18: 73–130.

——— 1996. 'La question scolaire à Boukhara et au Turkestan Russe, du "premier renouveau" à la soviétisation (fin du 18ᵉ siècle-1937)', *Cahier du Monde Russe* 37(1/2): 133–210.

——— 2001. 'Status, Strategies and Discourses of a Muslim "Clergy" under a Christian Law: Polemics about the Collection of the *zakât* in Late Imperial Russia', in S.A. Dudoignon and H. Komatsu (eds), *Islam in Politics in Russia and Central Asia (Early Eighteenth to Late Twentieth Centuries)*. London: Kegan Paul, pp.43–73.

——— 2004a. 'Faction Struggles among the Bukhran Ulama During the Colonial, the Revolutionary and the Early Soviet Periods (1868–1929): A Paradigm for History Writing?' in S. Tsugitaka (ed.), *Muslim Societies: Historical and Comparative Aspects*. London: Routledge, pp.62–96.

———— 2004b. 'Les "tribulations" du juge Żiyā: Histoire et mémoire du clientélisme politique à Boukhara (1868–1929)', *Asie Centrale* 5/6: 1095–1138.

———— 2004c. 'Local Lore, the Transmission of Learning, and Communal Identity in late Twentieth-century Tajikistan: The *Khujand-nāma* of 'Ārifjān Yahyāzād Khujandī', in S.A. Dudoignon (ed.), *Devout Societies versus Impious States?* Berlin: Schwarz, pp.213–42.

Eickelman, D.F. and J.W. Anderson (eds) 1999. *New Media in the Muslim World. The Emerging Public Sphere.* Bloomington: Indiana University Press.

Eickelman, D.F. and J.P. Piscatori. 1996. *Muslim Politics.* Princeton: Princeton University Press.

Eisenstadt, S.N. 1956. *From Generation to Generation: Age Groups and Social Structure.* New York: Free Press.

———— 1988. 'Youth, Generational Consciousness, and Historical Change', in J. Kuczyński, S.N. Eisenstadt, B. Ly and L. Sakar (eds), *Perspectives on Contemporary Youth.* Hong Kong: United Nations, pp.91–110.

Eloundou-Enyegue, P.M., C.S. Stokes and G.T. Cornwell. 2000. 'Are There Crisis-led Fertility Declines? Evidences from Central Cameroon', *Population Research and Policy Review* 19: 47–72.

El-Shamy, H. 1981. 'The Brother-sister Syndrome in Arab Family Life: Sociocultural Factors in Arab Psychiatry: A Critical Review', *International Journal of Sociology of the Family* 2: 313–23.

Elster, J. 1986. *Karl Marx: A Reader.* Cambridge: Cambridge University Press.

Elwert, G. 1989. 'Nationalismus und Ethnizität. Über die Bildung von Wir-Gruppen', *Kölner Zeitschrift für Soziologie und Sozialpsychologie* 41: 440–64.

———— 1994. 'Feldforschung – vom literarischen Bericht zur methodischen angeleiteten qualitativen und quantitativen Forschung', *Skripte zu den Kulturwissenschaften* 1. Frankfurt an der Oder: Europa-Universität.

———— 2004. 'Anthropologische Perspektiven auf Konflikt', in J.M. Eckert (ed.), *Anthropologie der Konflikte: Georg Elwerts konflikttheoretische Thesen in der Diskussion.* Bielefeld: Transcript, pp.26–38.

Elwert, G., S. Feuchtwang and D. Neubert. 1999. *Dynamics of Violence: Processes of Escalation and De-escalation in Violent Group Conflicts.* Berlin: Duncker and Humblot.

Elwert, G., M. Kohli and H. Müller (eds). 1990. *Im Lauf der Zeit: Ethnographische Studien zur gesellschaftlichen Konstruktion von Lebensaltern.* Saarbrücken: Breitenbach.

Engels, F. 2004[1884]. *The Origin of the Family, Private Property and the State.* Chippendale: Resistance Books.

Epkenhans, T. 2010. 'Islam and Islamic Education in the Republic of Tajikistan', in M. Kemper, R. Motika and S. Reichmuth (eds), *Islamic Education in the Soviet Union and its Successor States.* London: Routledge, pp.313–48.

———— 2011. 'Defining Normative Islam: Some Remarks on Contemporary Islamic Thought in Tajikistan – Hoji Akbar Turajonzoda's *Sharia and Society*', *Central Asian Survey* 30(1): 81–96.

Faroughi, P. 1999. '1998 Socio-economic Survey of Households, Farms and Bazaars in Tajikistan'. Unpublished report submitted to Save the Children.

Fathi, H. 2004. 'Islamisme et pauvreté dans le monde rural de l'Asie centrale postsoviétique', *Programme de l'UNRISD Société Civile et Movements Sociaux* 14.

Fedtke, E. 1998. 'Jadids, Young Bukharans, Communists and the Bukharan Revolution: From an Ideological Debate in the Early Soviet Union', in A. v. Kügelgen, M. Kemper and A.J. Frank (eds), *Muslim Culture in Russia and Central Asia from the Nineteenth to the Early Twentieth Centuries*, Vol. 2. Berlin: Klaus Schwarz, pp.483–512.

Fierman, W. 1988. 'Western Popular Culture and Soviet Youth: A Case Study of the "Muslim" Regions', *Central Asian Survey* 7(1): 7–36.

———— (ed.). 1991. *Soviet Central Asia: The Failed Transformation*. Oxford: Westview.

Fischer, H. 1996. *Lehrbuch der genealogischen Methode*. Berlin: Reimer.

———— 1997. 'Zensusaufnahme – das Beispiel Gabsonkeg', in W. Schulze, H. Fischer and H. Lang (eds), *Geburt und Tod: Ethnodemographische Probleme, Methoden und Ergebnisse*. Berlin: Reimer, pp.37–90.

Fortes, M. 1933. 'Notes on Juvenile Delinquency', *Sociological Review* 25: 14–24 and 153–58.

———— 1962a[1958]. 'Introduction', in J. Goody (ed.), *The Developmental Cycle of Domestic Groups*. Cambridge: Cambridge University Press, pp.1–14.

———— 1962b. 'Introduction', in M. Fortes (ed.), *Marriage in Tribal Societies*. Cambridge: Cambridge University Press, pp.1–13.

———— 1967[1949]. *The Web of Kinship among the Tallensi*. London: Oxford University Press.

———— 1970. *Kinship and the Social Order: The Legacy of Lewis Henry Morgan*. London: Routledge.

Fuller, G.E. 2003. 'The Youth Factor: The New Demographics of the Middle East and the Implications for U.S. Policy', *Analysis Paper 3*. Washington, DC: Saban Center for Middle East Policy, Brookings Institution.

———— 2004. *The Youth Crisis in Middle Eastern Society*. Michigan: Institute for Social Policy and Understanding.

Gaijsina, L. 2008. 'Asia-Plus'. Retrieved 22 June 2008 from: *www.asiaplus.tj/en/*.

Geertz, C. 1973. *The Interpretation of Cultures*. New York: Perseus.

Geiss, G.P. 2001. 'Mahalla and Kinship Relations: A Study on Residential Communal Commitment Structures in Central Asia of the Nineteenth Century', *Central Asian Survey* 20(1): 97–106.

Gellner, E. 1990[1983]. *Nations and Nationalism*. Oxford: Blackwell.

Georgeon, F. 2007. 'Les jeunes Turcs était-ils jeunes? Sur le phénomène des générations, de l'Empire ottoman à la république Turque', in F. Georgeon and K. Kreise (eds), *Enfance et jeunesse dans le monde musulman*. Paris: Maisonneuve et Larose, pp.147–74.

Ghobarah, H., P. Huth and B. Russett. 2001. 'Civil Wars Kill and Maim People – Long after the Shooting Stops', *Center for Basic Research in the Social Sciences*. Retrieved 30 June 2002 from: www.cbrss.harvard.edu/programs/hsecurity/papers/civilwar.pdf.

Ghufronov, D., and A. Yuldoshev. 2008. 'Women in Gharm Demonstrate Demanding Collection of Illegally Possessed Weapons', *Asia Plus*. Retrieved 31 September 2008: from www.asiaplus.tj/en/.

Giddens, A. 1979. *Central Problems in Social Theory*. London: Macmillan.

Gillis, J.R. 1974. *Youth and History: Tradition and Change in European Age Relations 1770 to the Present*. New York: Academic Press.

Girard, R. 1979. *Violence and the Sacred*. Baltimore: Johns Hopkins University Press.

Gluckman, M. 1963. *Order and Rebellion in Tribal Africa*. London: Cohen and West.

Goldstein, J.R. 2011. 'A Secular Trend toward Earlier Male Sexual Maturity: Evidence from Shifting Ages of Male Young Adult Mortality'. *PLoS ONE* 6(8): e14826. doi:10.1371/journal.pone.0014826

Goldstone, J.A. 1991. *Revolution and Rebellion in the Early Modern World*. Berkeley: University of California Press.

Goody, J. 1972. 'Domestic Groups', *Addison-Wesley Modular Publications* 28: 1–32.

Guboglo, M. 1990. 'Demography and Language in the Capitals of the Union Republics', *Journal of Soviet Nationalities* 1(4): 1–42.

Gulzoda, S. 2011. 'Davlati Javon va Hukumati Solkhūrda' [A young state and an old government], *Faraj* 31(241): 8–9.

Hahn, J.W. 1969. 'The Komsomol Kollektiv as an Agency of Political Socialization', *Youth and Society* 1(2): 219–39.

——— 1971. 'Political Socialization in the USSR: The Komsomol and the Educational System', Ph.D. diss. Durham, NC: Department of Political Science, Duke University.

Hajnal, J. 1982. 'Two Kinds of Preindustrial Household Formation System', *Population and Development Review* 8(3): 449–94.

Halbach, U. 1996. 'Der Islam in der GUS: Die regionale und einzelstaatliche Ebene'. *Berichte des Bundesinstituts für Ostwissenschaftliche und Internationale Studien*. Cologne: Bundesinstitut für Ostwissenschaftliche und Internationale Studien.

Hall, G.S. 1904. *Adolescence: Its Psychology and its Relations to Physiology, Anthropology, Sociology, Sex, Crime, Religion and Education*. New York: D. Appleton and Company.

Hall, M. 2005. 'Tajikistan at the Crossroads of Democracy and Authoritarianism', in B.N. Schlyter (ed.), *Prospects for Democracy in Central Asia*. London: Tauris, pp.25–39.

Hammel, E.A., and D.S. Friou. 1997. 'Anthropology and Demography: Marriage, Liaison, or Encounter?' in D. Kertzer (ed.), *Anthropological Demography*. Chicago: University of Chicago Press, pp.175–200.

Hamroboyeva, N. 2008. 'Tajik OMON Commander Killed in Shootout in Eastern Tajikistan', *Asia Plus*. Retrieved 4 February 2008 from: *www.asia-plus.tj/en/*.

Harris, C. 2002. 'Muslim Views on Population: The Case of Tajikistan', in J. Meuleman (ed.), *Islam in the Era of Globalization: Muslim Attitudes towards Modernity and Identity*. London: Routledge, pp.211–22.

——— 2004. *Control and Subversion: Gender Relations in Tajikistan*. London: Pluto.

——— 2006. *Muslim Youth: Tensions and Transitions in Tajikistan*. Boulder, CO: Westview.

Harwin, J. 1996. *Children of the Russian State: 1917–1995*. Aldershot: Avebury.

Haub, C. 1994. 'Population Change in the Former Soviet Republics', *Population Bulletin* 49(4): 2–52.

Hayit, B. 1992. *'Basmatschi' Nationaler Kampf Turkestans in den Jahren 1917 bis 1934*. Cologne: Dreisam.

Heady, P. 2007. 'What Can Anthropological Methods Contribute to Demography – and How?', *Demographic Research* 16(18): 555–58.

Heald, S. 2000. 'Tolerating the Intolerable: Cattle Raiding among the Kuria of Kenya', in G. Aijmer and J. Abbink (eds), *Meanings of Violence: A Cross Cultural Perspective*. Oxford: Berg, pp.101–22.

Heathershaw, J. 2005. 'The Paradox of Peacebuilding: Peril, Promise, and Small Arms in Tajikistan', *Central Asian Survey* 24(1): 21–38.

——— 2009. *Post-conflict Tajikistan: The Politics of Peacebuilding and the Emergence of Legitimate Order*. London: Routledge.

Hebdige, D. 1988. *Hiding in the Light: On Images and Things*. London: Routledge.

Hechter, M. 1988. *Principles of Group Solidarity*. Berkeley: University of California Press.

Heinsohn, G. 2006. *Söhne und Weltmacht: Terror im Aufstieg und Fall der Nationen*. Zurich: Füssli.

Helms, M. 1988. *Ulysses' Sail: An Ethnographic Odyssey of Power, Knowledge, and Geographic Distance*. Princeton: Princeton University Press.

Herzfeld, M. 1980. 'Honour and Shame: The Problem in the Comparative Analysis of Moral Systems', *Man* 15(2): 339–51.

Hetmanek, A. 1993. 'Islamic Revolution and Jihad Come to the Former Soviet Central Asia: The Case of Tajikistan', *Central Asian Survey* 12(3): 365–78.

Hobsbawm, E. 1999. *Nations and Nationalism since 1780: Programme, Myth, Reality.* Cambridge: Cambridge University Press.

Hohmann, S., S. Roche and M. Garenne. 2010. 'The Changing Sex Rations at Birth during the Civil War in Tajikistan: 1992–1995', *Journal of Biosocial Science* 42(6): 773–86.

Holzwarth, W. 1978. 'Abgabesysteme und dörfliche Organisation der Tajiken Badakhshans im 19. und 20. Jahrundert', M.A. diss. Berlin: Free University of Berlin.

Honwana, A., and F. de Boeck (eds). 2005. *Makers and Breakers: Children and Youth in Postcolonial Africa.* Oxford: Currey.

Howell, N. 1986. 'Demographic Anthropology', *Annual Review Anthropology* 15: 219–46.

Humphrey, C. 1983. *Karl Marx Collective: Economy, Society and Religion in a Siberian Collective Farm.* Cambridge: Cambridge University Press.

Huntington, S.P. 1998[1996]. *The Clash of Civilization and the Remaking of World Order.* London: Touchstone Books.

Islamov, S.I. 1988. *Sem'ya i byt.* [Family and way of life]. Dushanbe: Irfon.

Jacobson, J. 1998. *Islam in Transition. Religion and Identity among British Pakistan Youth.* London, New York: Routledge.

Jenkins, C., E. Crenshaw and K. Robinson. 2006. 'Ideologies of Violence: The Social Origins of Islamist and Leftist Transnational Terrorism', *Social Forces* 84(4): 2009–26.

Jenkins, R. 2003. 'Rethink Ethnicity: Identity, Categorization, and Power', in J. Stone and D. Rutledge (eds), *Race and Ethnicity: Comparative and Theoretical Approaches.* Malden, MA: Blackwell, pp.59–71.

Johnson-Hanks, J. 2002. 'On the Limits of Life Stages in Ethnography: Toward a Theory of Vital Conjunctures', *American Anthropologist* 104(3): 865–80.

Jones, E., and F.W. Grupp. 1987. *Modernization, Value Change and Fertility in the Soviet Union.* Cambridge: Cambridge University Press.

Jonker, G. 1997. 'Death, Gender and Memory: Remembering Loss and Burial as a Migrant', in D. Field, J. Hockey and N. Small (eds), *Death, Gender and Ethnicity.* London: Routledge, pp.187–201.

Joseph, S. 1994. 'Brother/Sister Relationships: Connectivity, Love and Power in the Reproduction of Patriarchy in Lebanon', *American Ethnologist* 21(1): 50–73.

Jum'aev, R. 2001. *Jashni arūsii Tojikoni vodii Hisor* [Celebration of the Tajik bride in Hisor Valley]. Dushanbe: Nashriyoti 'Amri ilm.

Jumhuri Todjikiston. 2007. *Sanadhoi me'jorii huquqi oid ba tanzimi an'ana va jashnu marosimho* [Standard document of law about custom and celebration and ceremonies]. Dushanbe: 'Sharqi Ozodi' Dastgohi ijroiyai Presidenti Jumhurii Tojikiston.

Juricic, A. 1994. 'The Faithful Assistant: The Komsomol in the Soviet Military and Economy, 1918–1932', Ph.D. diss. Edmonton: Department of History, University of Alberta.

Kagwanja, P.M. 2005. 'Clash of Generations? Youth Identity, Violence and the Politics of Transition in Kenya, 1997–2002', in J. Abbink and I. van Kessel (eds), *Vanguard or Vandals: Youth, Politics and Conflict in Africa*. Leiden: Brill, pp.81–109.

Kakpo, N. 2007. *L'islam un recours pour les jeunes*. Paris: Sciences Politique.

Kamp, M. 2006. *The New Woman in Uzbekistan: Islam, Modernity and Unveiling under Communism*. Seattle: University of Washington Press.

———— 2008. *Hamza. A Communist Martyr and Uzbek Collective Memory*. Bloomington: Department of Central Eurasian Studies, Indiana University.

Kandiyoti, D. 1999. 'Poverty in Transition: An Ethnographic Critique of Household Surveys in Post-Soviet Central Asia', *Development and Change* 30: 499–524.

———— 2007. 'The Politics of Gender and Soviet Paradox: Neither Colonized, Nor Modern?, *Central Asian Survey* 26(4): 601–23.

Karim, B. 1997. *Faryodi solho: Hujjat, dalel, tabsira, khulosa* [Recalling the years: Documents, proof, collections, conclusions]. Moscow: Transdornauka.

Kasten, H. 1999. *Geschwister. Vorbilder, Rivalen, Vertraute*. Munich: Ernst Reinhardt.

Kayumzoda, A. 2012 'Tūrajonzoda. "Safari mo ba Russia yagon hadafi siyosī nadosht"' [Tūrajonzoda: 'Our trip to Russia had no political goal'], *Ozodi*. Retrieved 25 September 2012 from: http://www.ozodi.org/content/article/24719452.html?page=5#relatedInfoContainer.

Kehl-Bodrogi, K. 2008. *'Religion Is Not So Strong Here': Muslim Religious Life in Khorezm after Socialism*. Berlin: Lit.

Kemper M., R. Motika and S. Reichmuth (eds). 2010. *Islamic Education in the Soviet Union and its Successor States*. London: Routledge.

Kertzer, D.I., and T. Fricke. 1997. 'Toward an Anthropological Demography', in D.I. Kertzer (ed.), *Anthropological Demography: Toward a New Synthesis*. Chicago: University of Chicago Press, pp.1–35.

Khalid, A. 1998. *The Politics of Muslim Cultural Reform*. Berkeley: University of California Press.

———— 2007. *Islam after Communism: Religion and Politics in Central Asia*. Berkeley: University of California Press.

Khan, A.R., and D. Ghai. 1979. *Collective Agriculture and Rural Development in Soviet Central Asia*. London: McMillan.

Khudjibaeva, M. 1999. 'Television and the Tajik Conflict', *Central Asia Monitor* 1: 11–16.

Kikuta, H. 2009 'A Master Is Greater than a Father: Rearrangements of Traditions Among Muslim Artisans in Soviet and Post-Soviet Uzbekistan', in D.W.

Wood (ed.), *Economic Development, Integration, and Morality in Asia and the Americas*. Bingley: Emerald Group, pp.89–122.

Kılavuz, I.T. 2009. 'The Role of Networks in Tajikistan's Civil War: Network Activation and Violence Specialists', *Nationalities Papers* 37(5): 693–717.

Kirmse, S. 2009. 'Youth in Post-Soviet Central Asia: Exploring Transition, Globalization and Youth Culture in the Ferghana Valley', Ph.D. diss. London: School of Oriental and African Studies.

Kislyakov, N.A. 1969. *Ocherki po istorii sem'i i braka u narodov sredney asii i kazakhstana* [Essay on the history of the family and marriage among the people of Central Asia and Kazakhstan]. Leningrad: Akademiya Nauk SSSR.

Kislyakov, N.A. and A. K. Pisarchik 1972. *Tadzhiki Karategina i Darvaza* [The Tajiks of Karategin and Darvaz], Vol. 1. Dushanbe: Donish.

——— 1976. *Tadzhiki Karategina i Darvaza* [The Tajiks of Karategin and Darvaz], Vol. 2. Dushanbe: Donish.

Kłoskowska, A. 1988. 'Analysis of Sociological Literature on Youth', in J. Kuczyński, S.N. Eisenstadt, B. Ly and L. Sakar (eds), *Perspectives on Contemporary Youth*. Hong Kong: United Nations, pp.3–18.

Kluckhohn, C. 1969. 'Recurrent Themes in Myths and Mythmaking', in H.A. Murray (ed.), *Myth and Mythmaking*. Boston: Beacon, pp.46–60.

Knörr, J. 2007. *Kreolität und postkoloniale Gesellschaft: Integration und Differenz in Jakarta*. Frankfurt: Campus.

Koehler, J. 2000. *Die Zeit der Jungs: Zur Organisation von Gewalt und der Austragung von Konflikten in Georgien*. Münster: Lit.

Kohl, C. 2010. 'Creole Identity, Interethnic Relations and Postcolonial Nation-building in Guinea-Bissau, West Africa', Ph.D. diss. Halle: Martin Luther University Halle-Wittenberg.

Kohli, M., and G. Elwert (eds). 1990. *Im Lauf der Zeit: ethnographische Studien zur gesellschaftlichen Konstruktion von Lebensaltern*. Saarbrücken: Breitenbach.

Komatsu, H. 2000. 'Migration in Central Asia as Reflected in the Jadid Writings', in H. Komatsu, O. Chika and J.S. Schoeberlein (eds), *Migration in Central Asia: Its History and Current Problems*. Osaka: Japan Center for Area Studies, National Museum of Ethnoglogy, pp.21–34.

Krader, L. 1971. *Peoples of Central Asia*. Bloomington: Indiana University Press.

Krämer, A. 2002. *Geistliche Autorität und islamische Gesellschaft im Wandel. Studien über Frauenälteste (otin und xalfa) im unabhängigen Usbekistan*. Berlin: Schwarz.

Kroehnert, S. n.d. 'Jugend und Kriegsgefahr', *Berlin-Institute for Population and Development*. Retrieved 14 November 2008 from: http://www.berlin-institut.org/fileadmin/user_upload/Studien/Kroehnert_Jugend_und_Kriegsgefahr.pdf.

Kuebart, F. 1989. 'The Political Socialisation of Schoolchildren', in J. Riordan (ed.), *Soviet Youth Culture*. Bloomington: Indiana University Press, pp.103–21.

Kuniansky, A.S. 1981. 'Fertility and Labor Force in USSR: Theories and Models', Ph.D. diss. Houston: University of Houston.

Kurbanova, M. 2008. 'Perviy General. 100-letnemu yubuleyu znamenitogo tadzhikskogo voenachal'nika M. Tashmukhammedova' [The first General: For the centenary anniversary of the famous Tajik military commander M. Tashmukhammedova], *Asia Plus*. Retrieved 12 March 2009 from: http://www.tj.moy.su/news/2008-01-26-922

Lacina, B., and N. Gleditsch. 2006. 'Monitoring Trends in Global Combat: A New Dataset of Battle Deaths', in H. Brunborg, E. Tabeau and H. Urdal (eds), *The Demography of Armed Conflict*. Dordrecht: Springer, pp.131–52.

Lamphear, J. 1998. 'Brothers in Arms: Military Aspects of East African Age-class Systems in Historical Perspective', in E. Kurimoto and S. Simonse (eds), *Conflict, Age and Power in North East Africa: Age Systems in Transition*. Oxford: Currey, pp.79–97.

Lang, H. 1982. 'Die Bedeutung des Zeithorizontes für die Planung von Sedentarisationsprojekten: Northern Rizeigat settlement project als Beispiel (Sudan)', in F. Scholz and J. Janzen (eds), *Nomadismus – ein Entwicklungsproblem?* Berlin: Reimer, pp. 65–72.

——— 1997. 'Ethnodemographie und Bedeutung von ethnographischen Zensuserhebungen', in W. Schulze, H. Fischer and H. Lang (eds), *Geburt und Tod: Ethnodemographische Probleme, Methoden und Ergebnisse*. Berlin: Reimer, pp.4–36.

Laslett, P. 1969. 'Size and Structure of the Household in England over Three Centuries', *Population Studies* 23(2): 199–223.

Last, M. 2005. 'Towards a Political History of Youth in Muslim Northern Nigeria, 1750–2000', in J. Abbink and I. van Kessel (eds), *Vanguard or Vandals: Youth, Politics and Conflict in Africa*. Leiden: Brill, pp.37–54.

Lee, R.D., and J.R. Goldstein. 2003. 'Rescaling the Life Cycle: Longevity and Proportionality', in J.R. Carey and S. Tuljapurkar (eds), *Life Span: Evolutionary, Ecological, and Demographic Perspectives*. New York: Population Council, pp.183–207.

Le Meur, P.-Y. 2008. 'Between Emancipation and Patronage: Changing Intergenerational Relationships in Central Benin', in E. Alber, S. van der Geest and S.R. Whyte (eds), *Generations in Africa: Connections and Conflicts*. Berlin: Lit, pp.209–36.

Lévi-Strauss, C. 1958. *Strukturale Anthropologie*. Frankfurt: Suhrkamp.

——— 1993[1949]. *Die elementaren Strukturen der Verwandtschaft*. Frankfurt: Suhrkamp.

Li, Q., and M. Wen. 2005. 'Conflict and Adult Mortality', *Journal of Peace Research* 42: 471–92.

Liechty, M. 2002. *Suitably Modern. Making Middle-class Culture in a New Consumer Society.* Princeton: Princeton University Press.

Lindstrom, D.P., and B. Berhanu. 1999. 'The Impact of War, Famine, and Economic Decline on Marital Fertility in Ethiopia', *Demography* 36(2): 247–61.

Livi-Bacci, M. 2001[1992]. *A Concise History of World Population.* Malden, MA: Blackwell.

Loy, T. 2005. *Jaghnob 1970: Erinnerungen an eine Zwangsumsiedlung in der Tadschikischen SSR.* Wiesbaden: Reichert.

Lublin, N. 1991. 'Implications of Ethnic and Demographic Trends', in W. Fierman (ed.), *Soviet Central Asia: The Failed Transformation.* Oxford: Westview, pp.36–61.

McBrien, J. 2008. 'The Fruit of Devotion. Islam and Modernity in Kyrgyzstan', Ph.D. diss. Halle: Martin Luther University Halle-Wittenberg.

McCaskie, T.C. 2008. 'Gun Culture in Kumasi', *Africa* 78(3): 433–54.

Macfarlane, A. 1968. 'Population Crisis: Anthropology's Failure', *New Society* 315: 519–21.

McIntyre, A. (ed.). 2005. *Invisible Stakeholders: Children and War in Africa.* Pretoria: Institute for Security Studies.

Mahmood, C.K. 1996. *Fighting for Faith and Nation: Dialogues with Sikh Militants.* Philadelphia: University of Pennsylvania Press.

Maira, S., and E. Soep (eds). 2005. *Youthscapes: The Popular, the National, the Global.* Philadelphia: University of Pennsylvania Press.

Makhamov, M. 1996. 'Islam and the Political Development of Tajikistan after 1985', in H. Malik (ed.), *Central Asia: Its Strategic Importance and Future Prospects.* London: Macmillian, pp.195–210.

Malinowski, B. 1927. *Sex and Repression in a Savage Society.* London: Kegan Paul.

―――― 1929. *The Sexual Life of Savages in North-Western Melanesia.* New York: Halcyon House.

Malthus, T.R. 1999[1798]. *An Essay on the Principle of Population.* Oxford: Oxford University Press.

Mandaville, P. 2001. *Transnational Muslim Politics. Reimagining the Umma.* London, New York: Routledge.

Mannheim, K. 1970[1964]. *Wissenssoziologie. Auswahl aus dem Werk.* Neuwied am Rhein: Luchterhand.

Marguerat, Y. 2005. 'From Generational Conflict to Renewed Dialogue: Winning the Trust of Street Children in Lomé, Togo', in J. Abbink and I. van Kessel (eds), *Vanguard or Vandals: Youth, Politics and Conflict in Africa.* Leiden: Brill, pp.207–27.

Martin, V. 2001. *Law and Customs in the Steppe: The Kazakhs of the Middle Horde and Russian Colonialism in the Nineteenth Century.* London: Routledge Curzon.

Marwat, F.-R.K. 1969. *The Basmachi Movement in Soviet Central Asia*. Peshawar: Emjay Books International.

Maxted, J. 2003. 'Youth and War in Sierra Leone', *African Identities* 1(1): 69–78.

Mead, M. 1970. *Jugend und Sexualität in primitiven Gesellschaften*, Vol. 1: *Kindheit und Jugend in Samoa*. Munich: Dt. Taschenbuch-Verlag.

——— 1973[1970]. *Der Konflikt der Generationen: Jugend ohne Vorbild*. Freiburg: Walter.

Meeker, M. 1976. 'Meaning and Society in the Near East: Examples from the Black Sea Turks and the Levantine Arabs', *International Journal of Middle East Studies* 7(3): 383–422.

Meekers, D. 1992. 'The Process of Marriage in African Societies: A Multiple Indicator Approach', *Population and Development Review* 18(1): 61–78.

Mesquida, C.G., and N.I. Wiener. 1999. 'Male Age Composition and Severity of Conflicts', *Politics and the Life Sciences* 18(2): 181–89.

Mirzobekova, R. 2008. 'Rakhmonov idyet v sud. Minobrazovaniya otdast tisyachi studentov pod sud' [Rakhimov goes to court: The Ministry of Culture and Education brought thousands of students to court], *Asia Plus*. Retrieved 17 September 2008 from: *www.asiaplus.tj/en/*.

Moller, H. 1968. 'Youth as a Force in the Modern World', *Comparative Studies in Society and History* 10(3): 237–60.

Monogarova, L.F. 1992. *Sovremennaya gorodskaya sem'ya tadzhikov*. [The modern urban Tajik family]. Moscow: Rossijskaya Akademiya Nauk, Institut Etnologii I Antropologii II.

Monogarova, L.F., and I. Mukhiddinov 1992. *Sovremennaya sel'skaya sem'ya tadzhikov*. [The modern rural Tajik family]. Moskva: Rossijskaya Akademiya Nauk, Institut Etnologii I Antropologii I.

Mughal, A.-G. 2007. 'Migration, Remittances, and Living Standards in Tajikistan'. Unpublished report for International Organization for Migration, Tajikistan.

Mühlfried, F., and S. Sokolovskiy. 2011. *Exploring the Edge of Empire: Soviet Era Anthropology in the Caucasus and Central Asia*. Berlin: Lit.

Müller, H.K. 1989. *Changing Generations: Dynamics of Generation and Age-sets in Southern Sudan (Toposa) and Northwestern Kenya (Turkana)*. Saarbrücken: Breitenbach.

Müller-Dempf, H. 2008. 'The Ngibokoi Dilemma: Generation-sets and Social System Engineering in Times of Stress – An Example from the Toposa of Southern Sudan', *Working Papers, No. 109*. Halle: Max Planck Institute for Social Anthropology.

Naimov, B. 2005. 'New Passport: Another Challenge for Traveling Tajiks', *Central Asia-Caucasus Analyst*. Retrieved 15 October 2008 from: http://www.cacianalyst.org/view_article.php?articleid=3890.

Navrūzshoh, Z. 2009. 'Tajlili Rūzi javonon dar Tojikiston' [The glorious day of youth in Tajikistan], *Asia Plus*. Retrieved *25 June 2009* from: *www.asiaplus. tj/en/*.

Neyzi, L. 2003. 'Object or Subject? The Paradox of "Youth" in Turkey', in B. Turner (ed.), *Islam and Social Movements*. London: Routledge, pp.357–81.

Nieswand, B. 2007. 'Ghanaian Migrants in Germany and the Status Paradox of Migration: A Multi-sited Ethnography of Transnational Pathways of Migrant Inclusion', Ph.D. diss. Halle: Martin Luther University Halle-Wittenberg.

Niyazi, A. 1994. 'Tajikistan', in M. Mesbahi (ed.), *Central Asia and the Caucasus after the Soviet Union*. Gainesville: University of Florida Press, pp.164–90.

———— 1999. 'Islam and Tajikistan's Human and Ecological Crisis', in M.H. Ruffin and D.C. Waugh (eds), *Civil Society in Central Asia*. Seattle: University of Washington Press, pp.180–97.

———— 2000. 'Migration, Demography and Socio-ecological Processes in Tajikistan', in H. Komatsu, O. Chika and J.S. Schoeberlein (eds), *Migration in Central Asia: Its History and Current Problems*. Osaka: Japan Center for Area Studies, National Museum of Ethnology, pp.169–78.

Nora, P. 1996. 'Generation', in P. Nora (ed.), *Realms of Memory: Rethinking the French Past*, trans. A. Goldhammer. New York: Columbia University Press, pp.499–531.

Nordstrom, C. 1999. 'Requiem for the Rational War', in S.P. Reyna (ed.), *Deadly Developments: Capitalism, States and War*. Amsterdam: Gordon and Breach, pp.153–75.

Nourzhanov, K. 1998. 'Traditional Kinship Structure in Contemporary Tajik Politics', in D. Christian and C. Benjamin (eds), *Silk Road Studies II: Worlds of the Silk Roads, Ancient and Modern*. Brepols: Turnhout, pp.147–64.

———— 2005. 'Saviours of the Nation or Robber Barons? Warlord Politics in Tajikistan', *Central Asian Survey* 24(2): 109–30.

Obermeyer, C.M. 1992. 'Islam, Women and Politics: The Demography of Arab Countries', *Population and Development Review* 18(1): 33–60.

Olcott, M.B. 1992. 'Introduction', in S.P. Poliakov, *Islam, Religion and Tradition in Rural Central Asia*. New York: Sharpe, pp.xiii–xxvi.

Olimova, S. 2000. 'Islam and the Tajik Conflict', in R. Sagdeev and S. Eisenhower (eds), *Islam and Central Asia*. Washington, DC: Center for Political and Strategic Studies, pp.59–71.

———— 2002. 'Zur gesellschaftlichen Wahrnehmung von gemäßigten und radikalen Islam', in A. Kreikmeyer and A.C. Seifert (eds), *Zur Vereinbarkeit von politischem Islam und Sicherheit im OSZE-Raum: Dokumente eines islamisch-säkularen Dialogs in Tadschikistan*. Baden-Baden: Nomos Verlagsgesellschaft, pp.31–45.

———— 2004. 'Opposition in Tajikistan: Pro et Contra', in Y. Ro'i (ed.), *Democracy and Pluralism in Muslim Eurasia*. London: Frank Cass, pp.245–63.

———— 2006. 'Molodezh'i islam v Tadzhikistane' [Youth and Islam in Tajikistan], *Rasy i narody* 32: 157–79.

Olimova, S., and I. Bosc. 2003. *Labour Migration from Tajikistan*. Dushanbe: International Organization for Migration in cooperation with the Sharq Scientific Research Center.

Orywal, E. 2002. *Krieg oder Frieden. Eine vergleichende Untersuchung kultur-spezifischer Ideale – der Bürgerkrieg in Belutschistan/Pakistan*. Berlin: Reimer.

Pauli, J. 2000. *Das geplante Kind: Demographischer, wirtschaftlicher und sozialer Wandel in einer mexikanischen Gemeinde*. Münster: Lit.

Penati, B. 2008. 'Administrative Sources for the History of the Land-and-water Reform in Uzbekistan: Potential and Limitations', unpublished paper delivered at the conference 'Islamic Institutions and Muslim Culture in the Interwar Soviet Union (1919–1939)'. Halle: Centre for Oriental Studies, Martin Luther University Halle-Wittenberg, 11/12 December.

Peters, K. 2010. 'Generating Rebels and Soldiers: On the Socio-economic Crisis of Rural Youth in Sierra Leone before the War', in J. Knörr and W.T. Filho (eds), *The Powerful Presence of the Past: Historical Dimensions of Integration and Conflict in the Upper Guinea Coast*. Leiden: Brill, pp.323–55.

Peters, K., and P. Richards. 1998. 'Fighting with Open Eyes: Youth Combatants Talking about War in Sierra Leone', in P.J. Bracken and C. Petty (eds), *Rethinking the Trauma of War*. London: Free Association Books, pp.76–111.

Pétric, B.-M. 2002. *Pouvoir, don et réseaux en Ouzbékistan post-soviétique*. Paris: Presses Universitaire de France.

Pilkington, H. 1994. *Russia's Youth and its Culture: A Nation's Constructors and Constructed*. London: Routledge.

———— 2004. 'Youth Strategies for Local Living: Space, Power and Communication in Everyday Cultural Practice', in A. Bennett (ed.), *After Subculture: Critical Studies in Contemporary Youth Culture*. Basingstoke: Palgrave Macmillan, pp.119–34.

Pitt-Rivers, J. 1975. 'The Kith and the Kin', in J. Goody (ed.), *The Character of Kinship*. Cambridge: Cambridge University Press, pp.89–105.

Poliakov, S. 1992. *Everyday Islam: Religion and Tradition in Rural Central Asia*. London: M.E. Sharpe.

Qodirov, S. 1995. *Mehnat – asosi tarbiyai grajdanii javonon* [Work – the base of education of young citizens]. Dushanbe: Sino.

Rachewiltz, I. de. 2006. *The Secret History of the Mongols*, Vol. 1. Leiden: Brill.

Radcliffe-Brown, A.R. 1958[1950]. 'Introduction', in A.R. Radcliffe-Brown and D. Forde (eds), *African Systems of Kinship and Marriage*. London: Oxford University Press, pp.1–84.

Rahimov, R.R. 1989. *Hierarchy in Traditional Men's Associations of Centra Asia: Ecology and Empire*. Los Angeles: Center for Visual Anthropology, University of Southern California.

Rakhimov, R.R. 1990. *'Muzhskie doma' v traditsionnoy kul'ture tadzhikov* [The 'male house' in the traditional culture of the Tajiks]. Leningrad: Akademiya Nauk SSSR.

Randal, S. 2005. 'The Demographic Consequence of Conflict, Exile and Repatriation: A Case Study of Malian Tuareg', *European Journal of Population* 21: 291–320.

Randall, B., and R.A. Olson. 2000. *Standard Tajik–English Dictionary*. Edmonds: Star Publication.

Rasanayagam, J. 2010. *Islam in Post-Soviet Uzbekistan: The Morality of Experience*. Cambridge: Cambridge University Press.

Rashid, A. 2003. *Jihad: The Rise of Militant Islam in Central Asia*. New Haven: Yale University Press.

Richards, P. 1996. *Fighting for the Rain Forest: War, Youth and Resources in Sierra Leone*. London: Heinemann.

Riordan, J. 1989. 'The Komsomol', in J. Riordan (ed.), *Soviet Youth Culture*. Houndmills: Macmillan, pp.16–44.

Rivers, W.H.R. 1900. 'A Genealogical Method of Collecting Social and Vital Statistics', *Journal of Royal Anthropological Institute* 30: 74–82.

Roberts, S.R. 1998. 'Negotiating Locality, Islam, and National Culture in a Changing Borderland: The Revival of the Mäshräp Ritual among Young Uighur Men in the Ili Valley', *Central Asian Survey* 17(4): 673–99.

Roche, S. 2005. 'Bürgerkrieg und Wandel rechtlicher Flexibilität. Ethnographische Fallstudien von Konflikten in Vadi Rasht/Dushanbe (Tadschikistan)', M.A. diss. Berlin: Free University of Berlin.

——— 2009. 'Domesticating Youth: The Youth Bulge in Post-Civil War Tajikistan', Ph.D. diss. Halle: Martin Luther University Halle-Wittenberg.

——— 2010. 'Friendship Relations in Tajikistan: An Ethnographic Account', *Ab Imperio* 3: 273–98.

Roche, S., and J. Heathershaw. 2010a. 'Conflict in Tajikistan – Not Really about Radical Islam', *OpenDemocracy*. Retrieved 19 October 2010 from: www.opendemocracy.net.

——— 2010b. 'Tajikistan's Marginalised Youth', *OpenDemocracy*. Retrieved 20 October 2010 from: www.opendemocracy.net.

Roche, S., and S. Hohmann. 2011. 'Wedding Rituals and the Struggle over National Identities', *Central Asian Survey* 30(1): 71–86.

Roche, S., and A. Ismailbekova. 2010. 'Demography and Patronage: The Dynamics of the Youth Bulge in Kyrgyzstan', *Orient* 4: 33–43.

Ro'i, Y. 2000. *Islam in the Soviet Union: From the Second World War to Gorbachev*. New York: Columbia University Press.

Rousseau, C., T.M. Said, M.-J. Gangé and G. Bibeau. 1998. 'Between Myth and Madness: The Premigration Dream of Leaving among Young Somali Refugees', *Culture, Medicine and Psychiatry* 22: 385–411.

Roy, O. 1998. 'Is the Conflict in Tajikistan a Model for Conflicts throughout Central Asia?' in M.-R. Djalili, F. Grare and S. Akiner (eds), *Tajikistan: The Trials of Independence*. Richmond: Curzon, pp.132–47.

———— 1999. 'Kolkhoz and Civil Society in the Independent States of Central Asia', in M.H. Ruffin and D. Waugh (eds), *Civil Society in Central Asia*. Seattle: University of Washington Press, pp.109–21.

———— 2000. *The New Central Asia: The Creation of Nations*. London: Tauris.

———— 2004[2002]. *Globalised Islam: The Search for a New Ummah*. New York: Columbia University.

Rubin, B.R. 1998. 'Russian Hegemony and State Breakdown in the Periphery', in B.R. Rubin and J. Snyder (eds), *Post-Soviet Political Order, Conflict and State Building*. London: Routledge, pp.128–61.

Rzehak, L. 2001. *Vom Persischen zum Tadschikischen. Sprachliches Handeln und Sprachplanung in Transoxanien zwischen Tradition, Moderne und Sowjetmacht (1900–1956)*. Wiesbaden: Reichert.

Schiewek, E. 1998. 'On Mahallas and Their Use for Tadjikistan's Problems', unpublished document produced for *ACTED*.

Schiffauer, W. 1987. *Die Bauern von Subay: Das Leben in einem türkischen Dorf*. Stuttgart: Klett-Cotta.

Schlee, G. 1979. *Das Glaubens- und Sozialsystem der Rendille: Kamelnomaden Nordkenias*. Berlin: Dietrich Reimer Verlag.

———— 1989. *Identities on the Move: Clanship and Pastoralism in Northern Kenya*. Manchester: Manchester University Press.

———— 2001. 'Einleitung', in A. Horstmann and G. Schlee (eds), *Integration durch Verschiedenheit: Lokale und globale Formen interkultureller Kommunikation*. Bielefeld: Transcript, pp.17–46.

———— 2006. *Wie Feindbilder entstehen: Eine Theorie religiöser und ethnischer Konflikte*. Munich: Beck.

———— 2008. *How Enemies Are Made: Towards a Theory of Ethnic and Religious Conflicts*. Oxford: Berghahn.

Schlee, G., and E.E. Watson (eds). 2009a. *Changing Identifications and Alliances in North-East Africa: Ethiopia and Kenya*. Oxford: Berghahn.

———— 2009b. *Changing Identifications and Alliances in North-East Africa: Sudan, Uganda and the Ethiopia-Sudan Borderlands*. Oxford: Berghahn.

Schlee, G., and K. Werner. 1996. 'Inklusion und Exklusion: Die Dynamik von Grenzziehungen im Spannungsfeld von Markt, Staat und Ethnizität', in G. Schlee and K. Werner (eds), *Inklusion und Exklusion*. Cologne: Rüdiger Köppe, pp. 9–36.

Schoeberlein-Engel, J.S. 1994. 'Identity in Central Asia: Construction and Contention in the Conceptions of "Özbek", "Tâjik", "Muslim", "Samarquandi" and other Groups', Ph.D. diss. Cambridge, MA: Harvard University.

Şenı, N. 2007. 'La jeunesse: une "non-génération". Rhétorique éducative dans la Turquie des années trente', in F. Georgeon and K. Kreise (eds), *Enfance et jeunesse dans le monde musulman*. Paris: Maisonneuve and Larose, pp.233–58.

Shemyakina, O.N. 2007. 'Armed Conflict, Education and the Marriage Market: Evidence from Tajikistan', Ph.D. diss. Los Angeles: University of Southern California.

Shepler, S. 2005. 'Globalizing Child Soldiers in Sierra Leone', in S. Maira and E. Soep (eds), *Youthscapes: The Popular, the National, the Global*. Philadelphia: University of Pennsylvania Press, pp.119–36.

Shukurov, M.Sh, V.A. Kapranov, R. Hoshim and N.A. Maʼsumī (eds). 1969. *Farhangi zaboni tojikī* [Dictionary of the Tajik language], vol. 1.Moscow: Sovetskaya Entsiklopediya.

Simons, A. 2000. 'Mobilizable Male Youth, Indigenous Institutions and War', unpublished paper delivered at the conference 'Vereinigung von Afrikanisten in Deutschland (VAD), 17. Tagung: Afrika 2000'. Leipzig, 30 March–1 April.

Simonse, S. 2005. 'Warriors, Hooligans and Mercenaries: Failed Statehood and the Violence of Young Male Pastoralists in the Horn of Africa', in J. Abbink and I. van Kessel (eds), *Vanguard or Vandals: Youth, Politics and Conflict in Africa*. Leiden: Brill, pp.243–66.

Snesarev, G.P. 1963. *Traditsiya Muzhskikh Soyuzov v eyo Pozdneyshem Variante u Narodov Sredney Asii* [The tradition of male gatherings and their later development among the people of Central Asia]. Materialy Chorezmskoy Ekspedicii, vol. 7. Moscow, Petersburg: Institut Etnologii I antropologii RAN.

Sommers, M. 2006. 'Fearing Africa's Young Men: Male Youth, Conflict, Urbanization and the Case of Rwanda', in I. Bannon and M. Correia (eds), *The Other Half of Gender: Men's Issues in Development*. Washington, DC: World Bank, pp.137–58.

Stephan, M. 2006. '"You Come to Us Like a Black Cloud": Universal versus Local Islam in Tajikistan', in C. Hann (ed.), *The Postsocialist Religious Question: Faith and Power in Central Asia and East-Central Europe*. Münster: Lit, pp.147–67.

——— 2008. 'Das Bedürfnis nach Ausgewogenheit. Moralische Erziehung, Islam und Muslimsein in Tadschikistan zwischen Säkularisierung und religiöser Rückbesinnung', Ph.D. diss. Halle: Martin Luther University Halle-Wittenberg.

Sternberg, F. 1981[1935]. *Der Faschismus an der Macht*. Hildesheim: Gerstenberg.

Stewart, F.H. 1977. *Fundamentals of Age-group Systems*. New York: Academic Press.

Sulloway, F.J. 1997. *Born to Rebel: Birth Order, Family Dynamics, and Creative Lives*. New York: Vintage.

Tabeau, E., and J. Bijak. 2005. 'War-related Deaths in the 1992–1995 Armed Conflicts in Bosnia and Herzegovina: A Critique of Previous Estimates and Recent Results', *European Journal of Population* 21: 187–215.

Tadjbakhsh, S. 1994. 'Women and War in Tajikistan', *Central Asian Monitor* 1(26): 25–29.

Tchoroev, T. 2002. 'Historiography of Post-Soviet Kyrgyzstan', *International Journal of Middle Eastern Studies* 34: 351–74.

Tett, G. 1995. 'Guardians of the Faith? Gender and Religion in an (ex)Soviet Tajik Village', in C.F. El-Solh and J. Mabro (eds), *Muslim Women's Choices: Religious Belief and Social Reality*. Oxford: Berg, pp.128–51.

Tiger, L., and R. Fox. 1992[1971]. *The Imperial Animal*. London: Secker and Warburg.

Turner, R. 1993. 'Tajiks Have the Highest Fertility Rates in Newly Independent Central Asia', *Family Planning Perspectives* 35(3): 141–42.

Turner, V. 1995[1969]. *The Ritual Process: Structure and Anti-structure*. New York: Aldine de Gruyter.

Tutubalina, O. 2006. 'Poslednyaya okhota na 'zverya' [Last hunting of the 'beast']', *Asia Plus* 50(360): 6–7.

Umarov, K. 2006. 'External Labour Migration in Tajikistan: Root Causes, Consequences and Regulation', in R.R. Rios (ed.), *Migration Perspectives on Eastern Europe and Central Asia*. Vienna: International Organization for Migration, pp.91–102.

Urdal, H. 2004. 'The Devil in the Demographics: The Effect of Youth Bulges on Domestic Armed Conflict, 1950–2000', *Social Development Paper*. Washington, DC: Conflict Prevention and Reconstruction Unit, World Bank.

——— 2006. 'A Clash of Generations? Youth Bulges and Political Violence', *International Studies Quarterly* 50: 607–29.

——— 2007. 'The Demographics of Political Violence: Youth Bulges, Insecurity and Conflict', in L. Brainard and D. Chollet (eds), *Too Poor for Peace? Global Poverty, Conflict and Security in the 21st Century*. Washington, DC: Brookings Institution, pp.90–100.

Vakil, S. 2004. 'Iran: The Gridlock between Demography and Democracy', *SAIS Review* 24(2): 45–53.

Van der Geest, S. 2004. 'Participant Observation in Demographic Research: Fieldwork Experiences in a Ghanaian Community', in A.M. Basu and P. Aaby (eds), *The Methods and Uses of Anthropological Demography*. Oxford: Clarendon, pp.39–56.

Van Gennep, A. 1999[1909]. *Übergangsriten*. Frankfurt am Main: Campus.

Vaupel, J.W., and E. Loichinger. 2006. 'Redistributing Work in Aging Europe', *Science* 312(5782): 1911–13.

Verwimp, P., and J. van Bavel. 2005. 'Child Survival and Fertility of Refugees in Rwanda', *European Journal of Population* 21: 271–90.

Waldmann, P. 2002. 'Bürgerkriege', in W. Heitmeyer and J. Hagan (eds), *Internationales Handbuch der Gewaltforschung*. Wiesbaden: Westdeutscher Verlag, pp.368–89.

Weyland, P. 1993. *Inside the Third World Village*. London: Routledge.

Winckler, O. 2002. 'The Demographic Dilemma of the Arab World: The Employment Aspect', *Journal of Contemporary History* 37: 617–36.

Winter, J.M. 1992. 'War, Family, and Fertility in Twentieth-century Europe', in J.R. Gills (ed.), *The European Experience of Declining Fertility, 1850–1970: The Quiet Revolution*. Oxford: Blackwell, pp.291–309.

Wulff, H. 1995. 'Introducing Youth Culture in its own Rights: The State of the Art and New Possibilities', in V. Amit-Talai and H. Wulff (eds), *Youth Cultures: A Cross-Cultural Perspective*. London: Routledge, pp.1–18.

Wyn, J., and R. White. 1997. *Rethinking Youth*. London: Sage.

——— 1998. 'Youth Agency and Social Context', *Journal of Sociology* 34(3): 314–27.

Yurchak, A. 2006. *Everything Was Forever, Until It Was No More*. Princeton: Princeton University Press.

Zitelmann, T. 1991. 'Politisches Gemeinschaftshandeln, bewaffnete Gewalt, soziale Mythen: Die Oromo Liberation Front (OLF) in Äthiopien', in T. Scheffler (ed.), *Ethnizität und Gewalt*. Hamburg: Deutsche Orient-Institute, pp.251–72.

Zviagelskaya, I. 1998. 'The Tajik Conflict: Problems of Regulation', in M.-R. Djalili, F. Grare and S. Akiner (eds), *Tajikistan: The Trials of Independence*. Richmond: Curzon, pp.161–79.

Index